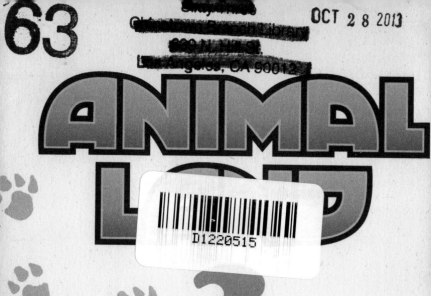

ANIMAL LAND

3

By Makoto Raiku

YOUNG ADULT

Translated and adapted by Stephen Paul

Lettered by Janice Chiang

KODANSHA
COMICS

Animal Land volume 3 is a work of fiction. Names, characters, places, and incidents are the products of the author's imagination or are used fictitiously. Any resemblance to actual events, locales, or persons, living or dead, is entirely coincidental.

A Kodansha Comics Trade Paperback Original

Animal Land volume 3 copyright © 2010 Makoto Raiku
English translation copyright © 2011 Makoto Raiku

Published in the United States by Kodansha Comics,
an imprint of Kodansha USA Publishing, LLC, New York.

Publication rights for this English edition arranged through
Kodansha Ltd., Tokyo.

First published in Japan in 2010 by Kodansha Ltd., Tokyo,
as *Doubutsu no Kuni*, volume 3.

ISBN 978-1-935429-15-9

Printed in the United States of America.

www.kodanshacomics.com

9 8 7 6 5 4 3 2 1

Translator/Adapter: Stephen Paul
Lettering: Janice Chiang

Every time I see a show on TV about traveling around the world, I always wish, "If only you could speak all the languages of mankind..." It would be so easy to visit all different countries and partake in their culture...

Makoto Raiku

Honorifics Explained

Throughout the Kodansha Comics books, you will find Japanese honorifics left intact in the translations. For those not familiar with how the Japanese use honorifics and, more important, how they differ from American honorifics, we present this brief overview.

Politeness has always been a critical facet of Japanese culture. Ever since the feudal era, when Japan was a highly stratified society, use of honorifics—which can be defined as polite speech that indicates relationship or status—has played an essential role in the Japanese language. When addressing someone in Japanese, an honorific usually takes the form of a suffix attached to one's name (example: "Asuna-san"), is used as a title at the end of one's name, or appears in place of the name itself (example: "Negi-sensei," or simply "Sensei!").

Honorifics can be expressions of respect or endearment. In the context of manga and anime, honorifics give insight into the nature of the relationship between characters. Many English translations leave out these important honorifics and therefore distort the feel of the original Japanese. Because Japanese honorifics contain nuances that English honorifics lack, it is our policy at Kodansha Comics not to translate them. Here, instead, is a guide to some of the honorifics you may encounter in Kodansha Comics.

-san: This is the most common honorific and is equivalent to Mr., Miss, Ms., or Mrs. It is the all-purpose honorific and can be used in any situation where politeness is required.

-sama: This is one level higher than "-san" and is used to confer great respect.

-dono: This comes from the word "tono," which means "lord." It is an even higher level than "-sama" and confers utmost respect.

-kun: This suffix is used at the end of boys' names to express familiarity or endearment. It is also sometimes used by men among friends, or when addressing someone younger or of a lower station.

-chan: This is used to express endearment, mostly toward girls. It is also used for little boys, pets, and even among lovers. It gives a sense of childish cuteness.

Bozu: This is an informal way to refer to a boy, similar to the English terms "kid" and "squirt."

Sempai/
Senpai: This title suggests that the addressee is one's senior in a group or organization. It is most often used in a school setting, where underclassmen refer to their upperclassmen as "sempai." It can also be used in the workplace, such as when a newer employee addresses an employee who has seniority in the company.

Kohai: This is the opposite of "sempai" and is used toward underclassmen in school or newcomers in the workplace. It connotes that the addressee is of a lower station.

Sensei: Literally meaning "one who has come before," this title is used for teachers, doctors, or masters of any profession or art.

-[blank]: This is usually forgotten in these lists, but it is perhaps the most significant difference between Japanese and English. The lack of honorific means that the speaker has permission to address the person in a very intimate way. Usually, only family, spouses, or very close friends have this kind of permission. Known as *yobisute*, it can be gratifying when someone who has earned the intimacy starts to call one by one's name without an honorific. But when that intimacy hasn't been earned, it can be very insulting.

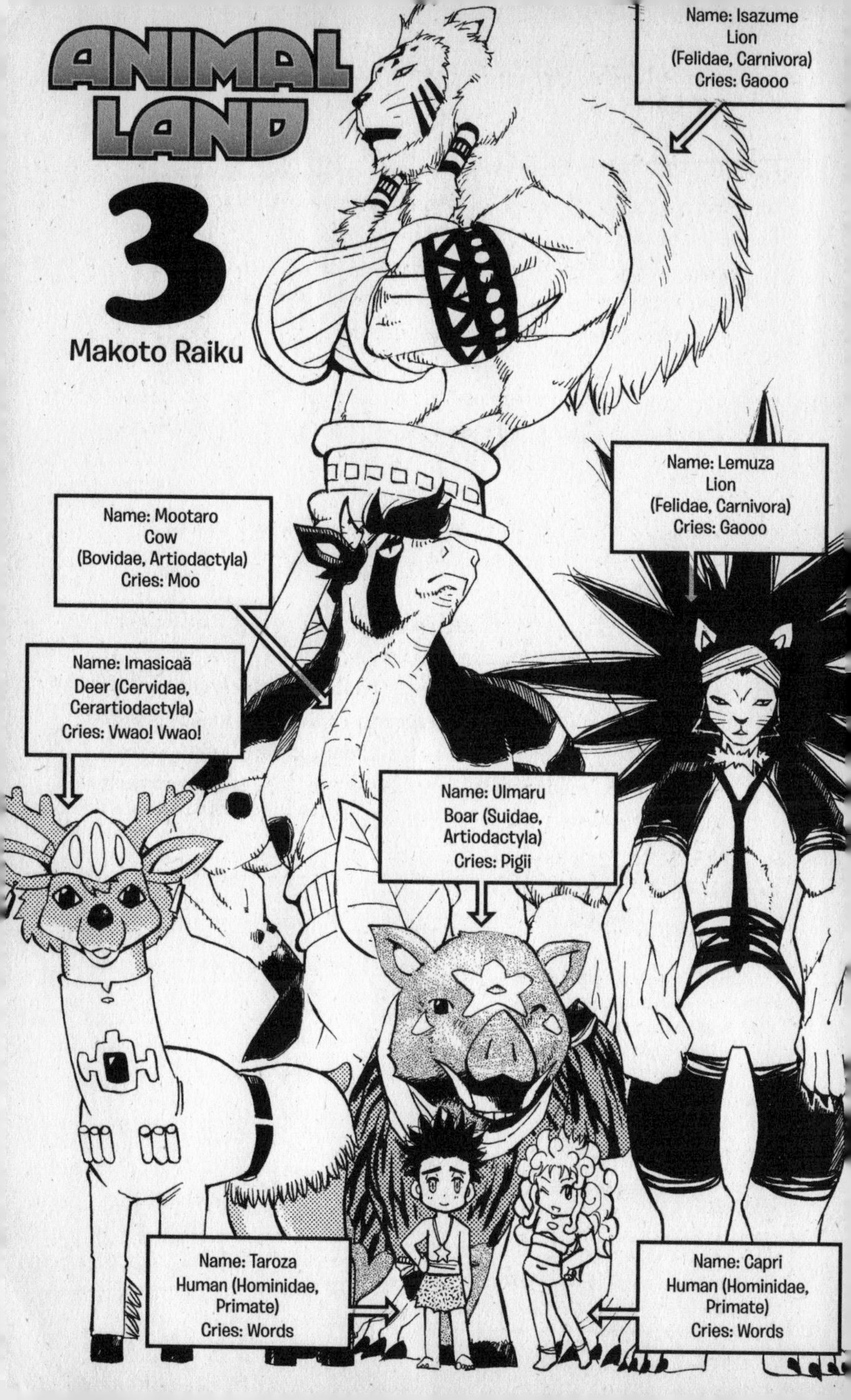
ANIMAL LAND
3
Makoto Raiku
Name: Isazume Lion (Felidae, Carnivora) Cries: Gaooo
Name: Lemuza Lion (Felidae, Carnivora) Cries: Gaooo
Name: Mootaro Cow (Bovidae, Artiodactyla) Cries: Moo
Name: Imasicaä Deer (Cervidae, Cerartiodactyla) Cries: Vwao! Vwao!
Name: Ulmaru Boar (Suidae, Artiodactyla) Cries: Pigii
Name: Capri Human (Hominidae, Primate) Cries: Words
Name: Taroza Human (Hominidae, Primate) Cries: Words

ANIMAL LAND

Character Profiles

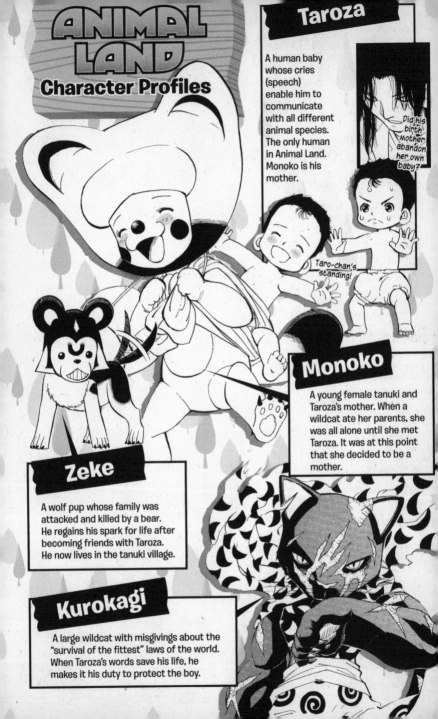

Taroza

A human baby whose cries (speech) enable him to communicate with all different animal species. The only human in Animal Land. Monoko is his mother.

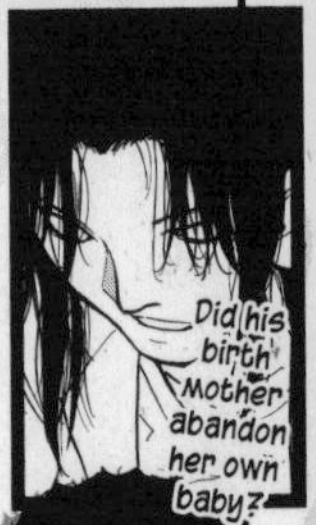
Did his birth Mother abandon her own baby?

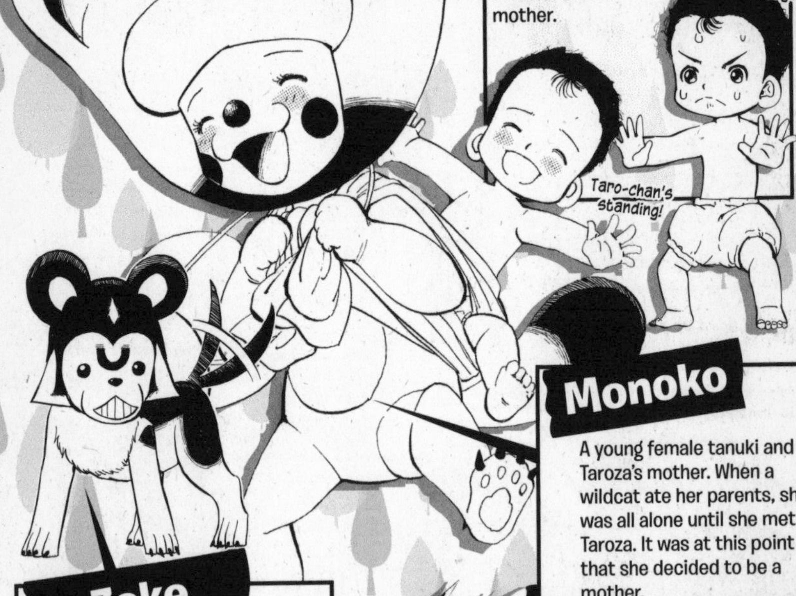
Taro-chan's standing!

Monoko

A young female tanuki and Taroza's mother. When a wildcat ate her parents, she was all alone until she met Taroza. It was at this point that she decided to be a mother.

Zeke

A wolf pup whose family was attacked and killed by a bear. He regains his spark for life after becoming friends with Taroza. He now lives in the tanuki village.

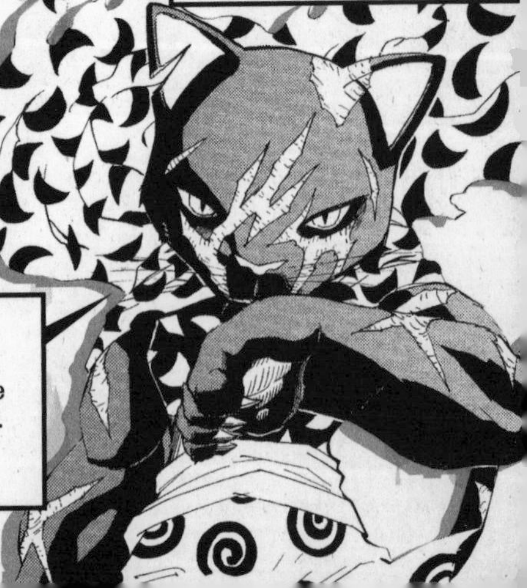

Kurokagi

A large wildcat with misgivings about the "survival of the fittest" laws of the world. When Taroza's words save his life, he makes it his duty to protect the boy.

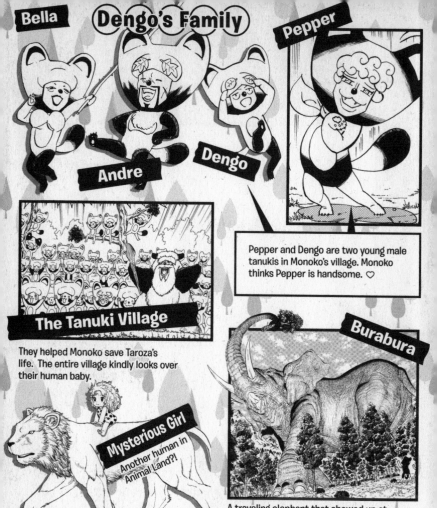

Dengo's Family

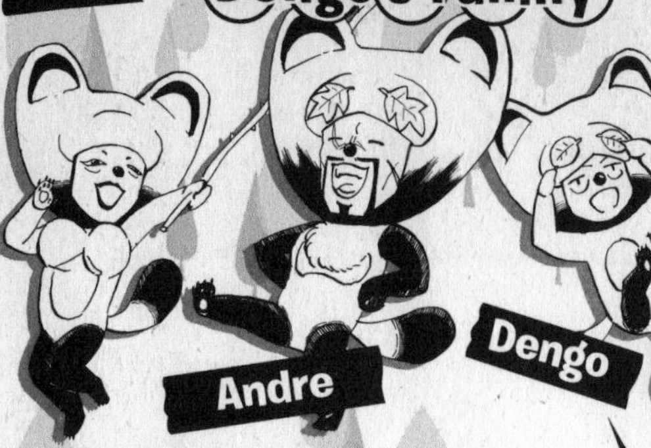
Bella
Andre
Dengo

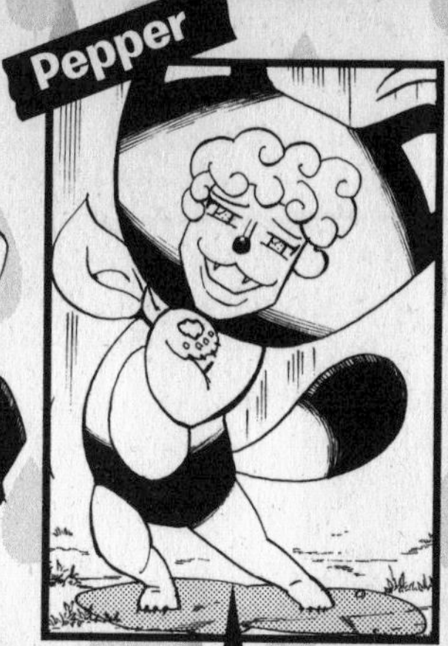
Pepper

Pepper and Dengo are two young male tanukis in Monoko's village. Monoko thinks Pepper is handsome. ♡

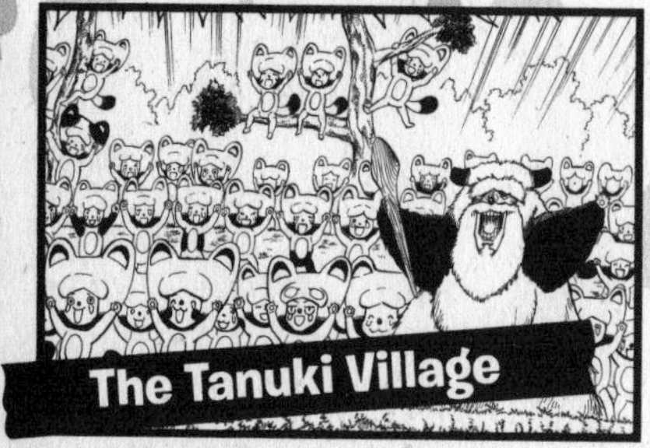
The Tanuki Village

They helped Monoko save Taroza's life. The entire village kindly looks over their human baby.

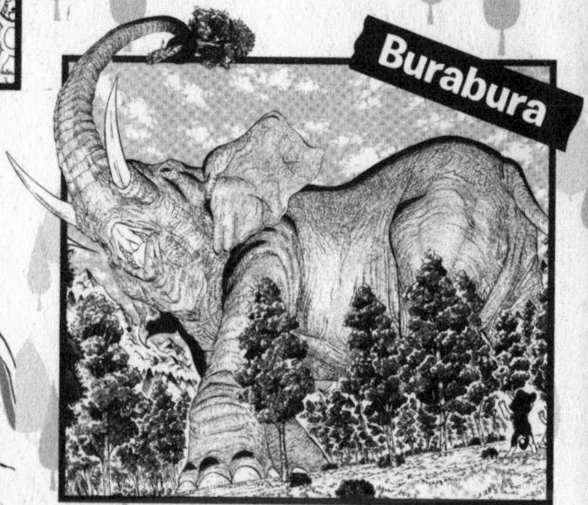
Burabura

A traveling elephant that showed up at the tanuki village. It is concerned over Taroza's cruel destiny.

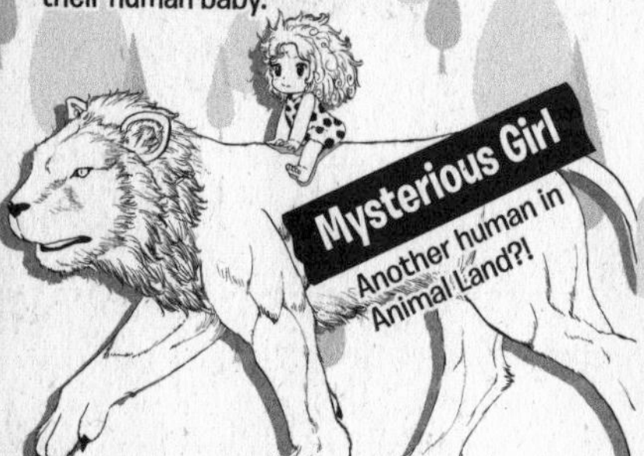
Mysterious Girl
Another human in Animal Land?!

In the previous volume...

Taroza, who is too weak and frail to get his own food, wants to help out by using his voice, which can communicate with all the animals in the world. But when the wandering elephant Burabura appears in town, it crushes Taroza's hopes by saying that his power should not exist in Animal Land. Despite this, Taroza is determined to use his power to make a world where all animals can be friends! Upon seeing him, Burabura is reminded of the sight of a little girl riding on the back of a lion...

Is this what will make the animals get along?!

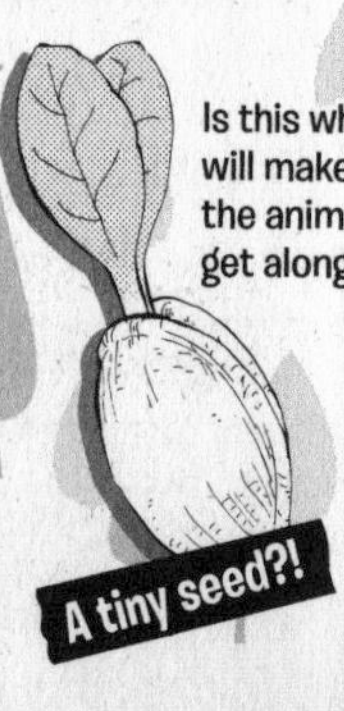
A tiny seed?!

CONTENTS

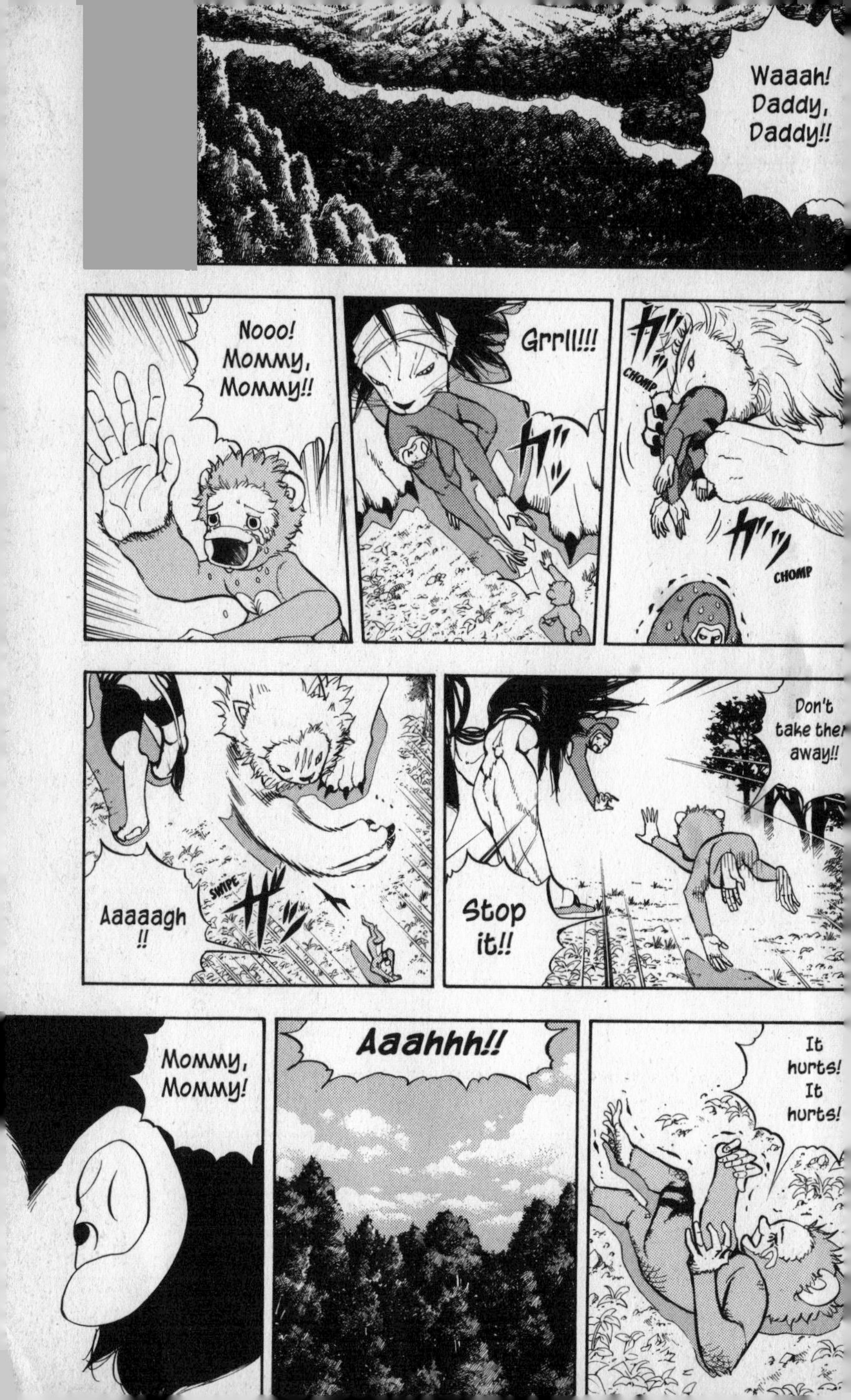
Waaah! Daddy, Daddy!!
CHOMP
CHOMP
Grrll!!!
Nooo! Mommy, Mommy!!
Don't take ther away!!
Stop it!!
SWIPE
Aaaaagh !!
It hurts! It hurts!
Aaahhh!!
Mommy, Mommy!

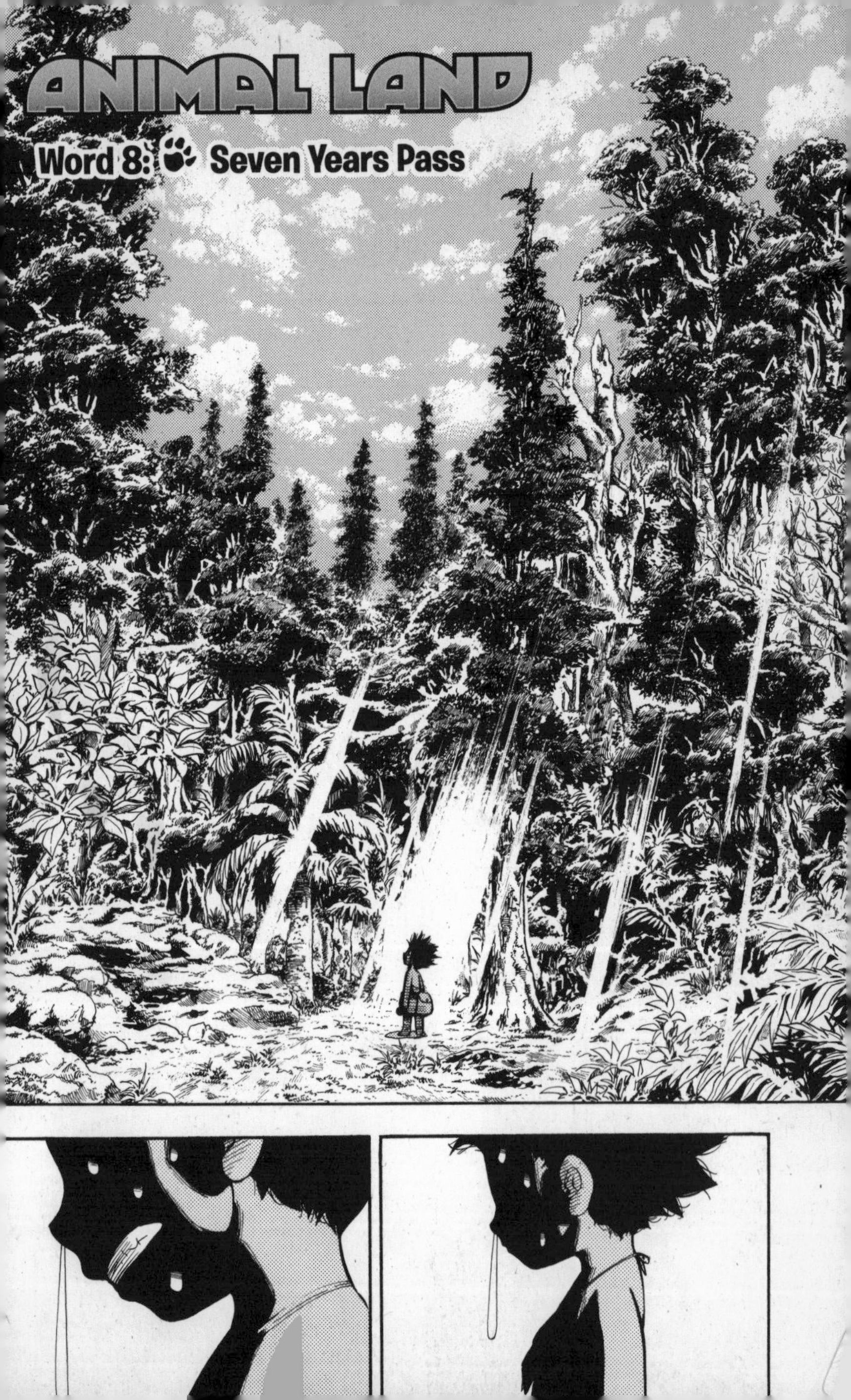
ANIMAL LAND
Word 8: Seven Years Pass

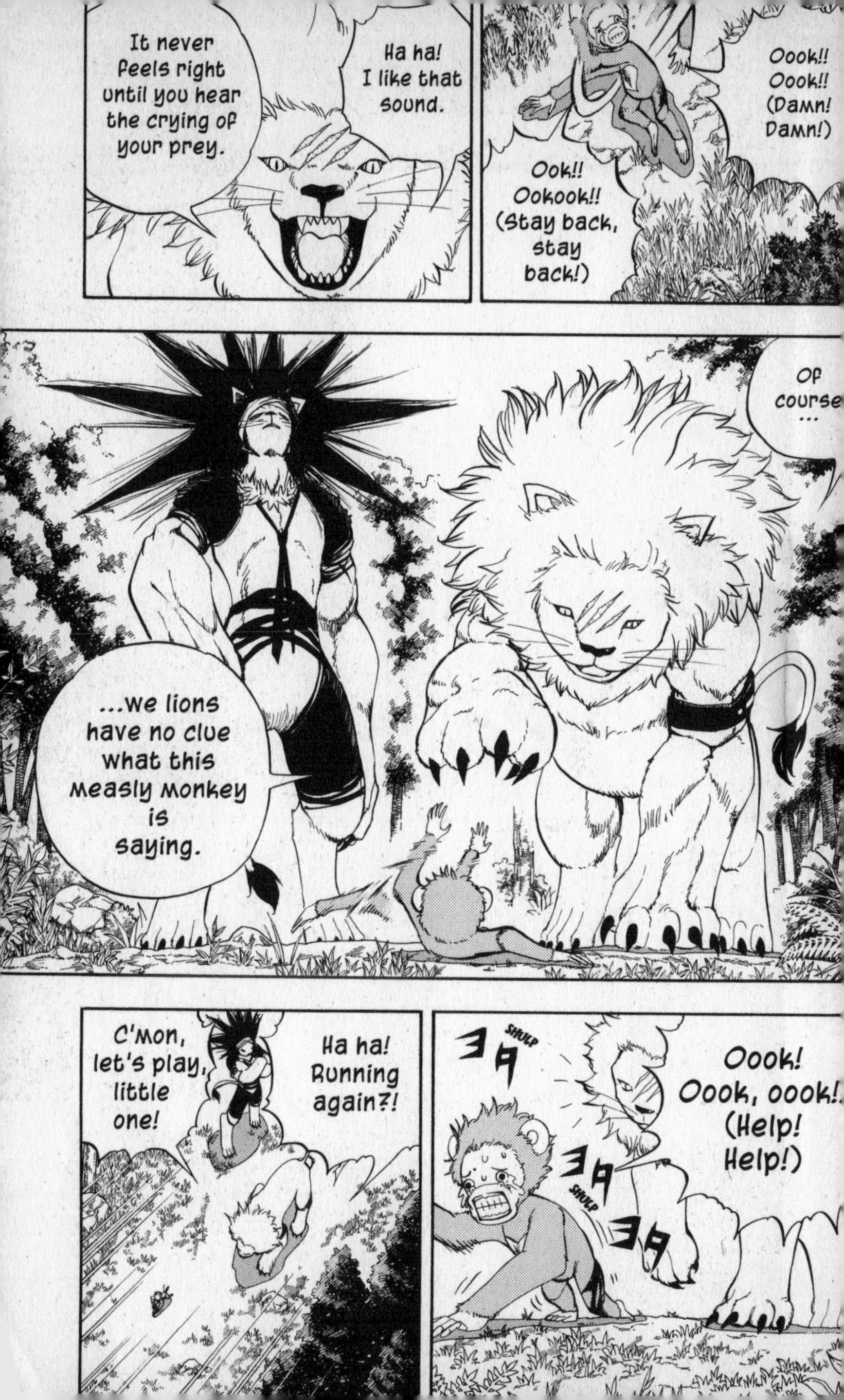
Oook!! Oook!! (Damn! Damn!)
Ook!! Ookook!! (Stay back, stay back!)
Ha ha! I like that sound.
It never feels right until you hear the crying of your prey.
Of course...
...we lions have no clue what this measly monkey is saying.
Oook! Oook, oook! (Help! Help!)
SHULP
SHULP
Ha ha! Running again?!
C'mon, let's play, little one!

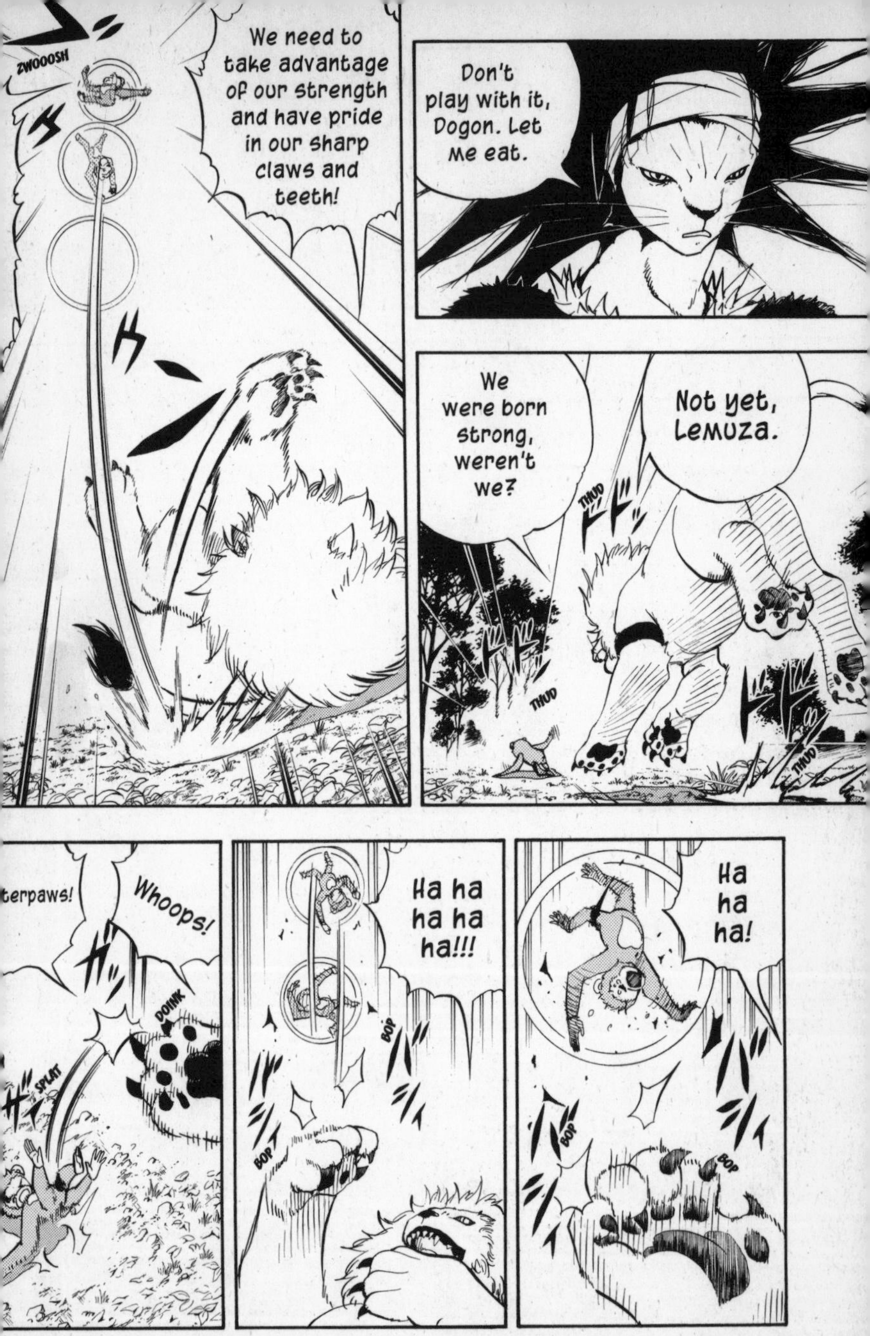
Don't play with it, Dogon. Let me eat.
Not yet, Lemuza.
We were born strong, weren't we?
THUD
THUD
THUD
We need to take advantage of our strength and have pride in our sharp claws and teeth!
ZWOOOSH
Ha ha ha!
BOP
BOP
Ha ha ha ha ha!!!
BOP
BOP
Whoops!
terpaws!
DOINK
SPLAT

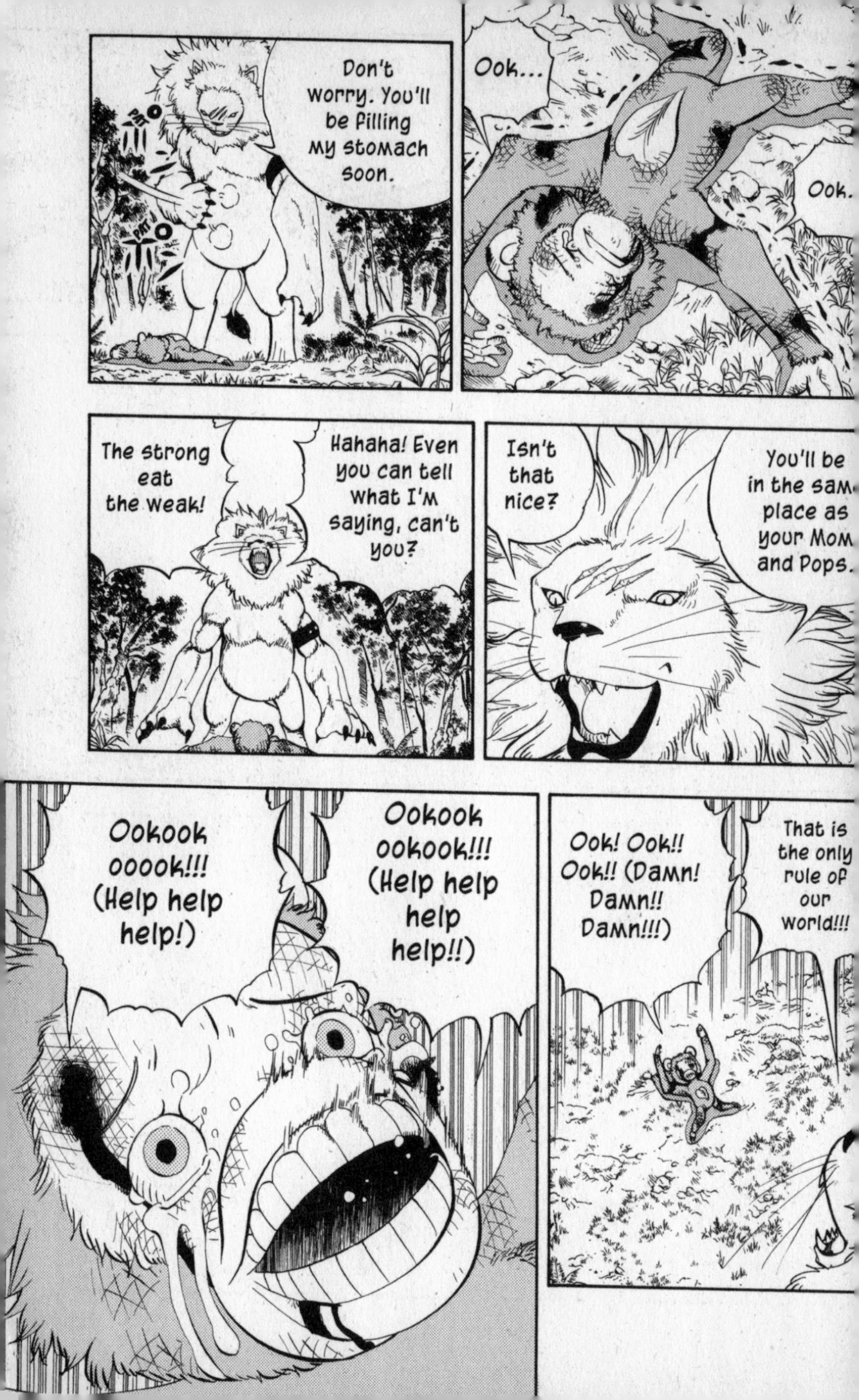

Ook...
Ook.
Don't worry. You'll be filling my stomach soon.
PAT
PAT
You'll be in the sam place as your Mom and Pops.
Isn't that nice?
Hahaha! Even you can tell what I'm saying, can't you?
The strong eat the weak!
That is the only rule of our world!!!
Ook! Ook!! Ook!! (Damn! Damn!! Damn!!!)
Ookook ookook!!! (Help help help help!!)
Ookook ooook!!! (Help help help!)

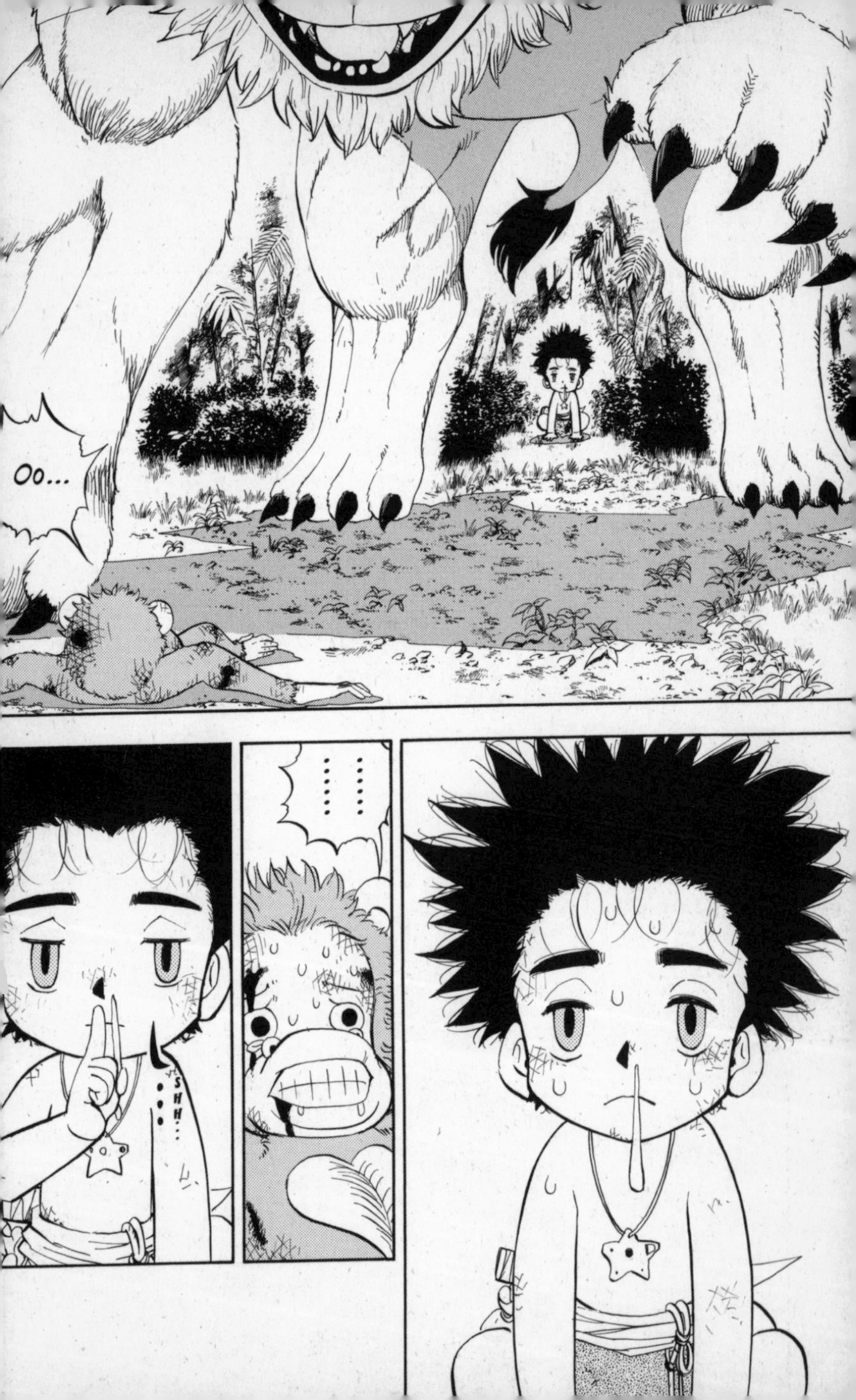
Oo...
......
SHH...

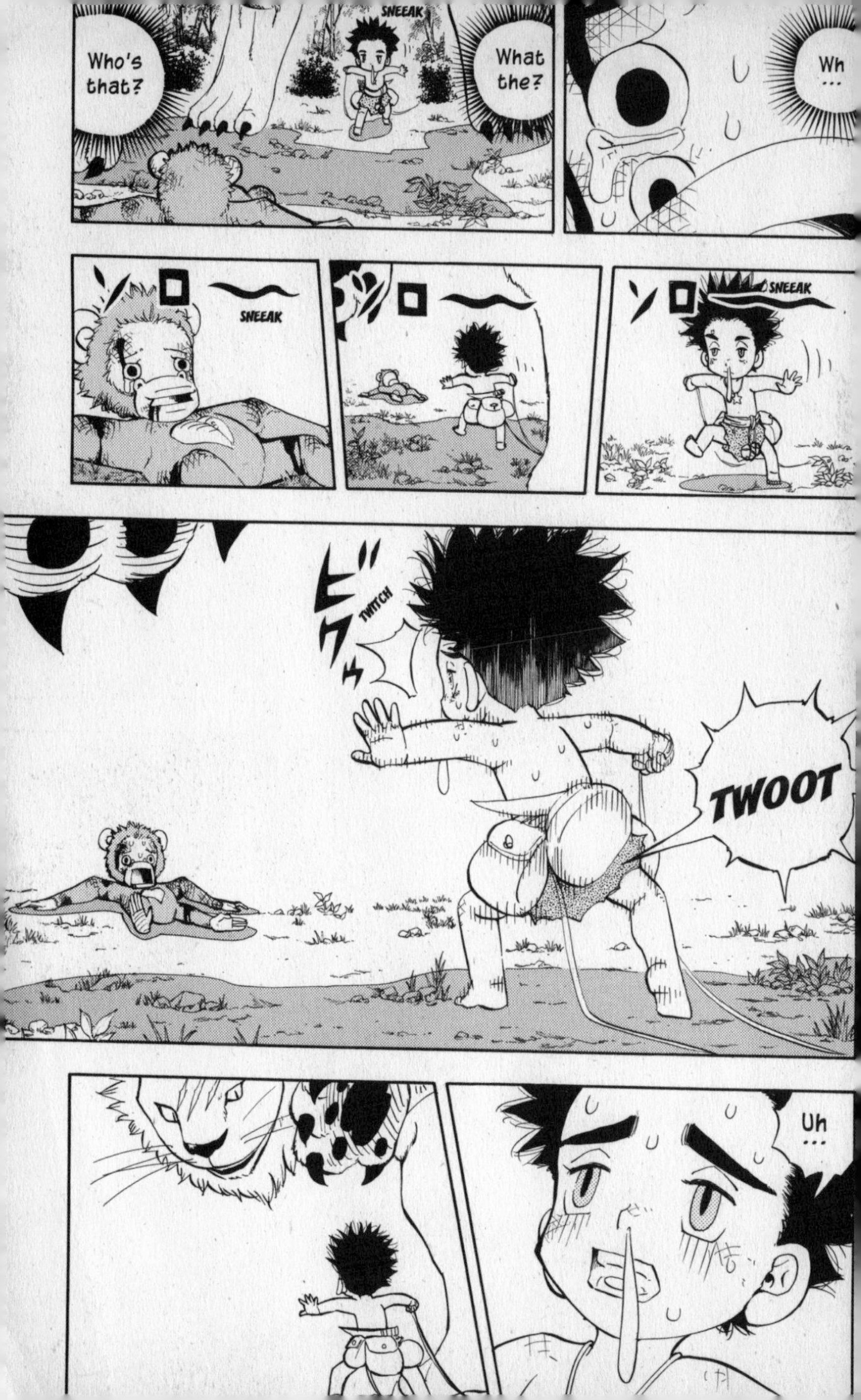
Wh ...
What the?
SNEEAK
Who's that?
ソロ
SNEEAK
ソロ
ソロ
SNEEAK
ビクッ
TWITCH
TWOOT
Uh ...

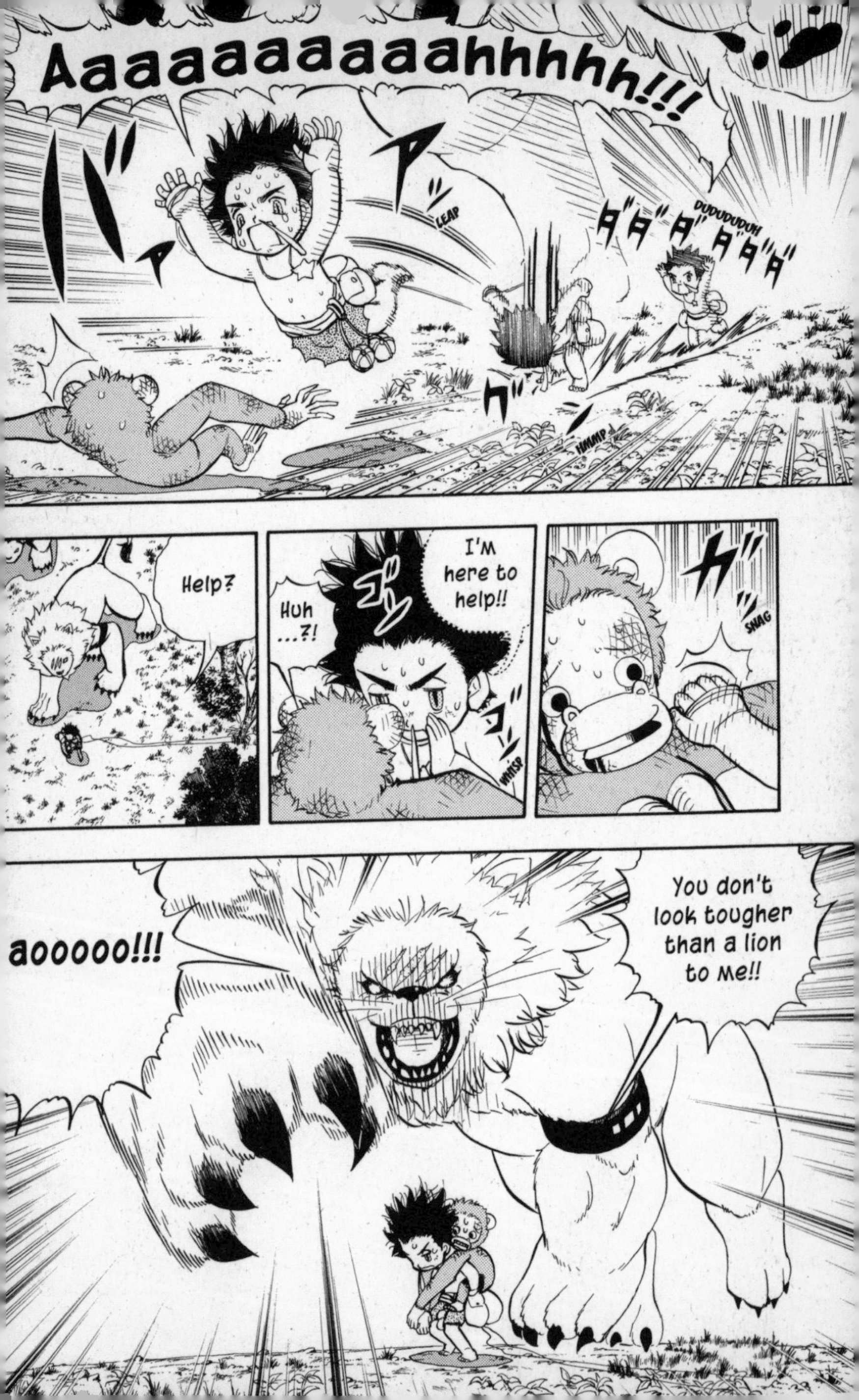
Aaaaaaaaaaaahhhhhh!!!
DUDUDUDUH
LEAP
HMMP
SNAG
I'M here to help!!
Huh ...?!
WHISP
Help?
You don't look tougher than a lion to me!!
aooooo!!!

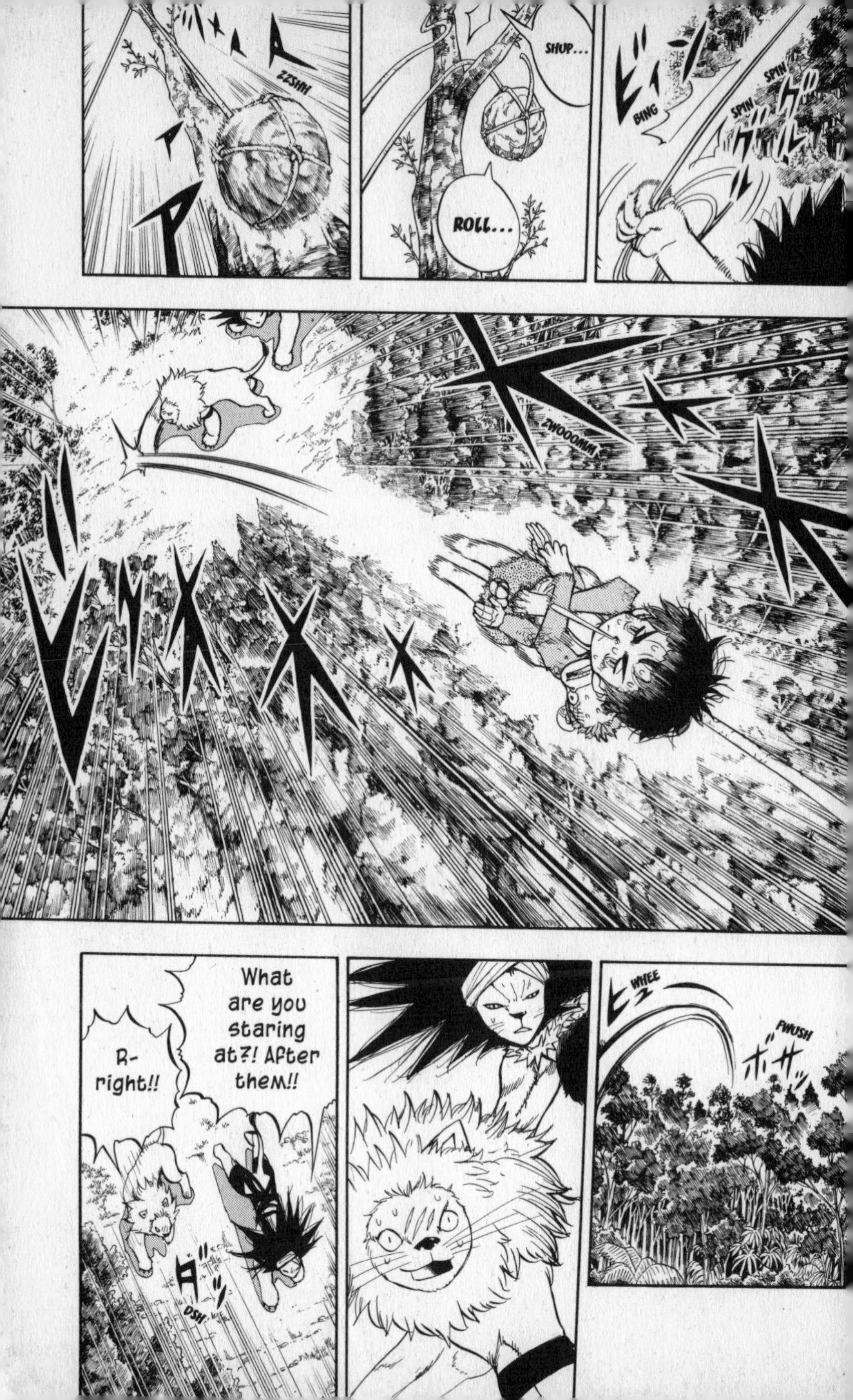
BING
SPIN
SPIN
SHUP...
ROLL...
ZZSHH
ZWOOOMM
WHEE
FWUSH
What are you staring at?! After them!!
R-right!!
DSH

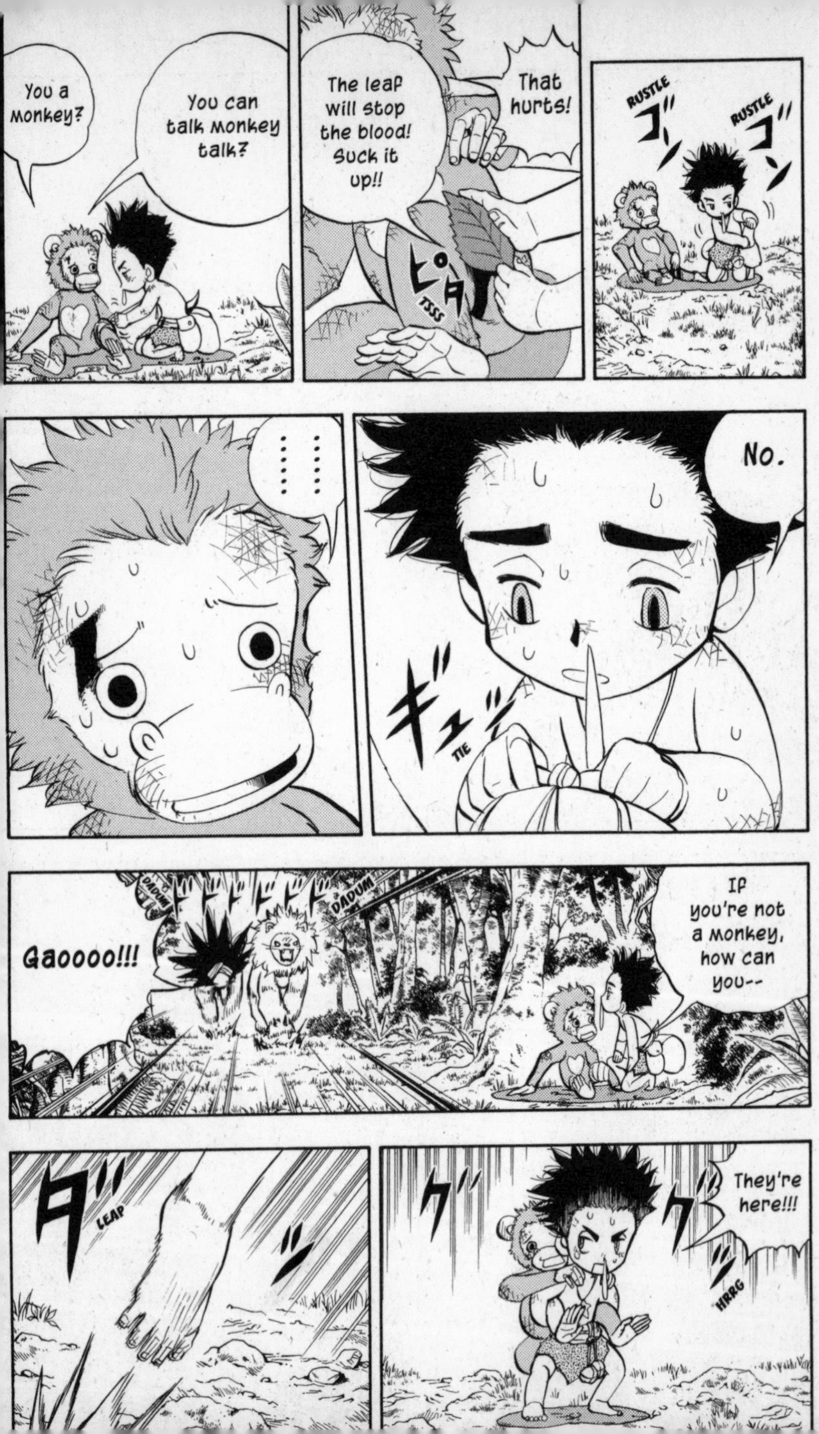
RUSTLE
RUSTLE
That hurts!
The leaf will stop the blood! Suck it up!!
TSSS
You can talk monkey talk?
You a monkey?
No.
TIE
......
If you're not a monkey, how can you--
DADUM
DADUM
Gaoooo!!!
They're here!!!
HRRG
LEAP

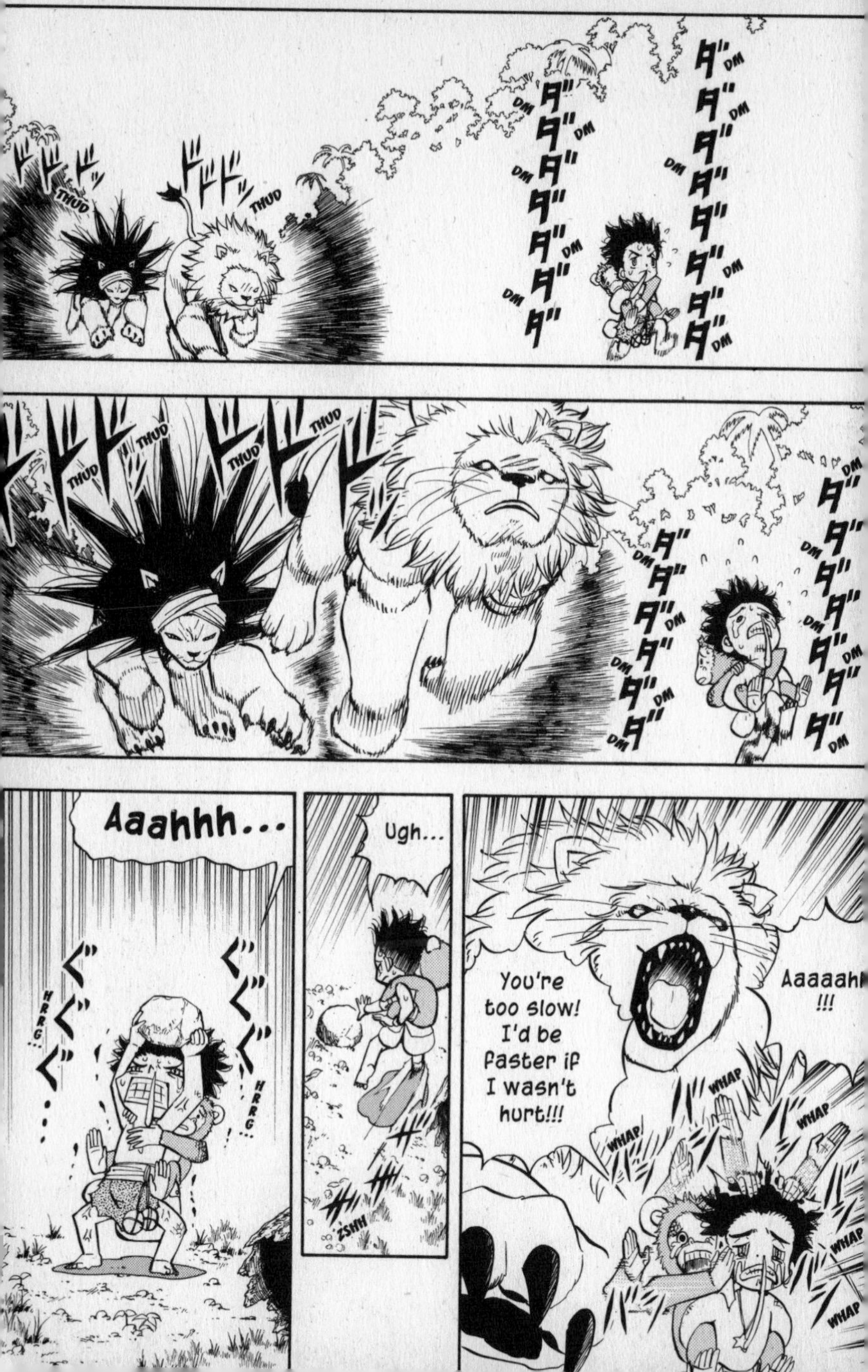

ダダダダダダダダ
DM DM DM DM DM
ダダダダダダ
DM DM DM DM
ドドドッ
THUD
ドドドッ
THUD
ダダダダダダダ
DM DM DM DM DM
ダダダダダ
DM DM DM DM
ドドドド
THUD THUD THUD
ドドドド
THUD THUD
Aaaaah!!!
You're too slow! I'd be faster if I wasn't hurt!!!
WHAP WHAP WHAP WHAP WHAP
Ugh...
ZSHH
Aaahhh...
ぐぐぐ
HRRG...
ぐぐぐ
HRRG...

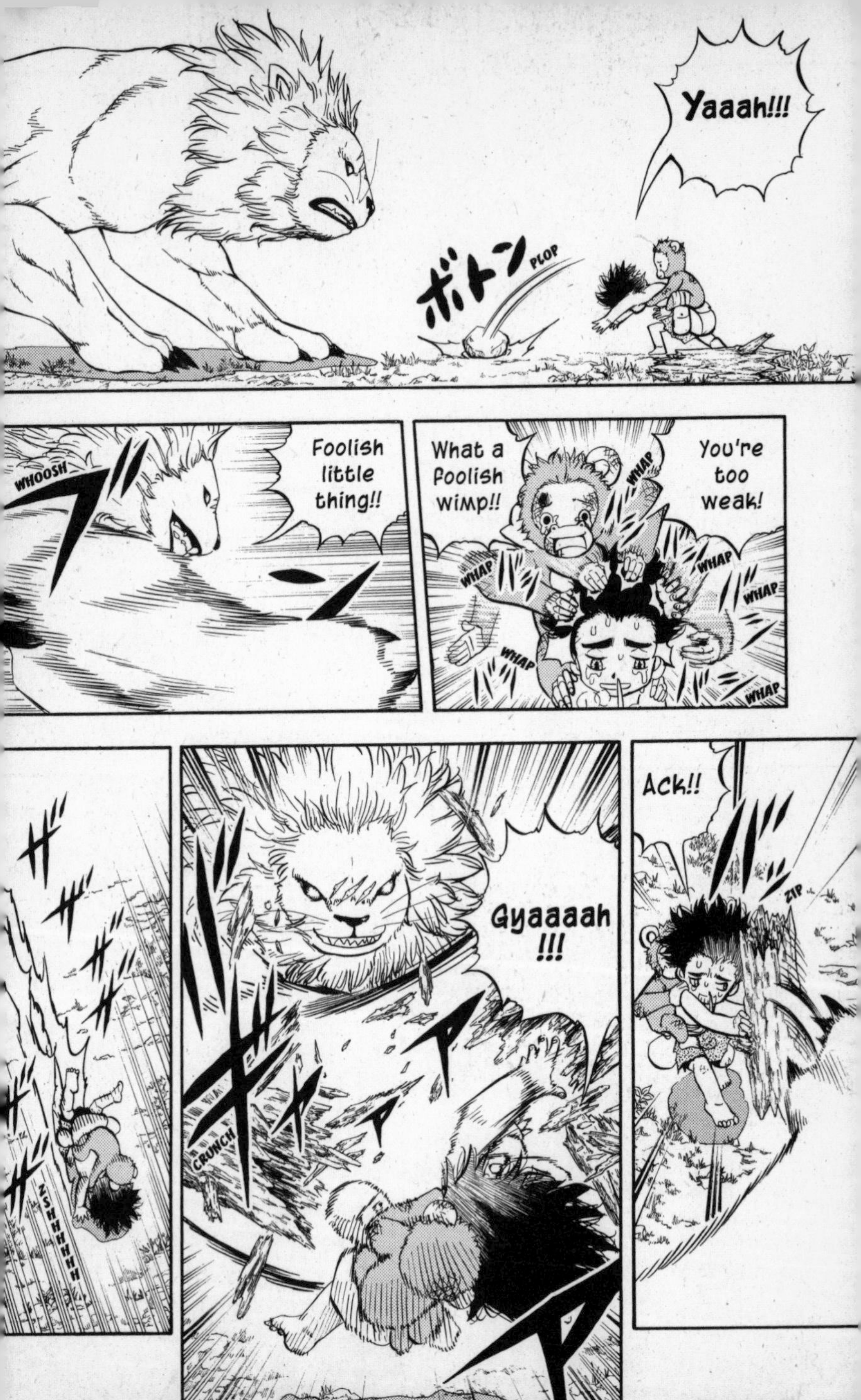
Yaaah!!!
ボトン
PLOP
You're too weak!
What a foolish wimp!!
WHAP
WHAP
WHAP
WHAP
WHAP
WHAP
Foolish little thing!!
WHOOSH
Ack!!
ZIP
Gyaaaah!!!
CRUNCH
ZSHHHHHH

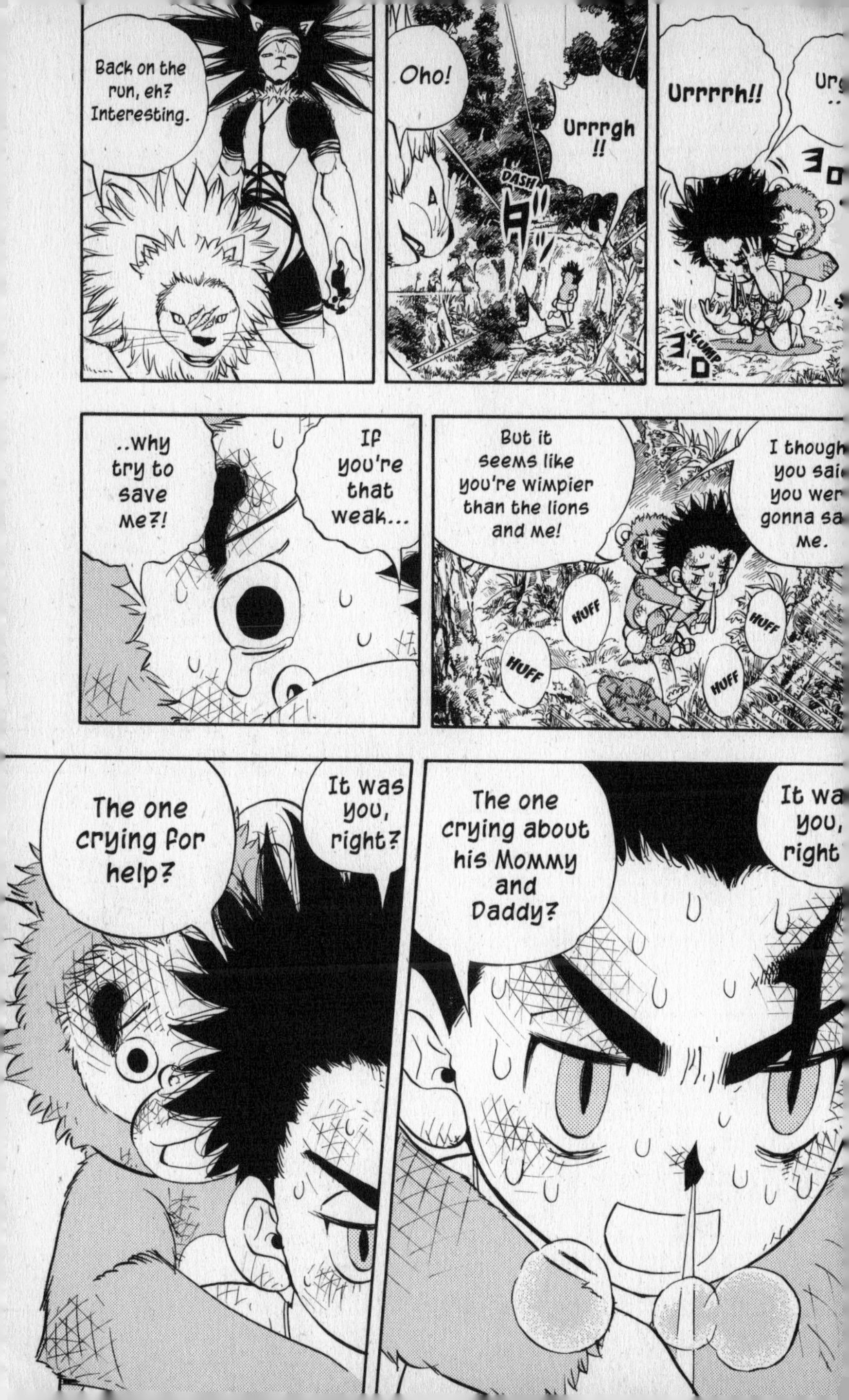
Urrrrh!!
SLUMP
Oho!
Urrrgh!!
DASH
Back on the run, eh? Interesting.
I though you sai you wer gonna sa me.
But it seems like you're wimpier than the lions and me!
HUFF
HUFF
HUFF
HUFF
If you're that weak...
..why try to save me?!
It wa you, right
The one crying about his Mommy and Daddy?
It was you, right?
The one crying for help?

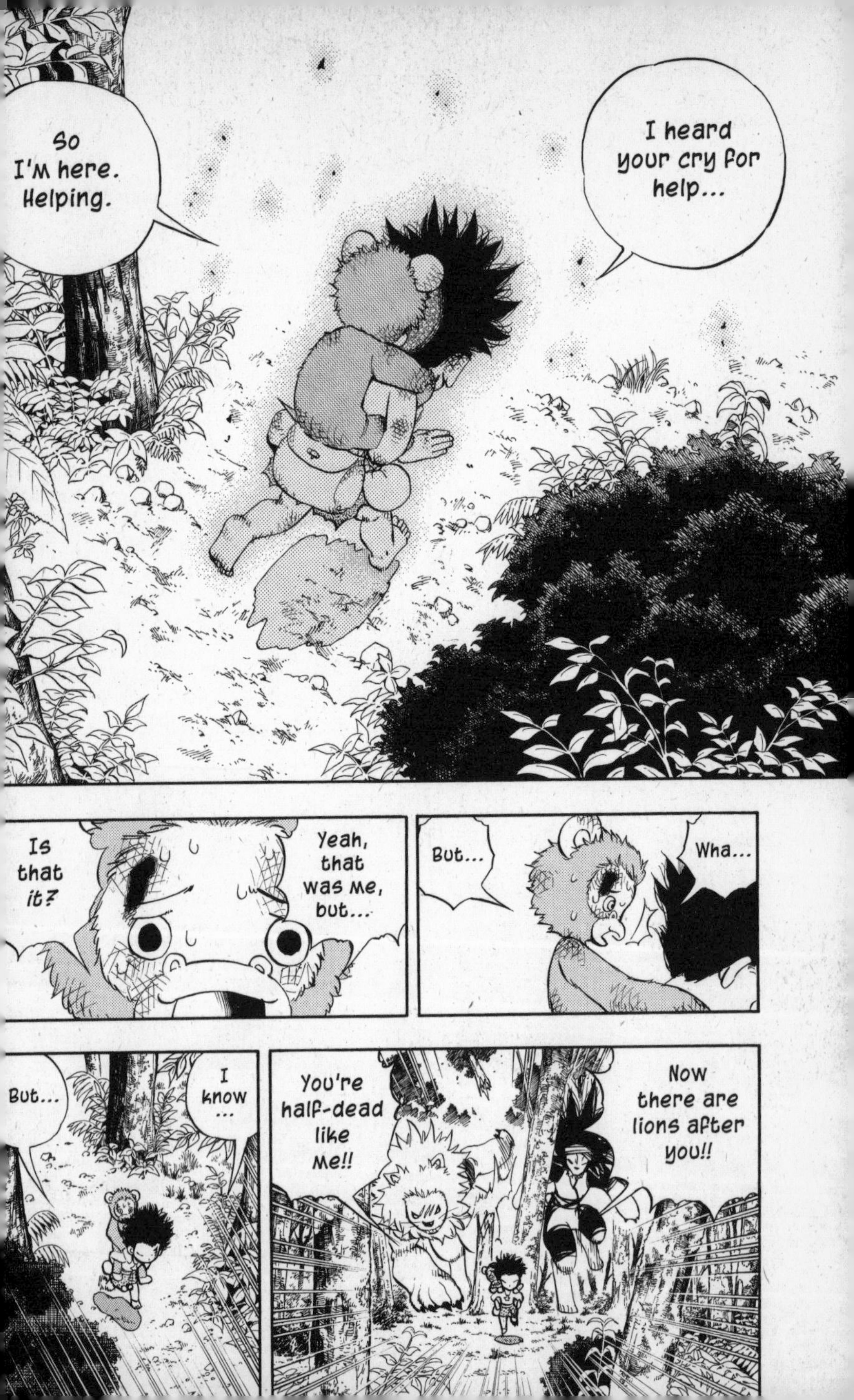
I heard your cry for help...
So I'm here. Helping.
Wha...
But...
Yeah, that was me, but...
Is that it?
Now there are lions after you!!
You're half-dead like me!!
I know...
But...

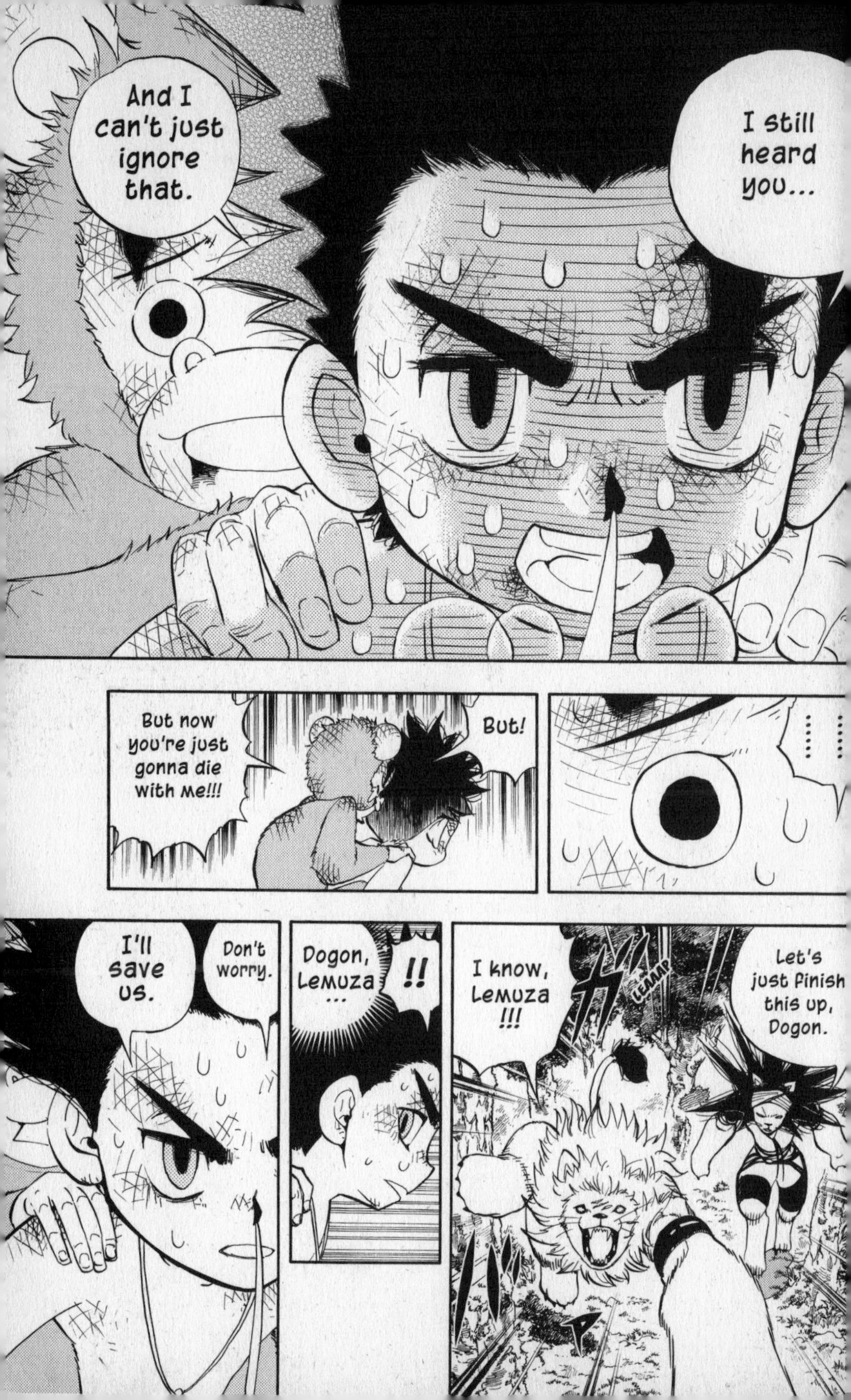
I still heard you...
And I can't just ignore that.
......
But!
But now you're just gonna die with me!!!
Let's just finish this up, Dogon.
LEAAAP
I know, Lemuza!!!
!!
Dogon, Lemuza...
Don't worry.
I'll save us.

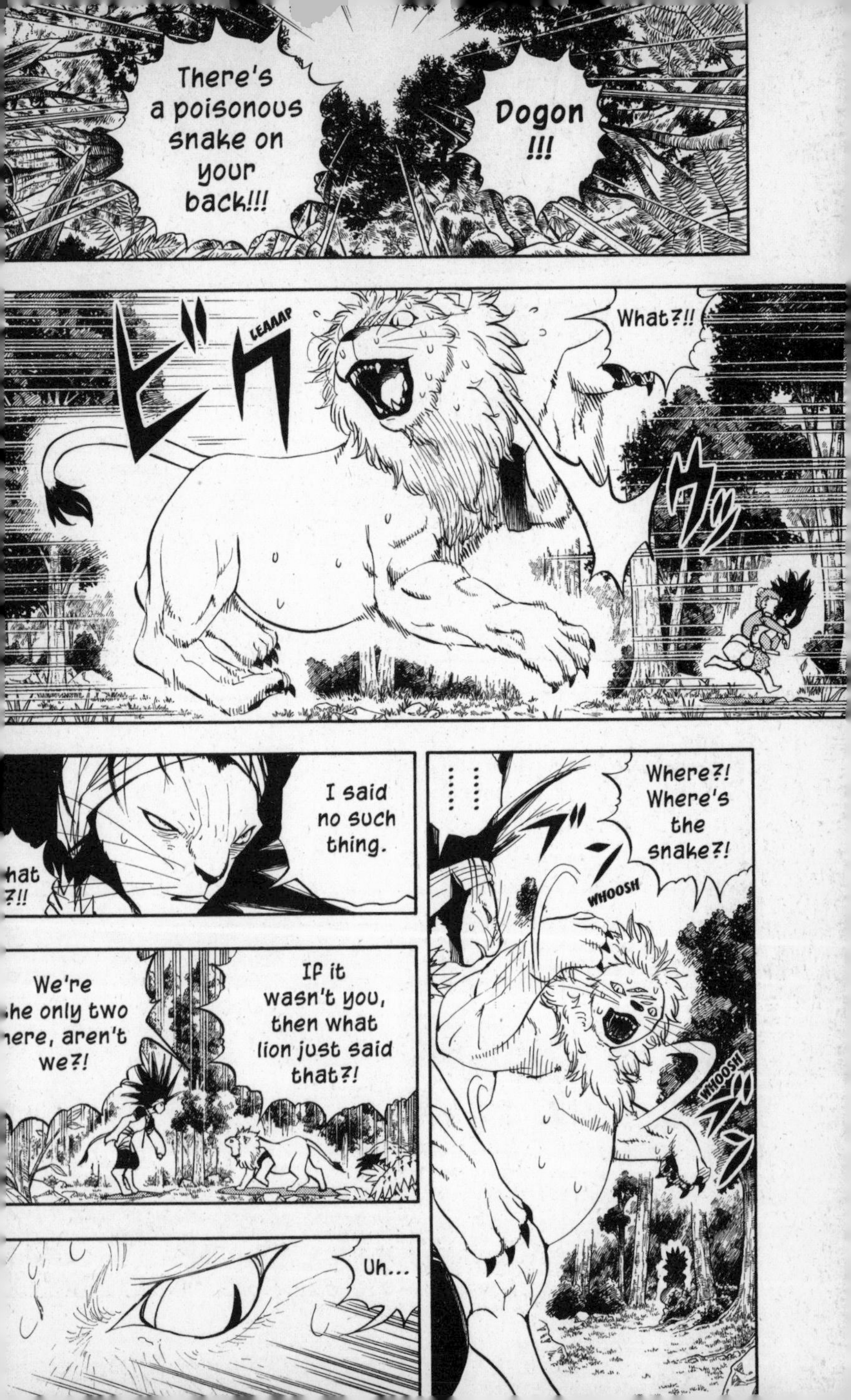
Dogon !!!
There's a poisonous snake on your back!!!
What?!!
LEAAAP
......
Where?! Where's the snake?!
WHOOSH
WHOOSH
I said no such thing.
hat ?!!
If it wasn't you, then what lion just said that?!
We're he only two ere, aren't we?!
Uh...

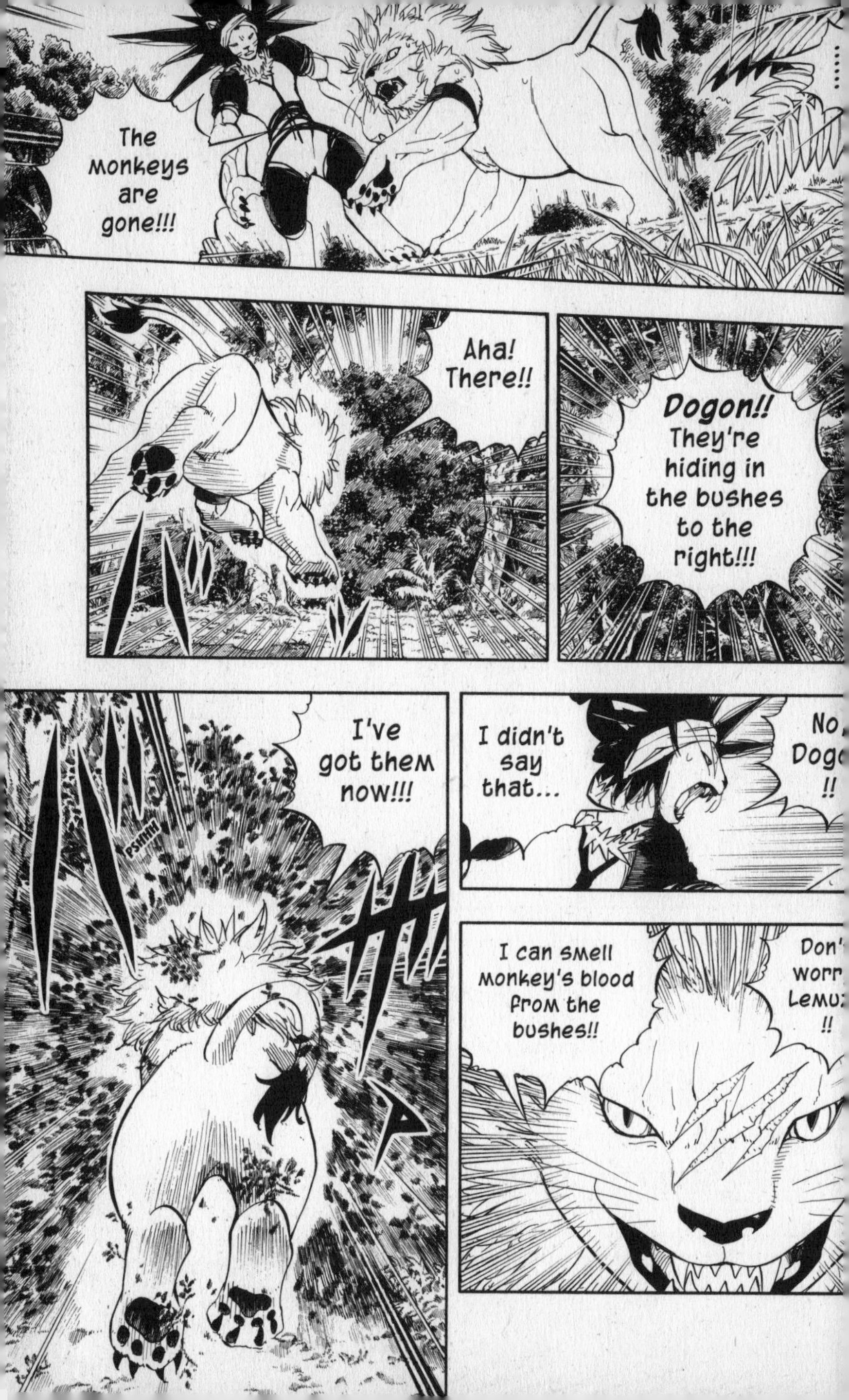
The monkeys are gone!!!
Dogon!! They're hiding in the bushes to the right!!!
Aha! There!!
No, Dogo !!
I didn't say that...
Don' worr Lemu !!
I can smell monkey's blood from the bushes!!
I've got them now!!!
PSHHH

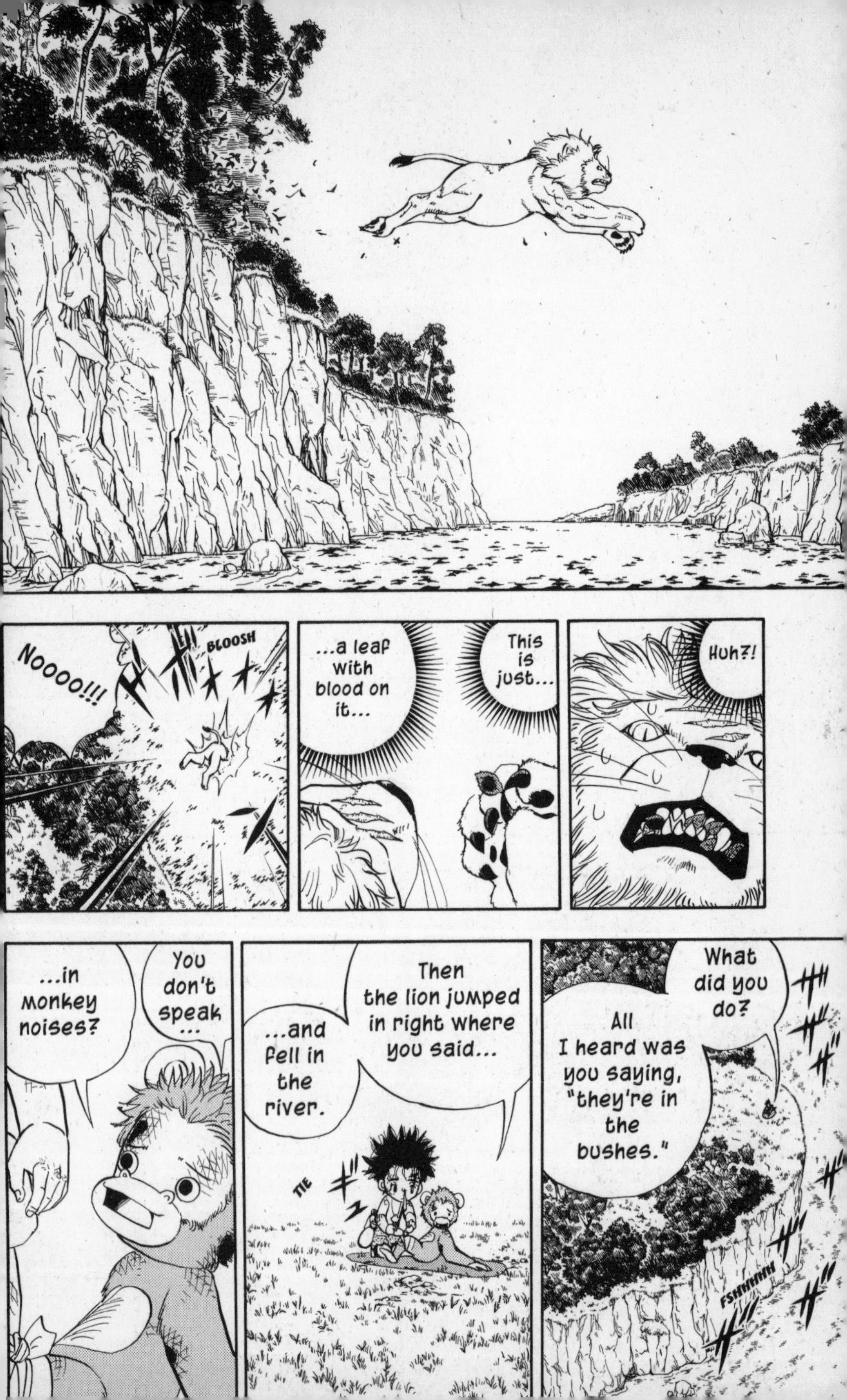
Huh?!
This is just...
...a leaf with blood on it...
Noooo!!!
BLOOSH
What did you do?
All I heard was you saying, "they're in the bushes."
FSHHHHH
Then the lion jumped in right where you said...
...and fell in the river.
TIE
You don't speak...
...in monkey noises?

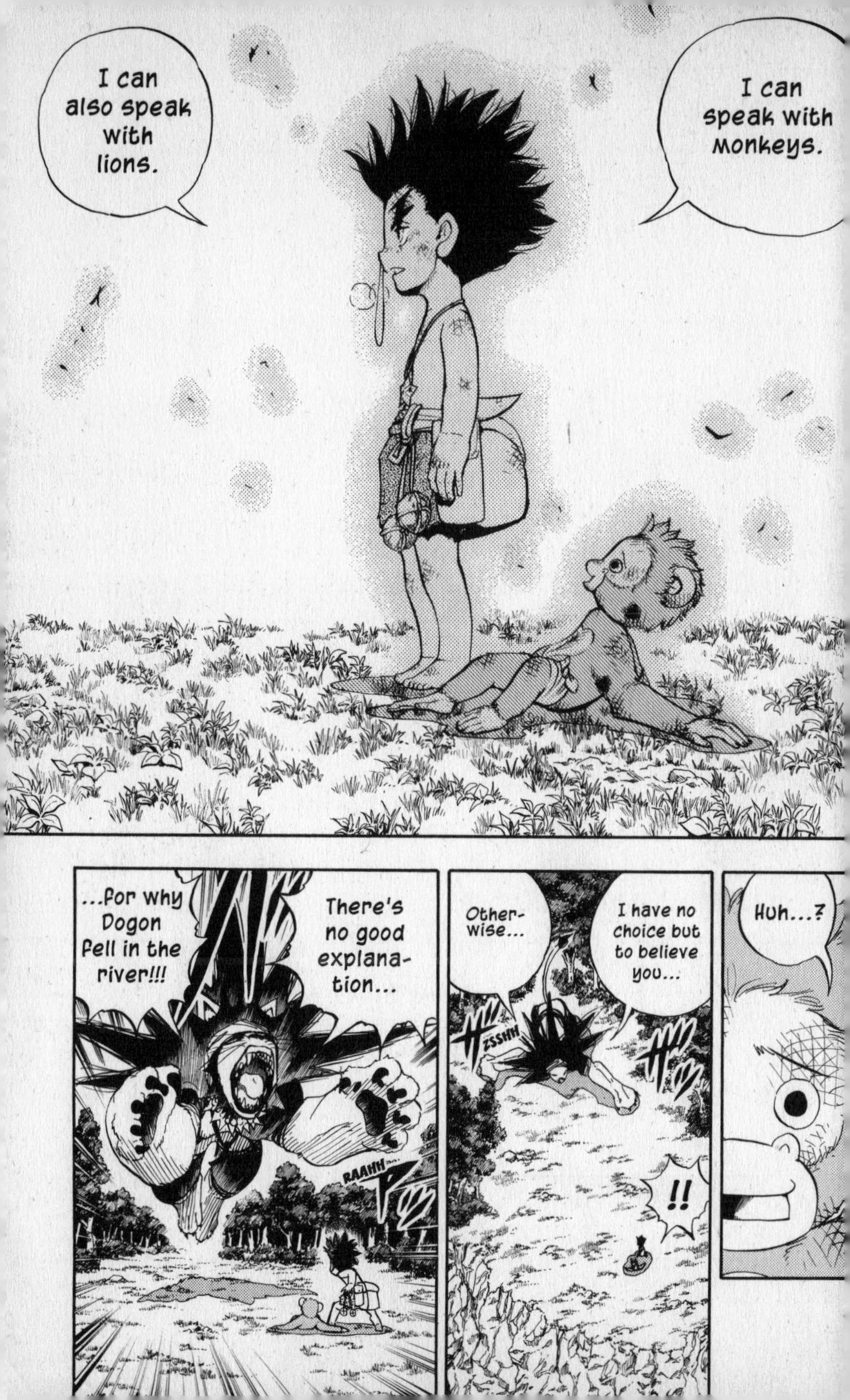
I can speak with monkeys.
I can also speak with lions.
Huh...?
I have no choice but to believe you...
Other-wise...
ZSSHH
!!
There's no good explana-tion...
...for why Dogon fell in the river!!!
RAAHH

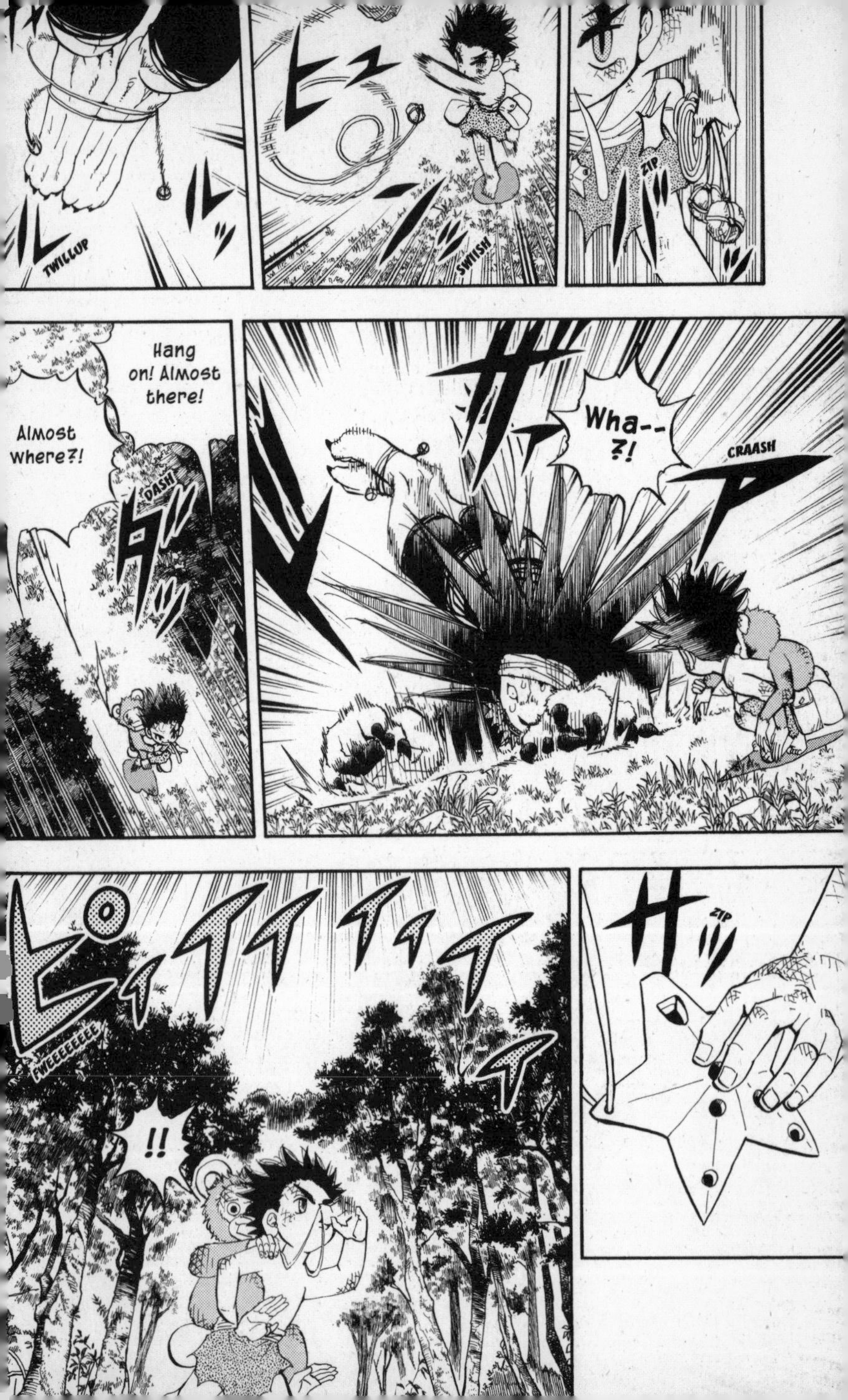
ZIP
SWISH
TWILLUP
Wha--?!
CRAASH
Hang on! Almost there!
Almost where?!
DASH
ZIP
FWEEEEEEEE
!!

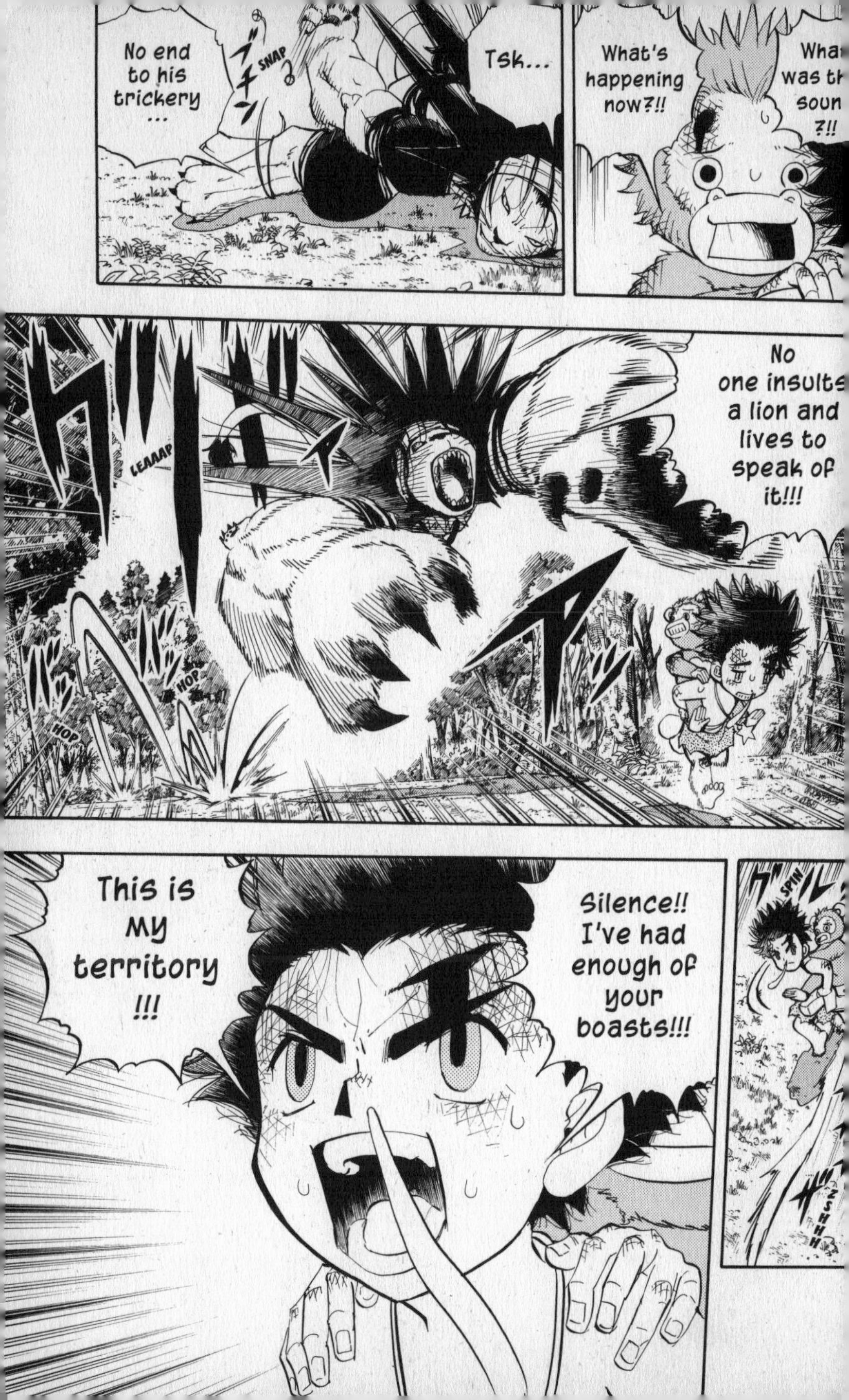
What's happening now?!!
Wha was th soun ?!!
Tsk...
SNAP
No end to his trickery ...
No one insults a lion and lives to speak of it!!!
LEAAAP
HOP
HOP
SPIN
ZSHHH
Silence!! I've had enough of your boasts!!!
This is my territory !!!

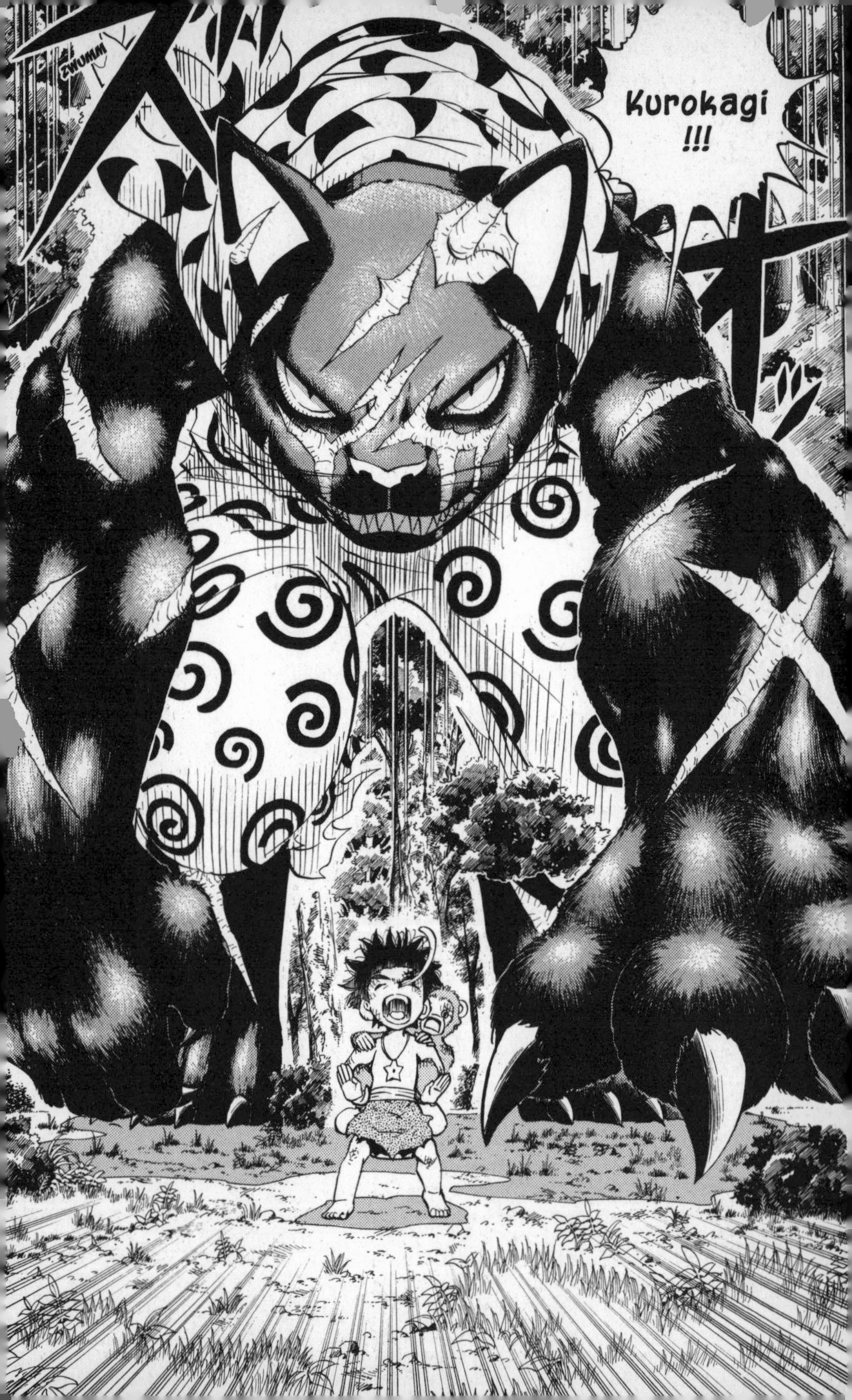
Kurokagi !!!
ZWUMM

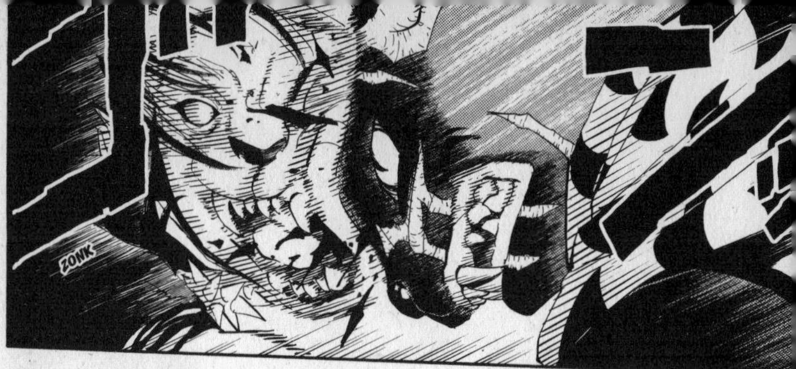
ZONK

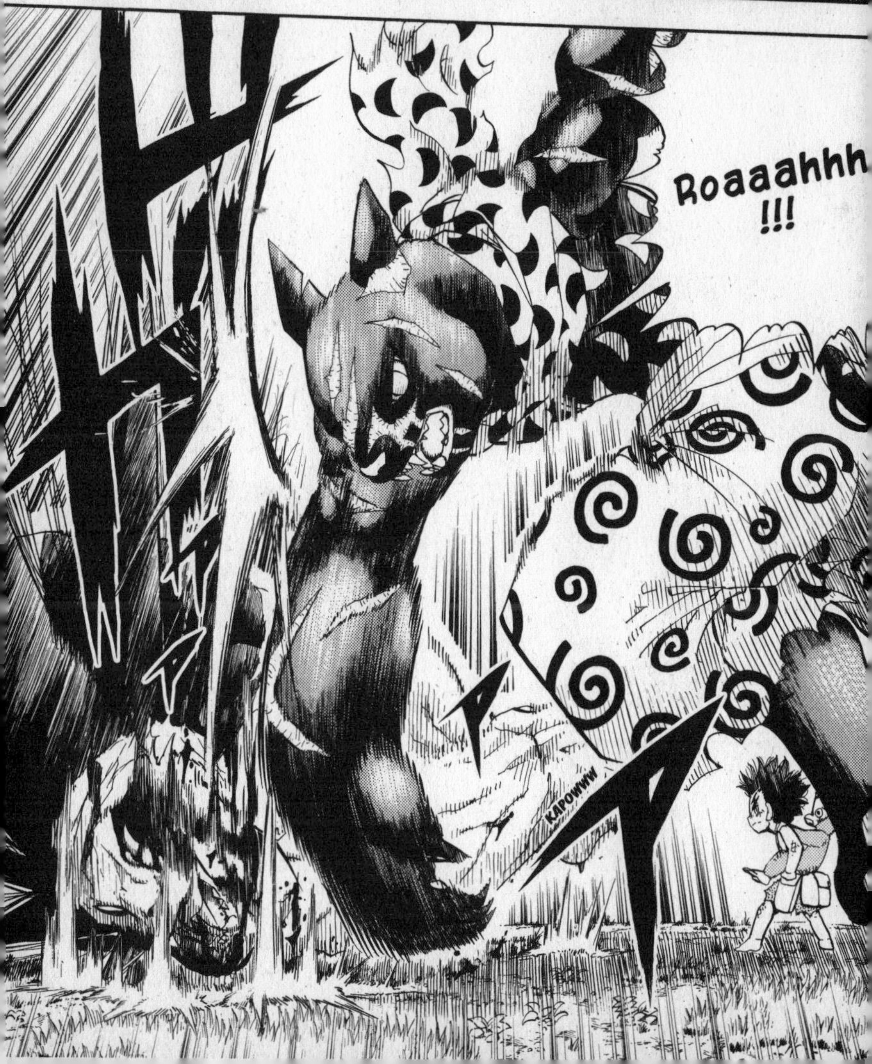
Roaaaahhh
!!!
KAPOWWW

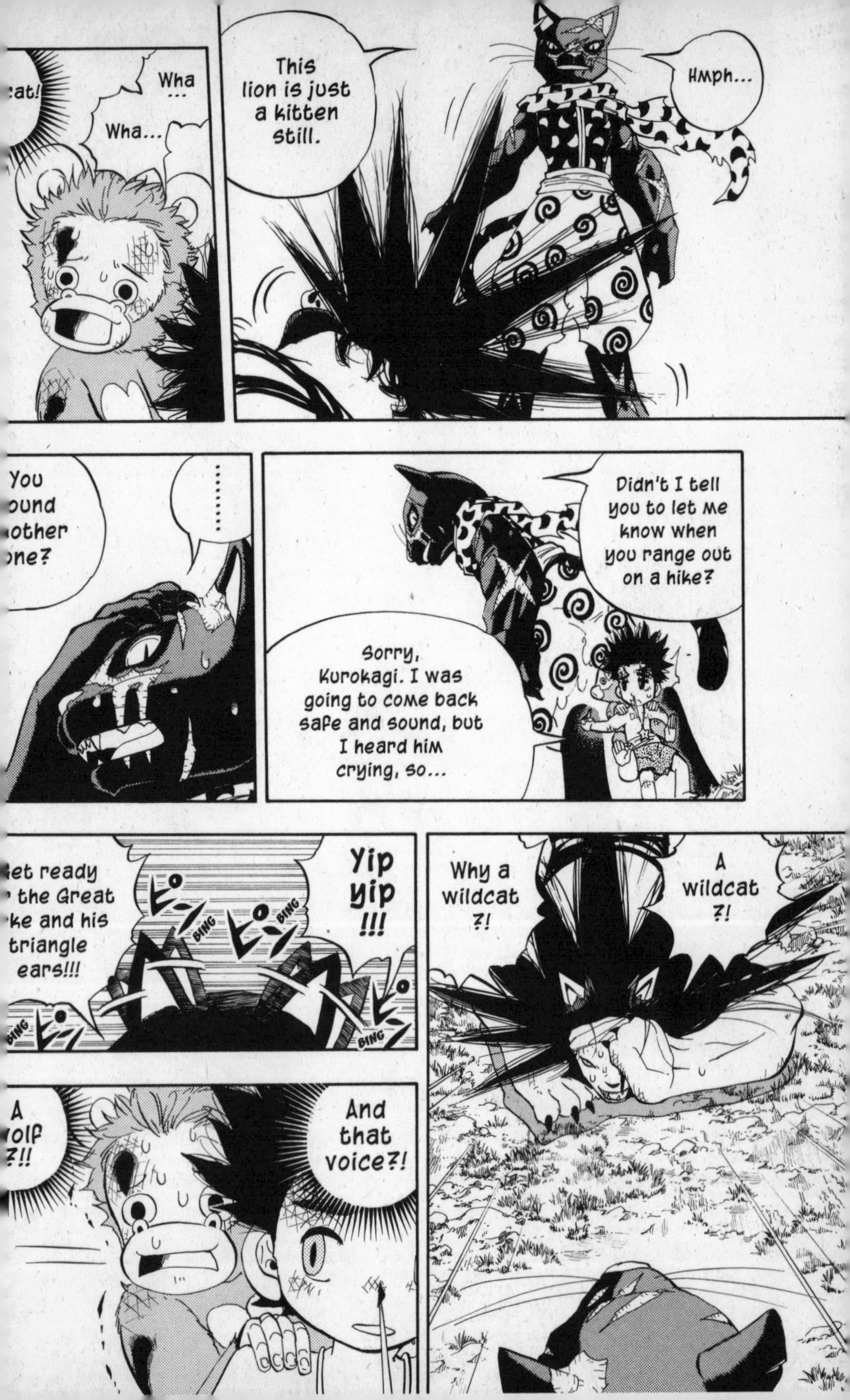

Hmph...
This lion is just a kitten still.
Wha...
Wha...
at!
Didn't I tell you to let me know when you range out on a hike?
Sorry, Kurokagi. I was going to come back safe and sound, but I heard him crying, so...
......
You ound other ne?
A wildcat ?!
Why a wildcat ?!
Yip yip !!!
BING
BING
BING
BING
et ready the Great ke and his triangle ears!!!
And that voice?!
A olf ?!!

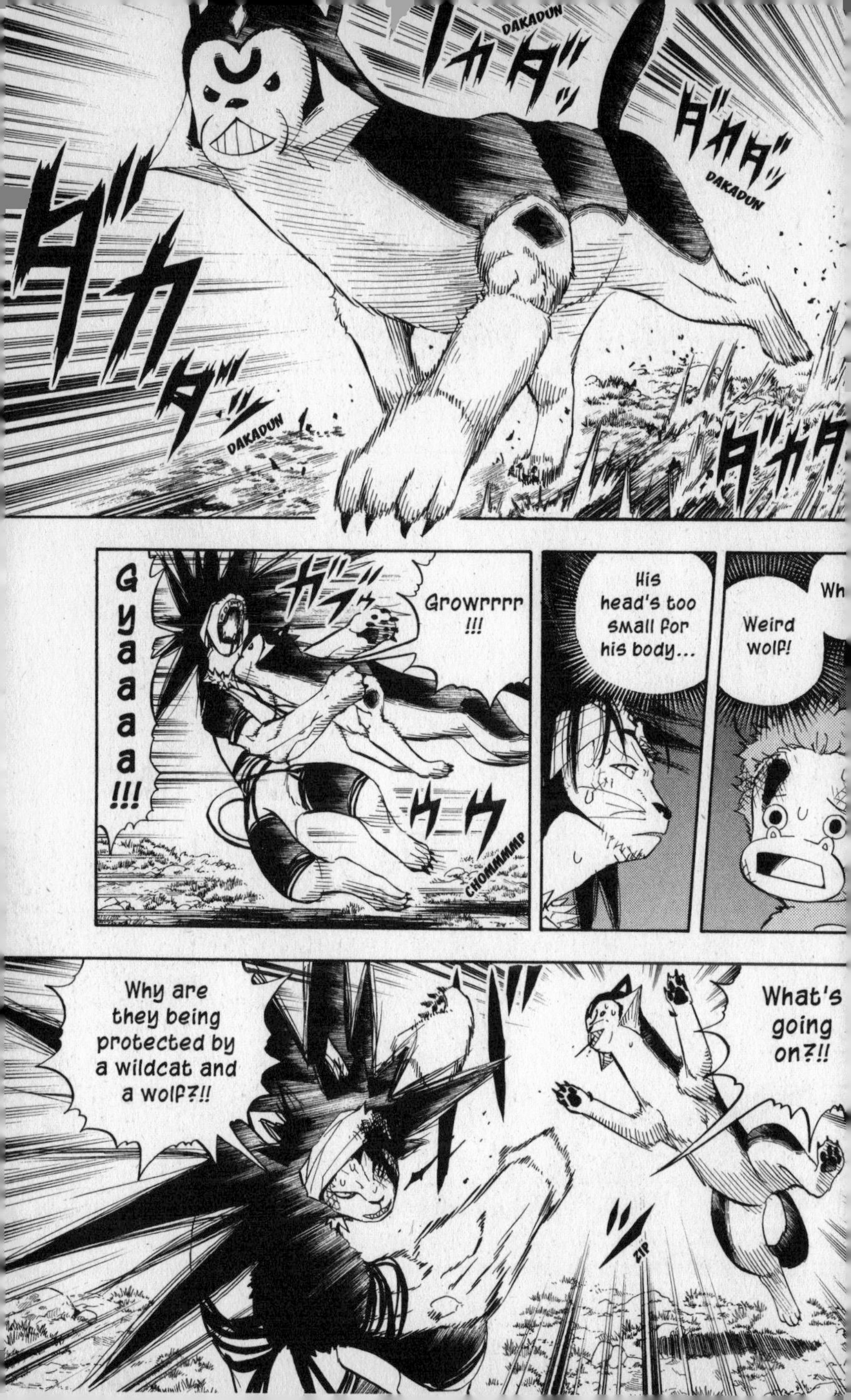
DAKADUN
DAKADUN
DAKADUN
Wh
Weird wolf!
His head's too small for his body...
Growrrrr !!!
Gyaaaaa!!!
CHOMMMMP
What's going on?!!
Why are they being protected by a wildcat and a wolf?!!
ZIP

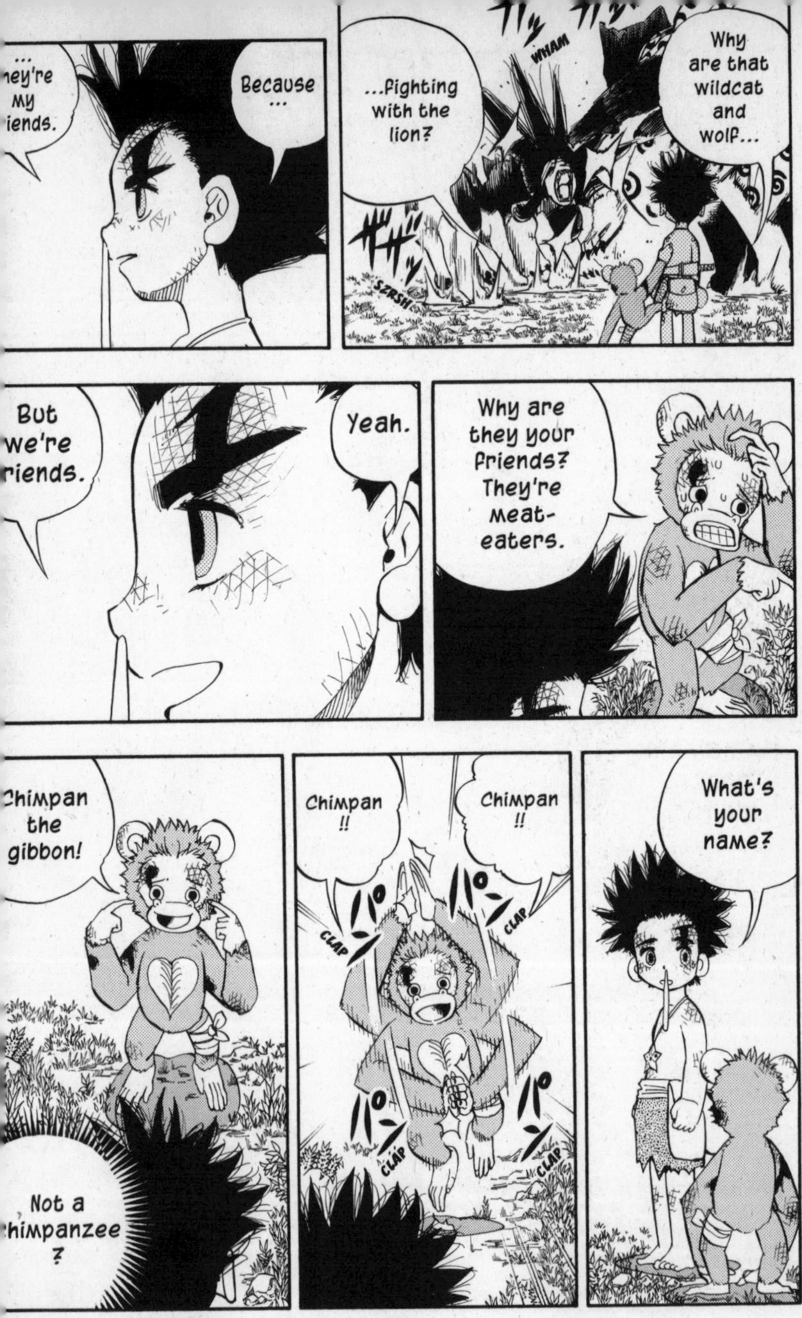

WHAM
Why are that wildcat and wolf...
...fighting with the lion?
SZRSH
Because ...
... ey're My iends.
Why are they your friends? They're meat-eaters.
Yeah.
But we're riends.
What's your name?
Chimpan !!
CLAP
CLAP
Chimpan !!
CLAP
CLAP
Chimpan the gibbon!
Not a himpanzee ?

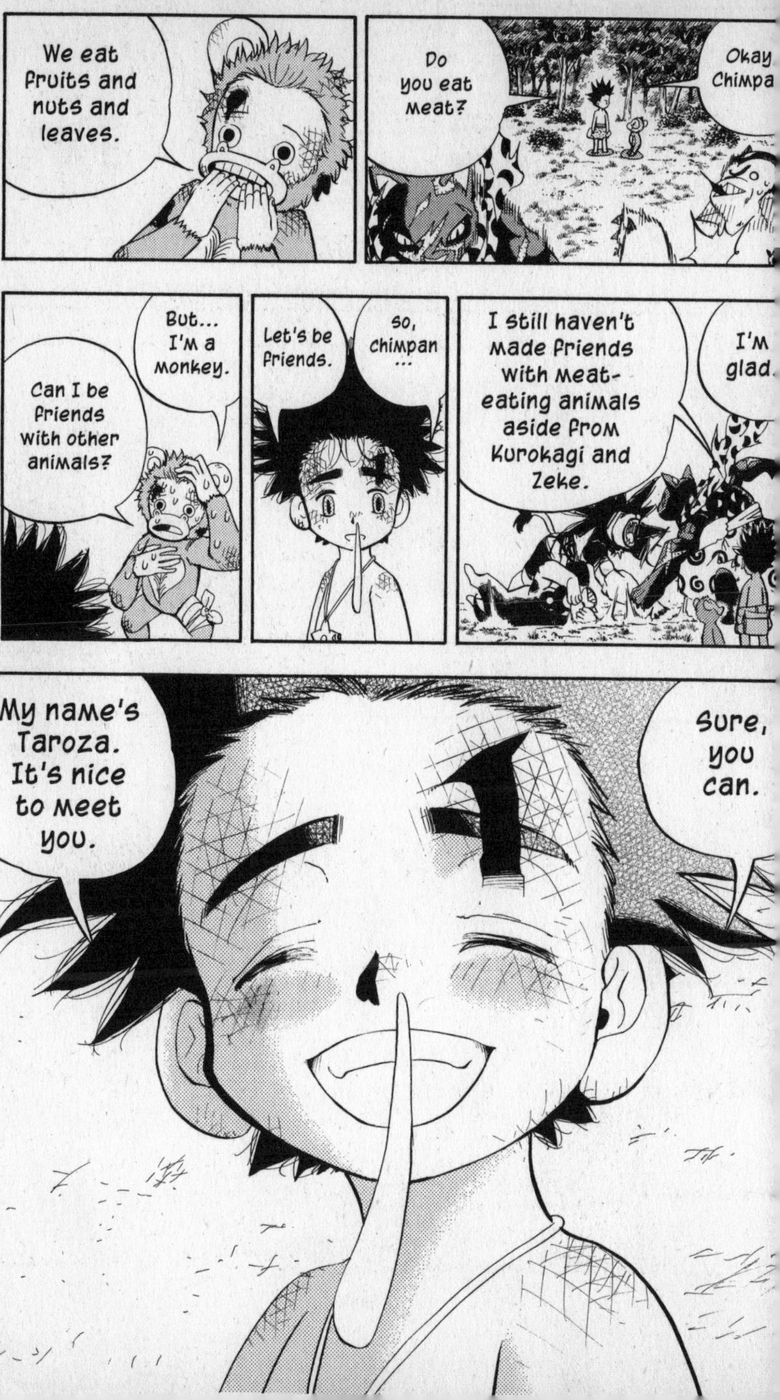
Okay Chimpa
Do you eat meat?
We eat fruits and nuts and leaves.
I'm glad.
I still haven't made friends with meat-eating animals aside from Kurokagi and Zeke.
So, Chimpan...
Let's be friends.
But... I'm a monkey.
Can I be friends with other animals?
Sure, you can.
My name's Taroza. It's nice to meet you.

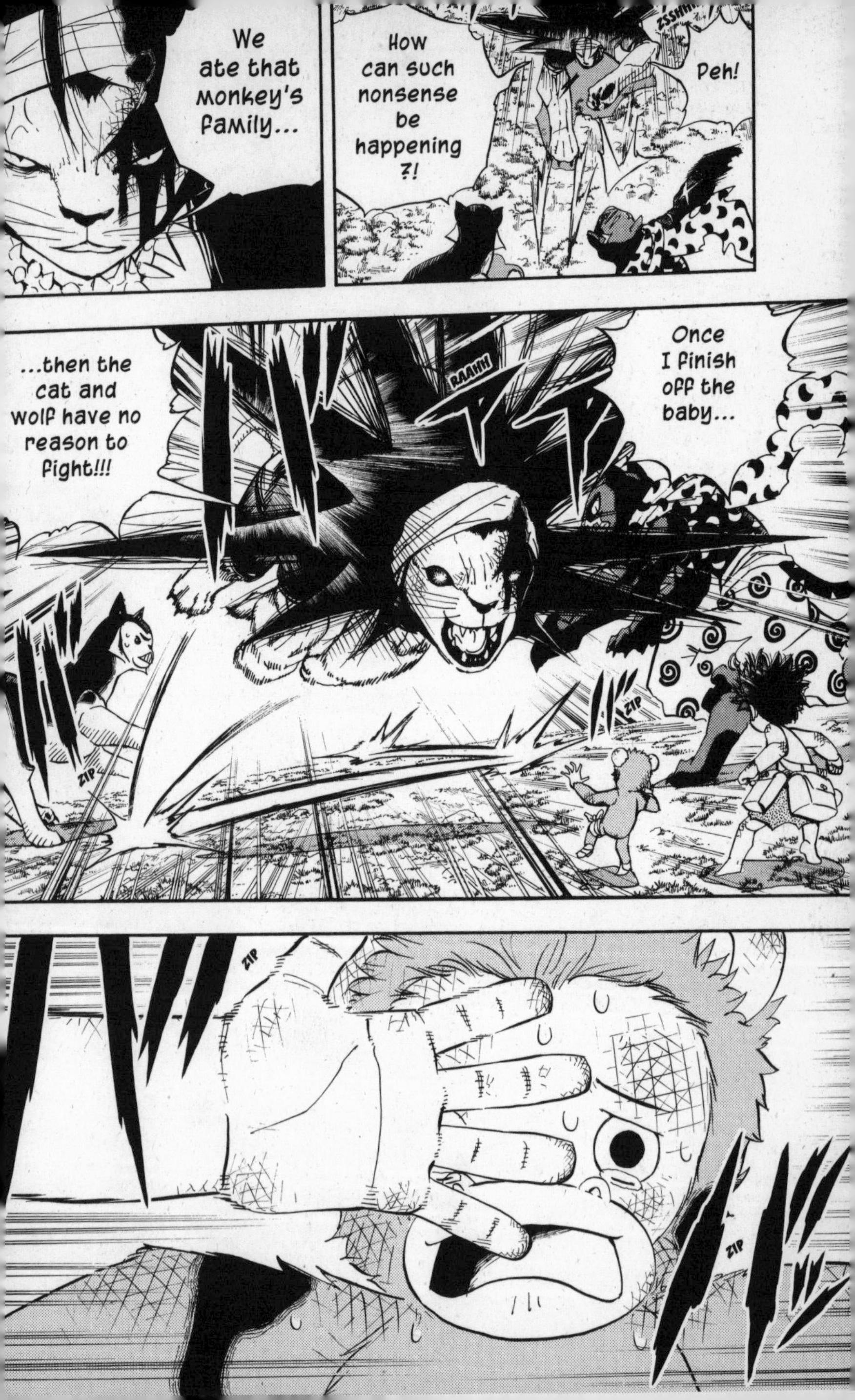
ZSSHHH
Peh!
How can such nonsense be happening ?!
We ate that monkey's family...
Once I finish off the baby...
RAAHH
ZIP
...then the cat and wolf have no reason to fight!!!
ZIP
ZIP
ZIP

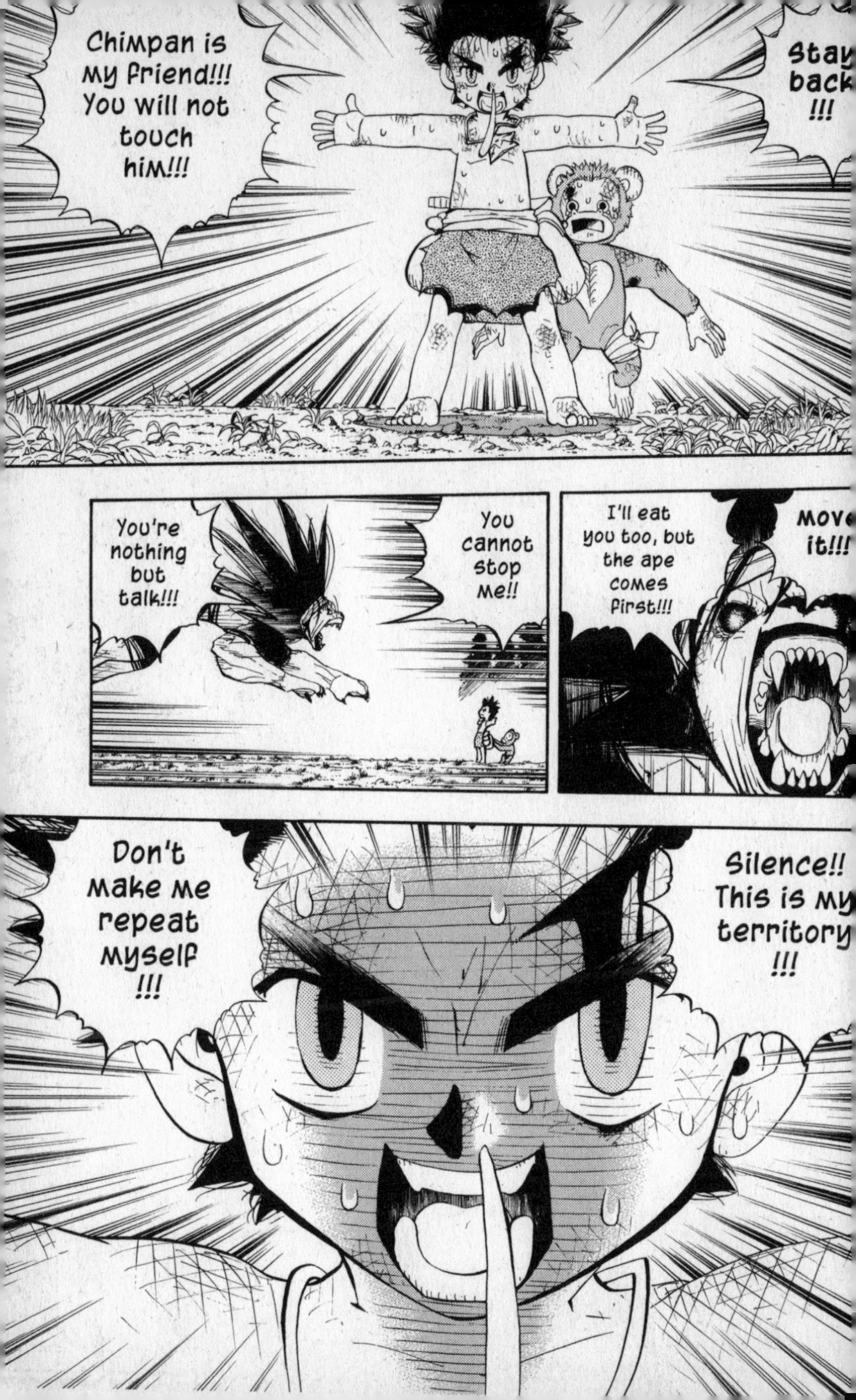
Stay back!!!
Chimpan is my friend!!! You will not touch him!!!
Move it!!!
I'll eat you too, but the ape comes first!!!
You cannot stop me!!
You're nothing but talk!!!
Silence!! This is my territory!!!
Don't make me repeat myself!!!

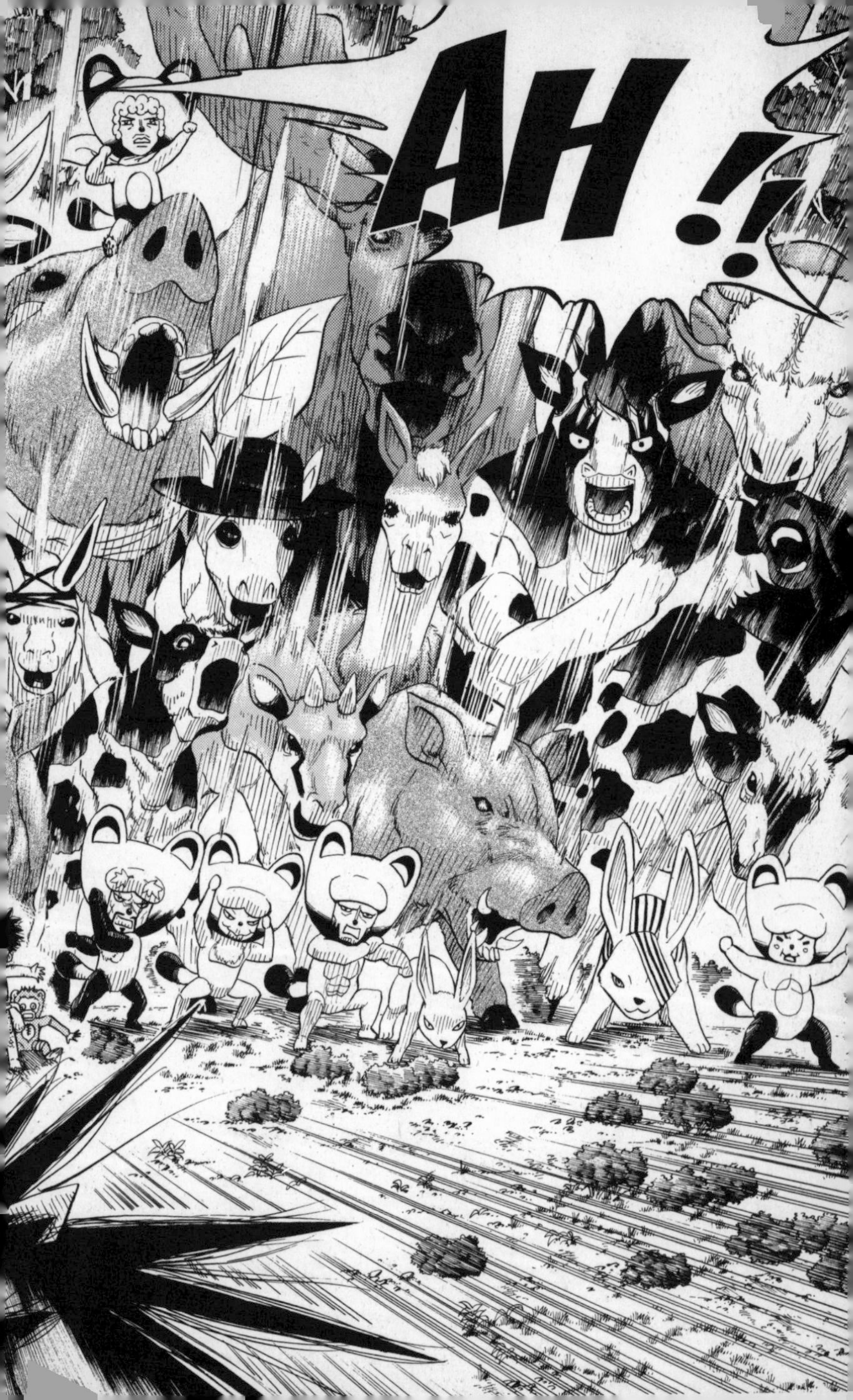
AH !!

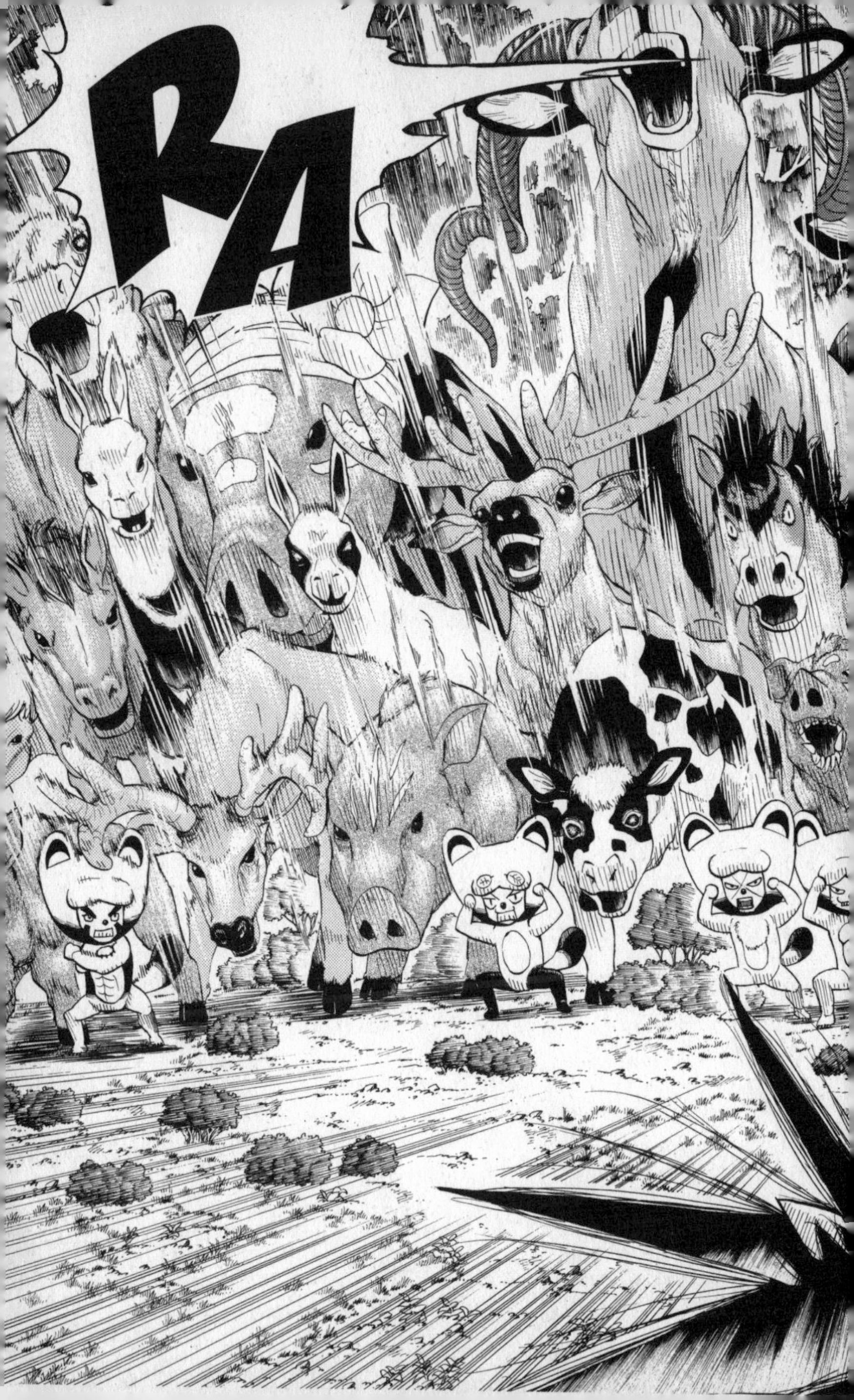
RA

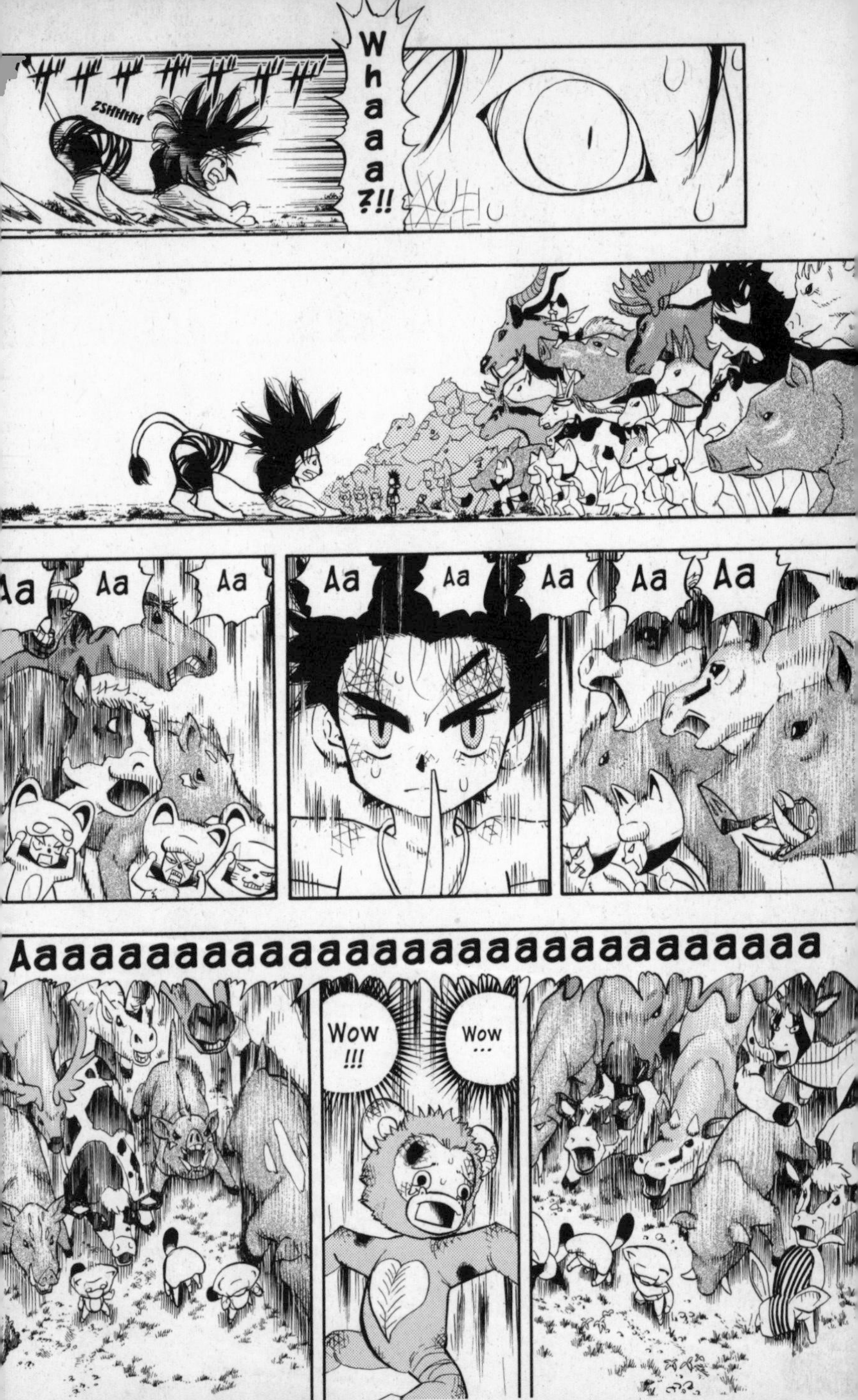
Whaaa?!!
ZSHHHH
ザザザザザザザ
Aa
Aa
Aa
Aa
Aa
Aa
Aa
Aa
Aaaaaaaaaaaaaaaaaaaaaaaaaaa
Wow...
Wow!!!

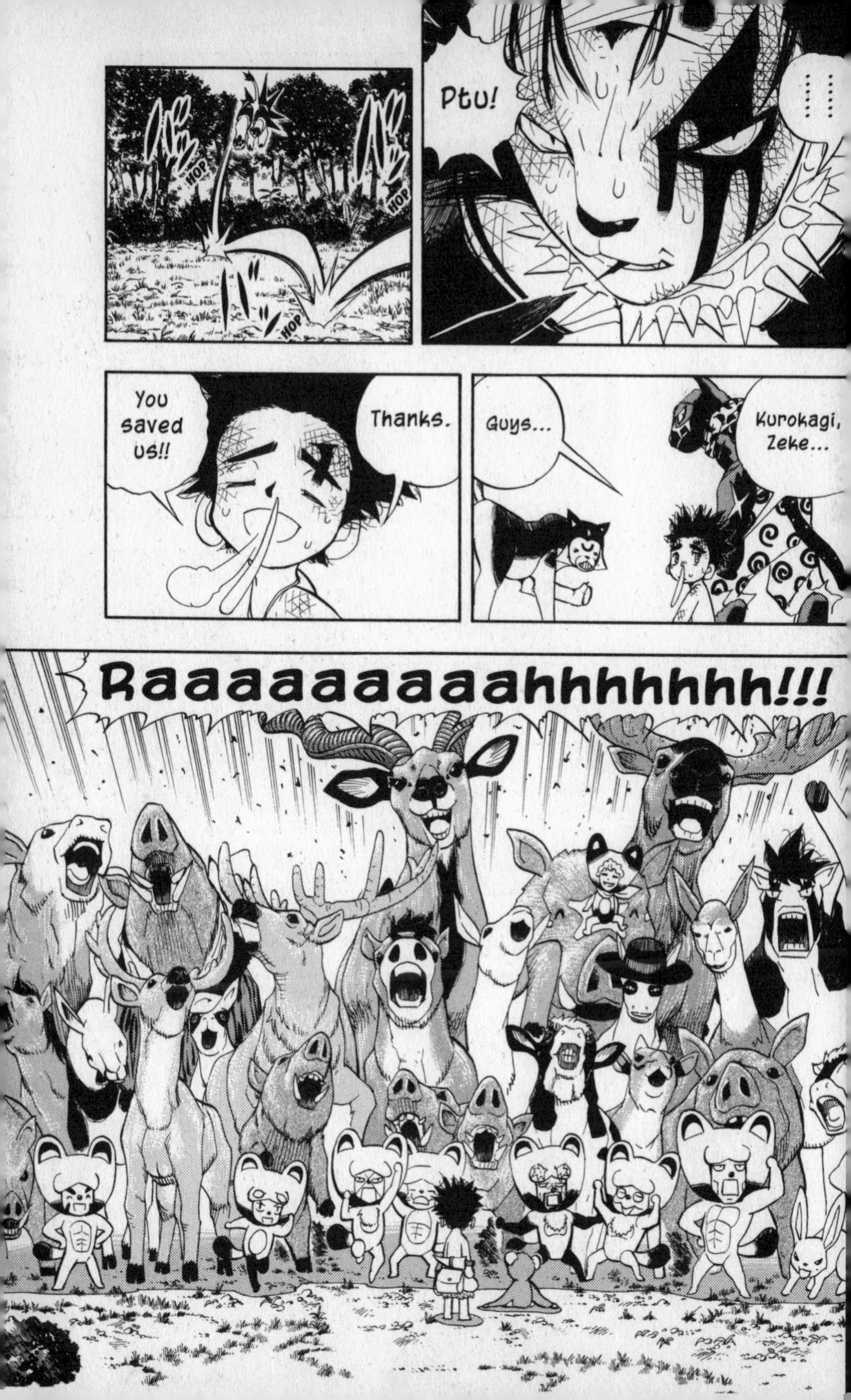
...
Ptu!
HOP
HOP
HOP
Kurokagi, Zeke...
Guys...
Thanks.
You saved us!!
Raaaaaaaaaahhhhhhh!!!

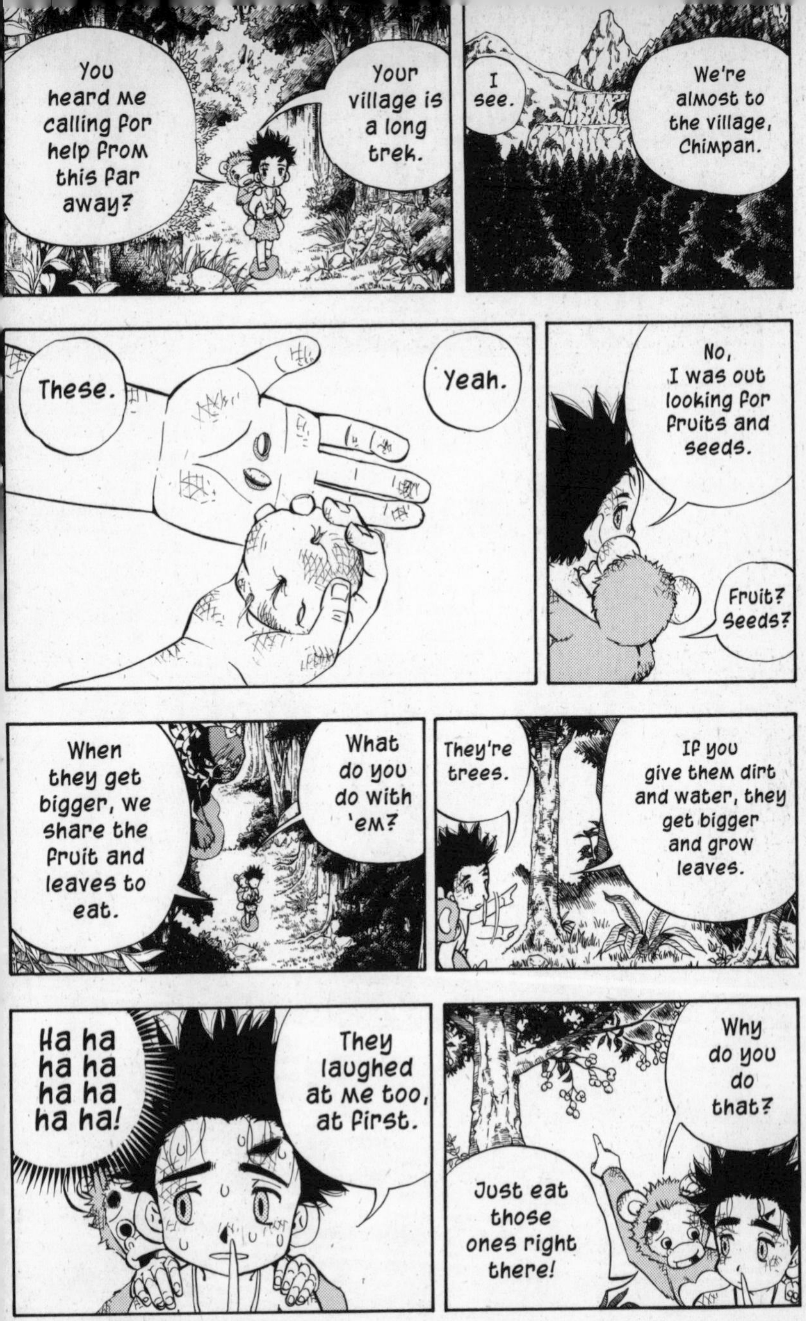
We're almost to the village, Chimpan.
I see.
Your village is a long trek.
You heard me calling for help from this far away?
No, I was out looking for fruits and seeds.
Fruit? Seeds?
Yeah.
These.
If you give them dirt and water, they get bigger and grow leaves.
They're trees.
What do you do with 'em?
When they get bigger, we share the fruit and leaves to eat.
Why do you do that?
Just eat those ones right there!
They laughed at me too, at first.
Ha ha ha ha ha ha ha ha!

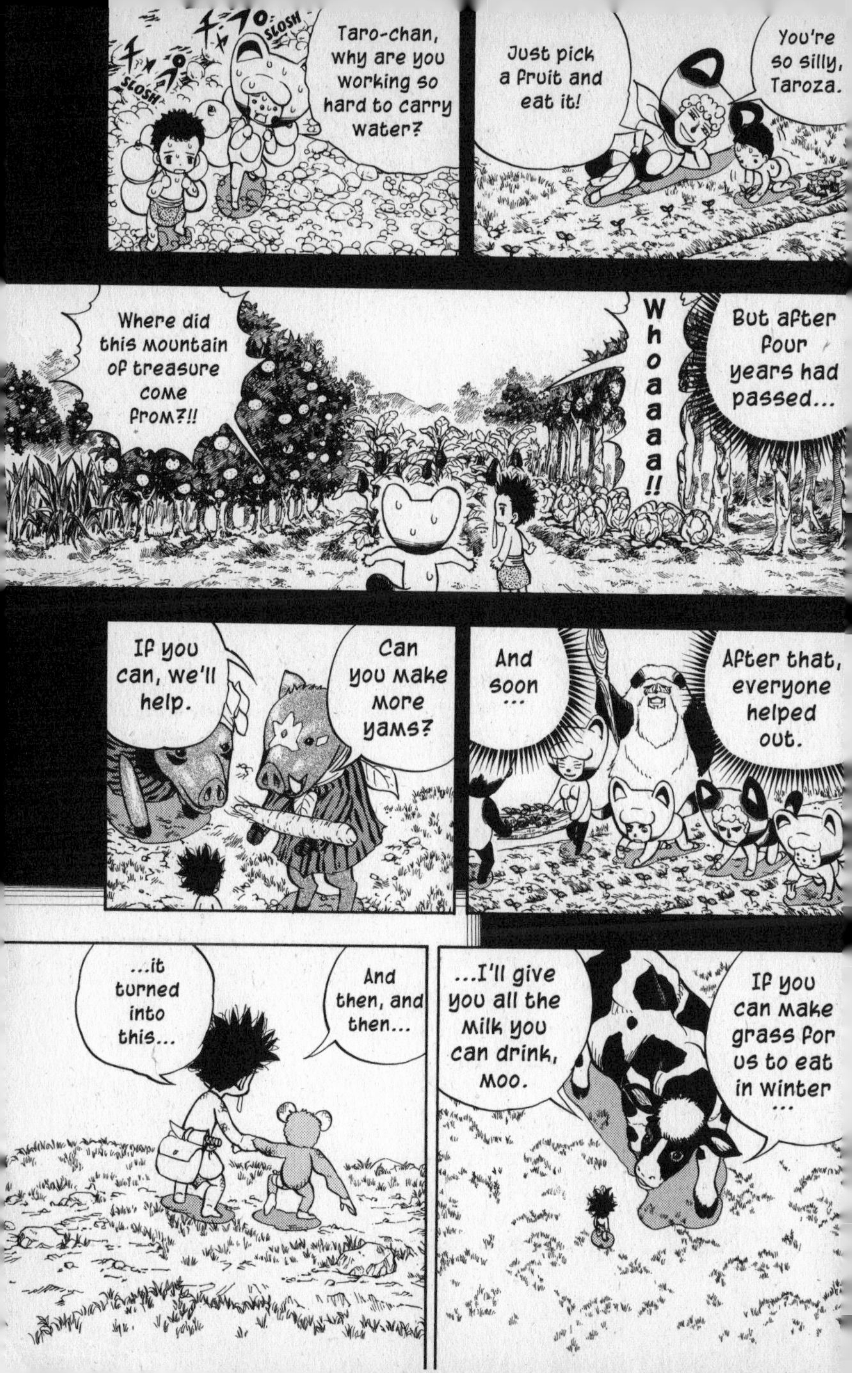
You're so silly, Taroza.
Just pick a fruit and eat it!
Taro-chan, why are you working so hard to carry water?
SLOSH
SLOSH
But after four years had passed...
Whoaaaaa!!
Where did this mountain of treasure come from?!!
After that, everyone helped out.
And soon...
Can you make more yams?
If you can, we'll help.
If you can make grass for us to eat in winter...
...I'll give you all the milk you can drink, moo.
And then, and then...
...it turned into this...

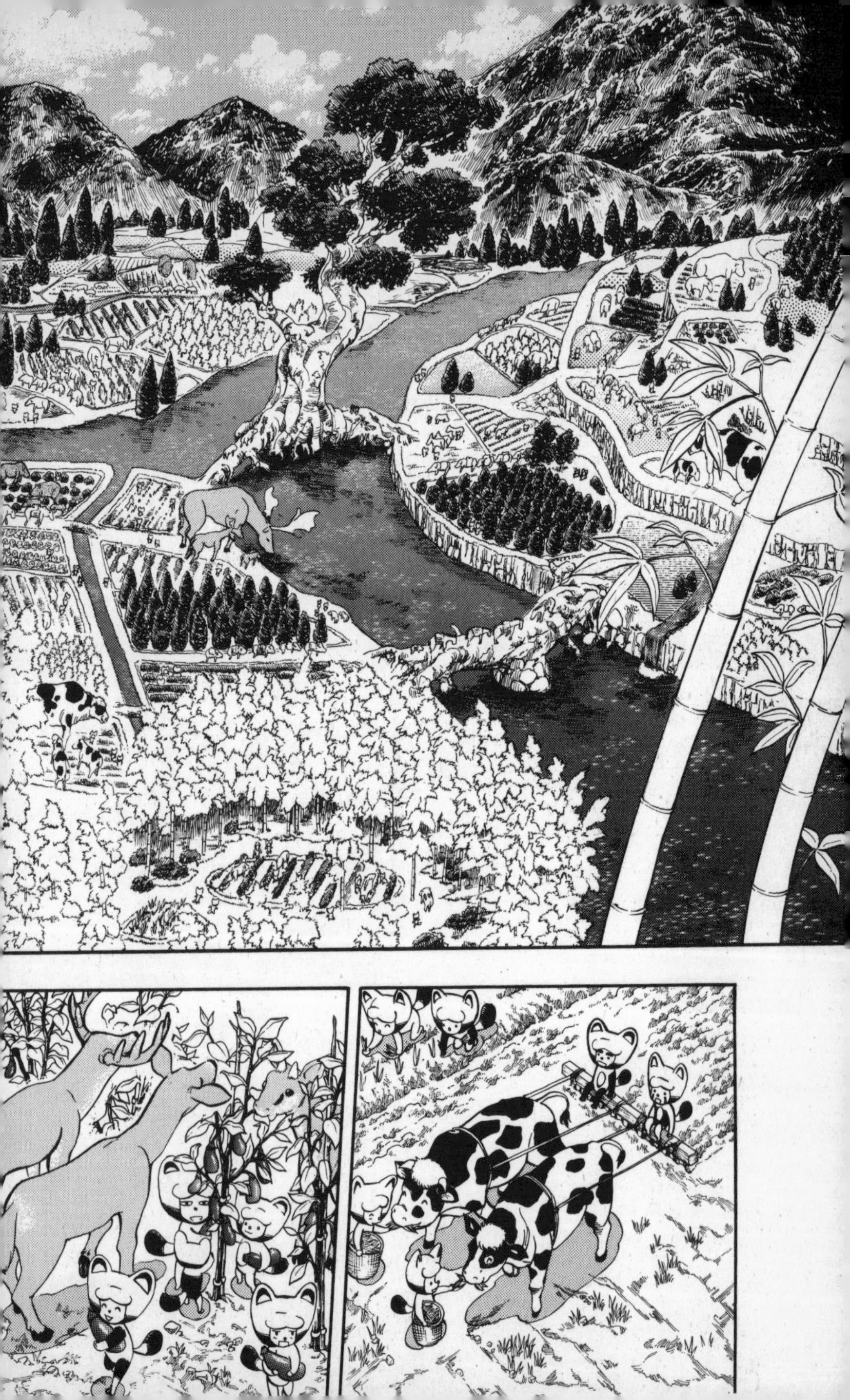

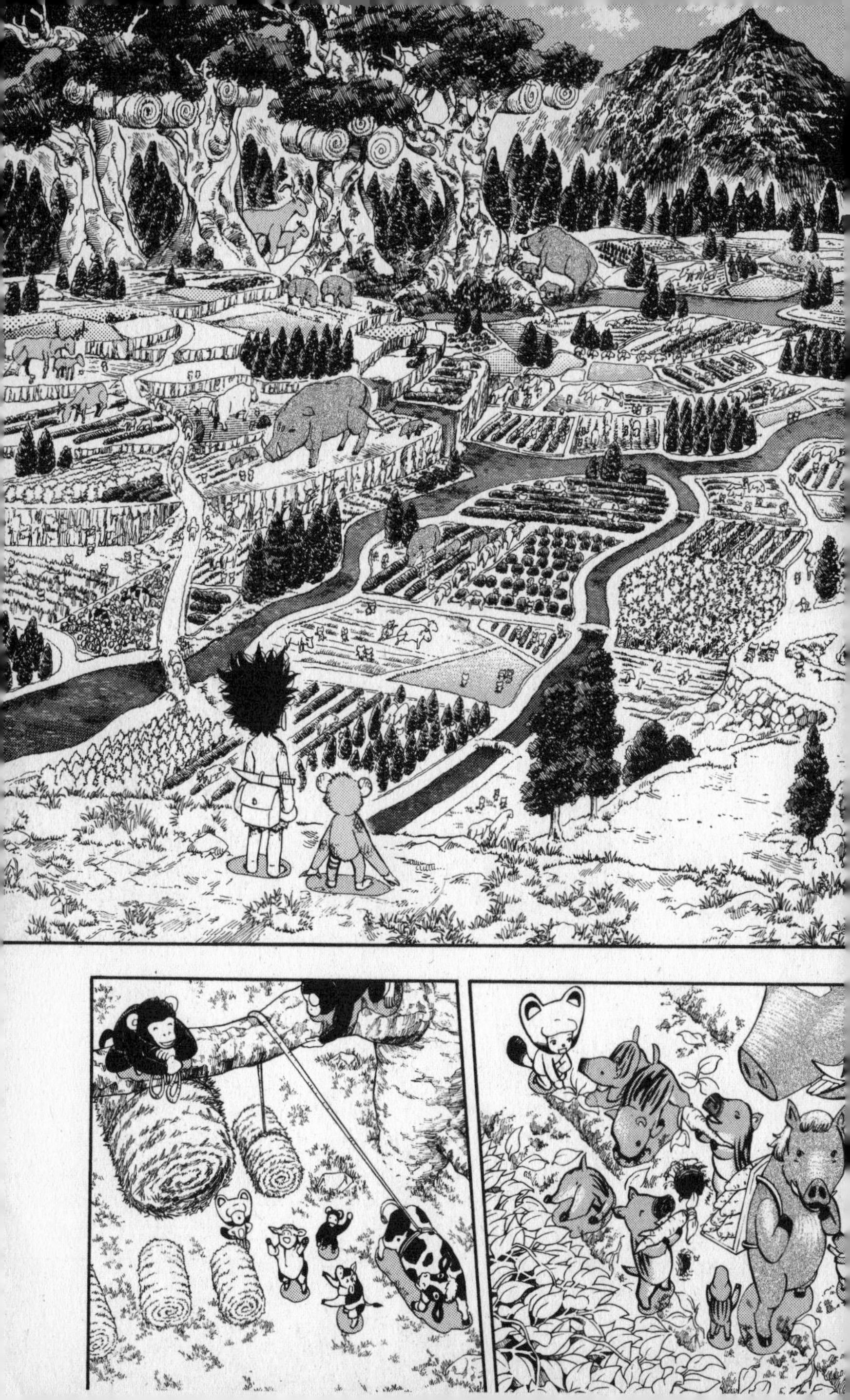

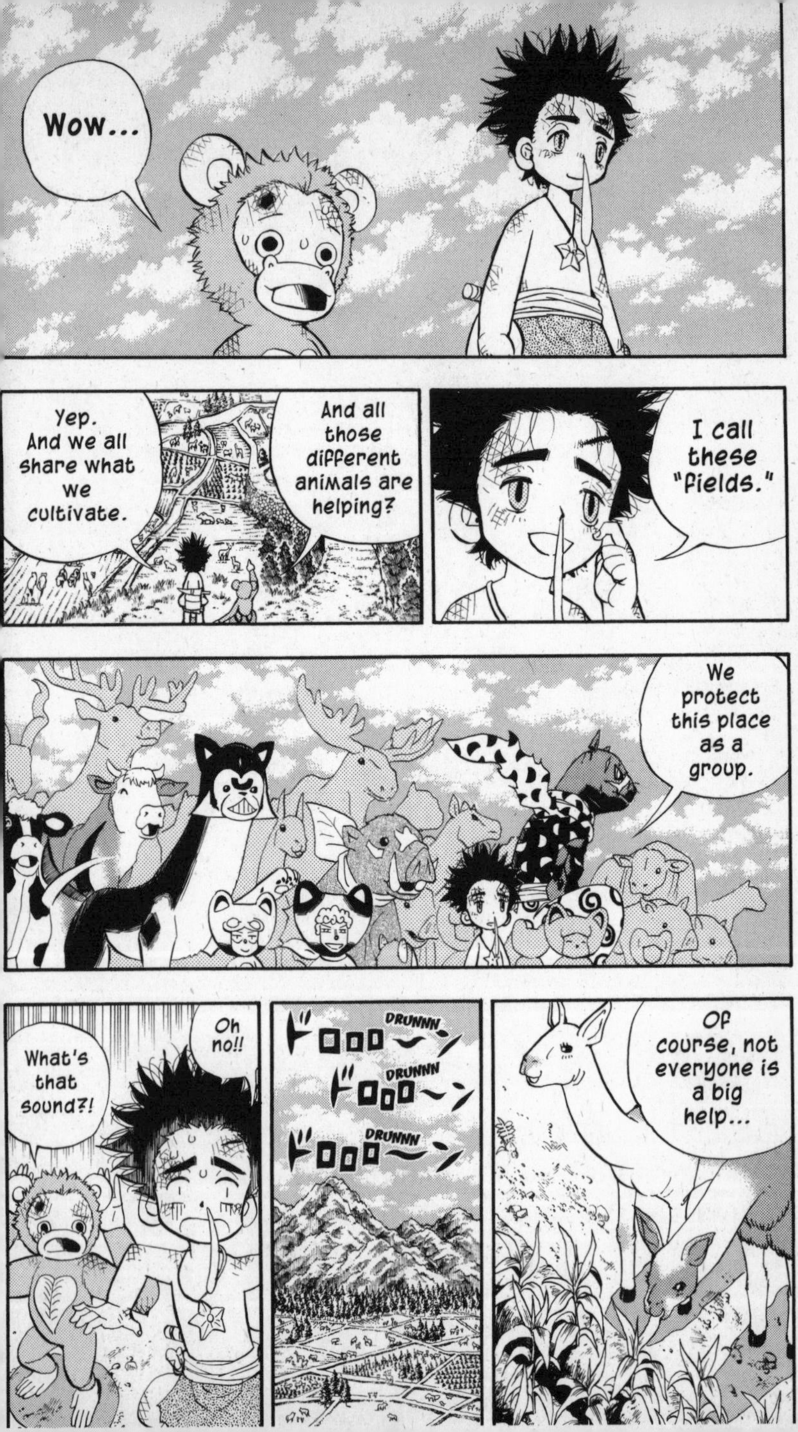

Wow...
I call these "fields."
And all those different animals are helping?
Yep. And we all share what we cultivate.
We protect this place as a group.
Of course, not everyone is a big help...
DRUNNN
DRUNNN
DRUNNN
Oh no!!
What's that sound?!

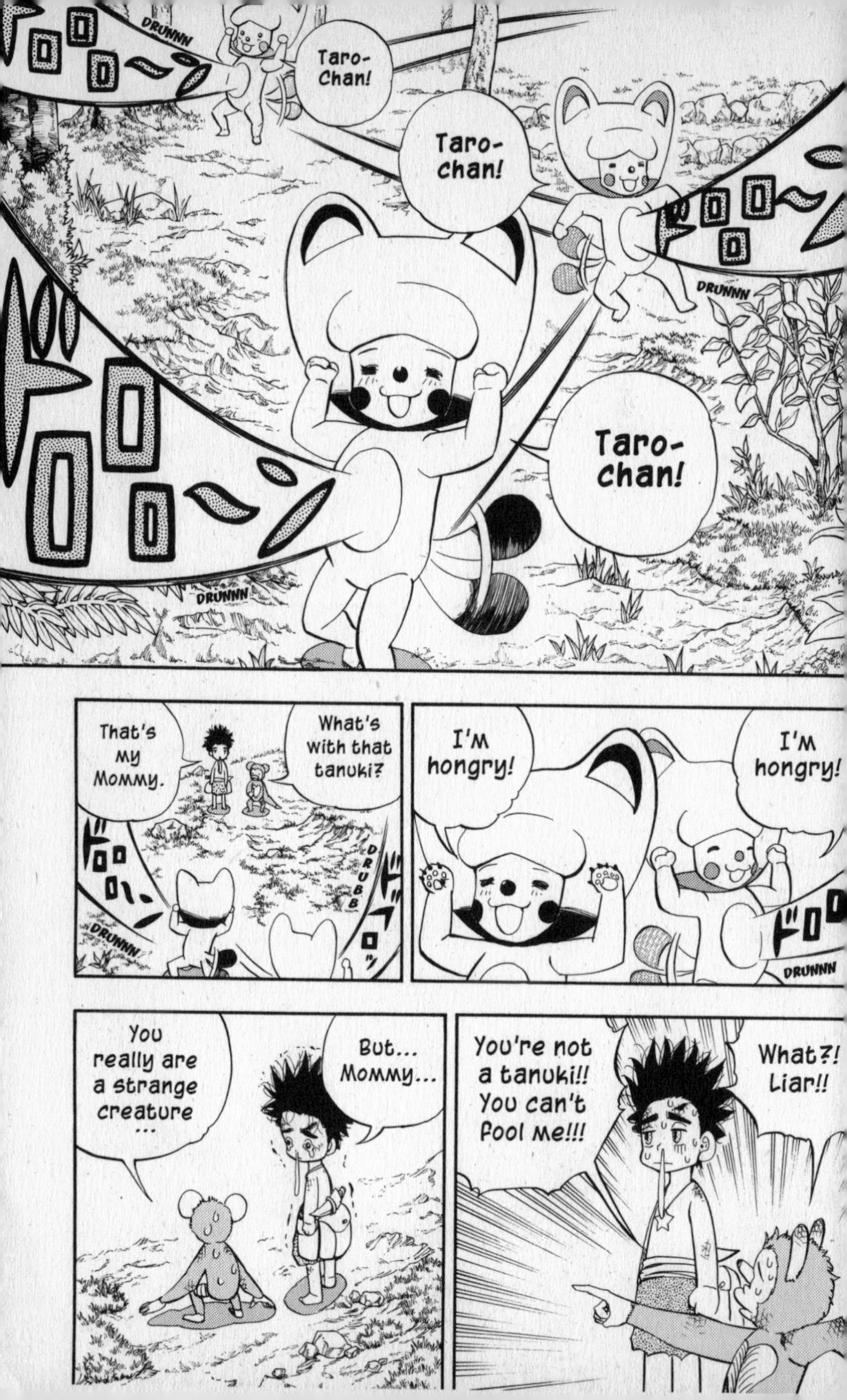
DRUNNN
Taro-Chan!
Taro-chan!
DRUNNN
Taro-chan!
DRUNNN
I'M hongry!
I'M hongry!
DRUNNN
What's with that tanuki?
That's my Mommy.
DRUBB
DRUNNN
What?! Liar!!
You're not a tanuki!! You can't fool me!!!
But... Mommy...
You really are a strange creature ...

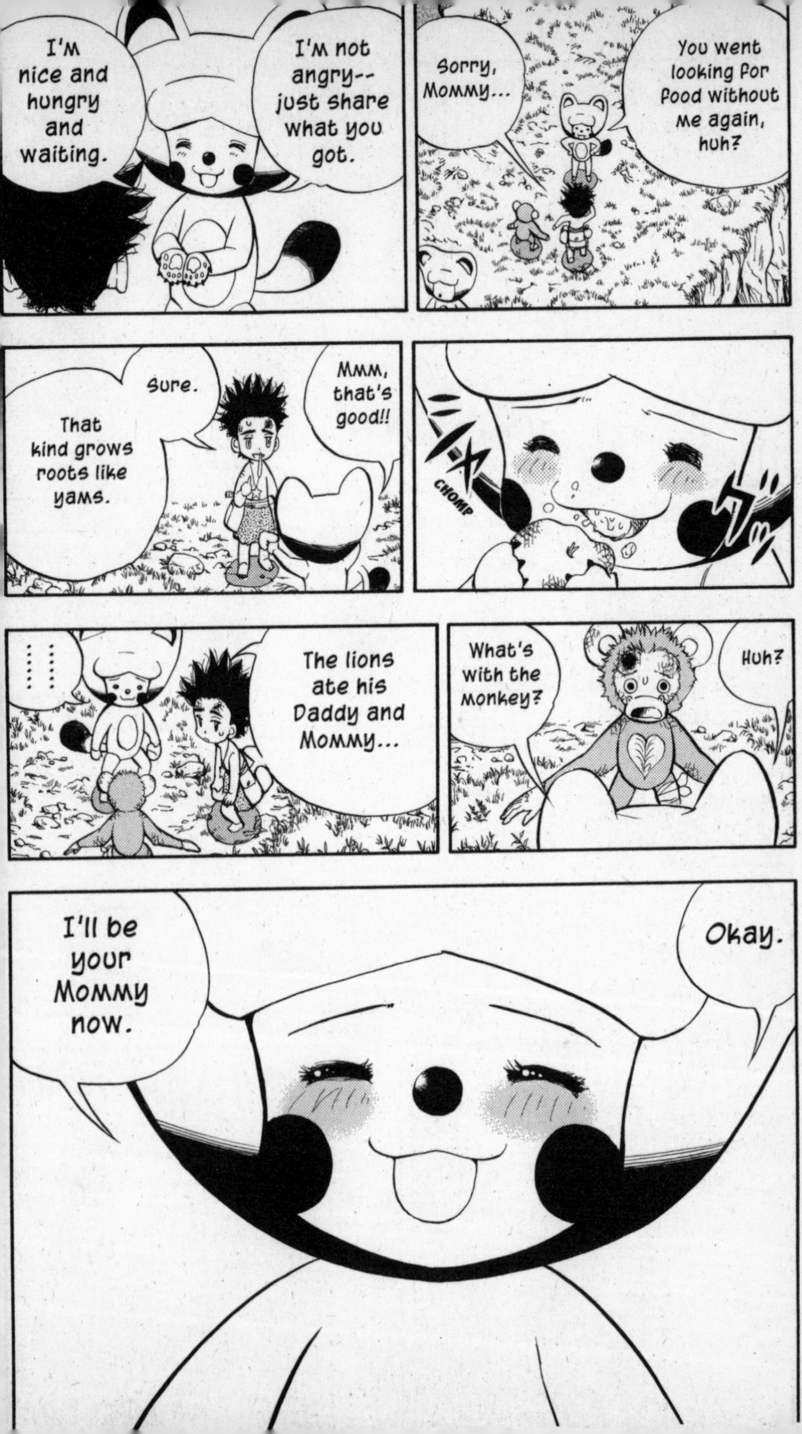
You went looking for food without me again, huh?
Sorry, Mommy...
I'm not angry-- just share what you got.
I'm nice and hungry and waiting.
CHOMP
Mmm, that's good!!
Sure.
That kind grows roots like yams.
Huh?
What's with the monkey?
The lions ate his Daddy and Mommy...
......
Okay.
I'll be your Mommy now.

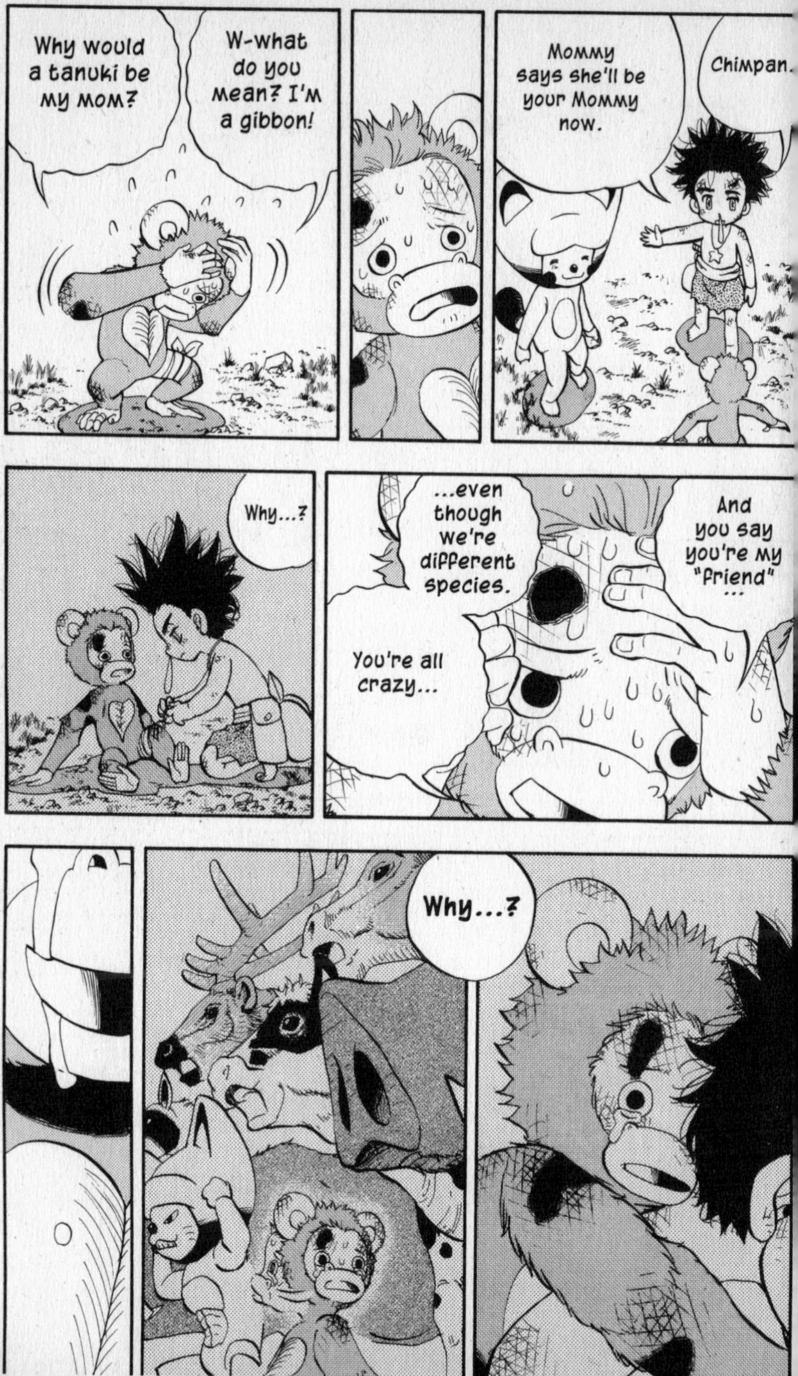
Chimpan.
Mommy says she'll be your Mommy now.
W-what do you mean? I'm a gibbon!
Why would a tanuki be my mom?
And you say you're my "friend" ...
...even though we're different species.
You're all crazy...
Why...?
Why...?

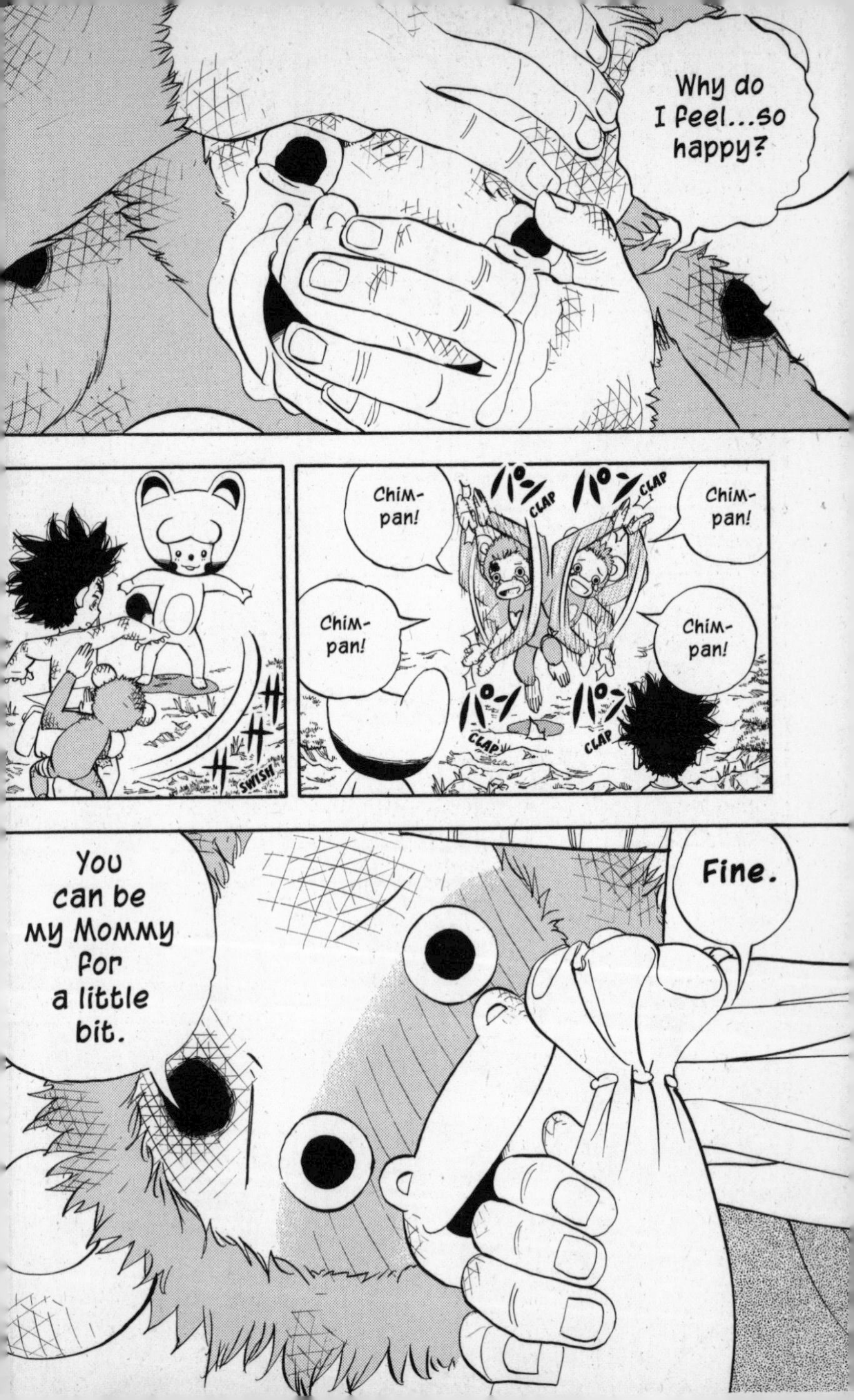
Why do I feel...so happy?
Chim-pan!
Chim-pan!
CLAP
CLAP
Chim-pan!
Chim-pan!
CLAP
CLAP
SWISH
Fine.
You can be my Mommy for a little bit.

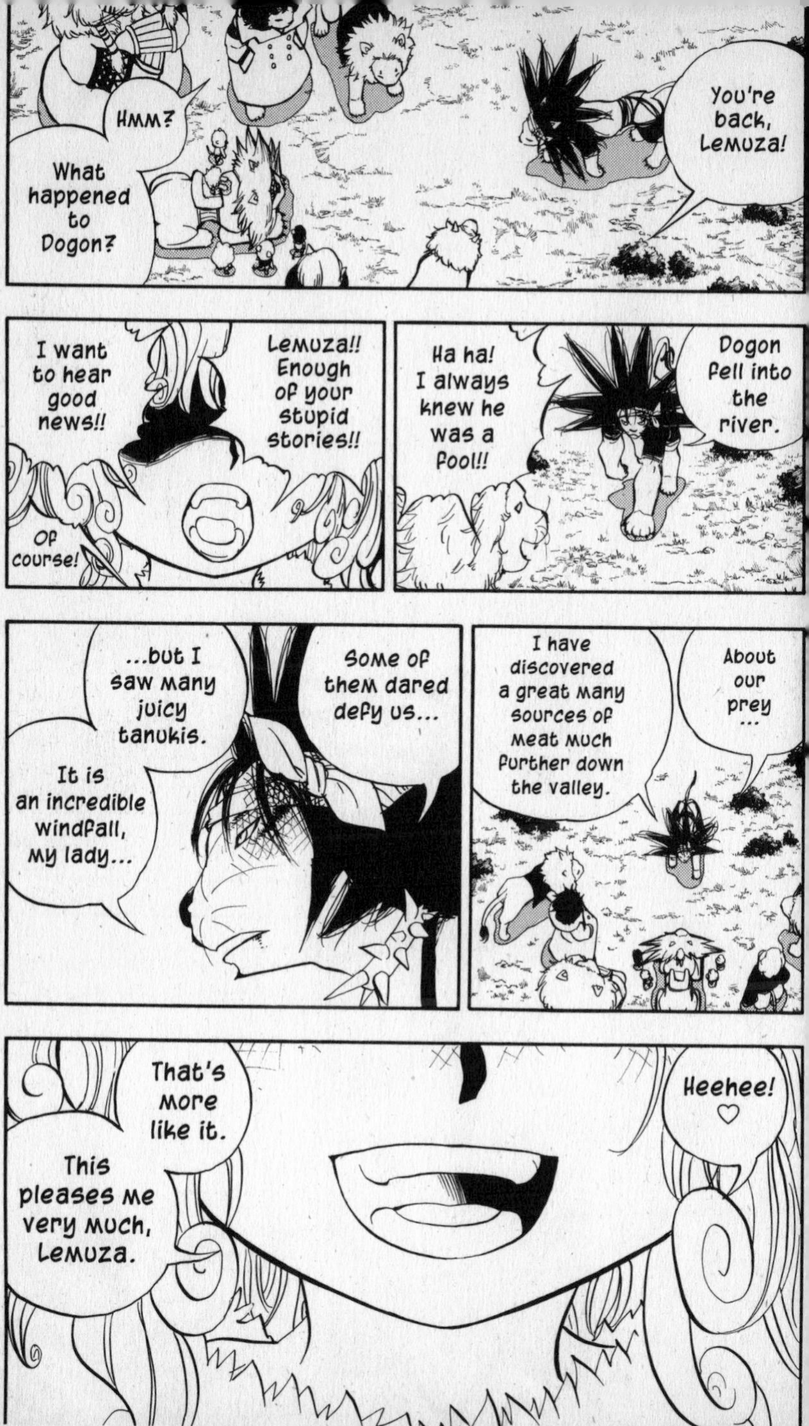
You're back, Lemuza!
Hmm?
What happened to Dogon?
Dogon fell into the river.
Ha ha! I always knew he was a fool!!
Lemuza!! Enough of your stupid stories!!
I want to hear good news!!
Of course!
About our prey...
I have discovered a great many sources of meat much further down the valley.
Some of them dared defy us...
...but I saw many juicy tanukis.
It is an incredible windfall, my lady...
Heehee! ♡
That's more like it.
This pleases me very much, Lemuza.

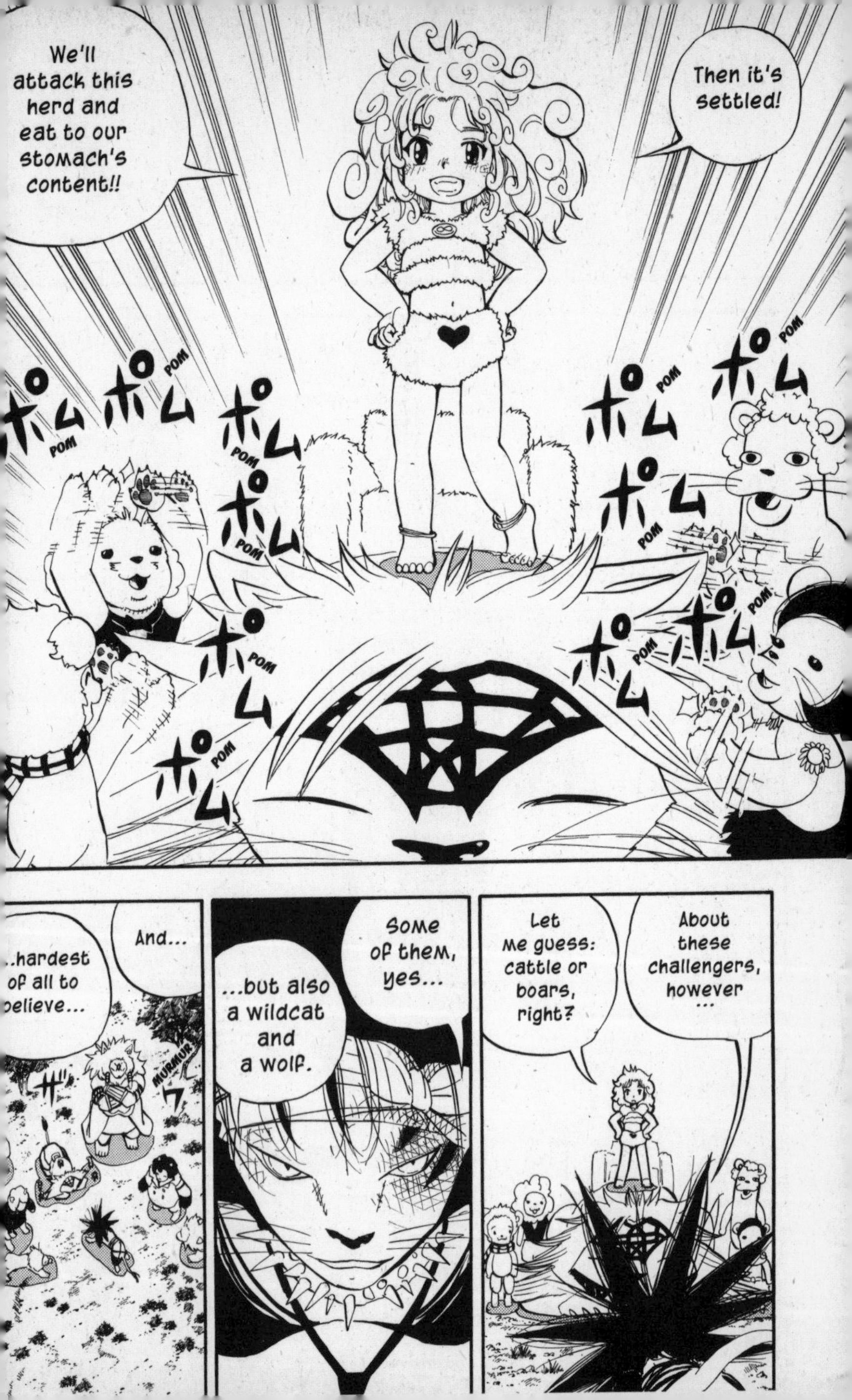
Then it's settled!
We'll attack this herd and eat to our stomach's content!!
POM
POM
POM
POM
POM
POM
POM
POM
POM
POM
POM
About these challengers, however ...
Let me guess: cattle or boars, right?
Some of them, yes...
...but also a wildcat and a wolf.
And...
..hardest of all to believe...
MURMUR

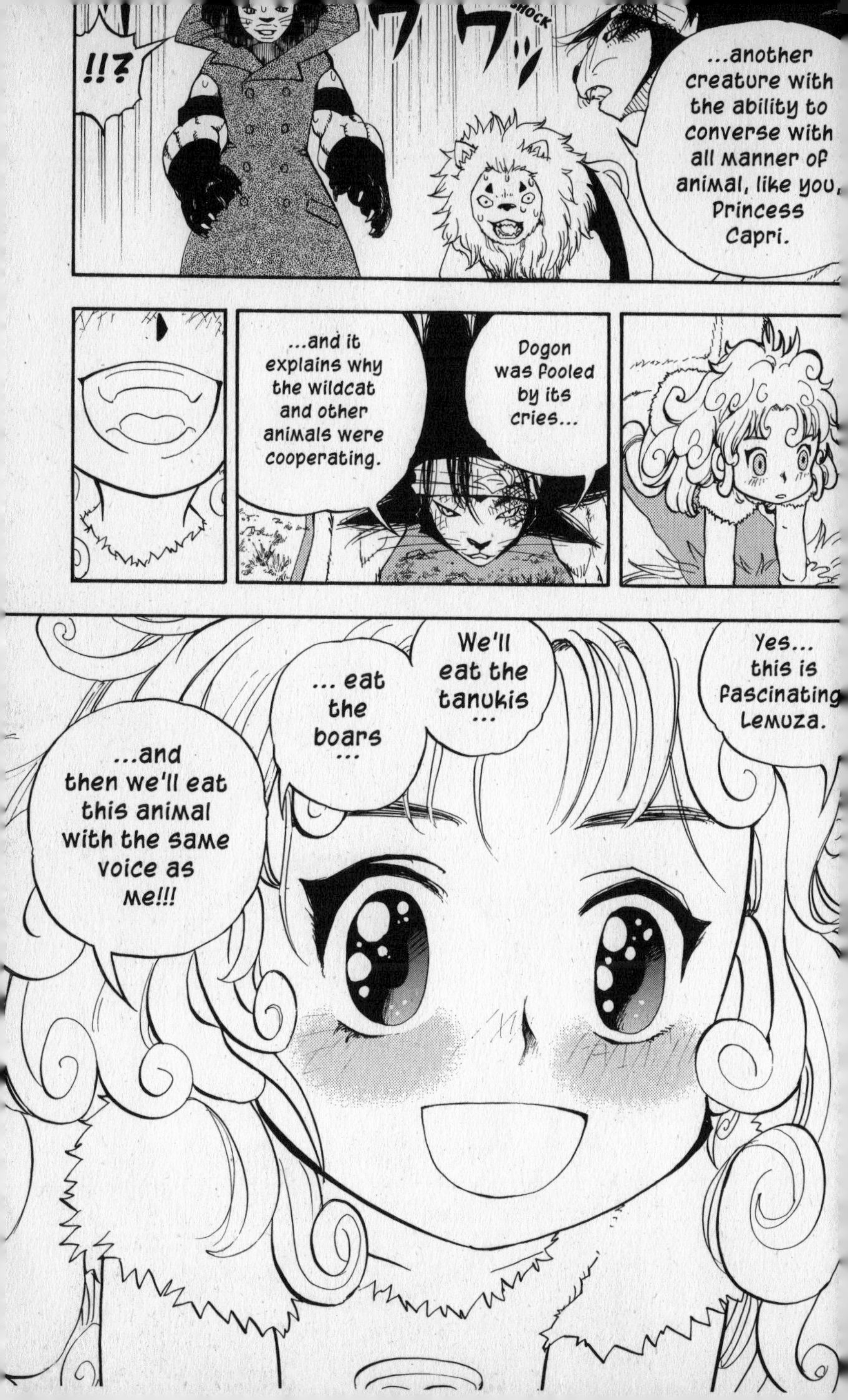
...another creature with the ability to converse with all manner of animal, like you, Princess Capri.
SHOCK
!!?
Dogon was fooled by its cries...
...and it explains why the wildcat and other animals were cooperating.
Yes... this is fascinating Lemuza.
We'll eat the tanukis...
... eat the boars...
...and then we'll eat this animal with the same voice as me!!!

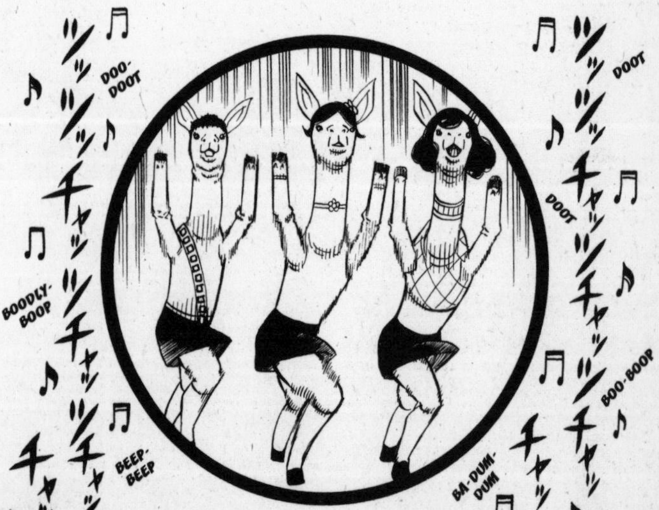
ツッツンツッチャッツンチャッツンチャッ
DOOT
DOOT
BOO-BOOP
チャッ
BA-DUM-DUM
ツッツンツッチャッツンチャッツンチャッ
DOO-DOOT
BOODLY-BOOP
BEEP-BEEP
チャッ

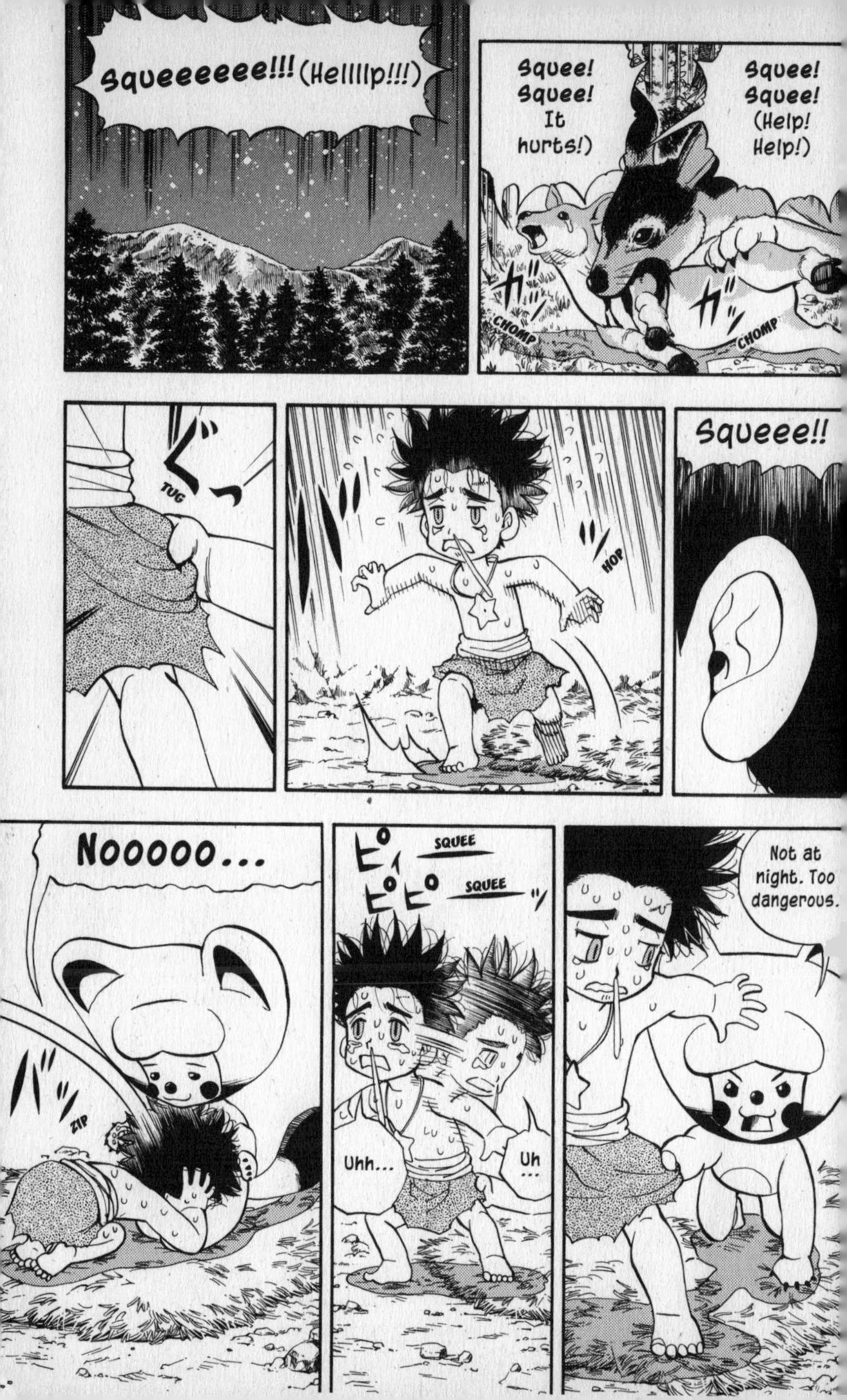
Squee! Squee! (Help! Help!)
Squee! Squee! It hurts!)
CHOMP
CHOMP
Squeeeeee!!! (Hellllp!!!)
Squeee!!
HOP
TUG
Not at night. Too dangerous.
SQUEE
SQUEE
Uh ...
Uhh...
Nooooo...
ZIP

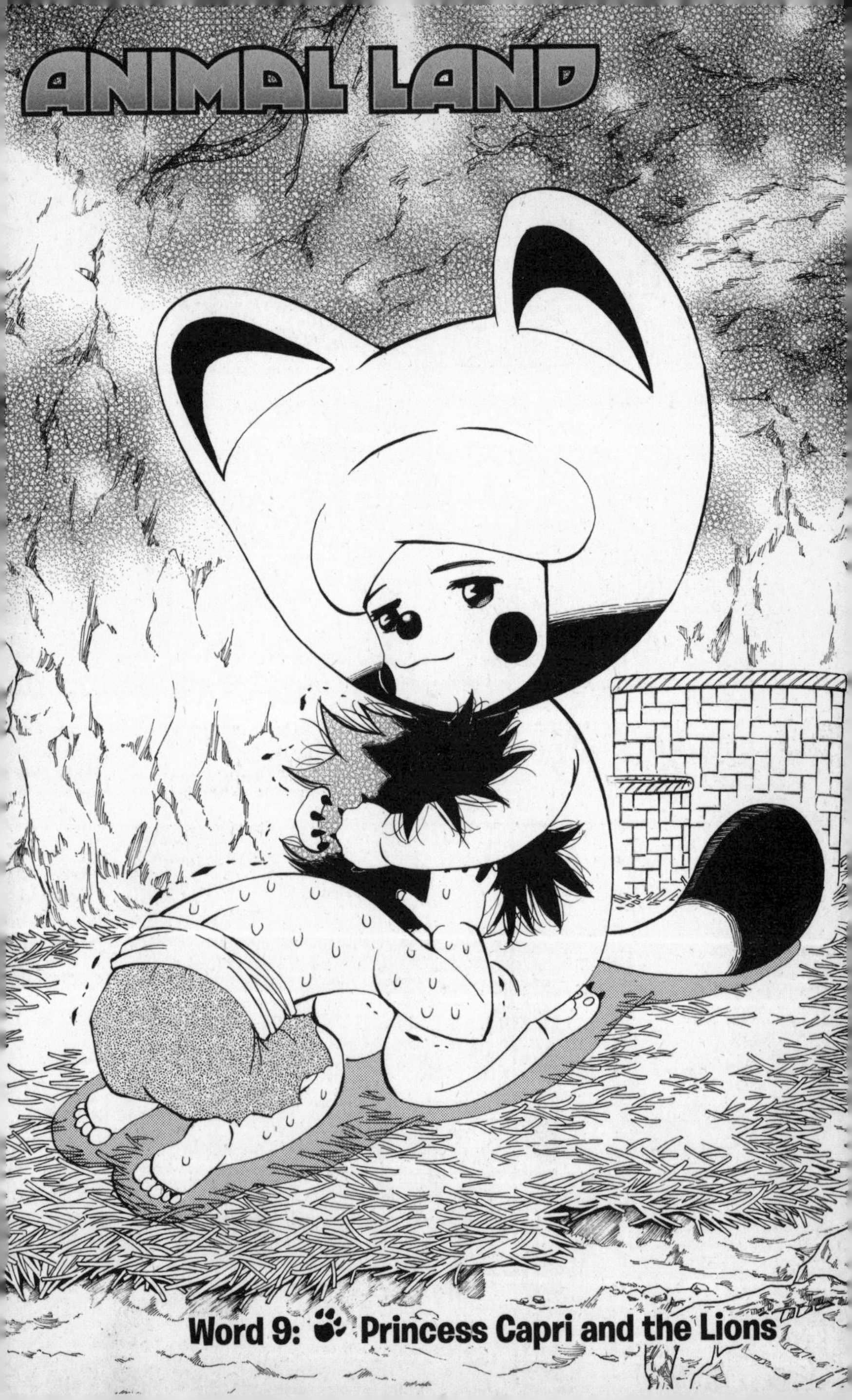
ANIMAL LAND
Word 9: Princess Capri and the Lions

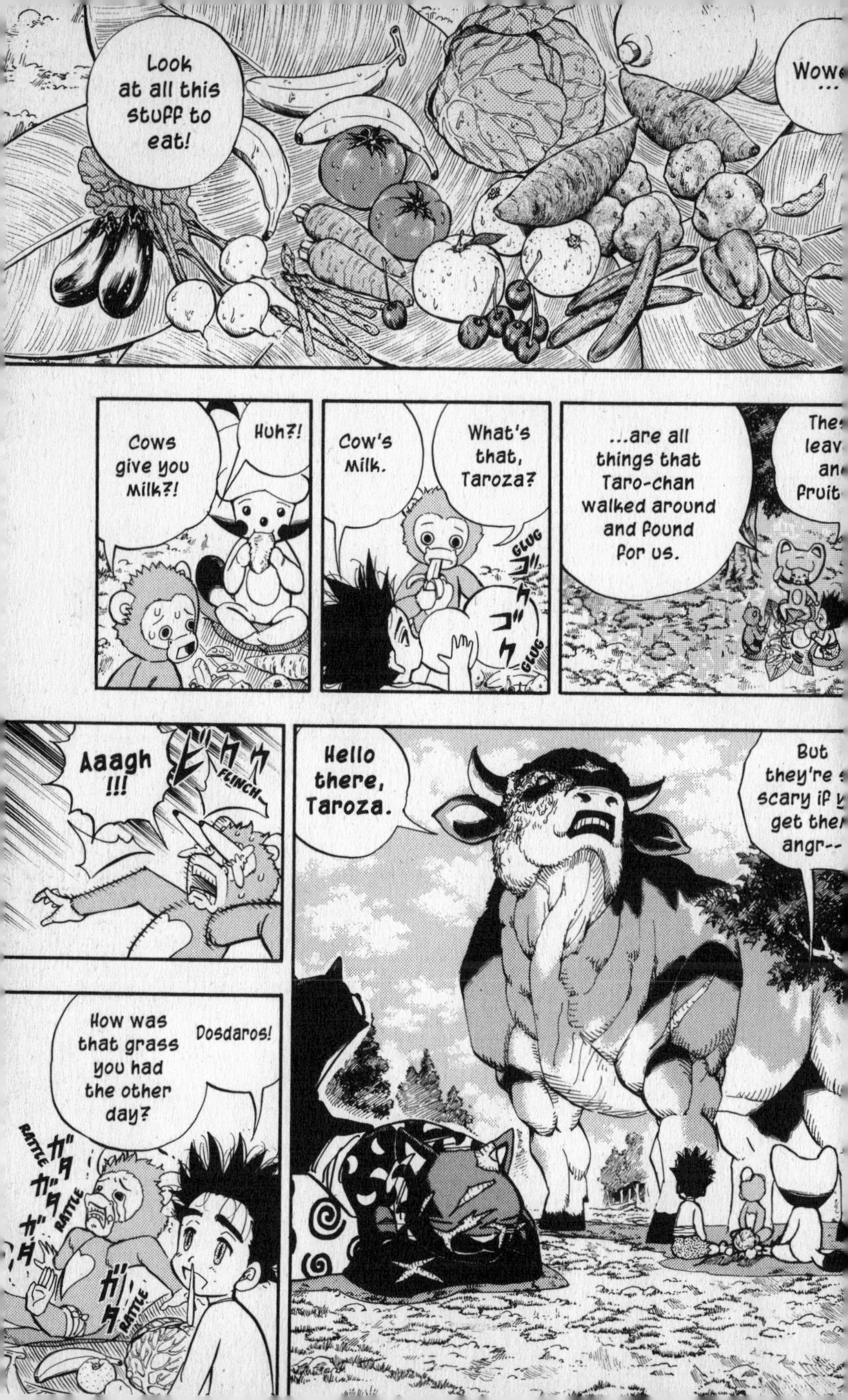
Wowe
...
Look at all this stuff to eat!
The
leav
an
fruit
...are all things that Taro-chan walked around and found for us.
What's that, Taroza?
Cow's milk.
GLUG
ゴクゴク
GLUG
Huh?!
Cows give you milk?!
But they're
scary if
get the
angr--
Hello there, Taroza.
ビクッ
FLINCH
Aaagh !!!
Dosdaros!
How was that grass you had the other day?
RATTLE
ガタ
RATTLE
ガタ
RATTLE
ガタ
RATTLE

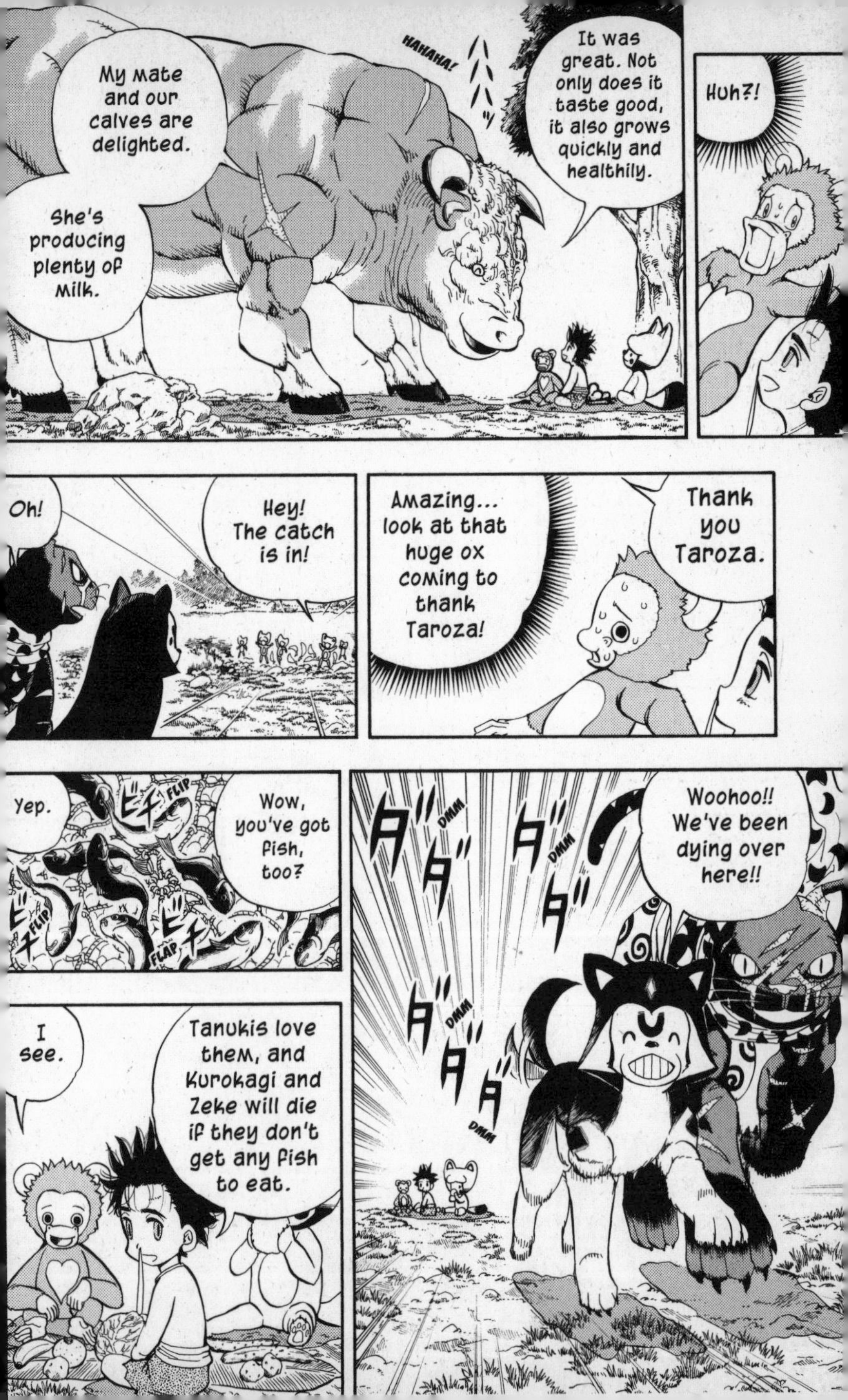

Huh?!
It was great. Not only does it taste good, it also grows quickly and healthily.
HAHAHA!
My mate and our calves are delighted.
She's producing plenty of milk.
Thank you Taroza.
Amazing... look at that huge ox coming to thank Taroza!
Hey! The catch is in!
Oh!
Woohoo!! We've been dying over here!!
DMM
DMM
DMM
DMM
Wow, you've got fish, too?
Yep.
FLIP
FLIP
FLAP
Tanukis love them, and Kurokagi and Zeke will die if they don't get any fish to eat.
I see.

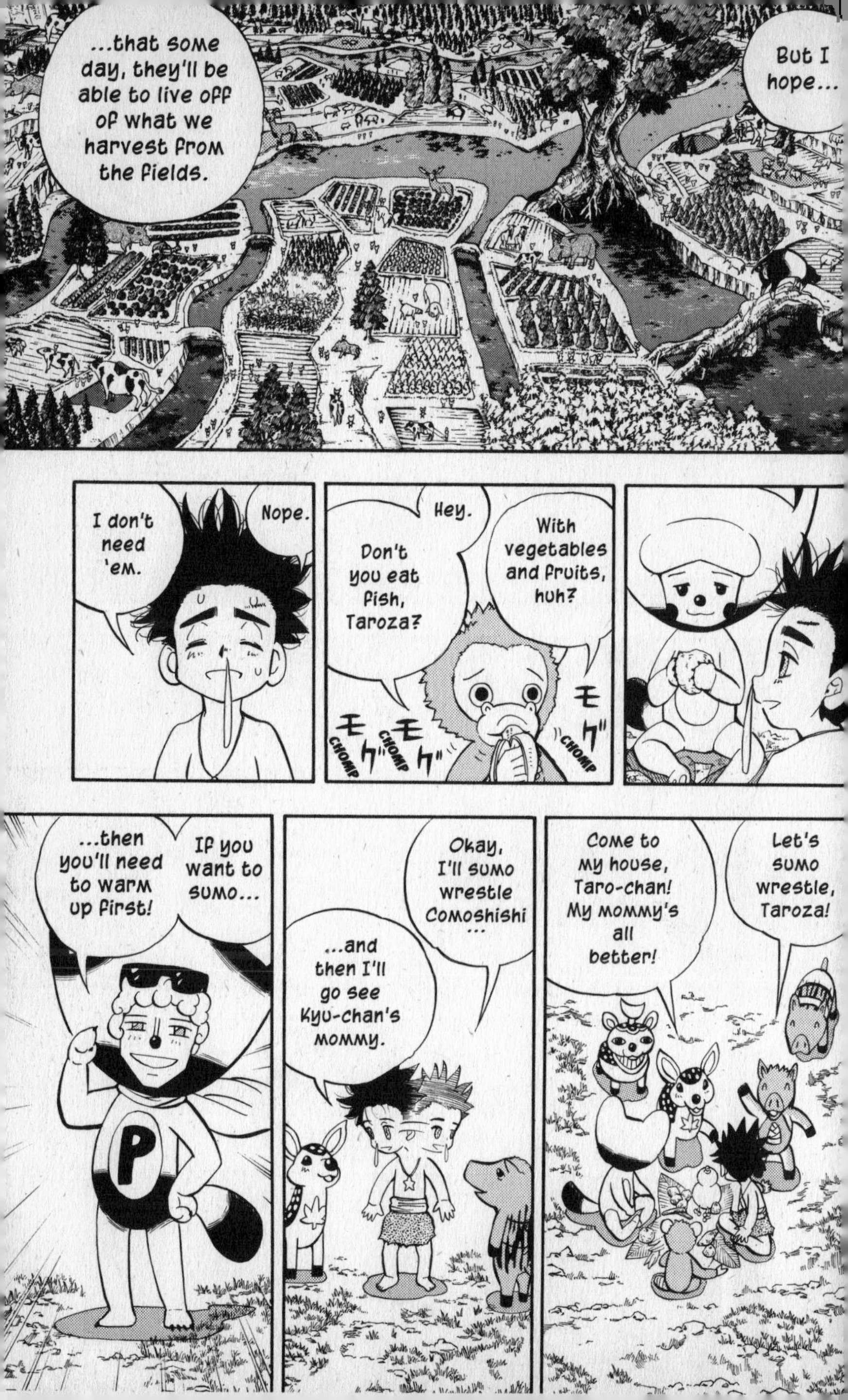
But I hope...
...that some day, they'll be able to live off of what we harvest from the fields.
With vegetables and fruits, huh?
Hey.
Don't you eat fish, Taroza?
モグ CHOMP
モグ CHOMP
モグ CHOMP
Nope.
I don't need 'em.
Let's sumo wrestle, Taroza!
Come to my house, Taro-chan! My mommy's all better!
Okay, I'll sumo wrestle Comoshishi ...
...and then I'll go see Kyu-chan's mommy.
If you want to sumo...
...then you'll need to warm up first!

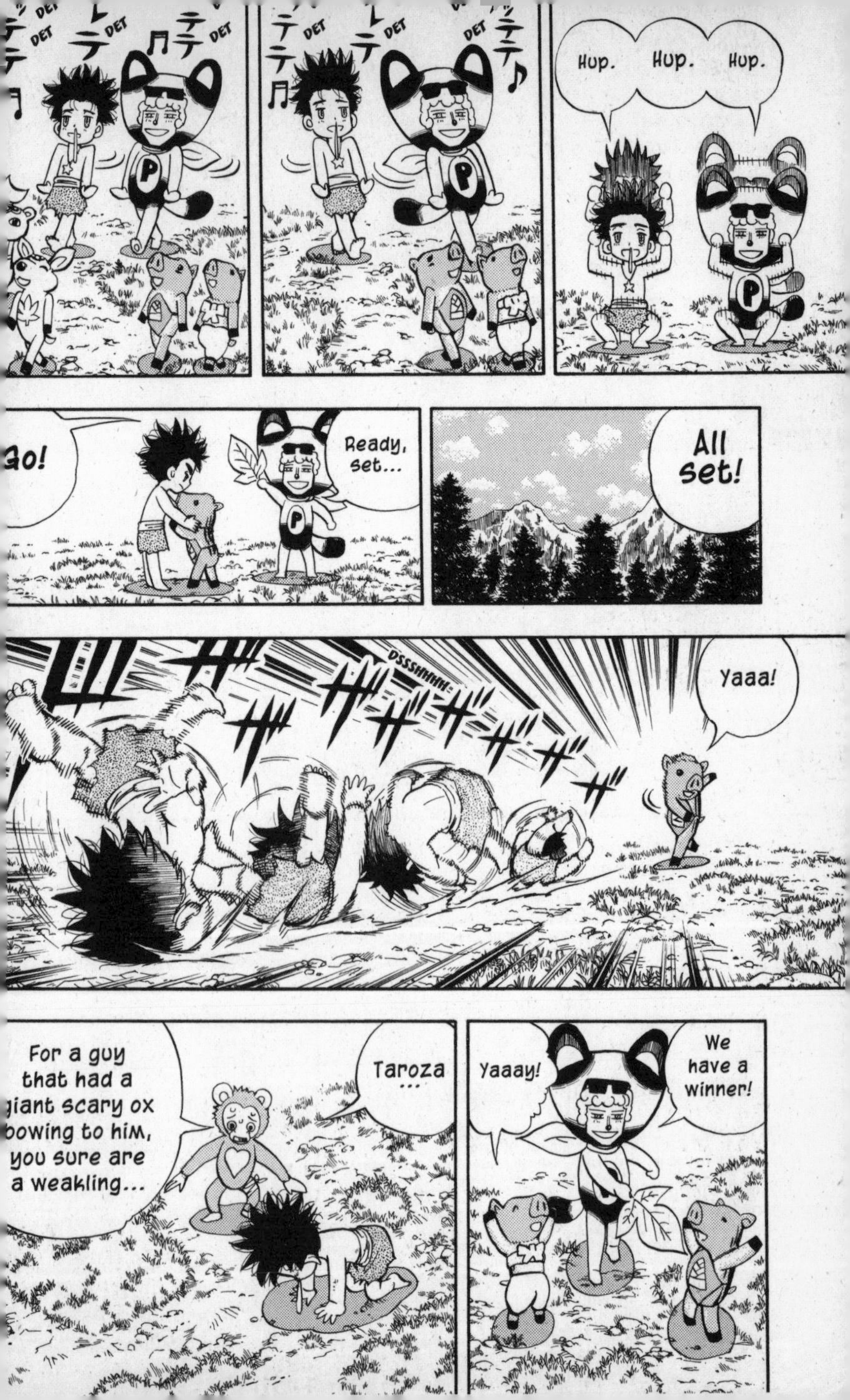
Hup. Hup. Hup.
テテ DET
テテ DET
テテ DET
DET DET
All set!
Ready, set...
Go!
Yaaa!
DSSSHHHH
We have a winner!
Yaaay!
Taroza ...
For a guy that had a giant scary ox bowing to him, you sure are a weakling...

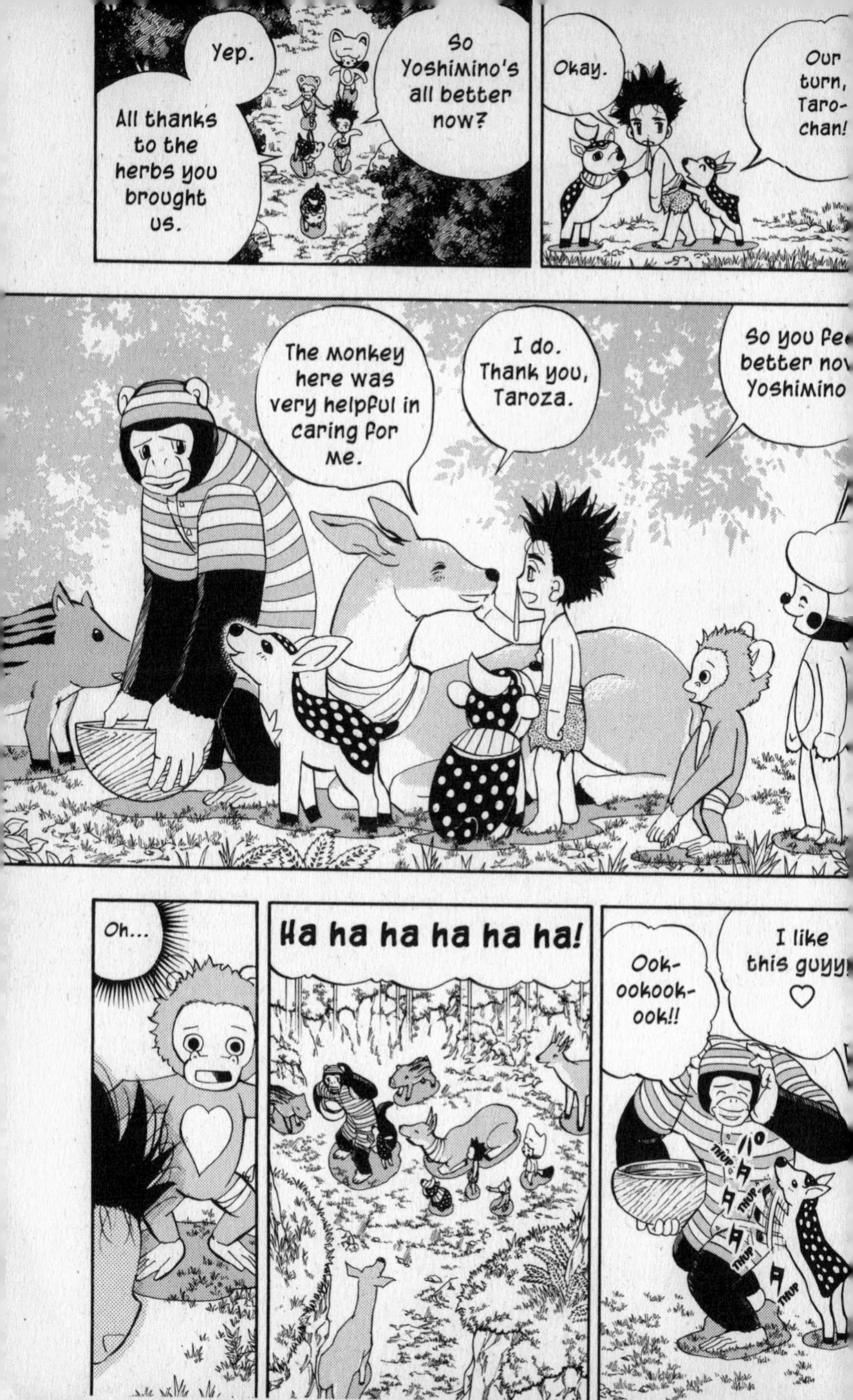
Our turn, Taro-chan!
Okay.
So Yoshimino's all better now?
Yep.
All thanks to the herbs you brought us.
So you fe better no Yoshimino
I do. Thank you, Taroza.
The monkey here was very helpful in caring for me.
I like this guyy! ♡
Ook-ookook-ook!!
THUP THUP THUP THUP
Ha ha ha ha ha ha!
Oh...

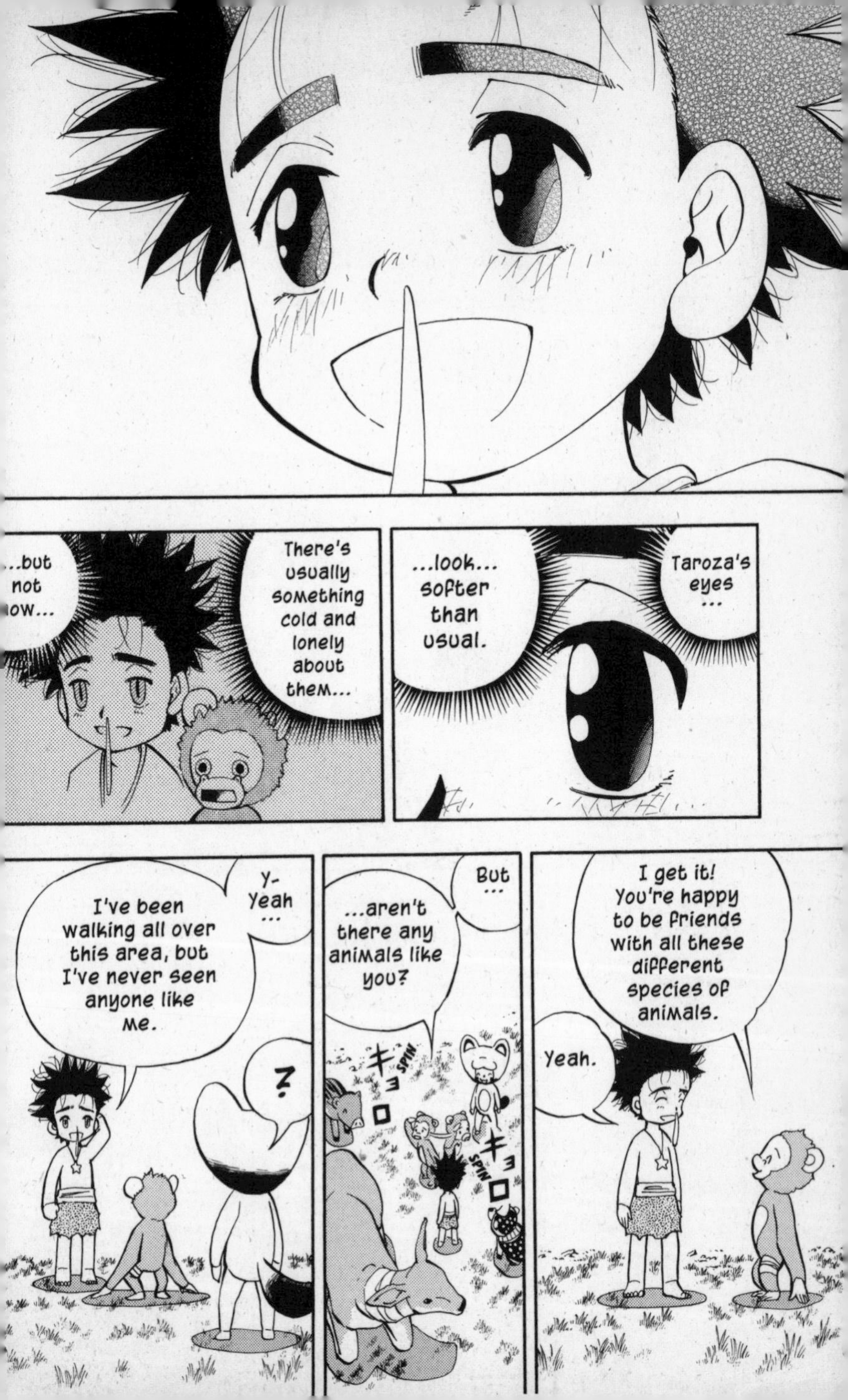
Taroza's eyes ...
...look... softer than usual.
There's usually something cold and lonely about them...
...but not ow...
I get it! You're happy to be friends with all these different species of animals.
Yeah.
But ...
...aren't there any animals like you?
キョロ SPIN
キョロ SPIN
Y-Yeah ...
I've been walking all over this area, but I've never seen anyone like me.
?

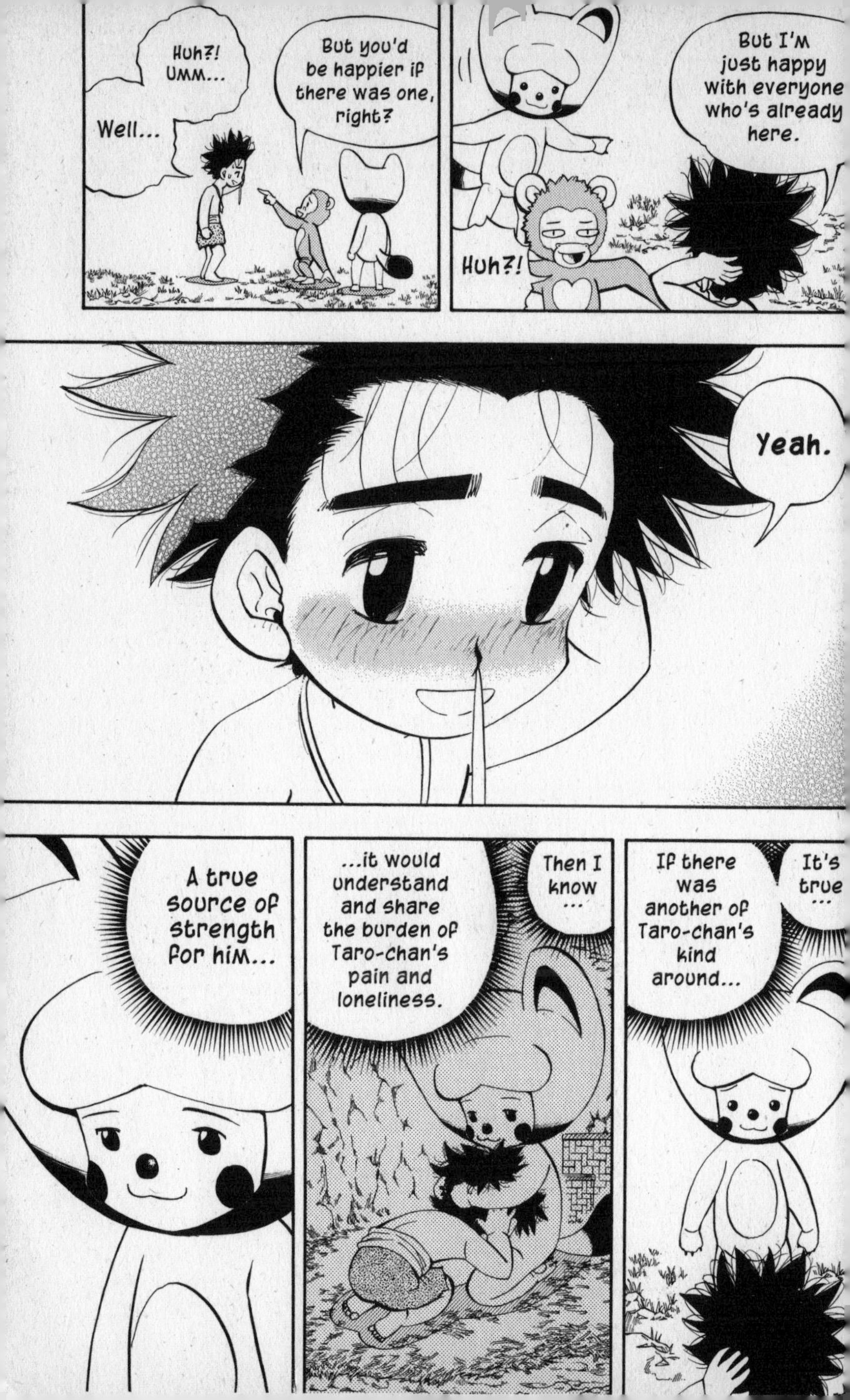
But I'm just happy with everyone who's already here.
Huh?!
But you'd be happier if there was one, right?
Huh?! Umm...
Well...
Yeah.
It's true...
If there was another of Taro-chan's kind around...
Then I know...
...it would understand and share the burden of Taro-chan's pain and loneliness.
A true source of strength for him...

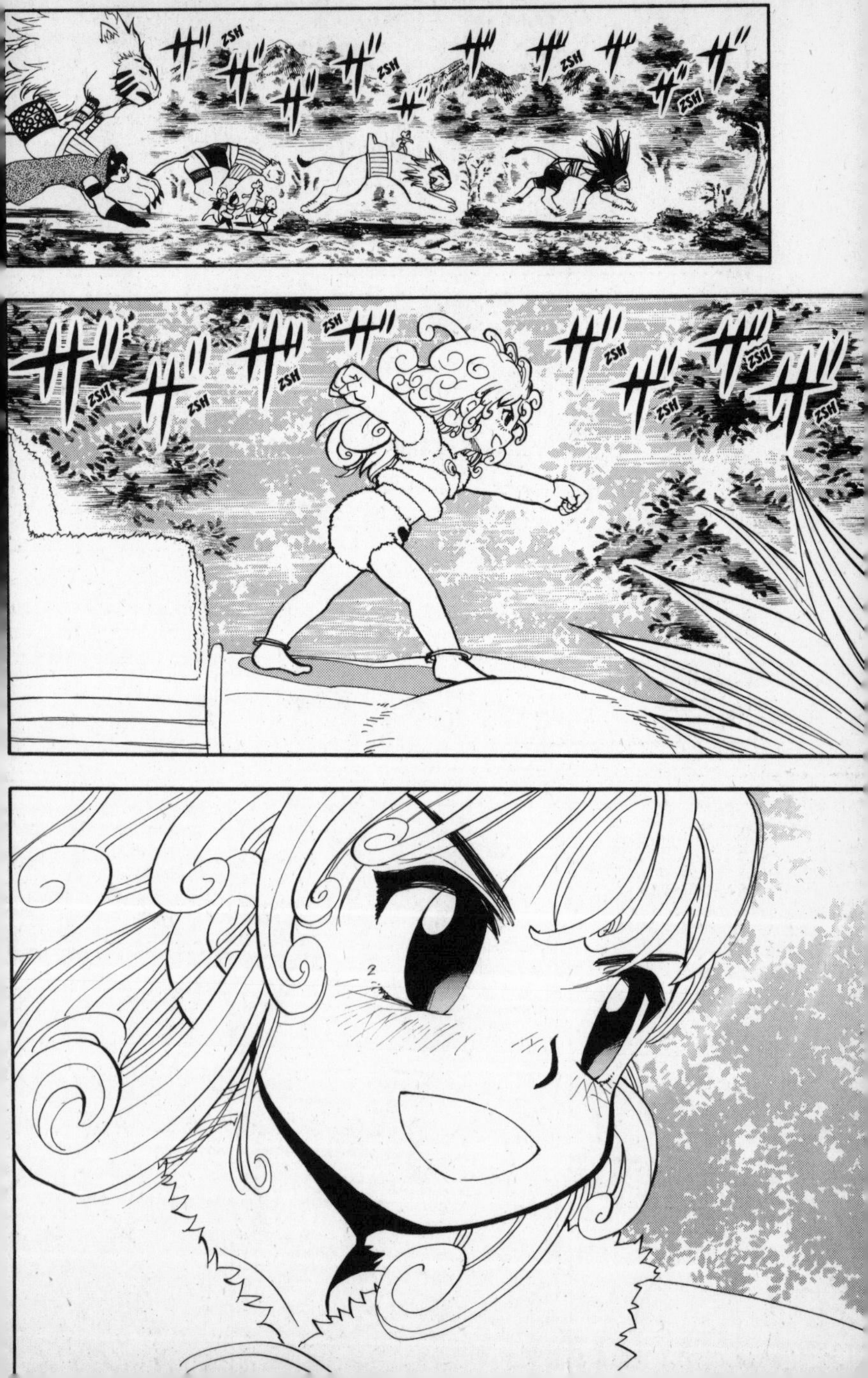
ザ
ザ
ZSH
ザ
ZSH
ザ
ザ
ザ
ZSH
ザ
ザ
ザ
ZSH
ザ
ザ
ZSH
ZSH
ザ
ZSH
ザ
ZSH
ZSH
ザ
ZSH
ザ
ZSH
ザ
ZSH
ザ
ZSH
ザ
ZSH
ザ
ZSH
ザ
ZSH

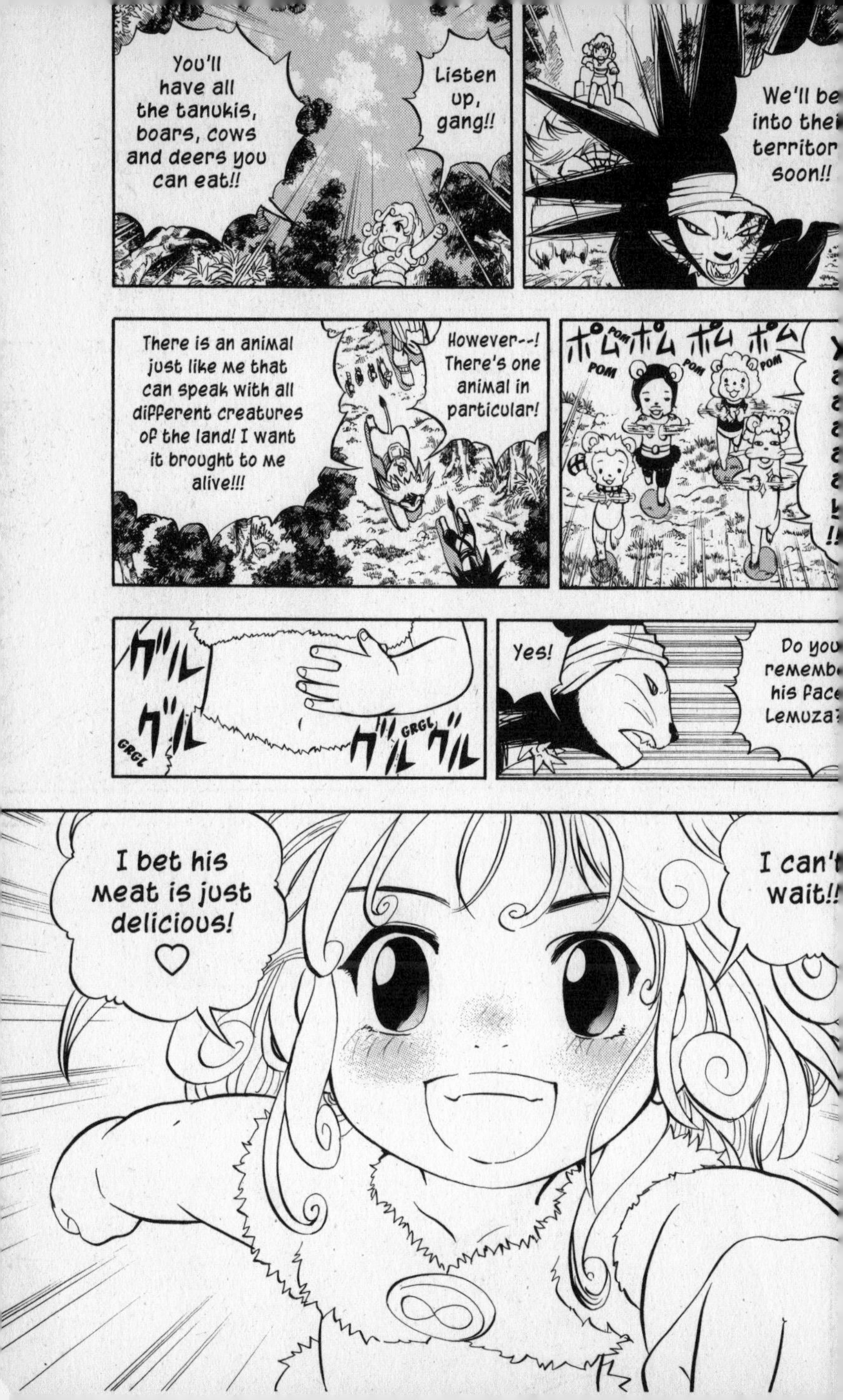
We'll be into thei territor soon!!
Listen up, gang!!
You'll have all the tanukis, boars, cows and deers you can eat!!
ポムポムポムポム
POM POM POM POM
However--! There's one animal in particular!
There is an animal just like me that can speak with all different creatures of the land! I want it brought to me alive!!!
Do you rememb his face Lemuza?
Yes!
グルグル グルグル
GRGL GRGL
I can't wait!!
I bet his meat is just delicious! ♡

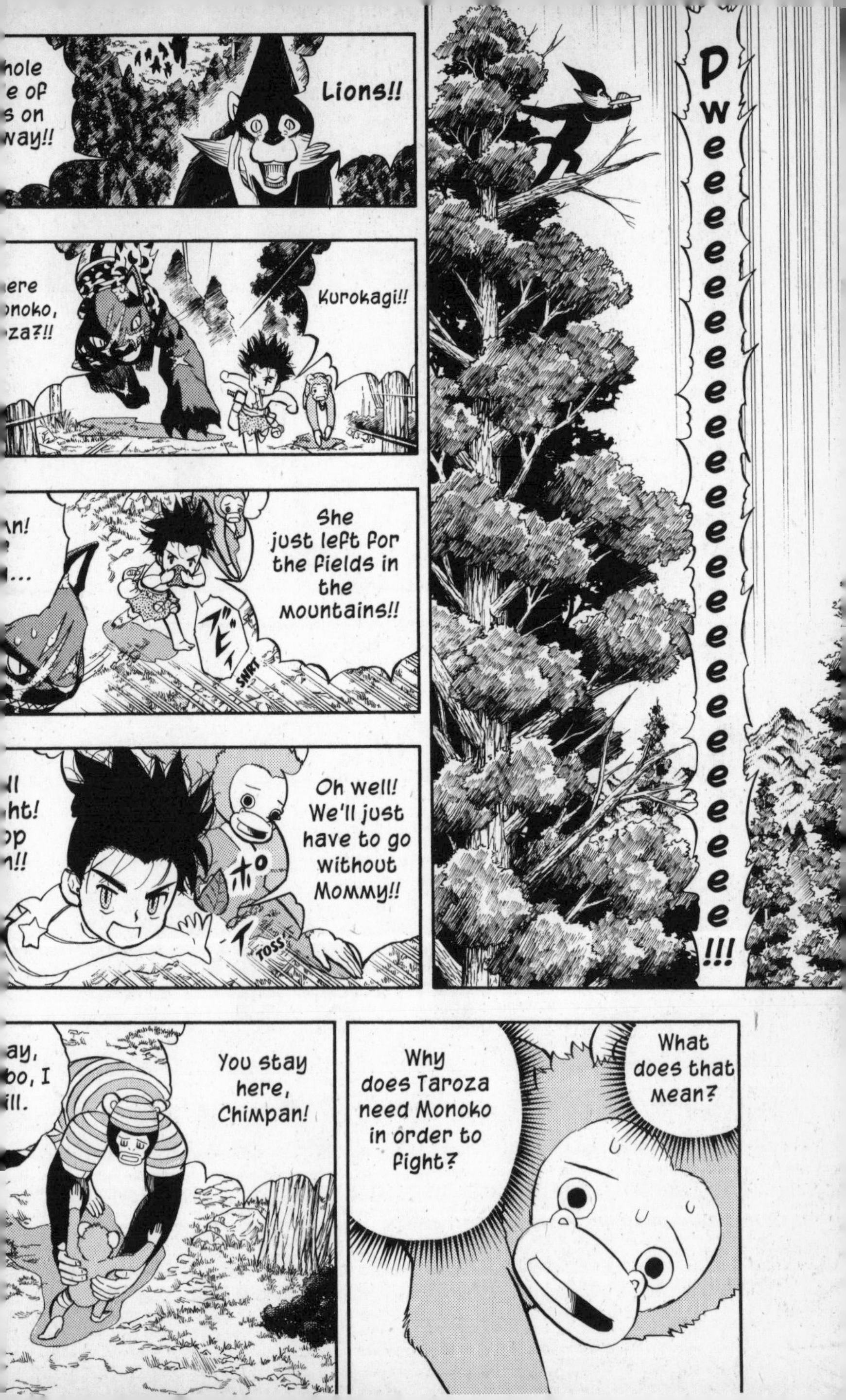
Pweeeeeeeeeeeeeeeeeeeeeee!!!
Lions!!
hole
e of
s on
way!!
Kurokagi!!
ere
onoko,
za?!!
She just left for the fields in the mountains!!
SNRT
n!
Oh well! We'll just have to go without Mommy!!
TOSS
ll
ht!
op
n!!
What does that mean?
Why does Taroza need Monoko in order to fight?
You stay here, Chimpan!
ay,
bo, I
ill.

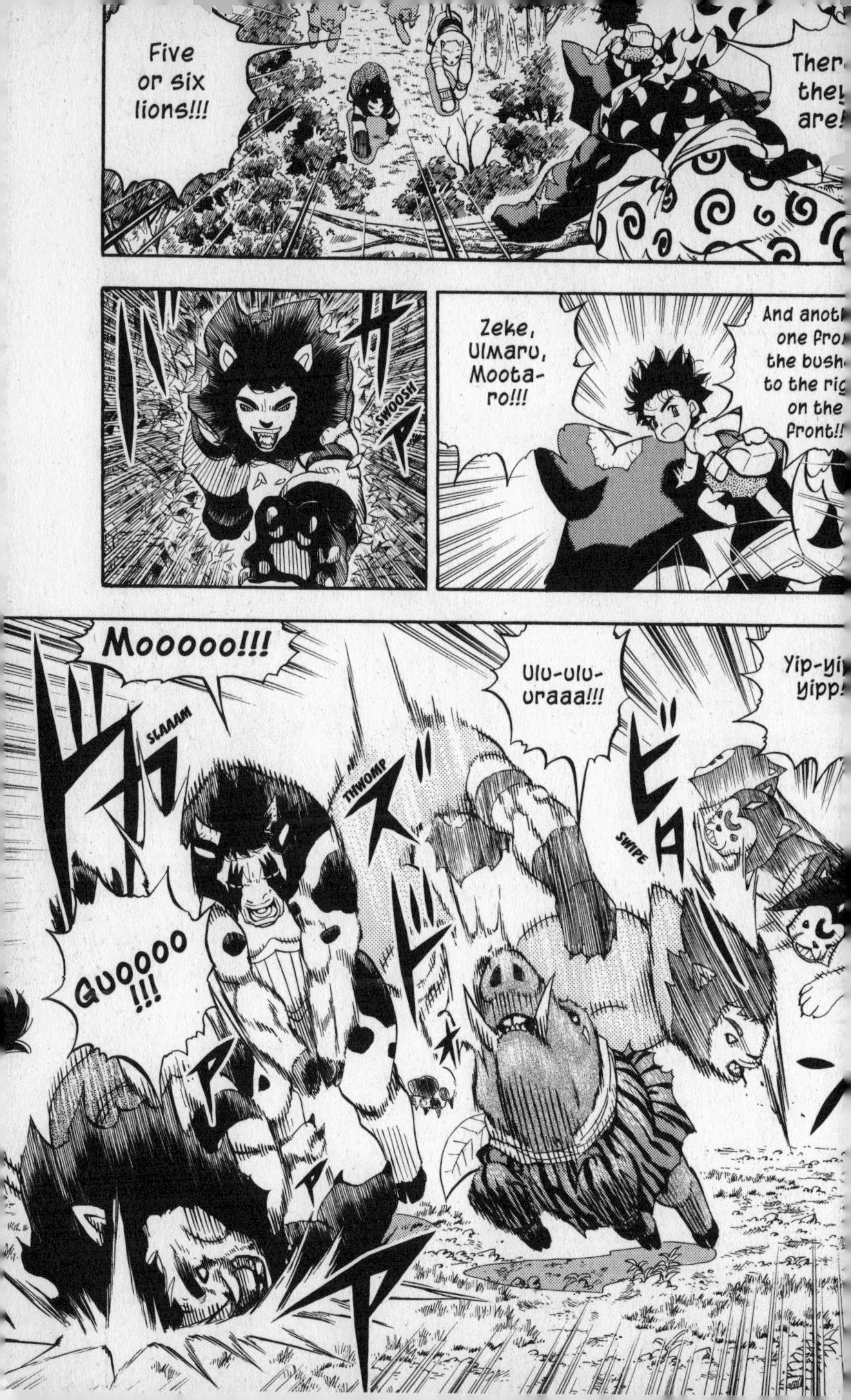

Ther they are!
Five or six lions!!!
And anoth one fro the bush to the rig on the front!!
Zeke, Ulmaru, Moota-ro!!!
SWOOSH
Yip-yip yipp!
Ulu-ulu-uraaa!!!
SWIPE
THWOMP
Mooooo!!!
SLAAAM
GUOOOO!!!

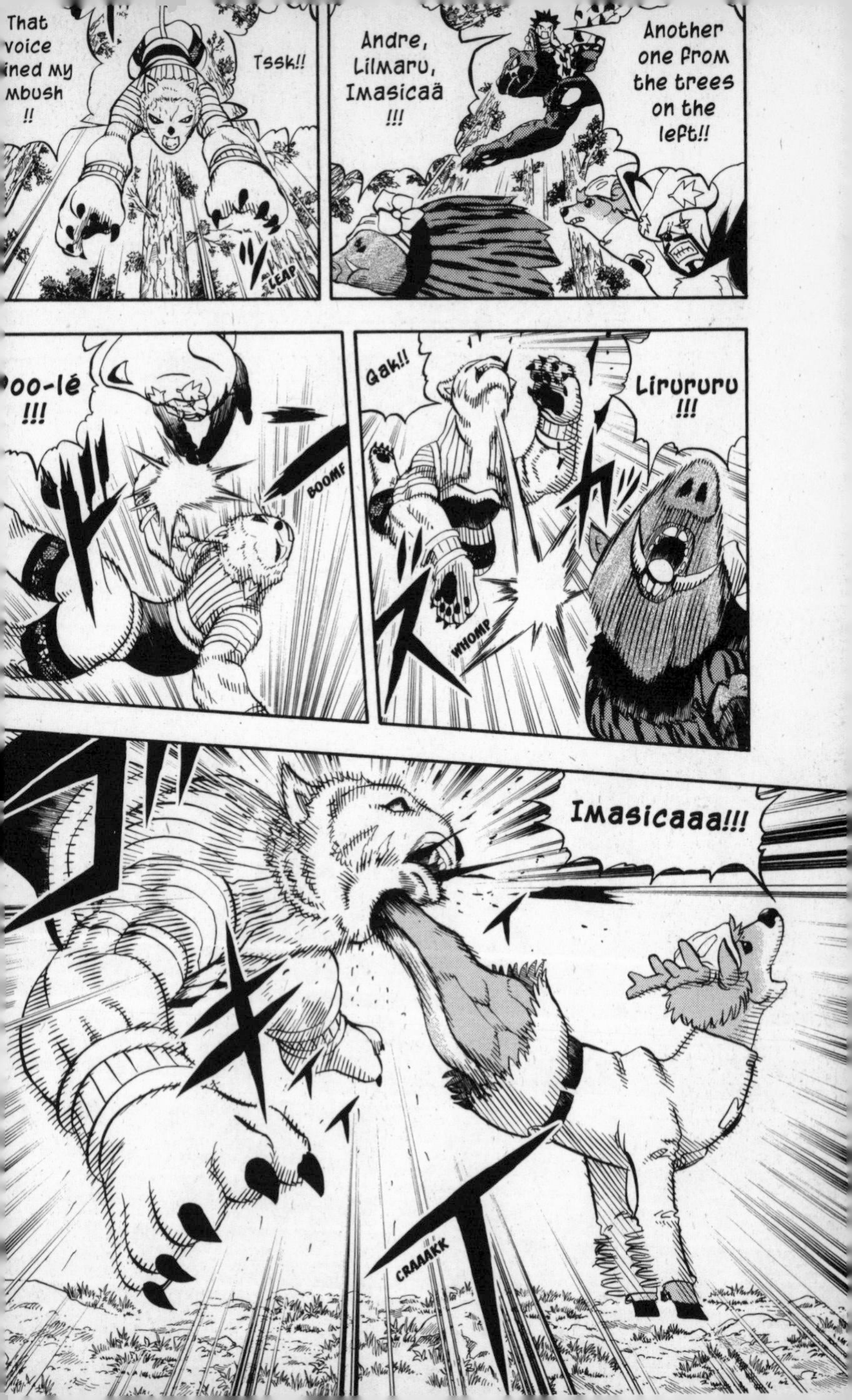

Another one from the trees on the left!!
Andre, Lilmaru, Imasicaä !!!
Tssk!!
That voice ined my mbush !!
LEAP
Lirururu !!!
Gak!!
WHOMP
BOOMF
oo-lé !!!
Imasicaaa!!!
CRAAAKK

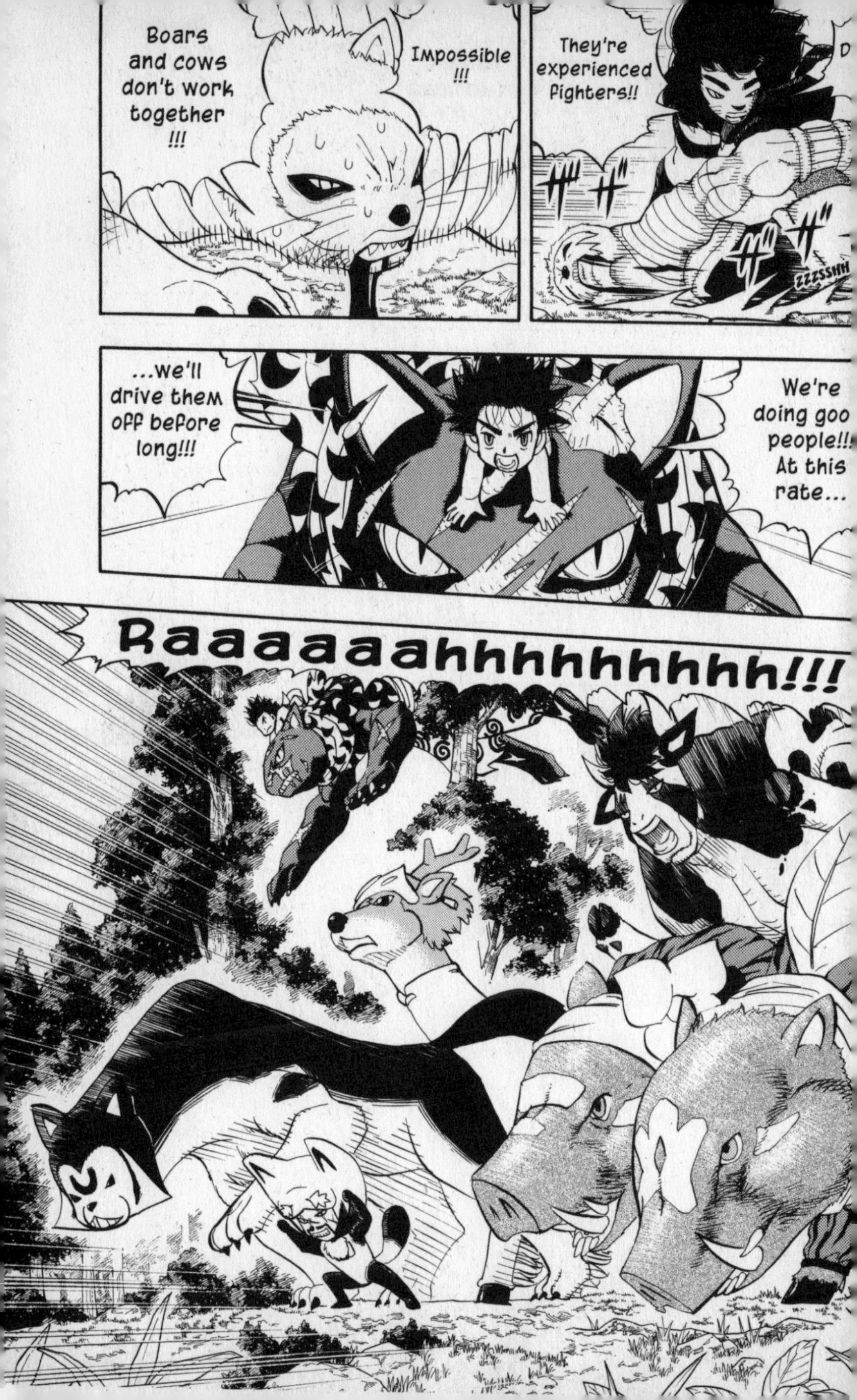
They're experienced fighters!!
D
ZZZSSHH
Impossible!!!
Boars and cows don't work together!!!
We're doing goo people!!! At this rate...
...we'll drive them off before long!!!
Raaaaaahhhhhhhh!!!

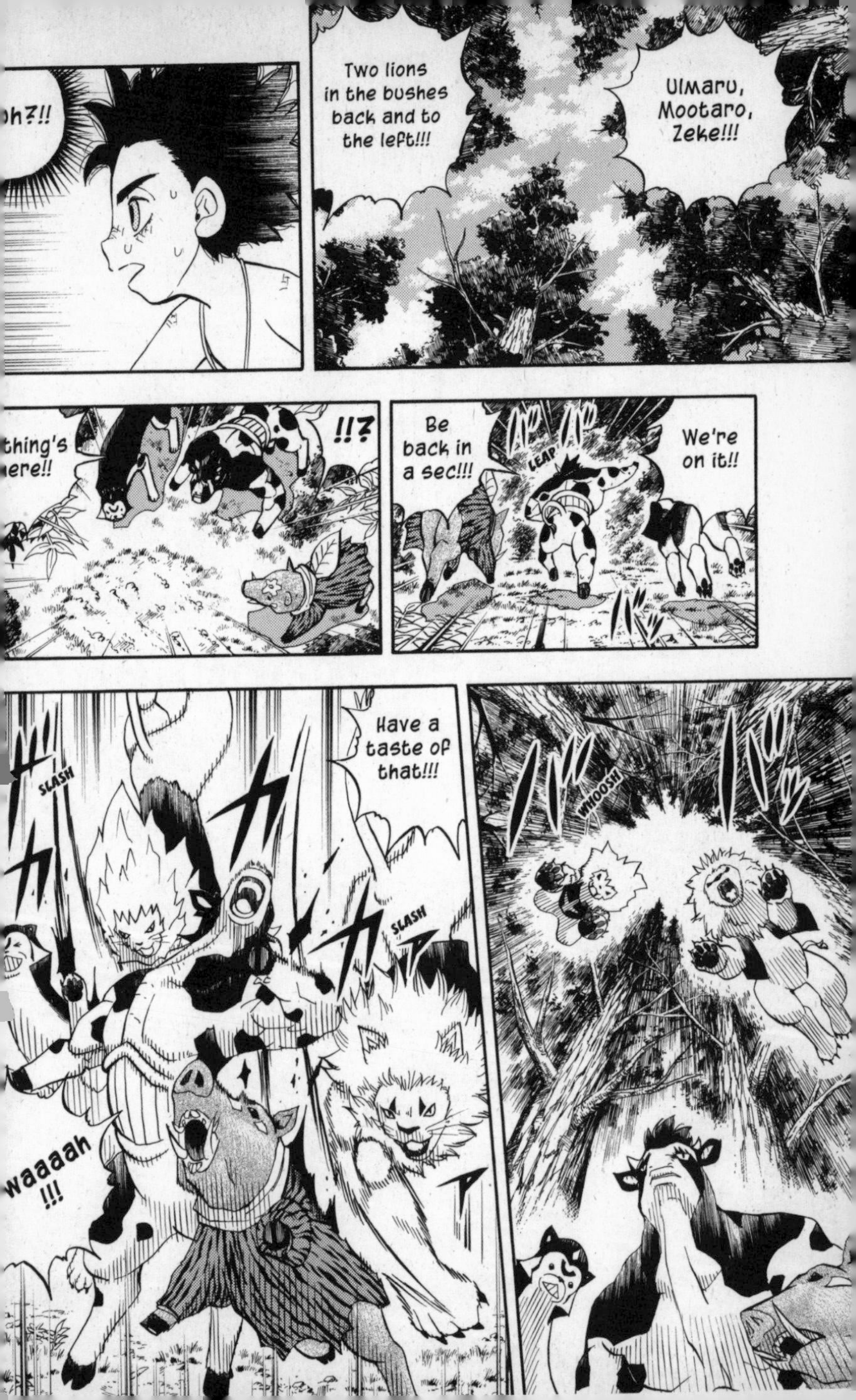
Ulmaru, Mootaro, Zeke!!!
Two lions in the bushes back and to the left!!!
h?!!
We're on it!!
LEAP
Be back in a sec!!!
!!?
thing's ere!!
WHOOSH
Have a taste of that!!!
SLASH
SLASH
Waaaah !!!

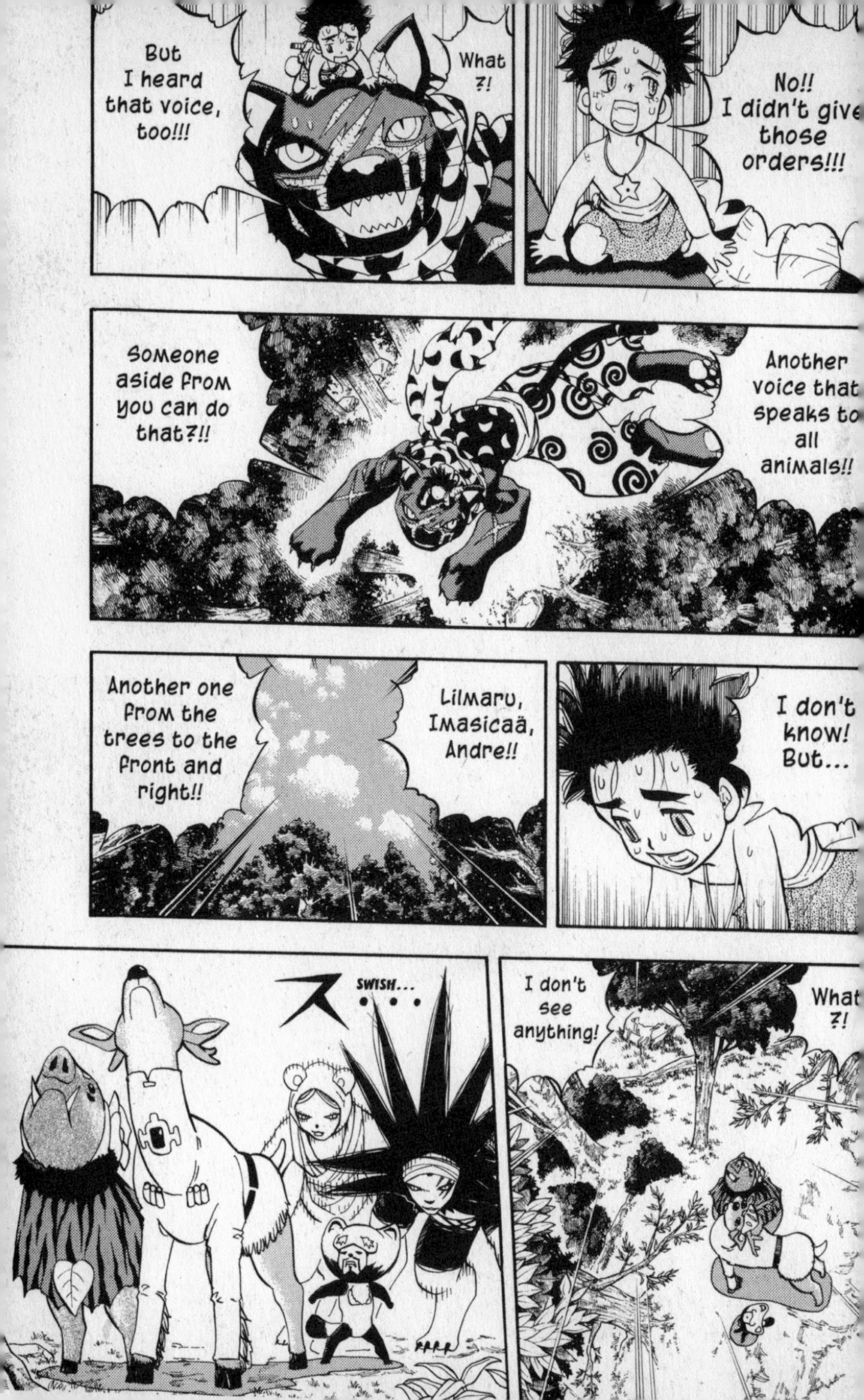
No!! I didn't give those orders!!!
What ?!
But I heard that voice, too!!!
Another voice that speaks to all animals!!
Someone aside from you can do that?!!
I don't know! But...
Lilmaru, Imasicaä, Andre!!
Another one from the trees to the front and right!!
What ?!
I don't see anything!
SWISH...

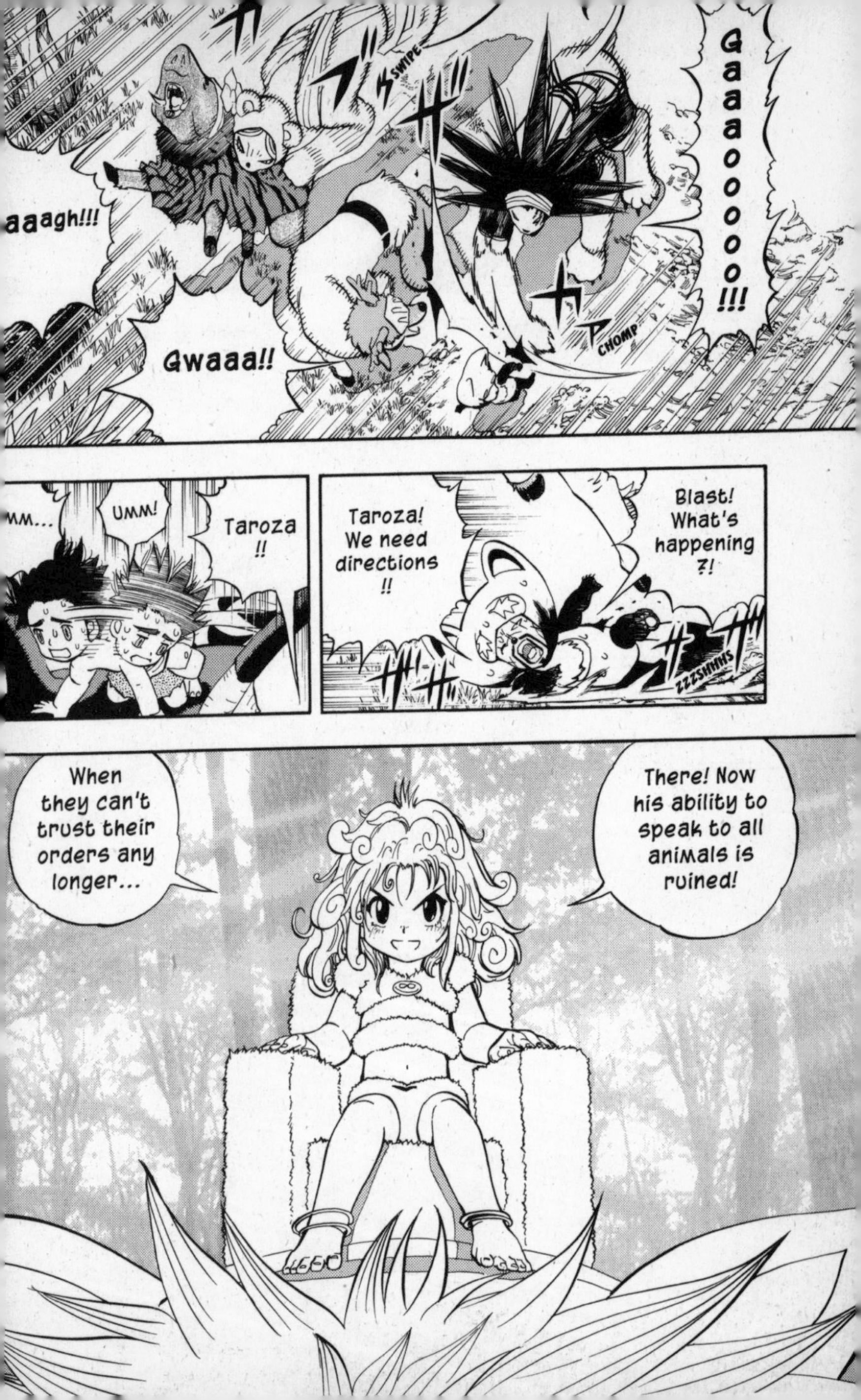
Gaaaoooooooo!!!
SWIPE
CHOMP
aaagh!!!
Gwaaa!!
Blast! What's happening ?!
Taroza! We need directions !!
ZZZSHHHS
Taroza !!
UMM!
MM...
There! Now his ability to speak to all animals is ruined!
When they can't trust their orders any longer...

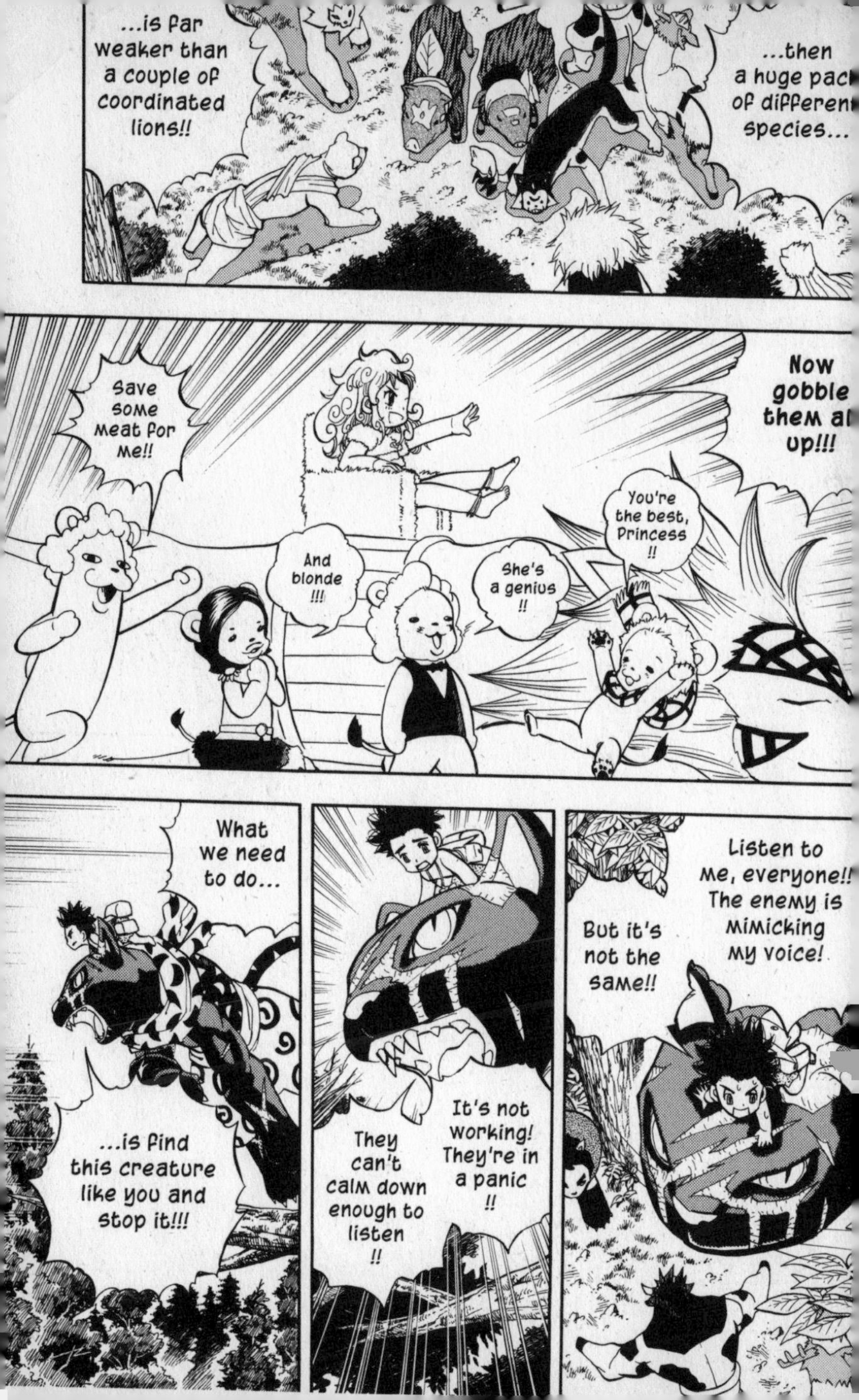
...then a huge pac of differen species...
...is far weaker than a couple of coordinated lions!!
Now gobble them al up!!!
You're the best, Princess !!
She's a genius !!
And blonde !!!
Save some meat for me!!
Listen to me, everyone!! The enemy is mimicking my voice!
But it's not the same!!
It's not working! They're in a panic !!
They can't calm down enough to listen !!
What we need to do...
...is find this creature like you and stop it!!!

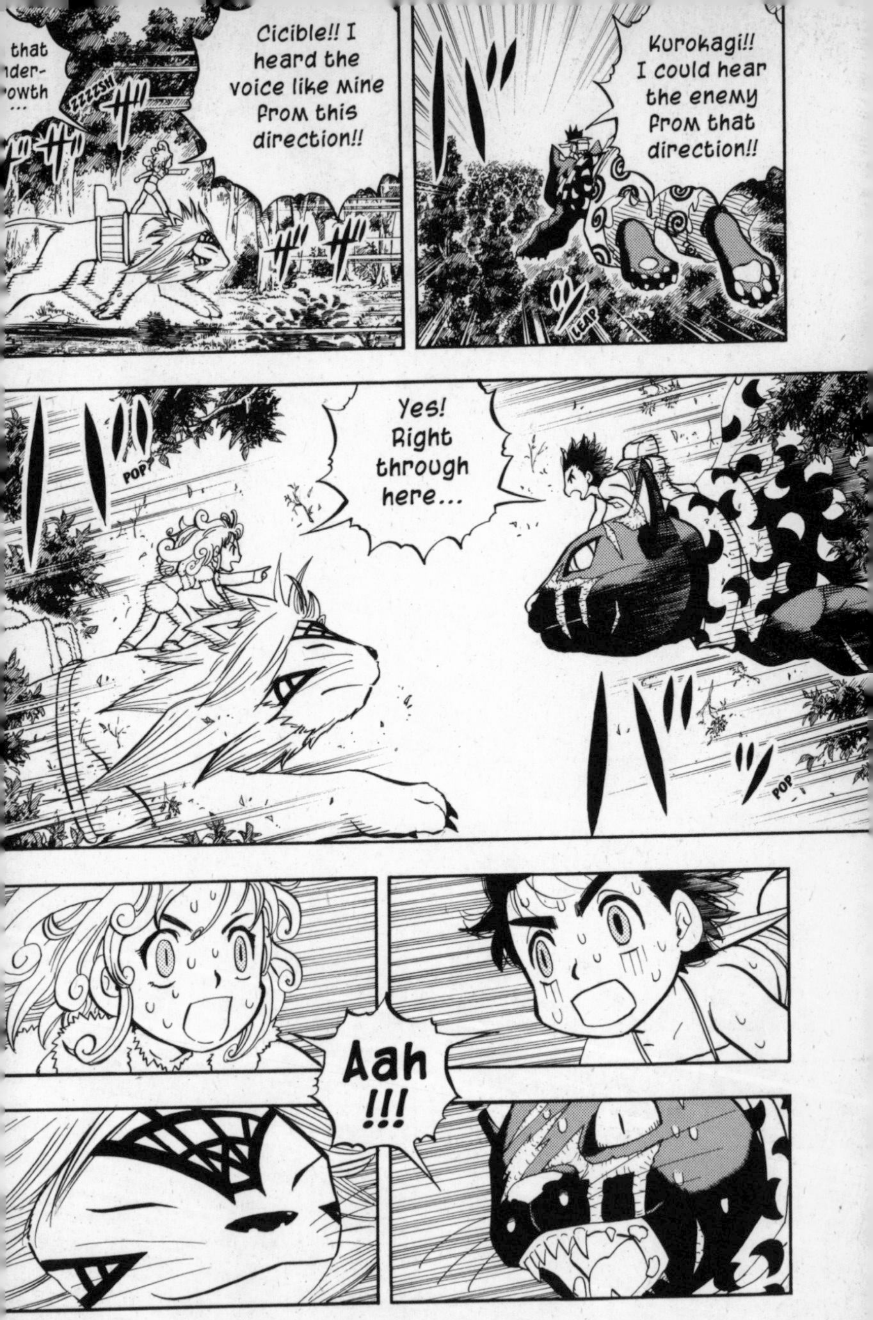
Kurokagi!! I could hear the enemy from that direction!!
LEAP
Cicible!! I heard the voice like mine from this direction!!
ZZZZSH
that
Yes! Right through here...
POP
POP
Aah !!!

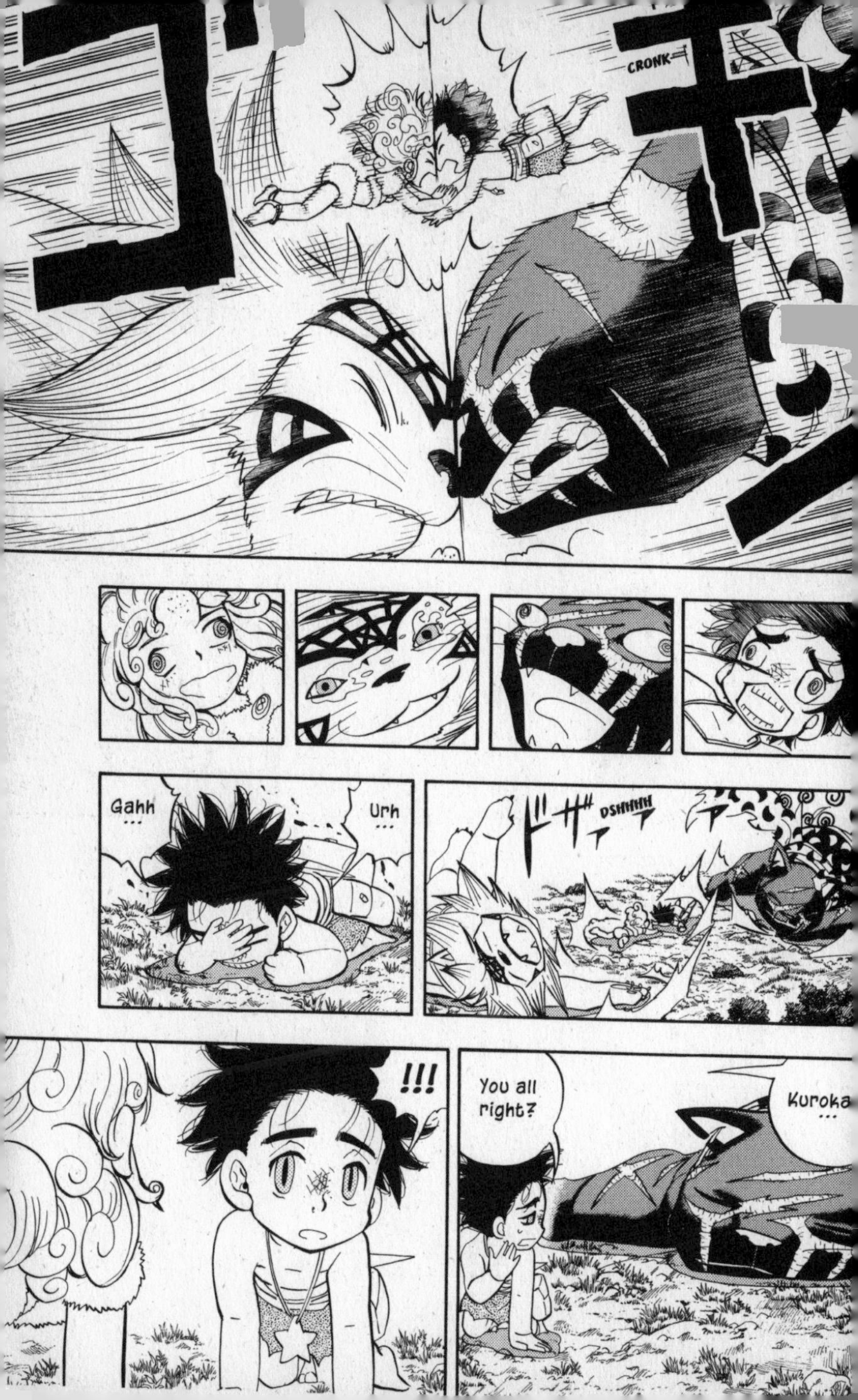
CRONK
Urh
...
Gahh
...
DSHHHH
!!!
Kuroka
...
You all right?

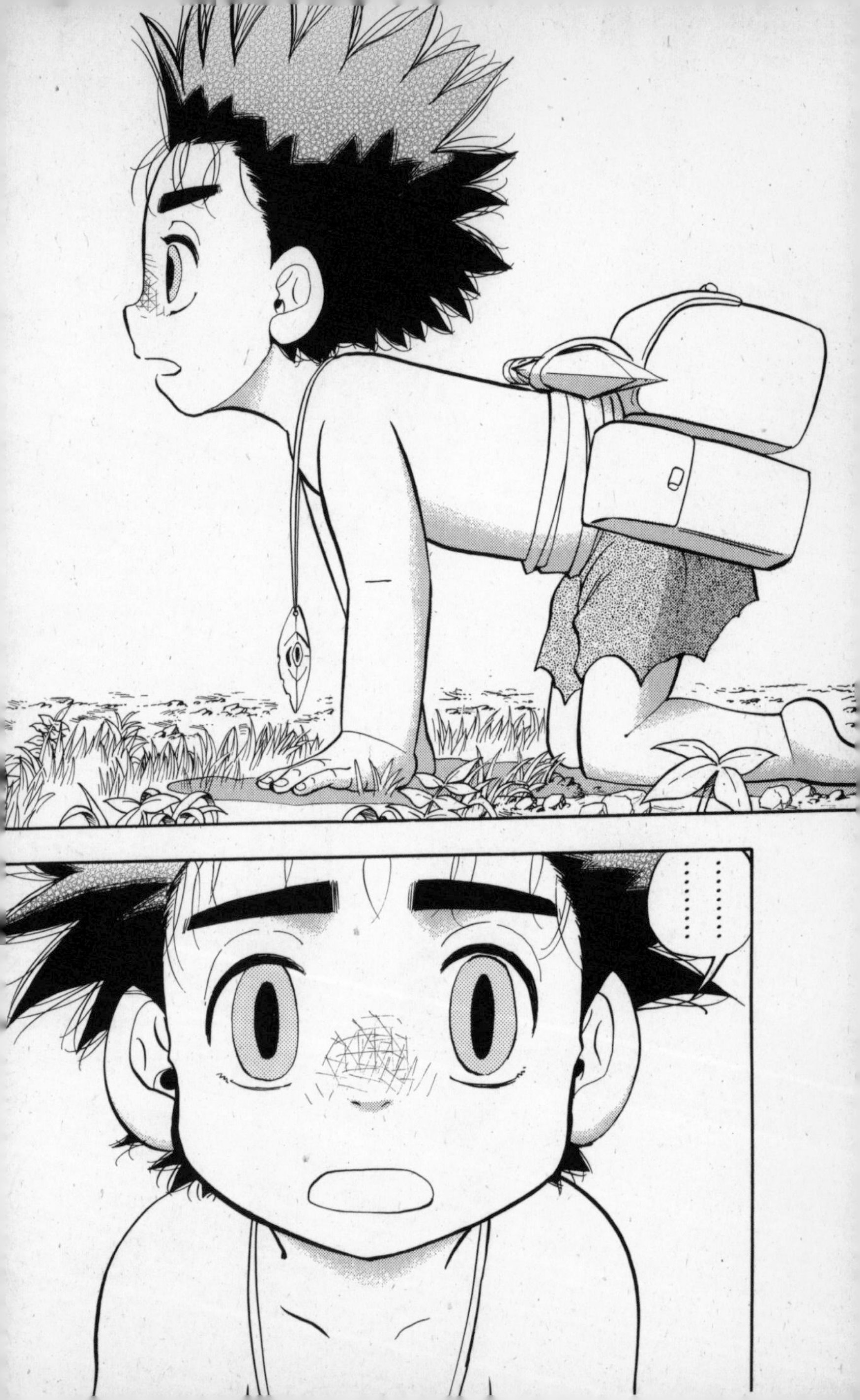
……

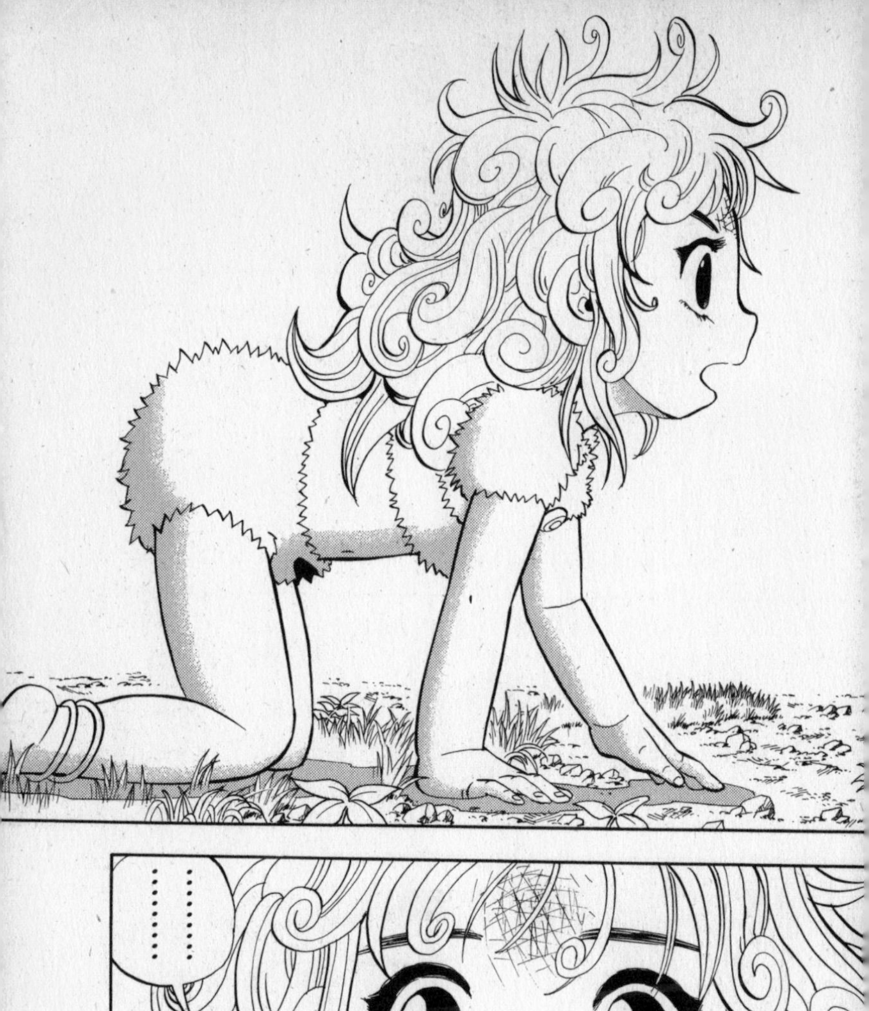

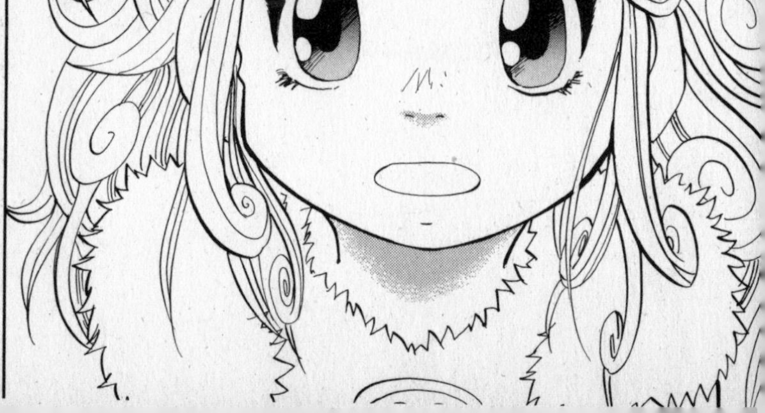
……

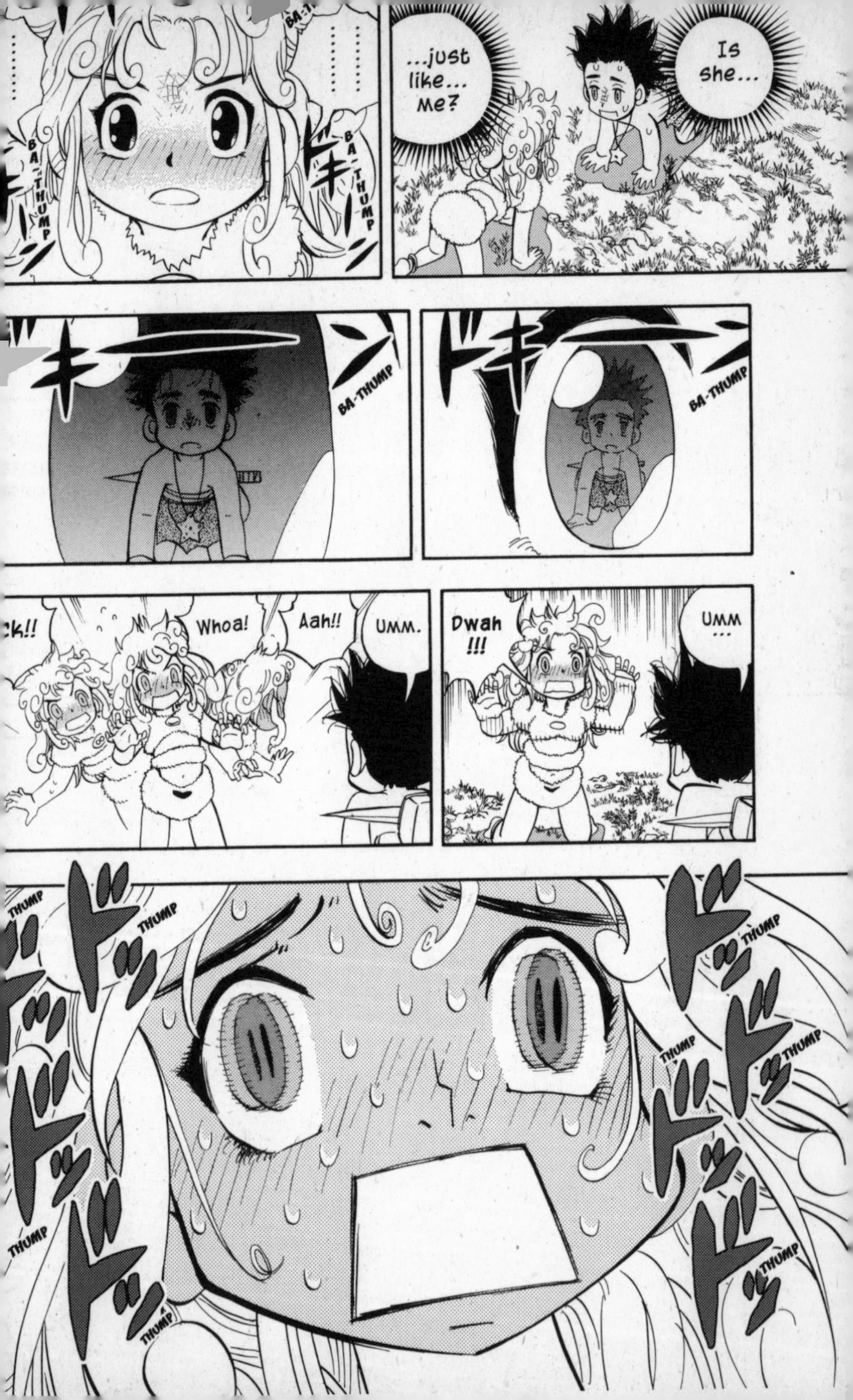

Is she...
...just like... me?
BA-THUMP
BA-THUMP
BA-THUMP
BA-THUMP
UMM ...
Dwah !!!
UMM.
Aah!!
Whoa!
ck!!
THUMP
THUMP
THUMP
THUMP
THUMP
THUMP
THUMP
THUMP

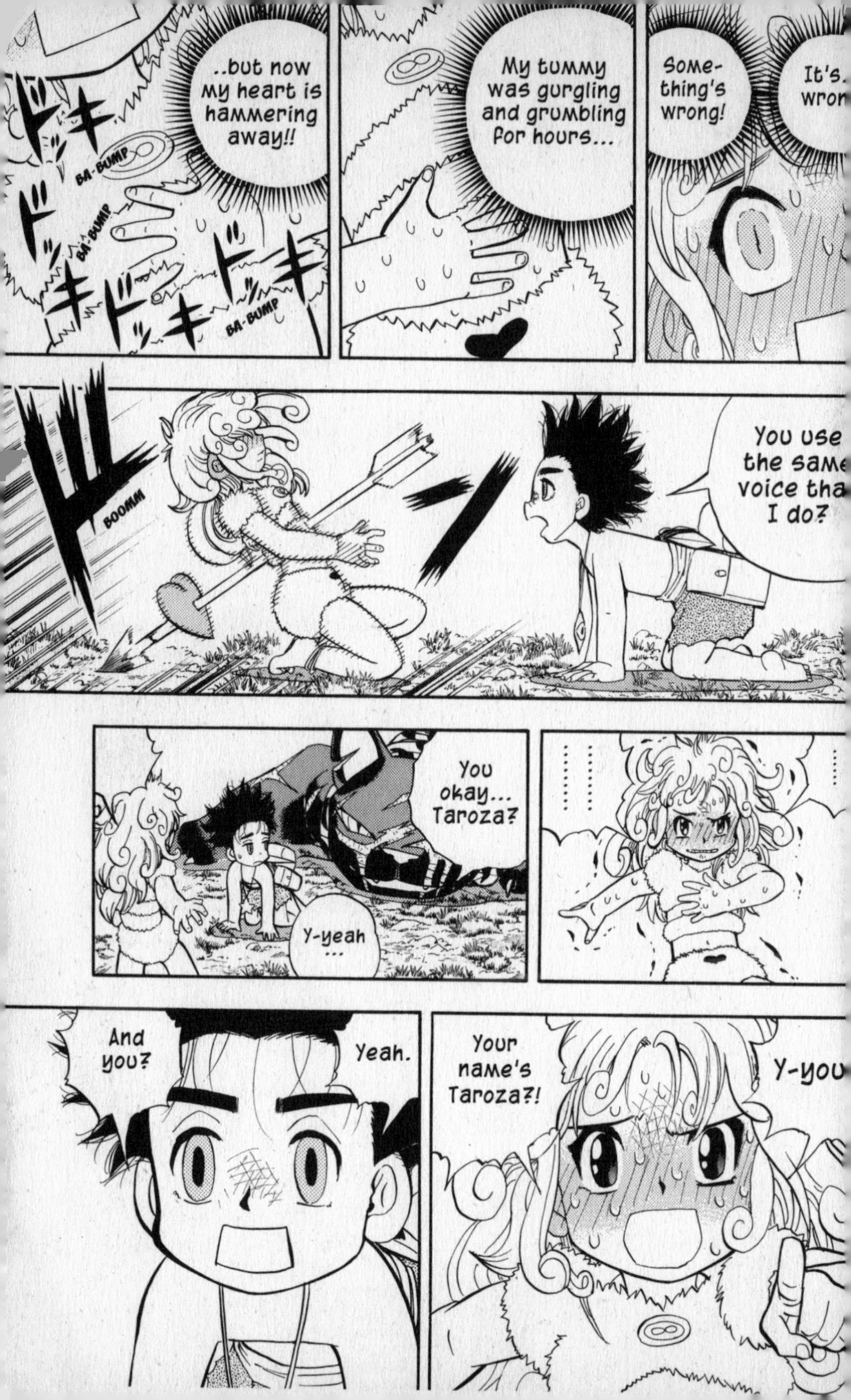

It's. wron
Some-thing's wrong!
My tummy was gurgling and grumbling for hours...
..but now my heart is hammering away!!
BA-BUMP
BA-BUMP
BA-BUMP
You use the same voice tha I do?
BOOMM
You okay... Taroza?
Y-yeah ...
Y-you
Your name's Taroza?!
Yeah.
And you?

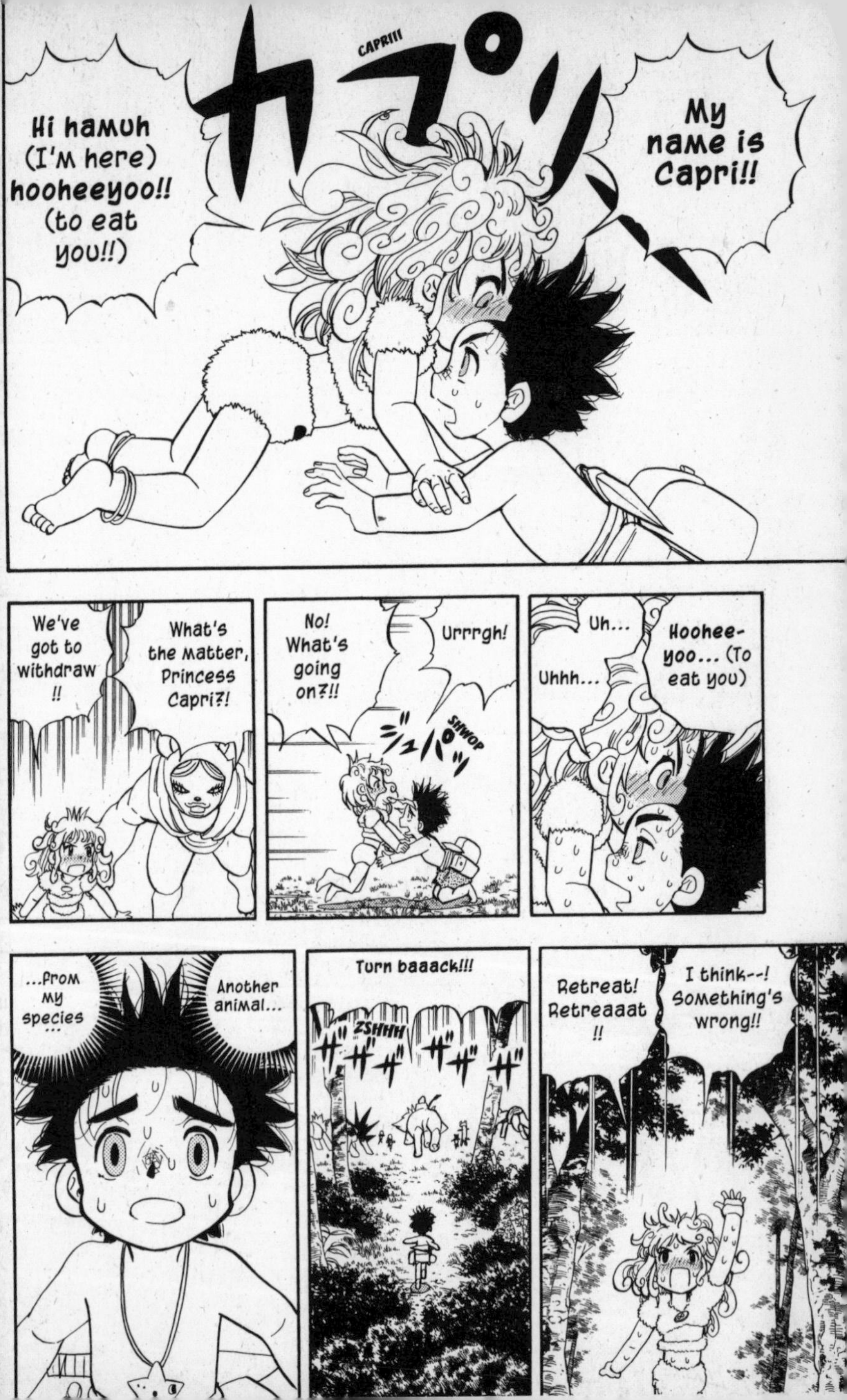
CAPRI!!
My name is Capri!!
Hi hamuh (I'm here) hooheeyoo!! (to eat you!!)
Hoohee-yoo... (To eat you)
Uh...
Uhhh...
Urrrgh!
No! What's going on?!!
SHWOP
What's the matter, Princess Capri?!
We've got to withdraw!!
I think--! Something's wrong!!
Retreat! Retreaaat!!
Turn baaack!!!
ZSHHH
Another animal...
...from my species...

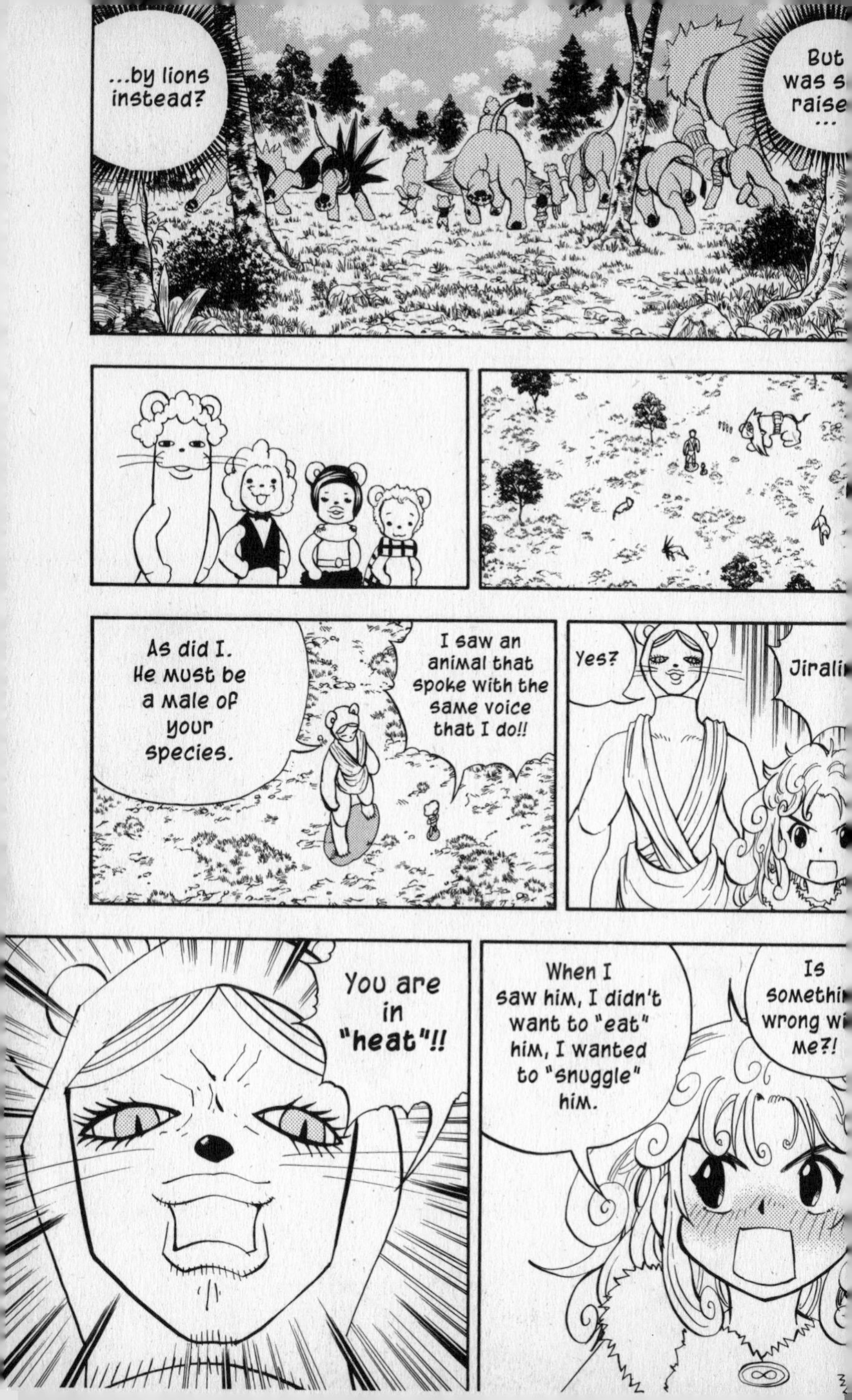
But was s raise ...
...by lions instead?
Jirali
Yes?
I saw an animal that spoke with the same voice that I do!!
As did I. He must be a male of your species.
Is somethi wrong wi me?!
When I saw him, I didn't want to "eat" him, I wanted to "snuggle" him.
You are in "heat"!!

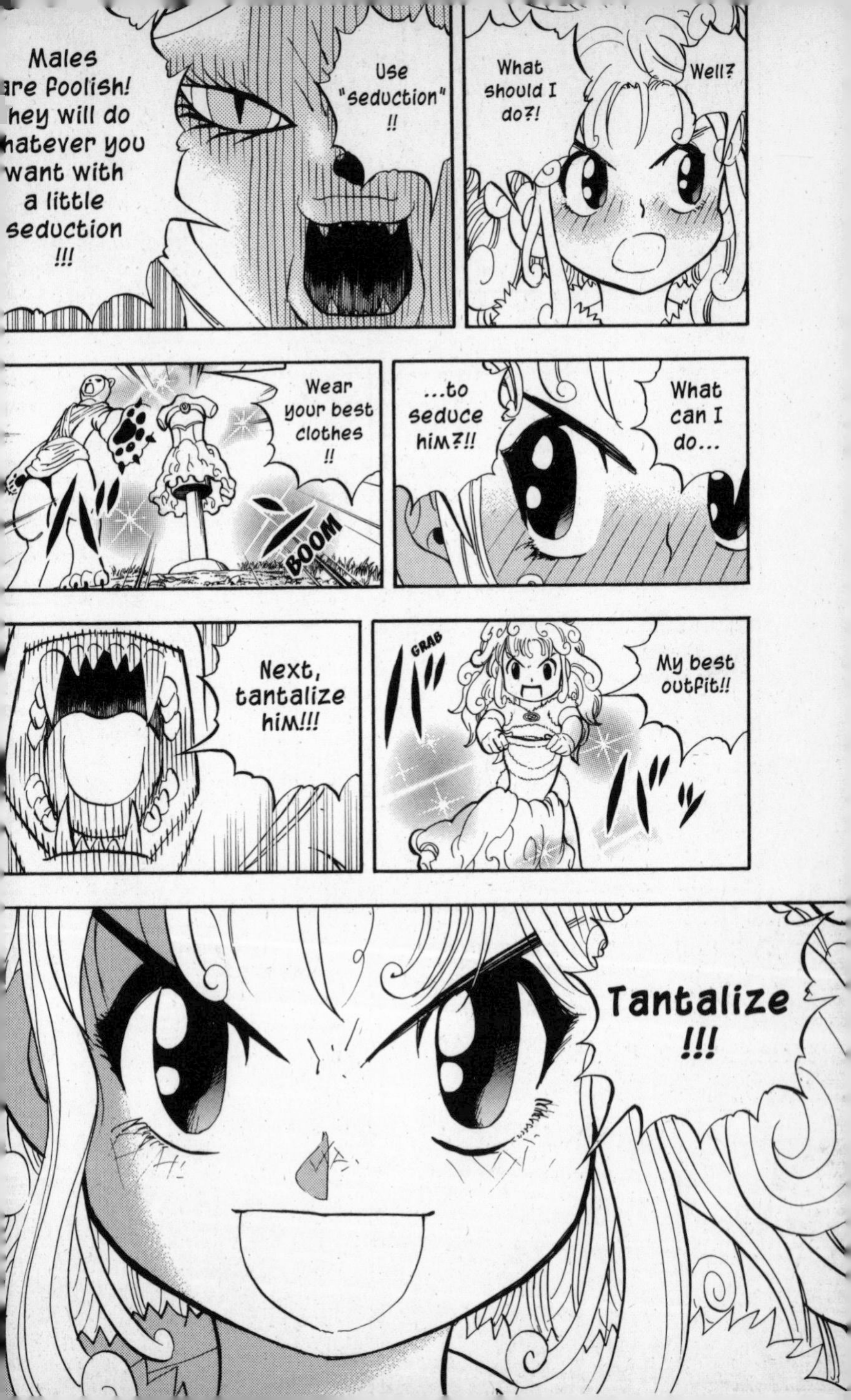
Well?
What should I do?!
Use "seduction" !!
Males are foolish! hey will do hatever you want with a little seduction !!!
What can I do...
...to seduce him?!!
Wear your best clothes !!
BOOM
GRAB
My best outfit!!
Next, tantalize him!!!
Tantalize !!!

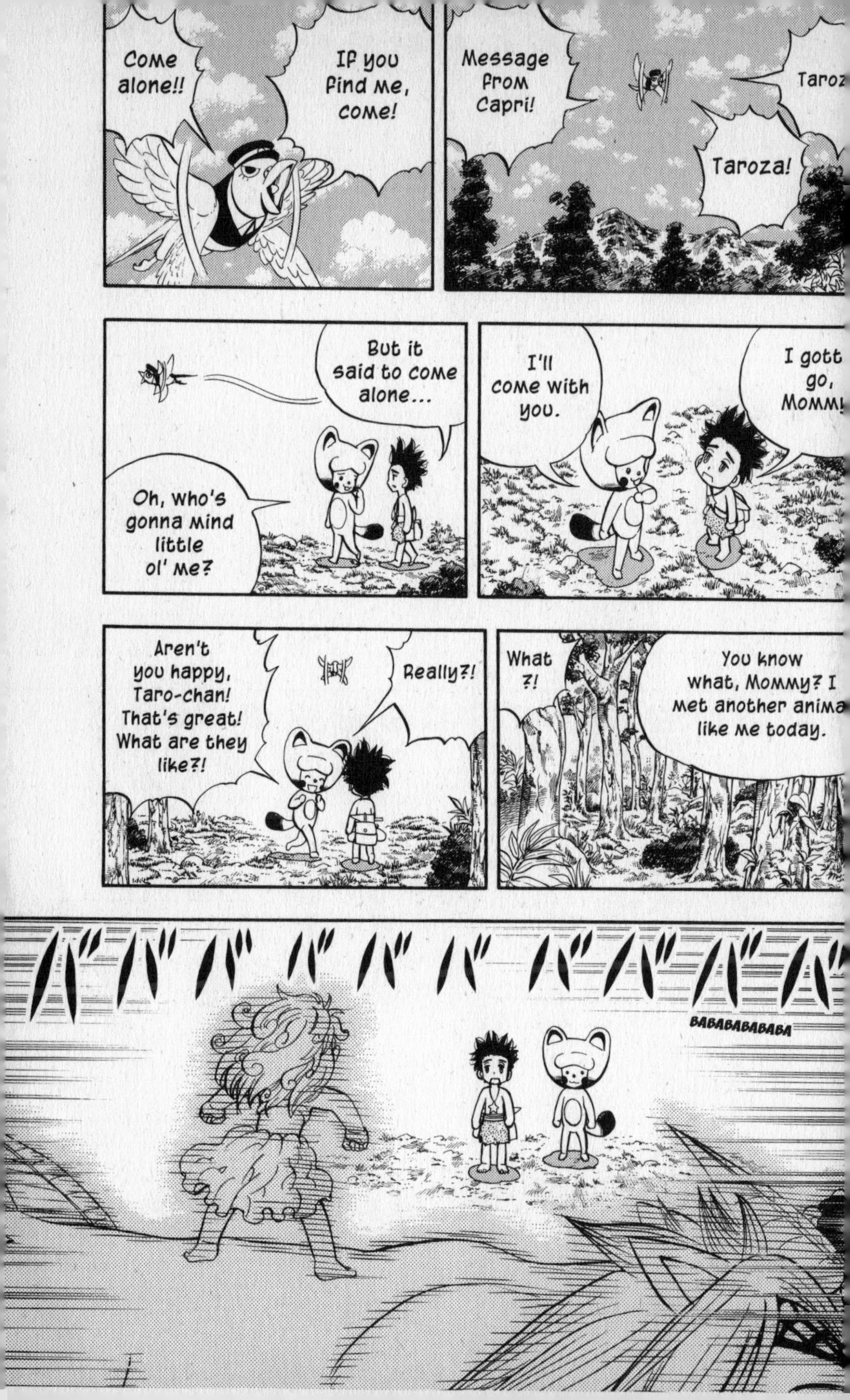
Taroz
Message from Capri!
Taroza!
If you find me, come!
Come alone!!
I gott go, Momm!
I'll come with you.
But it said to come alone...
Oh, who's gonna mind little ol' me?
You know what, Mommy? I met another anima like me today.
What ?!
Really?!
Aren't you happy, Taro-chan! That's great! What are they like?!
ババババババババババ
BABABABABABA

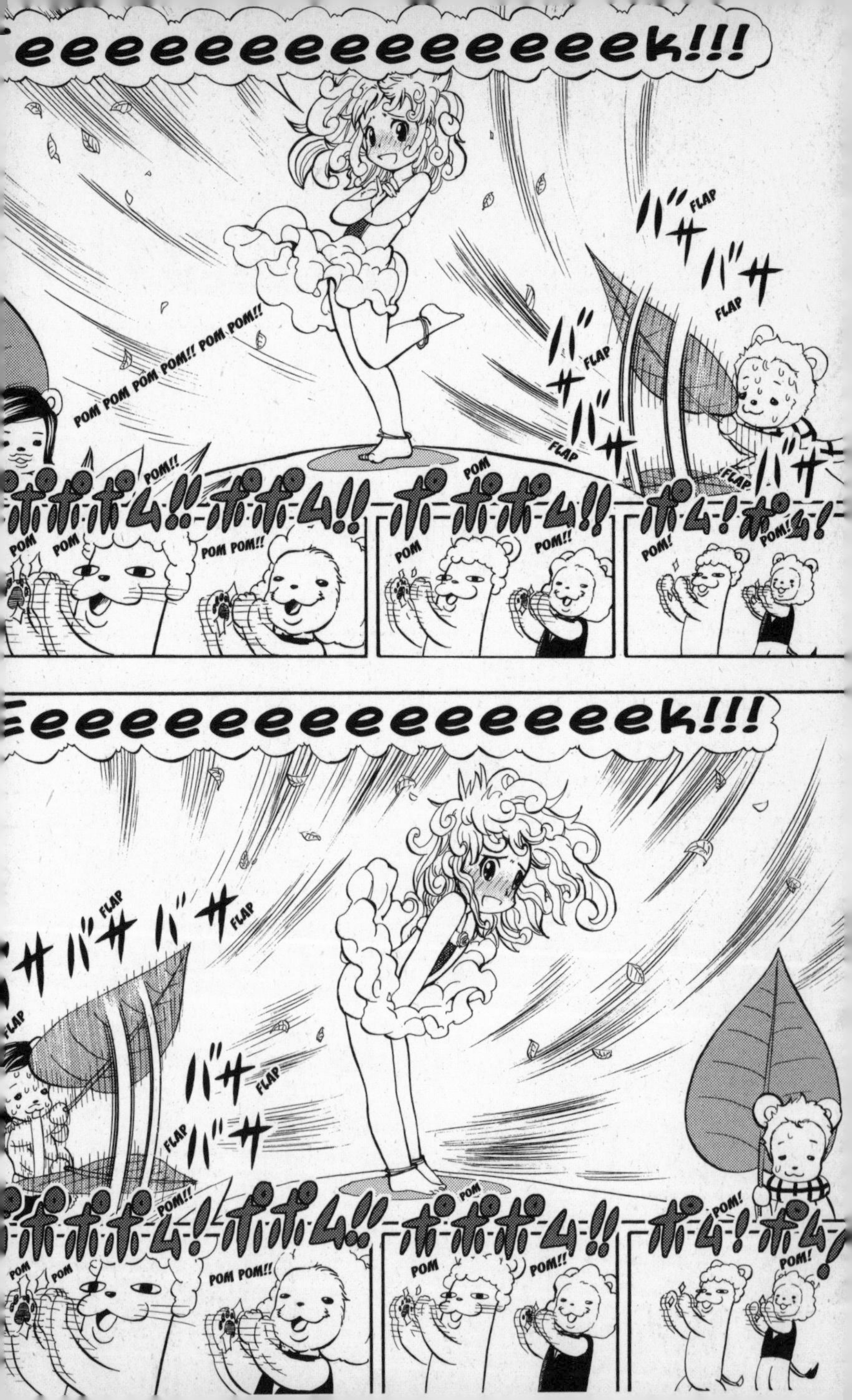

eeeeeeeeeeeeek!!!
バサバサ
FLAP
FLAP
バサバサ
FLAP
FLAP
バサ
FLAP
POM POM POM POM!! POM POM!!
POM!!
ポム!ポム!
POM!
POM!!
POM
ポポポム!!
POM
POM!!
ポポポム!!ポポム!!
POM
POM
POM POM!!
eeeeeeeeeeeeek!!!
バサバサ
FLAP
FLAP
バサバサ
FLAP
FLAP
FLAP
ポム!ポム!
POM!
POM!
POM
ポポポム!!
POM
POM!!
ポポポム!ポポム!!
POM!!
POM
POM
POM POM!!

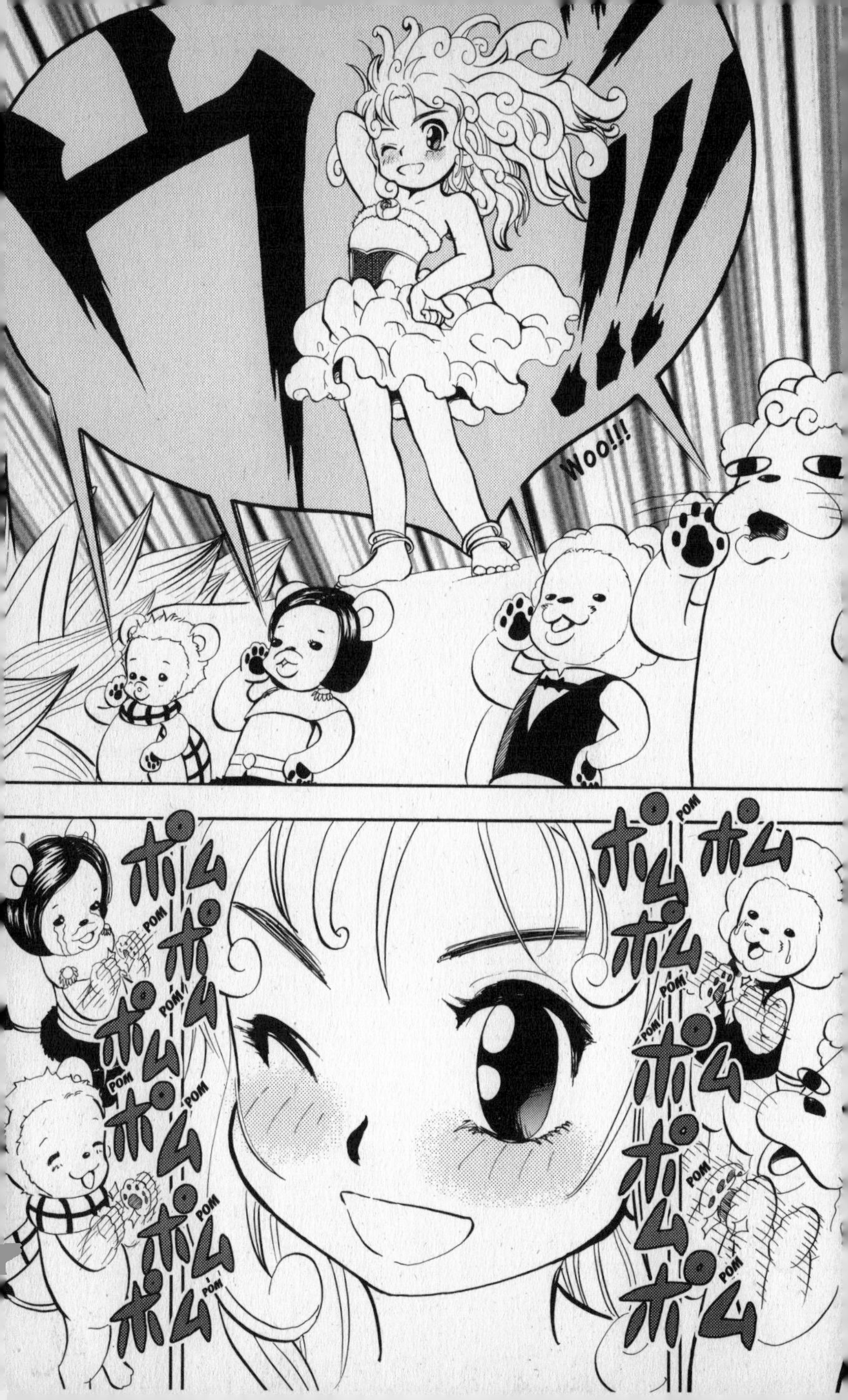
Woo!!!
ポムポムポムポムポムポム
POM POM POM POM POM
ポムポムポムポムポムポム
POM POM POM POM POM

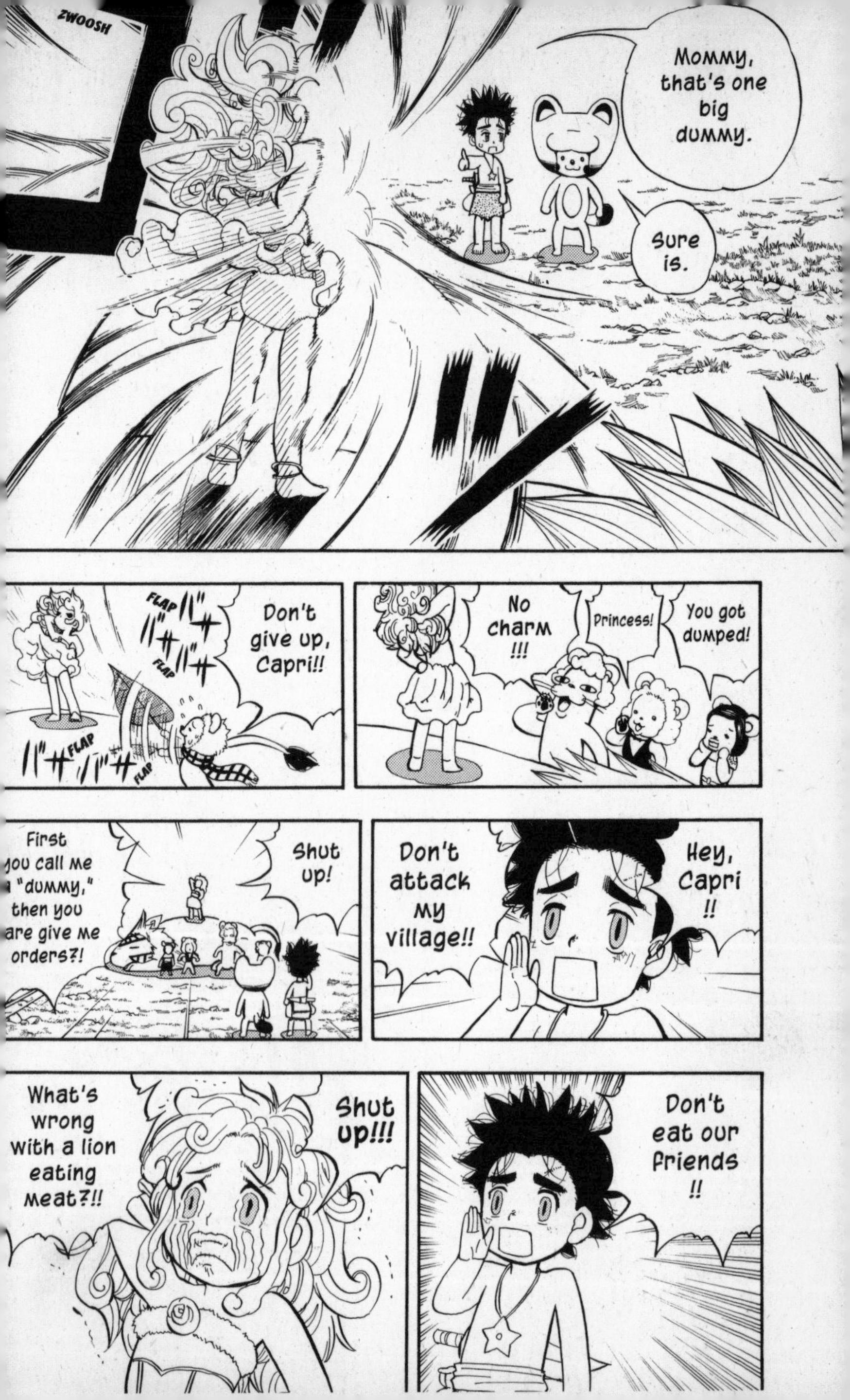
Mommy, that's one big dummy.
Sure is.
ZWOOSH
You got dumped!
Princess!
No charm !!!
Don't give up, Capri!!
FLAP
FLAP
FLAP
FLAP
Hey, Capri !!
Don't attack my village!!
Shut up!
First you call me a "dummy," then you are give me orders?!
Don't eat our friends !!
Shut up!!!
What's wrong with a lion eating meat?!!

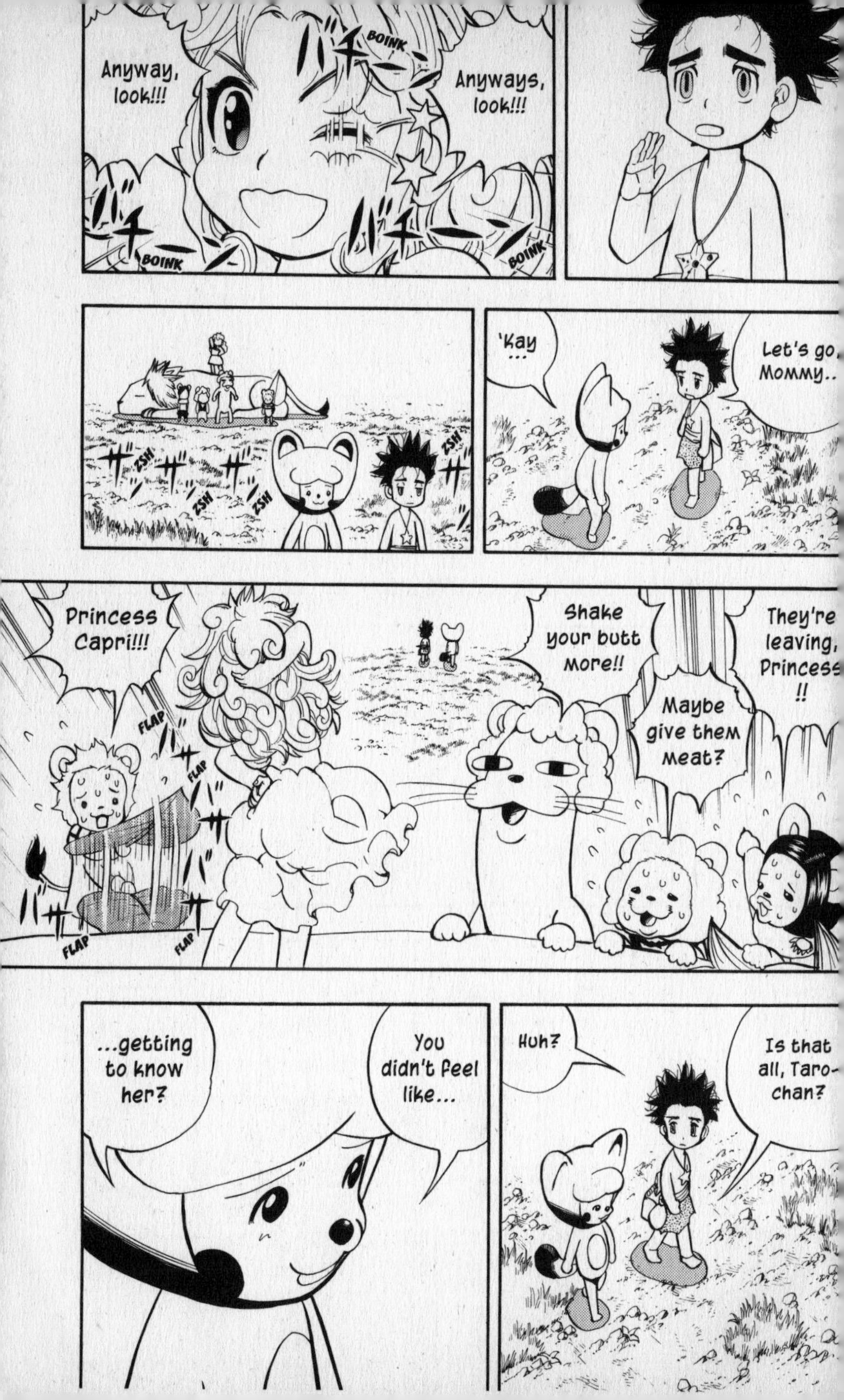
BOINK
Anyways, look!!!
Anyway, look!!!
BOINK
BOINK
Let's go, Mommy..
'Kay ...
ZSH
ZSH
ZSH
ZSH
They're leaving, Princess !!
Maybe give them meat?
Shake your butt more!!
Princess Capri!!!
FLAP
FLAP
FLAP
FLAP
Is that all, Taro-chan?
Huh?
You didn't feel like...
...getting to know her?

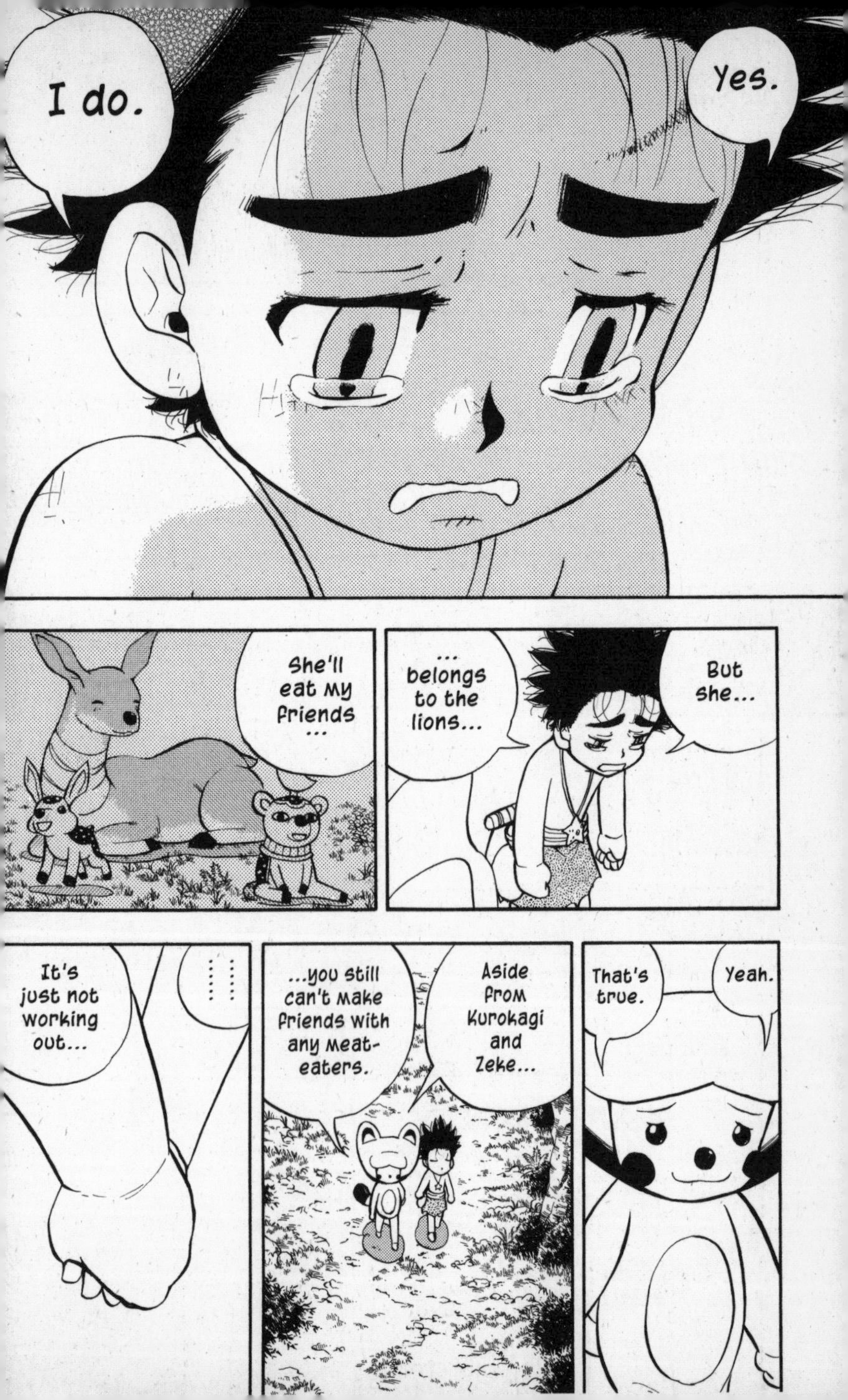
Yes.
I do.
But she...
...belongs to the lions...
She'll eat my friends ...
Yeah.
That's true.
Aside from Kurokagi and Zeke...
...you still can't make friends with any meat-eaters.
......
It's just not working out...

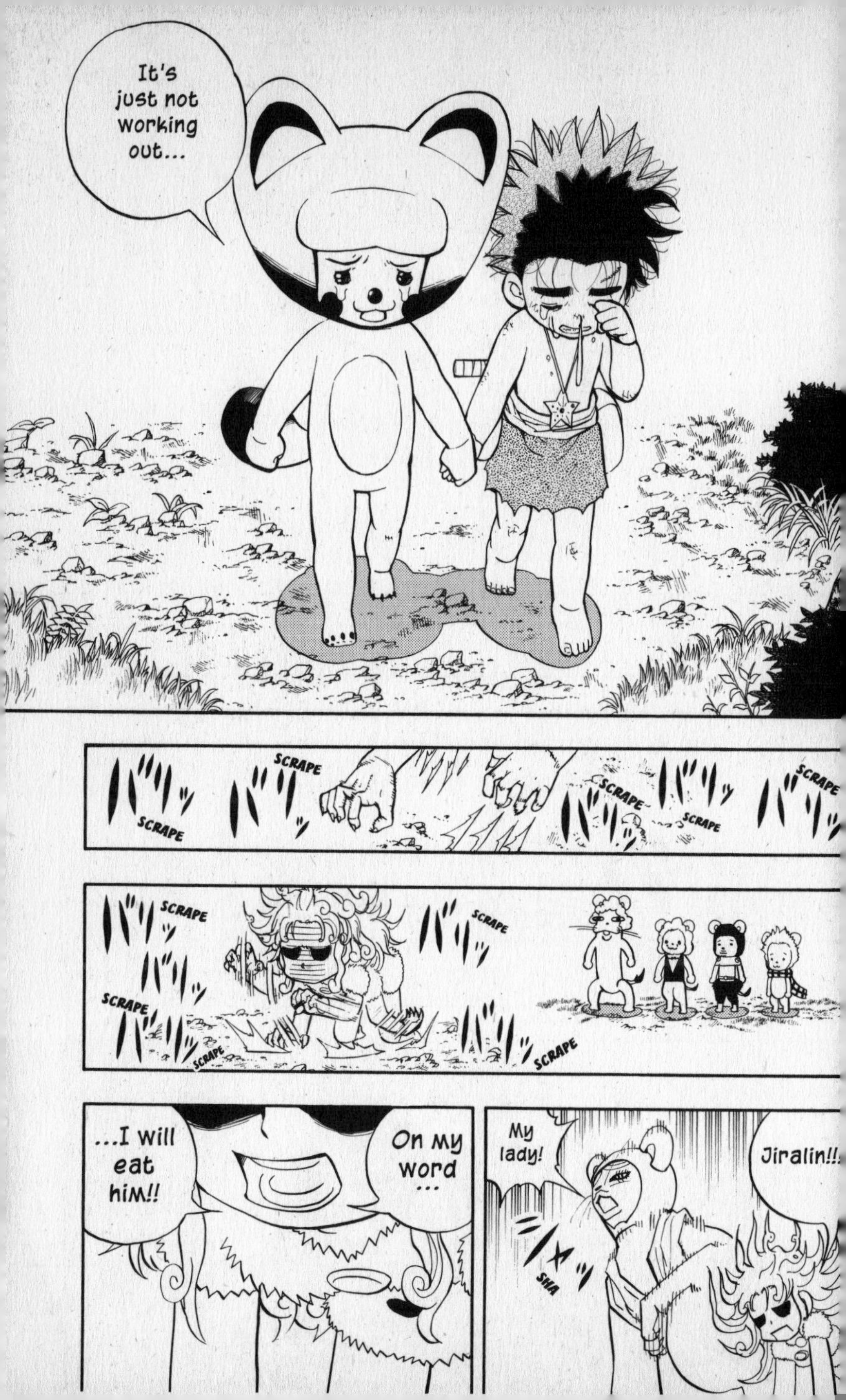
It's just not working out...
SCRAPE
SCRAPE
SCRAPE
SCRAPE
SCRAPE
SCRAPE
SCRAPE
SCRAPE
SCRAPE
SCRAPE
SCRAPE
Jiralin!!
My lady!
SHA
On my word...
...I will eat him!!

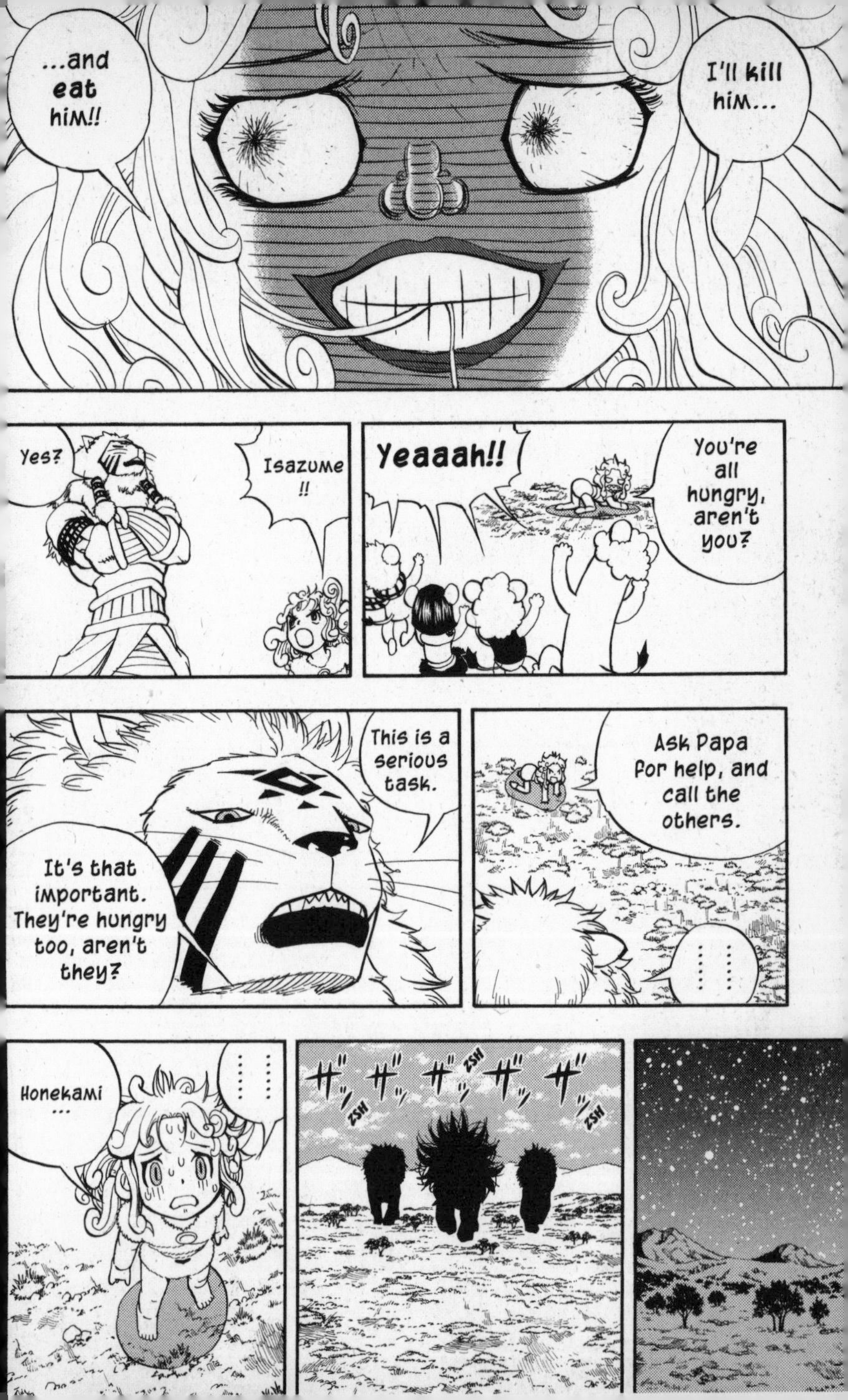
I'll kill him...
...and eat him!!
You're all hungry, aren't you?
Yeaaah!!
Isazume !!
Yes?
Ask Papa for help, and call the others.
......
This is a serious task.
It's that important. They're hungry too, aren't they?
ZSH
ZSH
ZSH
......
Honekami ...

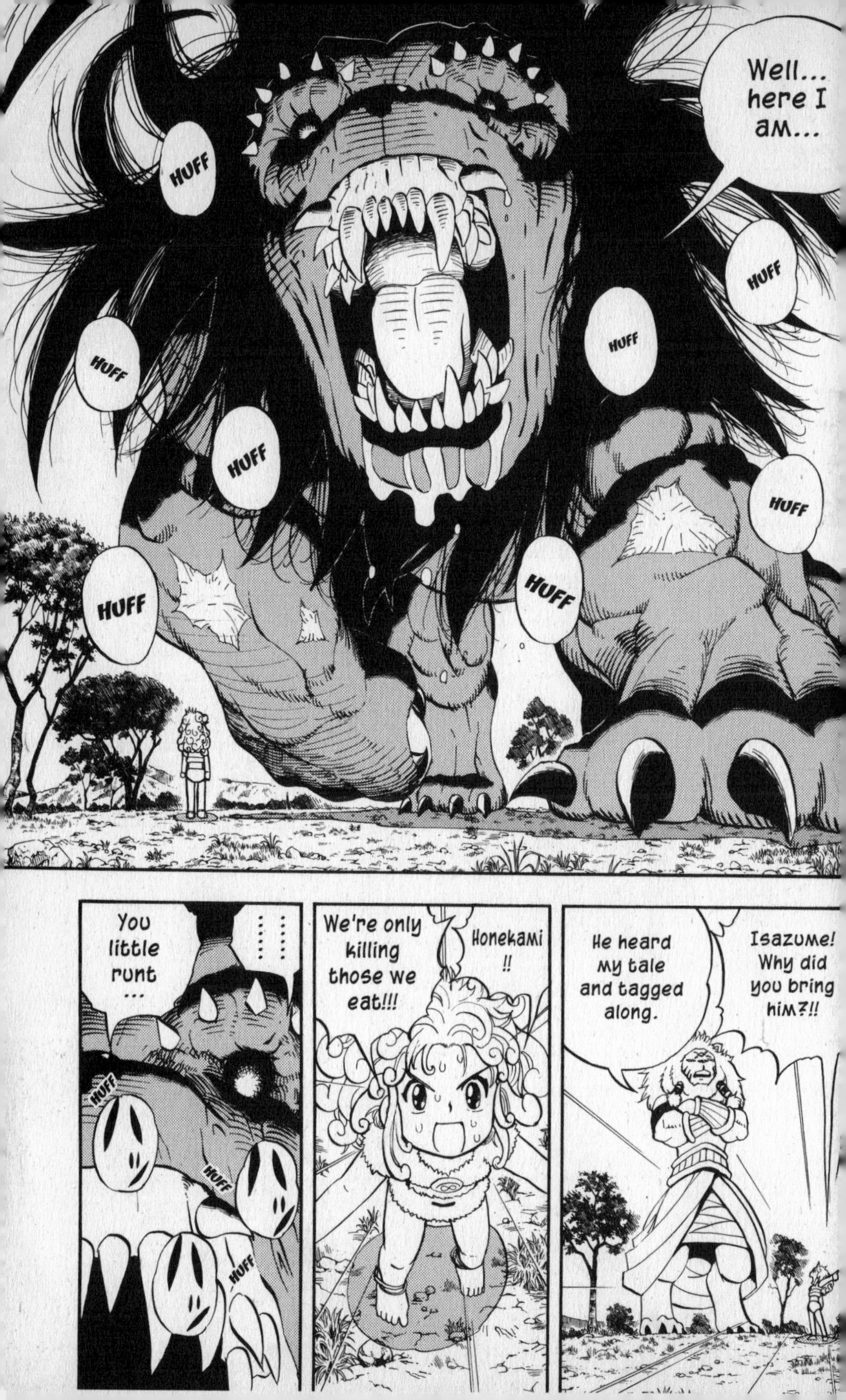
Well... here I am...
HUFF
HUFF
HUFF
HUFF
HUFF
HUFF
HUFF
HUFF
HUFF
Isazume! Why did you bring him?!!
He heard my tale and tagged along.
Honekami !!
We're only killing those we eat!!!
......
You little runt ...
HUFF
HUFF
HUFF

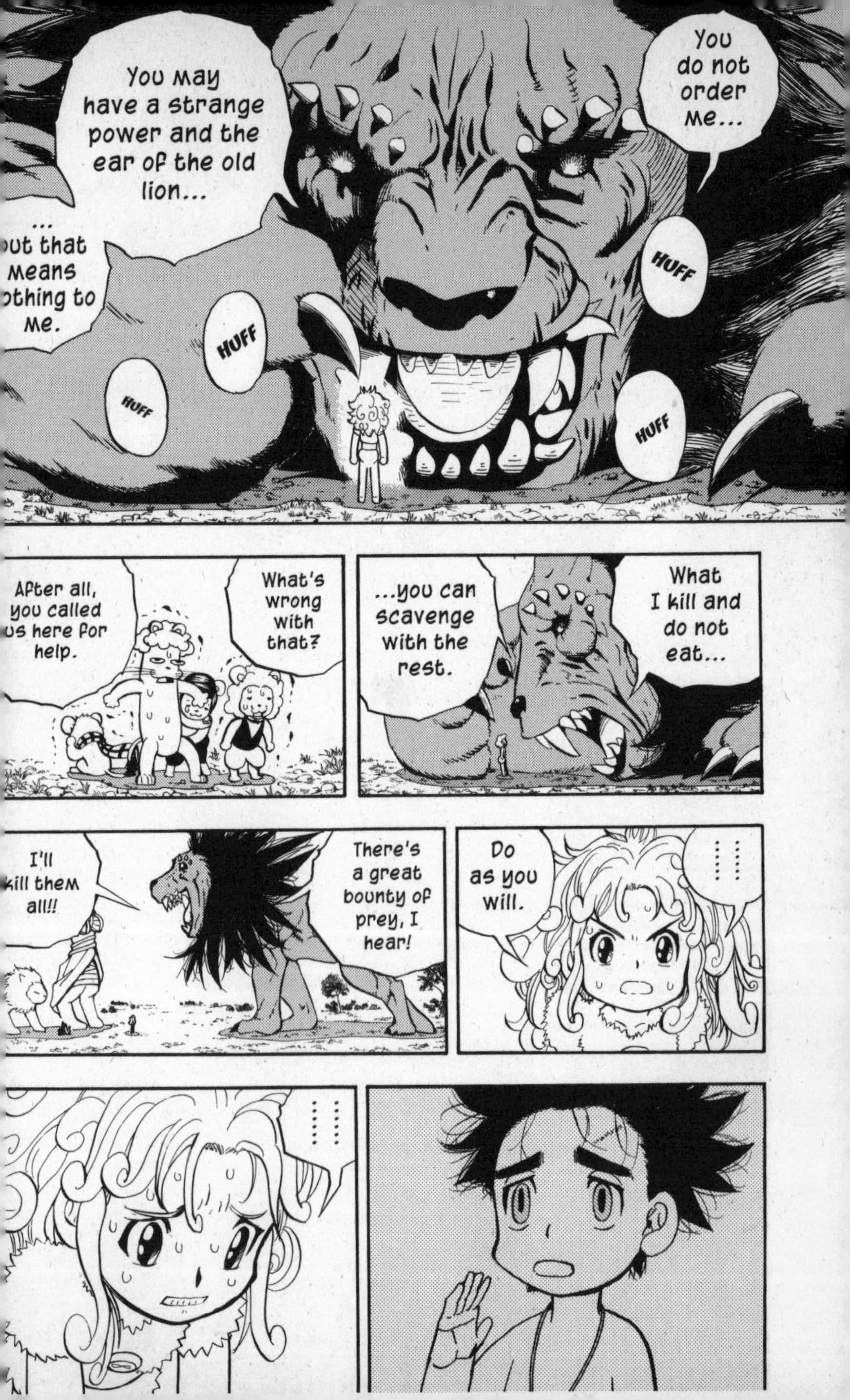
You do not order me...
You may have a strange power and the ear of the old lion...
... ut that means othing to me.
HUFF
HUFF
HUFF
HUFF
What I kill and do not eat...
...you can scavenge with the rest.
What's wrong with that?
After all, you called us here for help.
......
Do as you will.
There's a great bounty of prey, I hear!
I'll kill them all!!
......

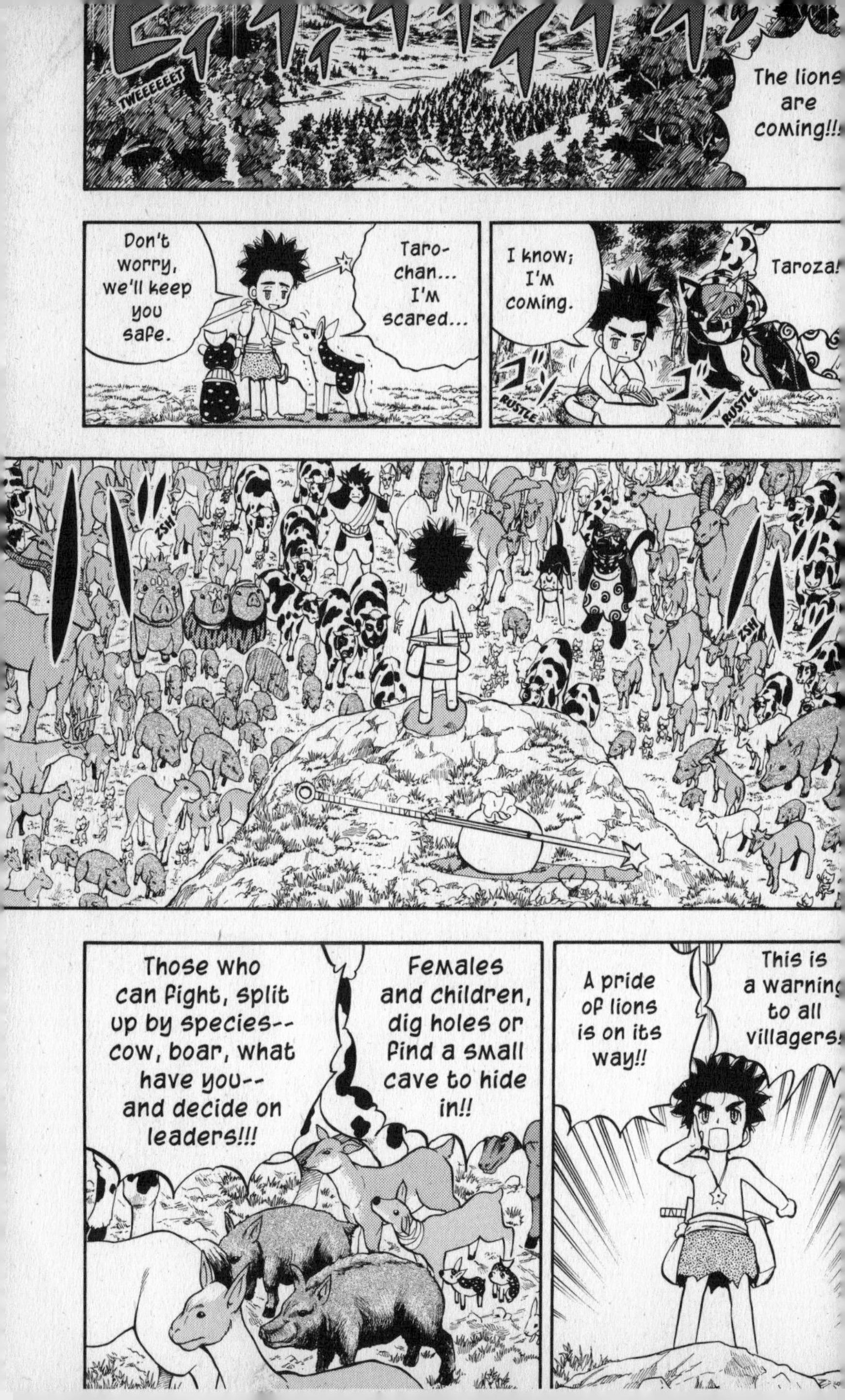
The lions are coming!!!
TWEEEEEET
Taroza!
I know; I'm coming.
RUSTLE
RUSTLE
Taro-chan... I'm scared...
Don't worry, we'll keep you safe.
ZSH
ZSH
This is a warning to all villagers!
A pride of lions is on its way!!
Females and children, dig holes or find a small cave to hide in!!
Those who can fight, split up by species--cow, boar, what have you--and decide on leaders!!!

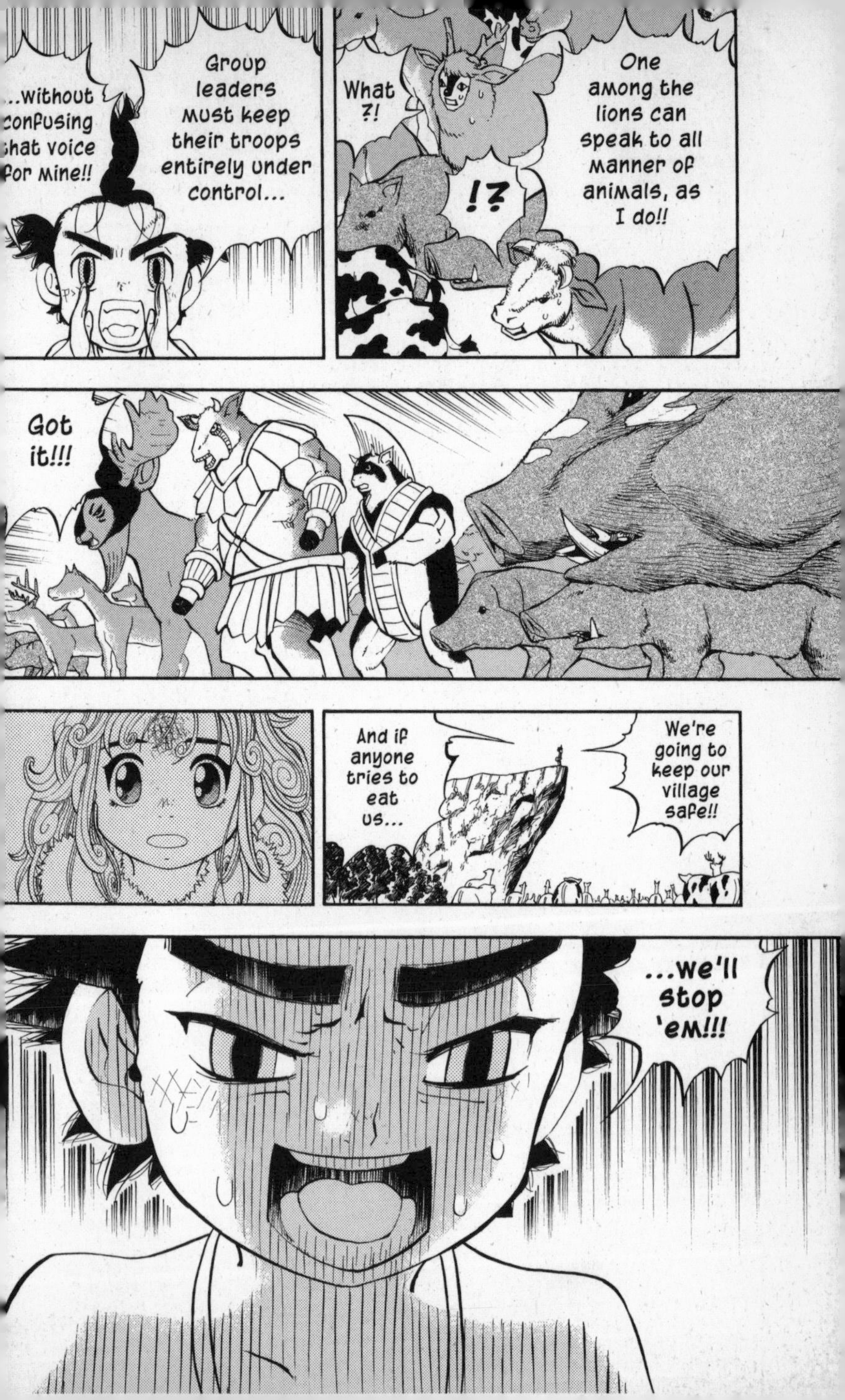

One among the lions can speak to all manner of animals, as I do!!
!?
What ?!
Group leaders must keep their troops entirely under control...
...without confusing that voice for mine!!
Got it!!!
We're going to keep our village safe!!
And if anyone tries to eat us...
...we'll stop 'em!!!

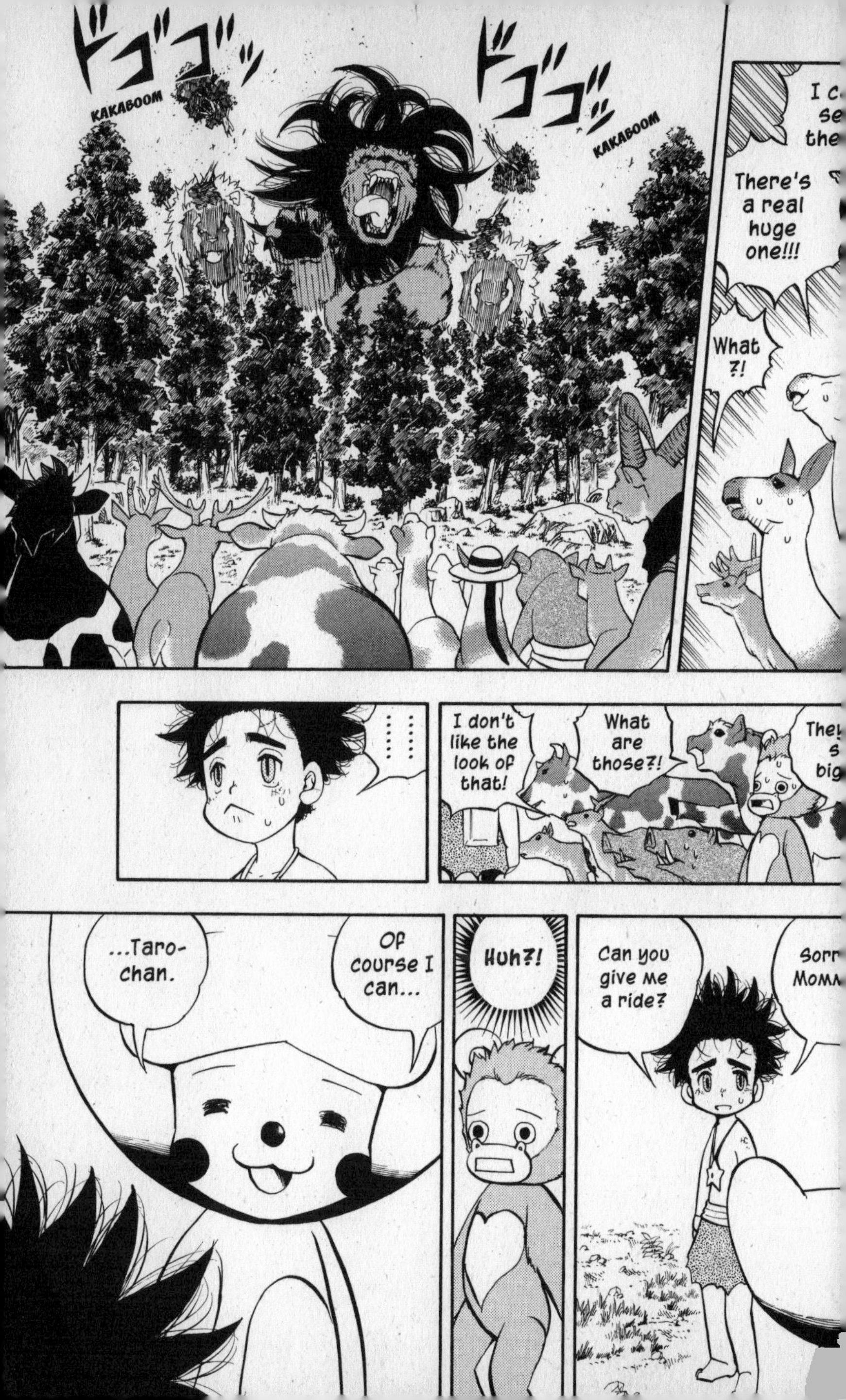

I c
se
the
There's a real huge one!!!
What?!
ドゴゴッ
KAKABOOM
ドゴゴッ
KAKABOOM
They
s
big
What are those?!
I don't like the look of that!
......
Sorr
MOMM
Can you give me a ride?
Huh?!
Of course I can...
...Taro-chan.

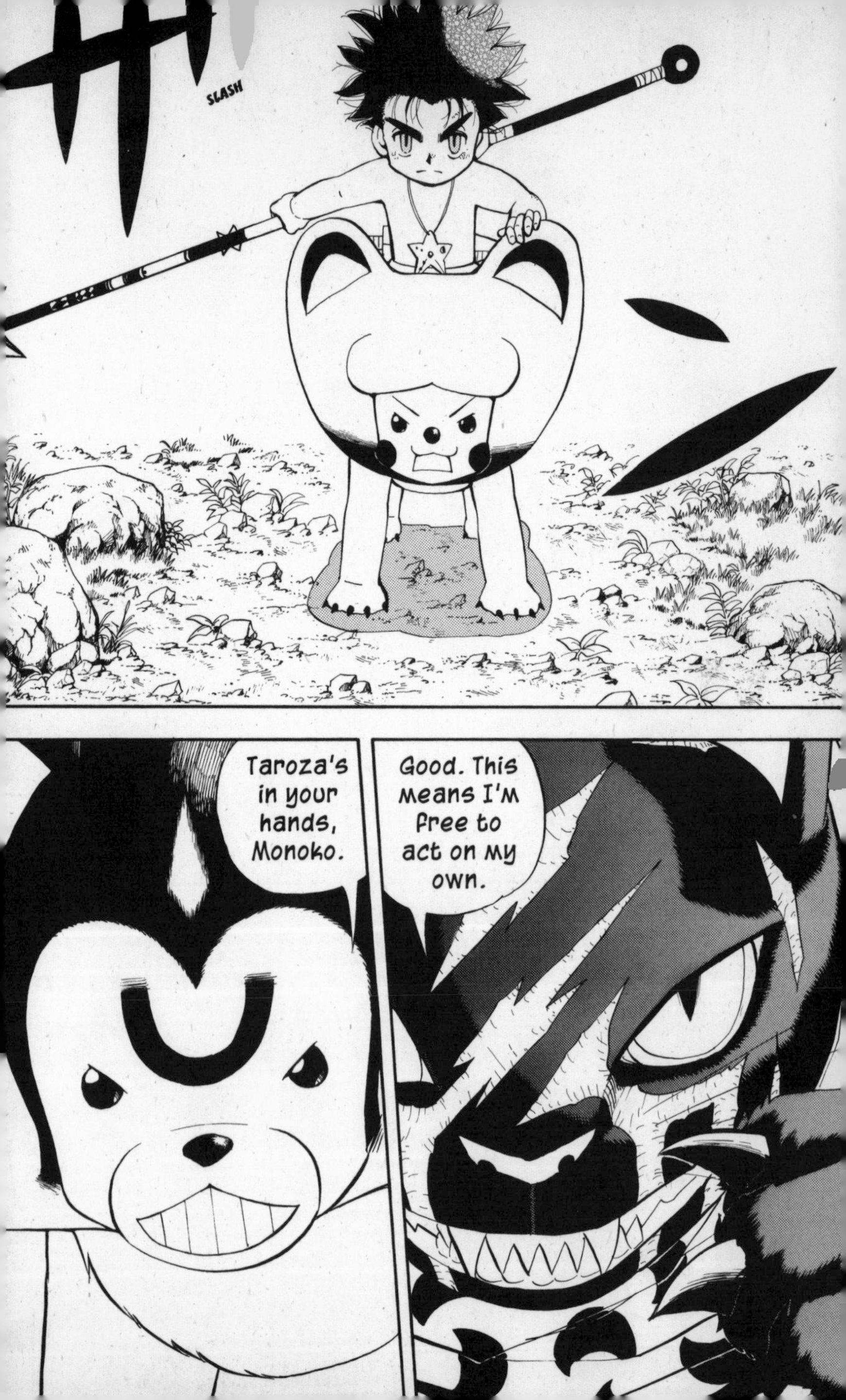
SLASH
Good. This means I'm free to act on my own.
Taroza's in your hands, Monoko.

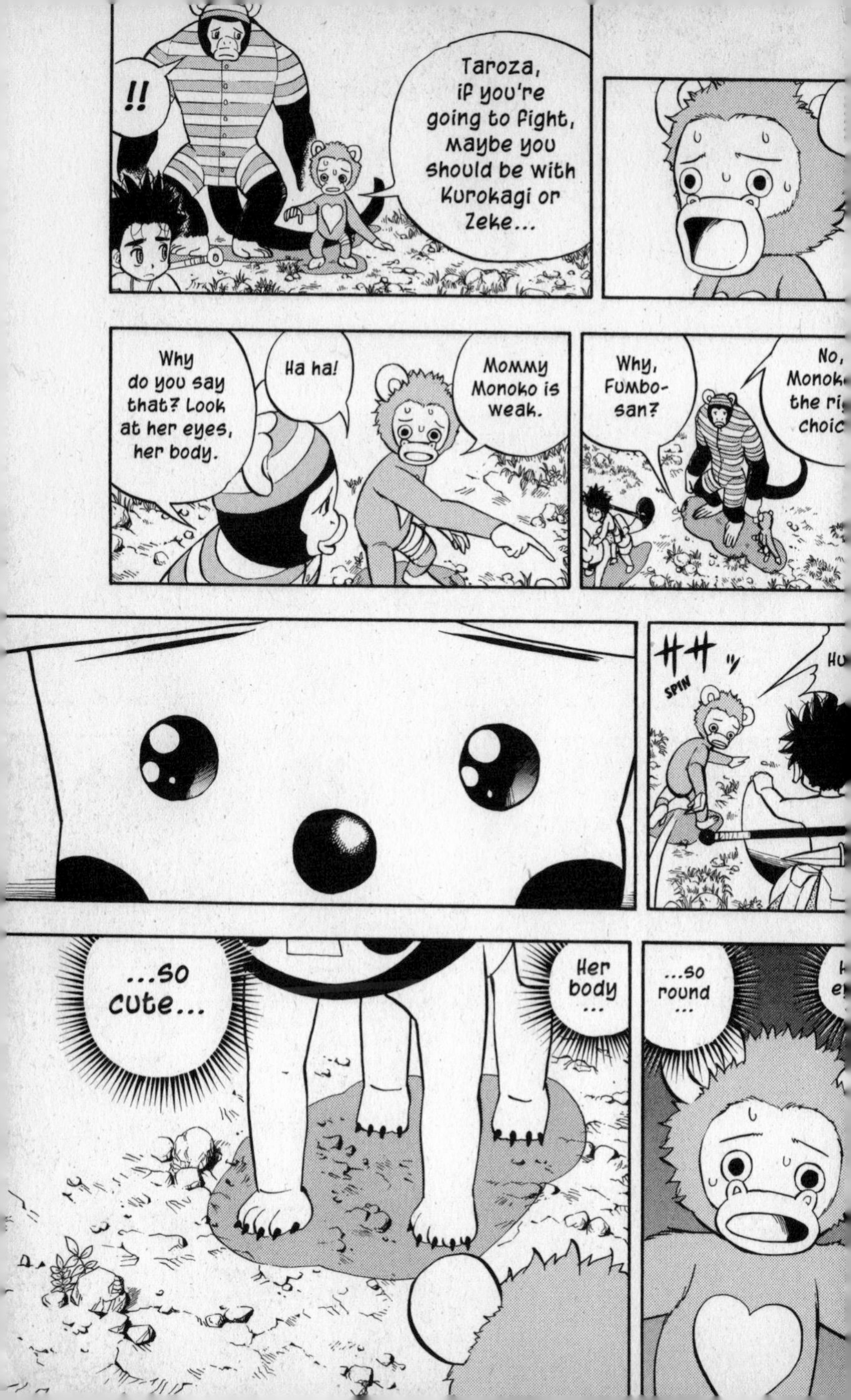
Taroza, if you're going to fight, maybe you should be with Kurokagi or Zeke...
!!
No, Monok the ri choic
Why, Fumbo-san?
Mommy Monoko is weak.
Ha ha!
Why do you say that? Look at her eyes, her body.
HU
SPIN
...so round ...
Her body ...
...so cute...

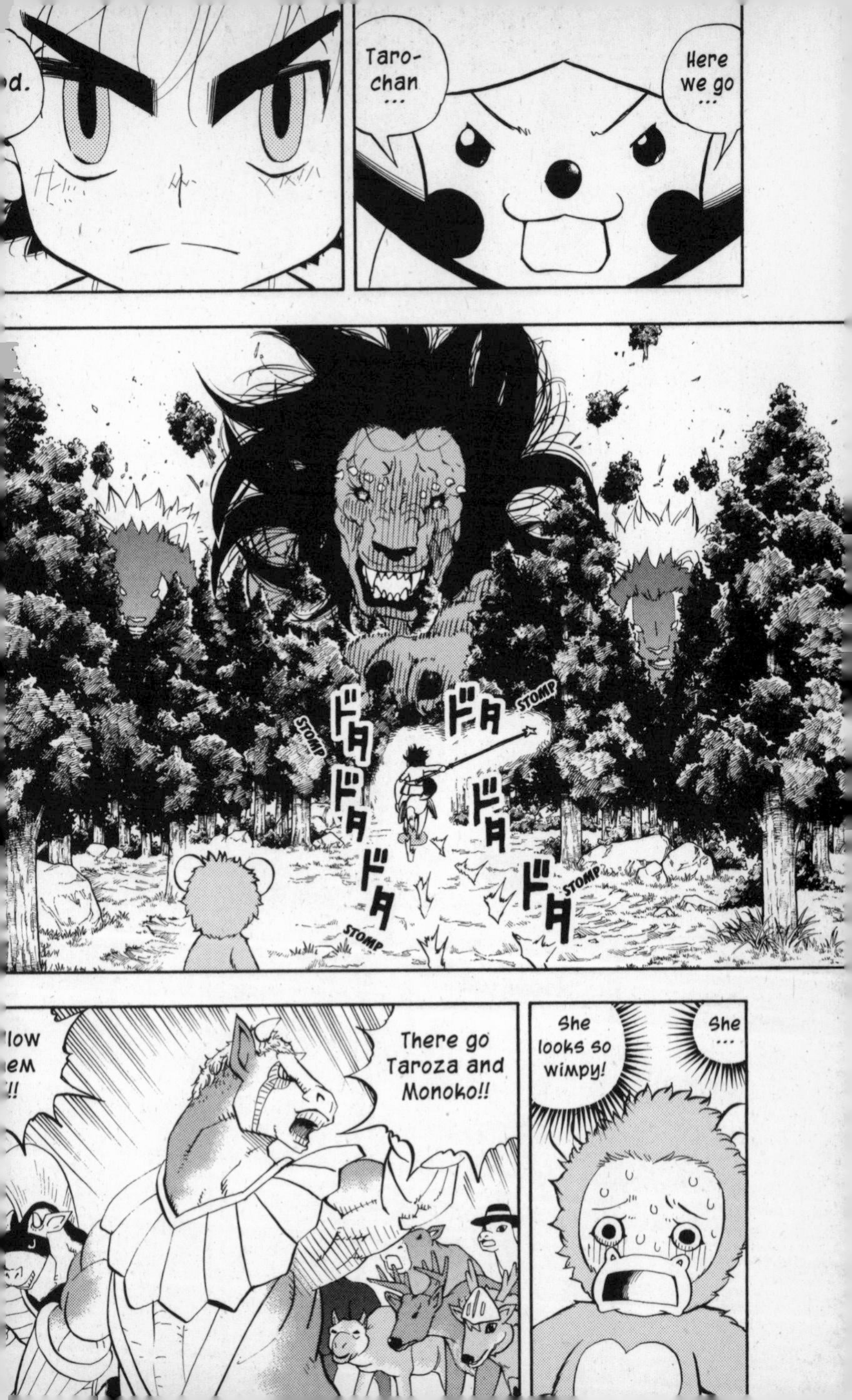
Here we go ...
Taro-chan ...
d.
ドタ
STOMP
ドタ
STOMP
ドタ
ドタ
ドタ
STOMP
ドタ
STOMP
She ...
She looks so wimpy!
There go Taroza and Monoko!!

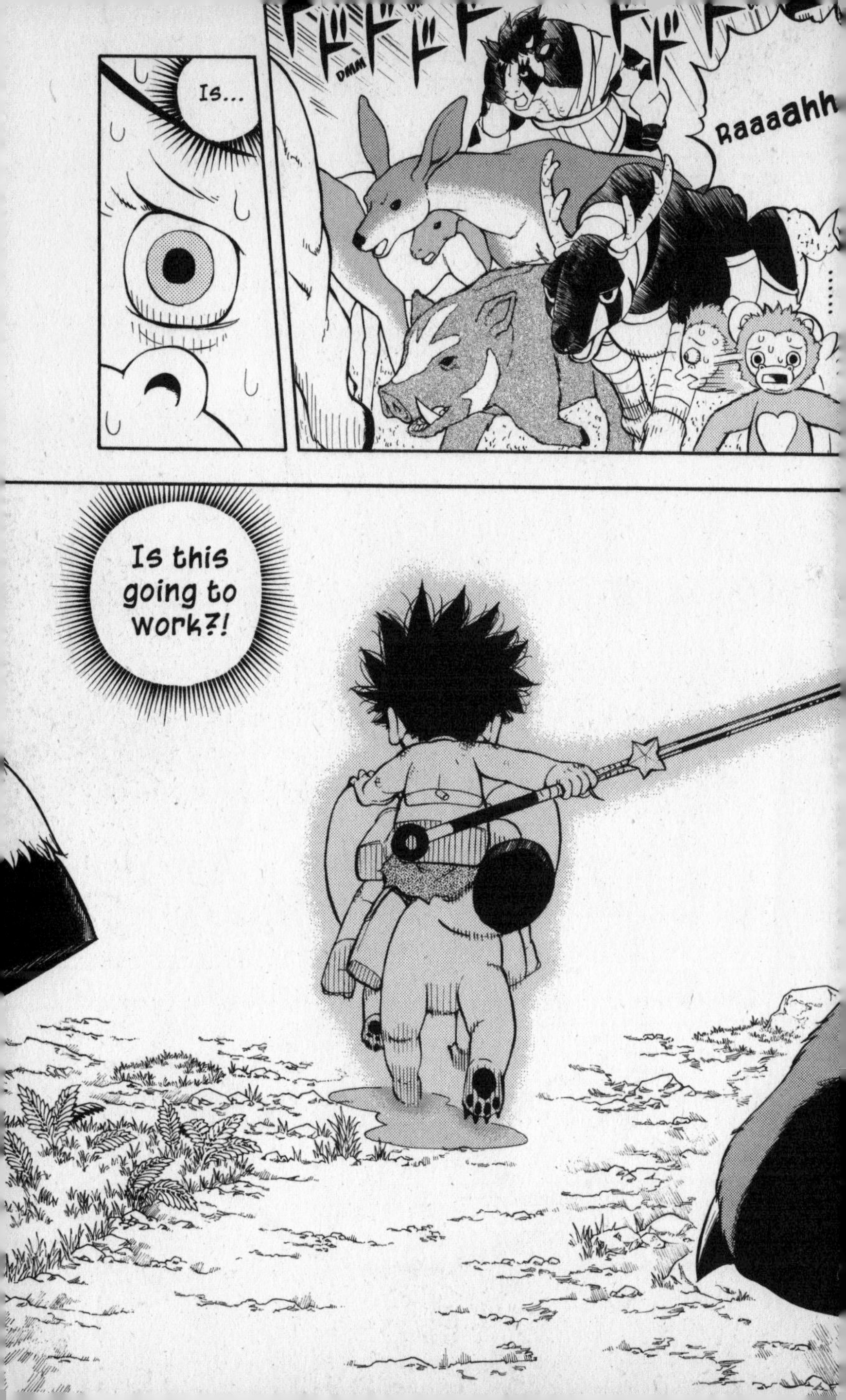

DMM
Raaaahh
Is...
Is this going to work?!

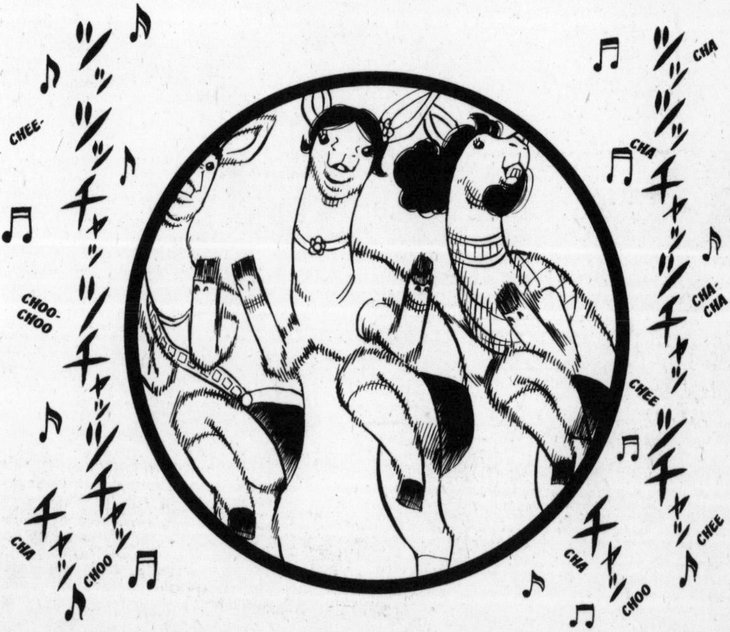
CHA
CHA
CHA-
CHA
CHEE
CHEE
CHA
CHOO
CHEE-
CHOO-
CHOO
CHOO
CHA

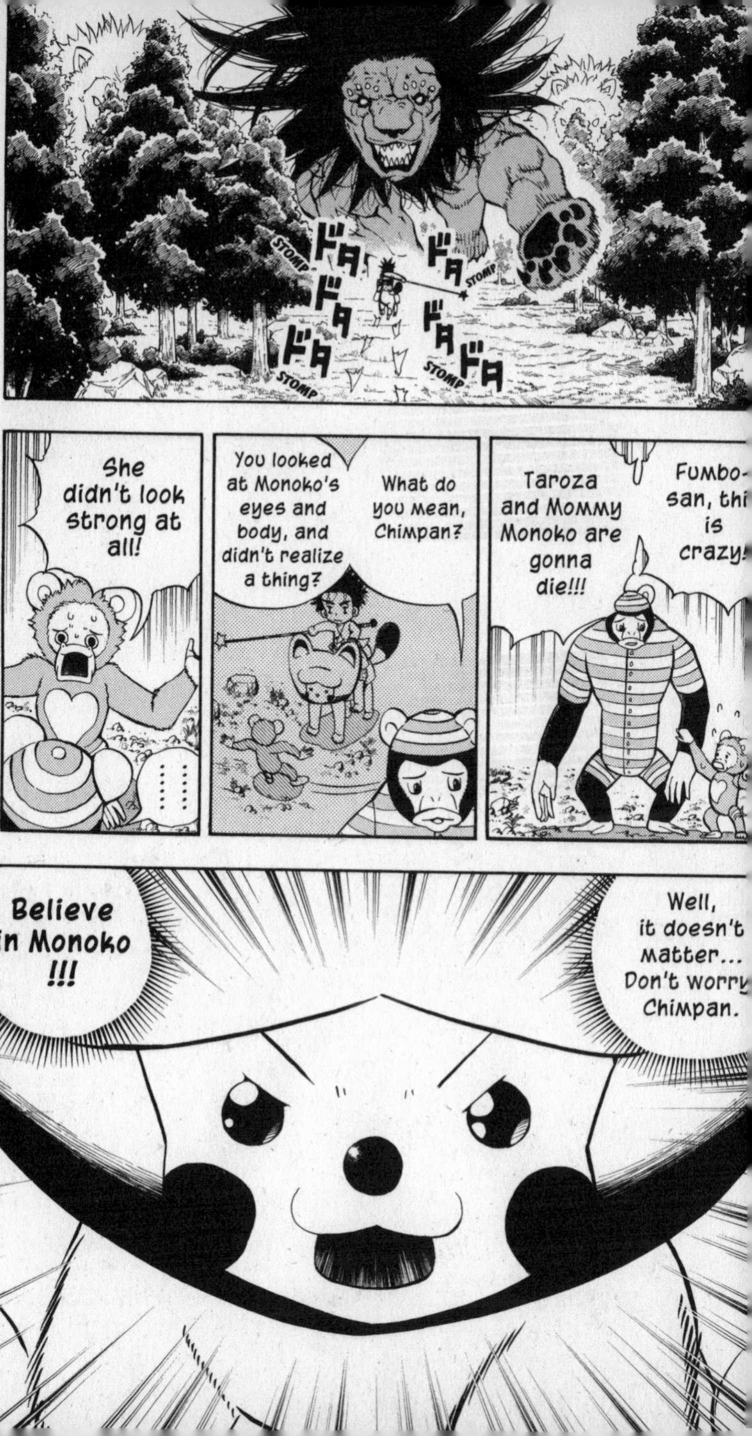

ドタ
STOMP
ドタドタ
STOMP
ドタ
ドタ
ドタ
STOMP
STOMP
Fumbo-san, thi is crazy!
Taroza and Mommy Monoko are gonna die!!!
What do you mean, Chimpan?
You looked at Monoko's eyes and body, and didn't realize a thing?
She didn't look strong at all!
......
Well, it doesn't matter... Don't worry Chimpan.
Believe in Monoko !!!

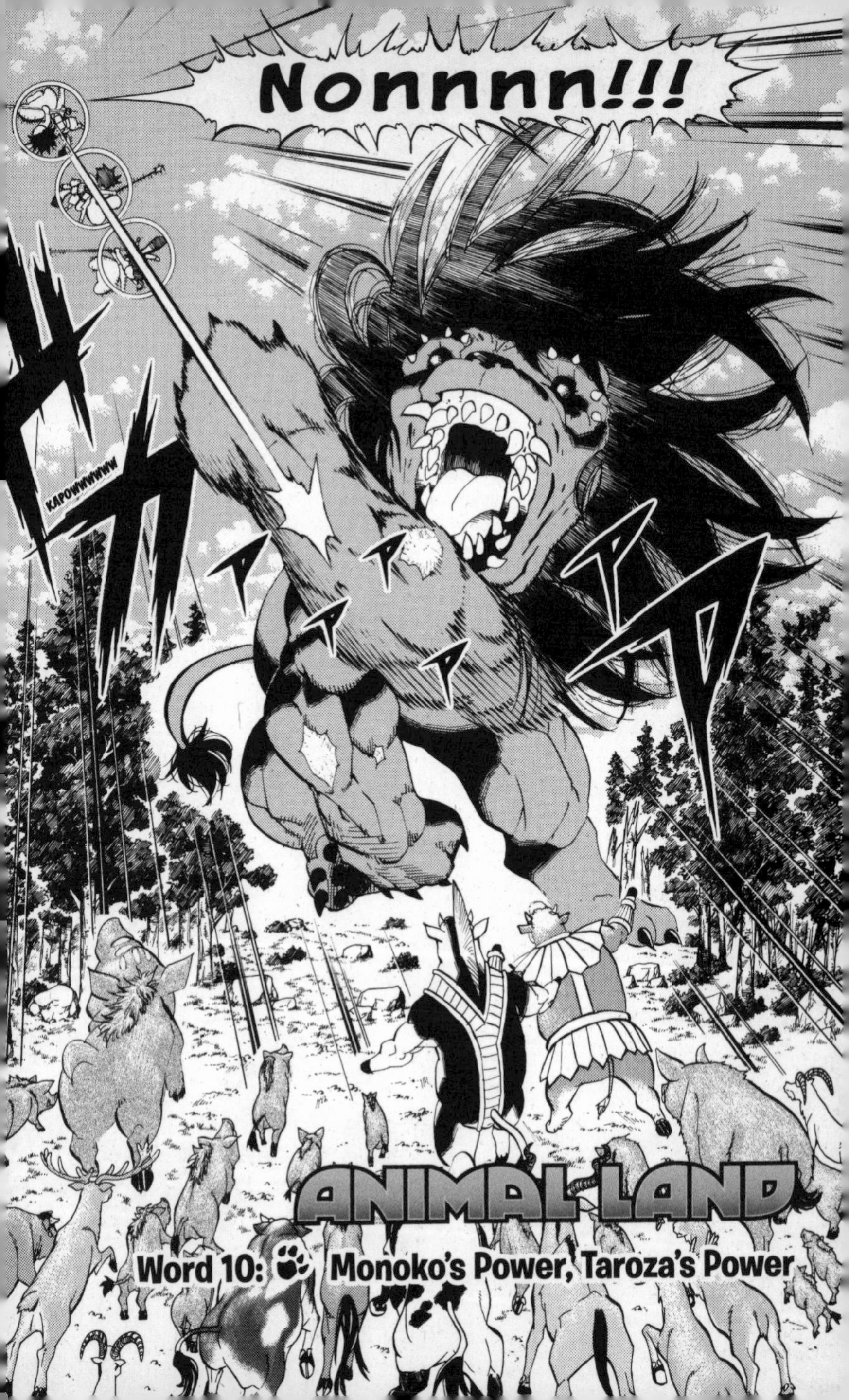
Nonnnn!!!
KAPOWWWWWWW
ANIMAL LAND
Word 10: Monoko's Power, Taroza's Power

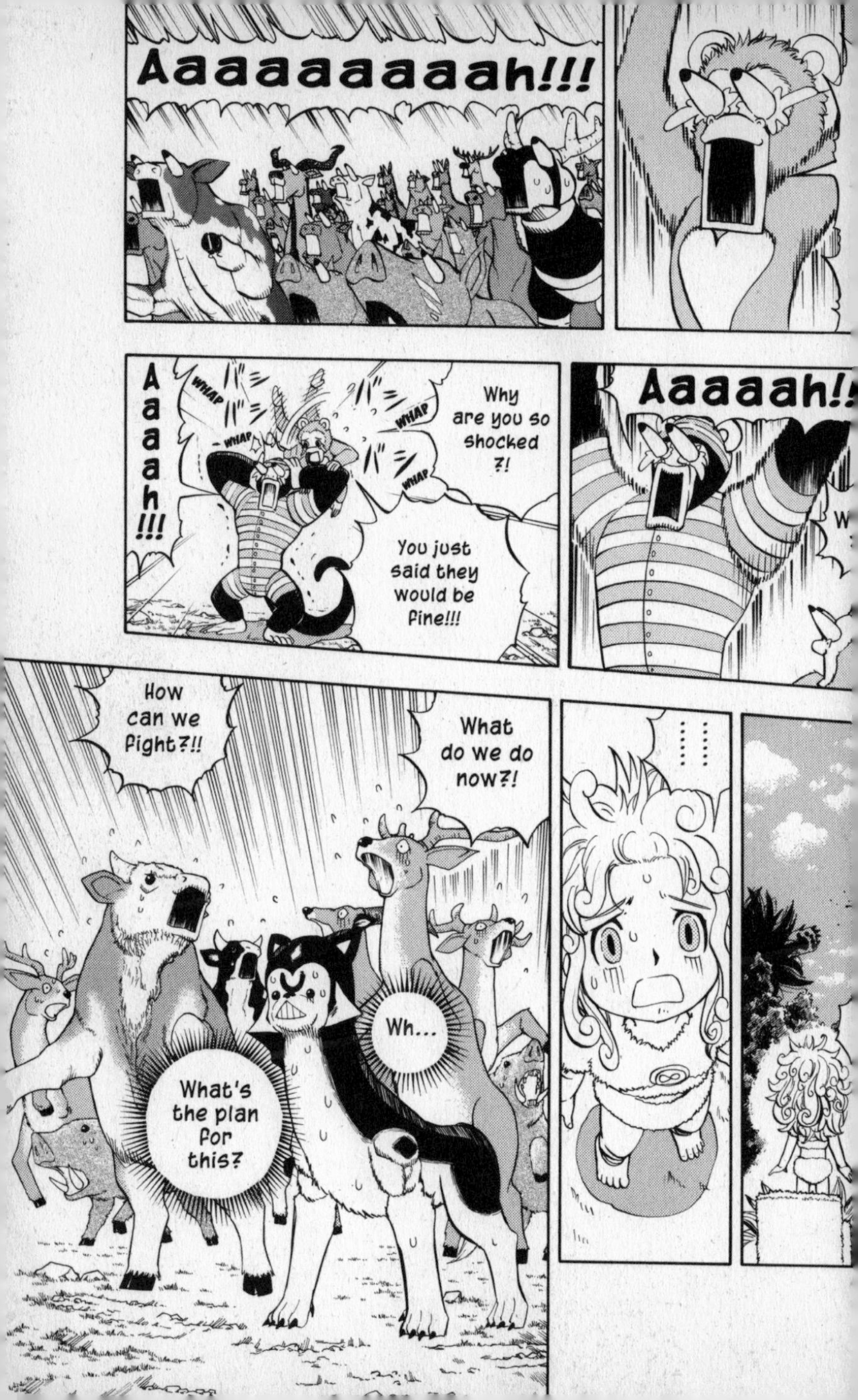
Aaaaaaaaaah!!!
Aaaaah!!
W
Why are you so shocked?!
WHAP
WHAP
WHAP
WHAP
You just said they would be fine!!!
Aaaaah!!!
......
What do we do now?!
How can we fight?!!
Wh...
What's the plan for this?

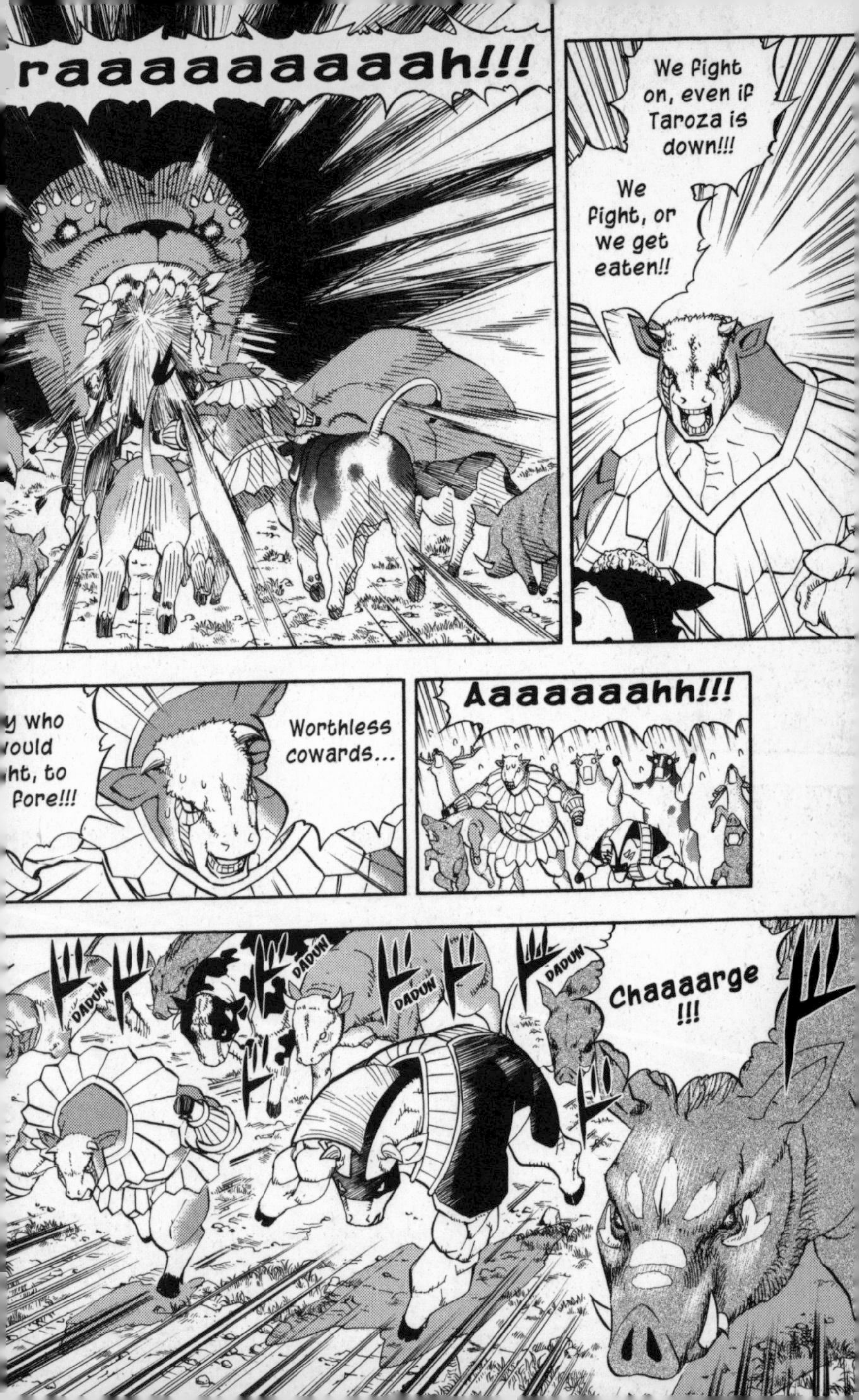
We fight on, even if Taroza is down!!!
We fight, or we get eaten!!
raaaaaaaaaaah!!!
Aaaaaaahh!!!
Worthless cowards...
y who would ht, to fore!!!
Chaaaarge!!!
DADUN
DADUN
DADUN
DADUN
DADUN

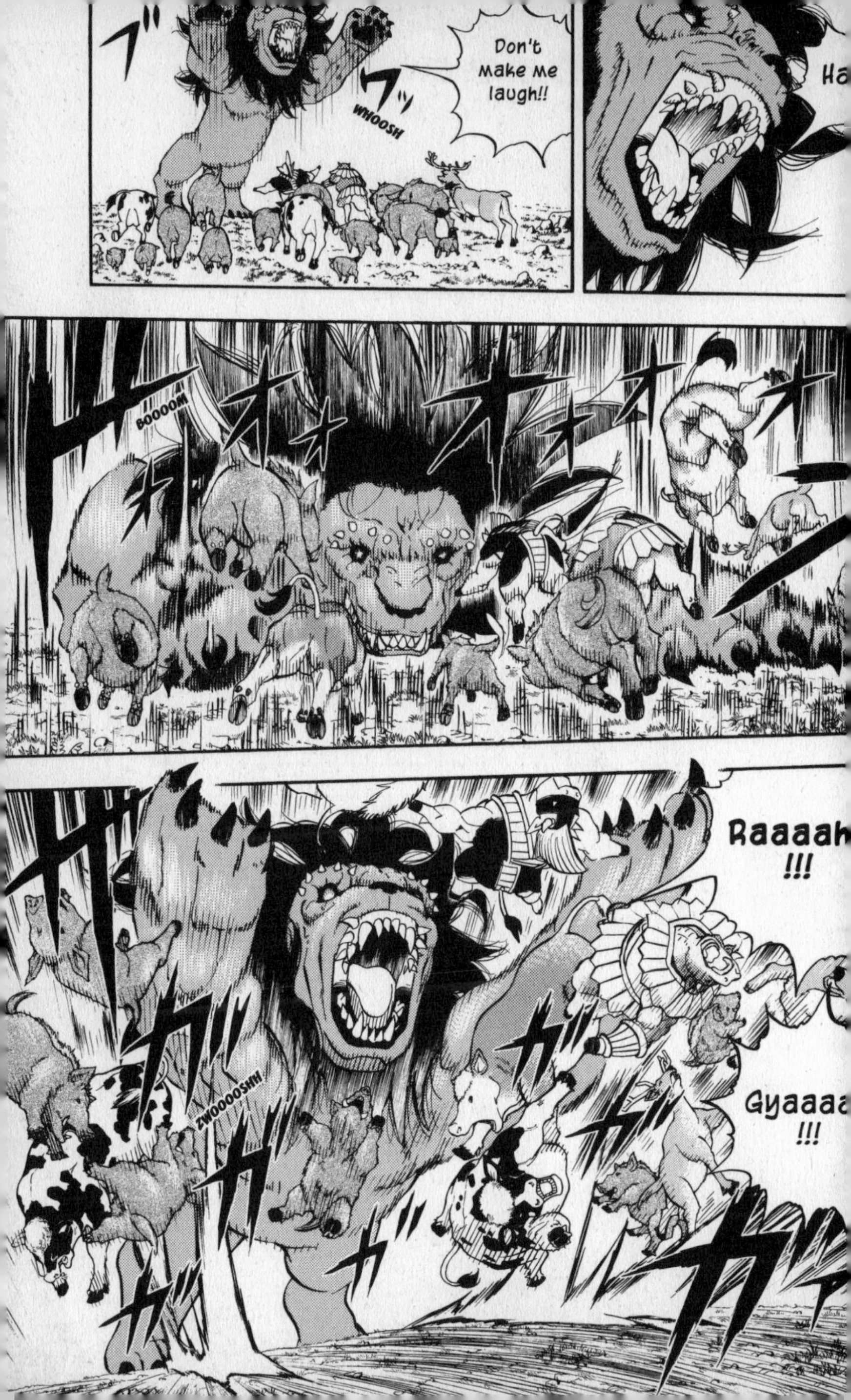
Ha
WHOOSH
Don't make me laugh!!
BOOOOM
Raaaah !!!
Gyaaaa !!!
ZWOOOOSHH

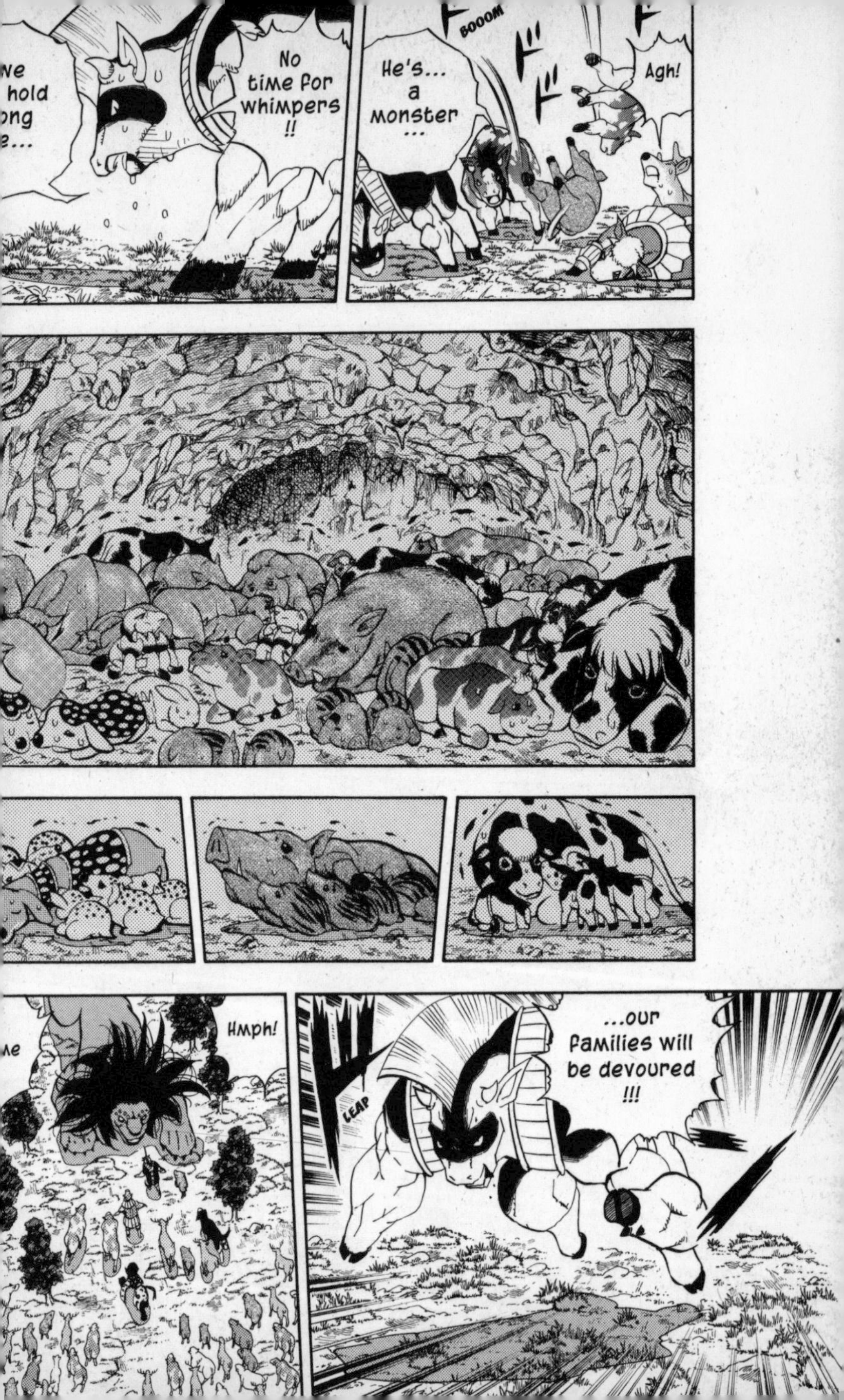
BOOOM
He's... a monster ...
Agh!
No time for whimpers !!
...our families will be devoured !!!
LEAP
Hmph!

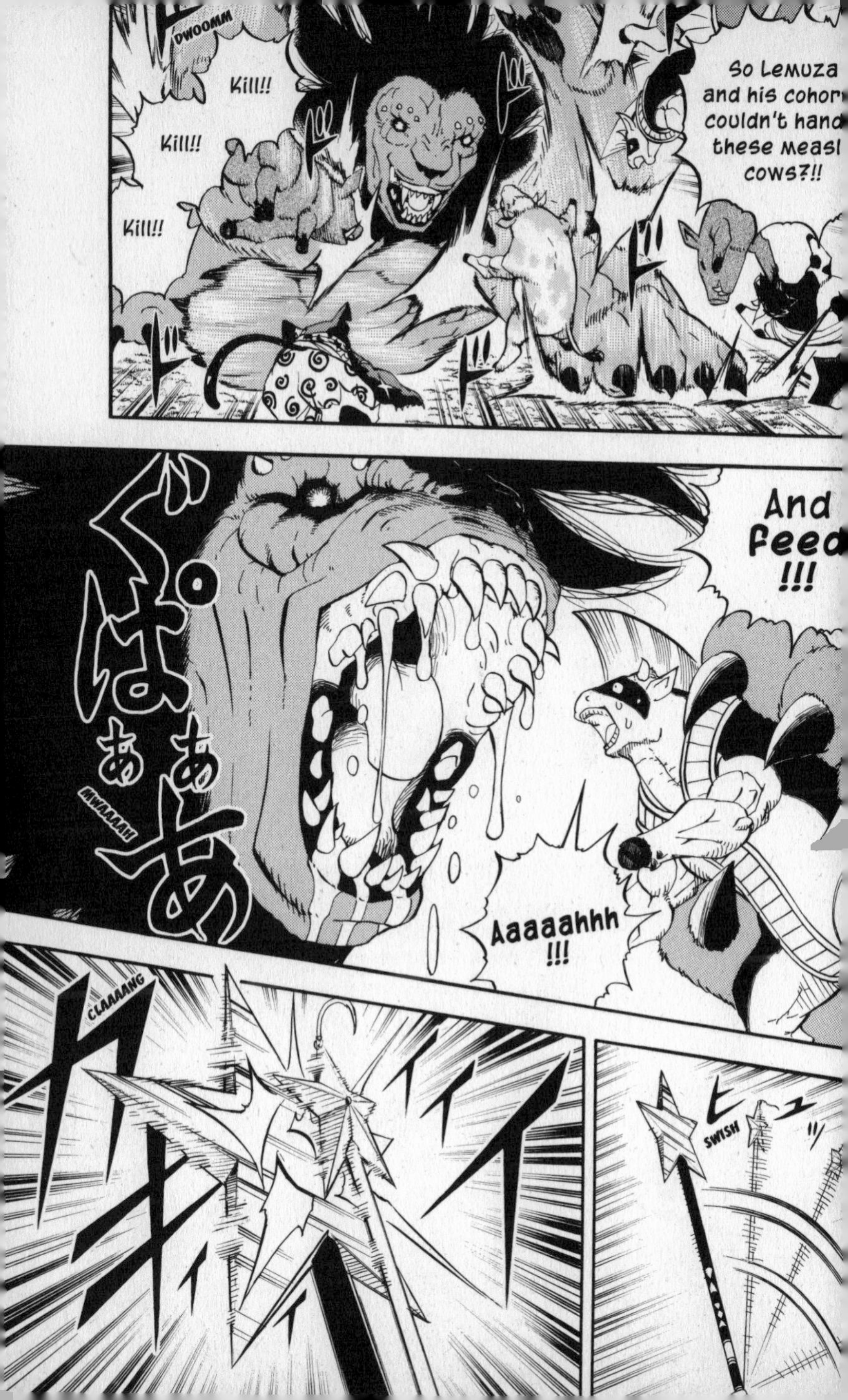
So Lemuza
and his cohor
couldn't hand
these measl
cows?!!
DWOOMM
Kill!!
Kill!!
Kill!!
And feed!!!
MWAAAAH
Aaaaahhh!!!
SWISH
CLAAAANG

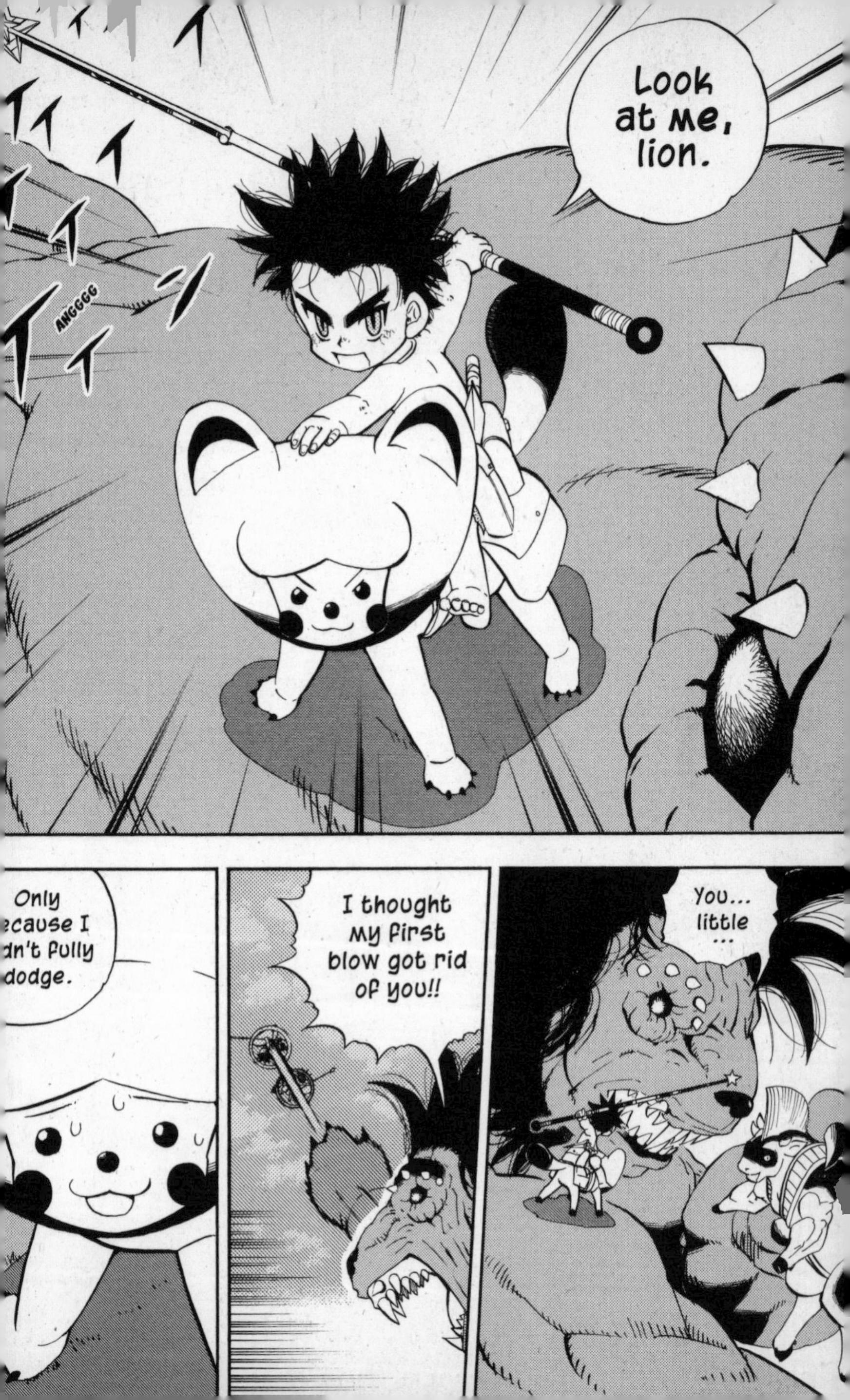
Look at me, lion.
ANGGGG
You... little ...
I thought my first blow got rid of you!!
Only ecause I dn't fully dodge.

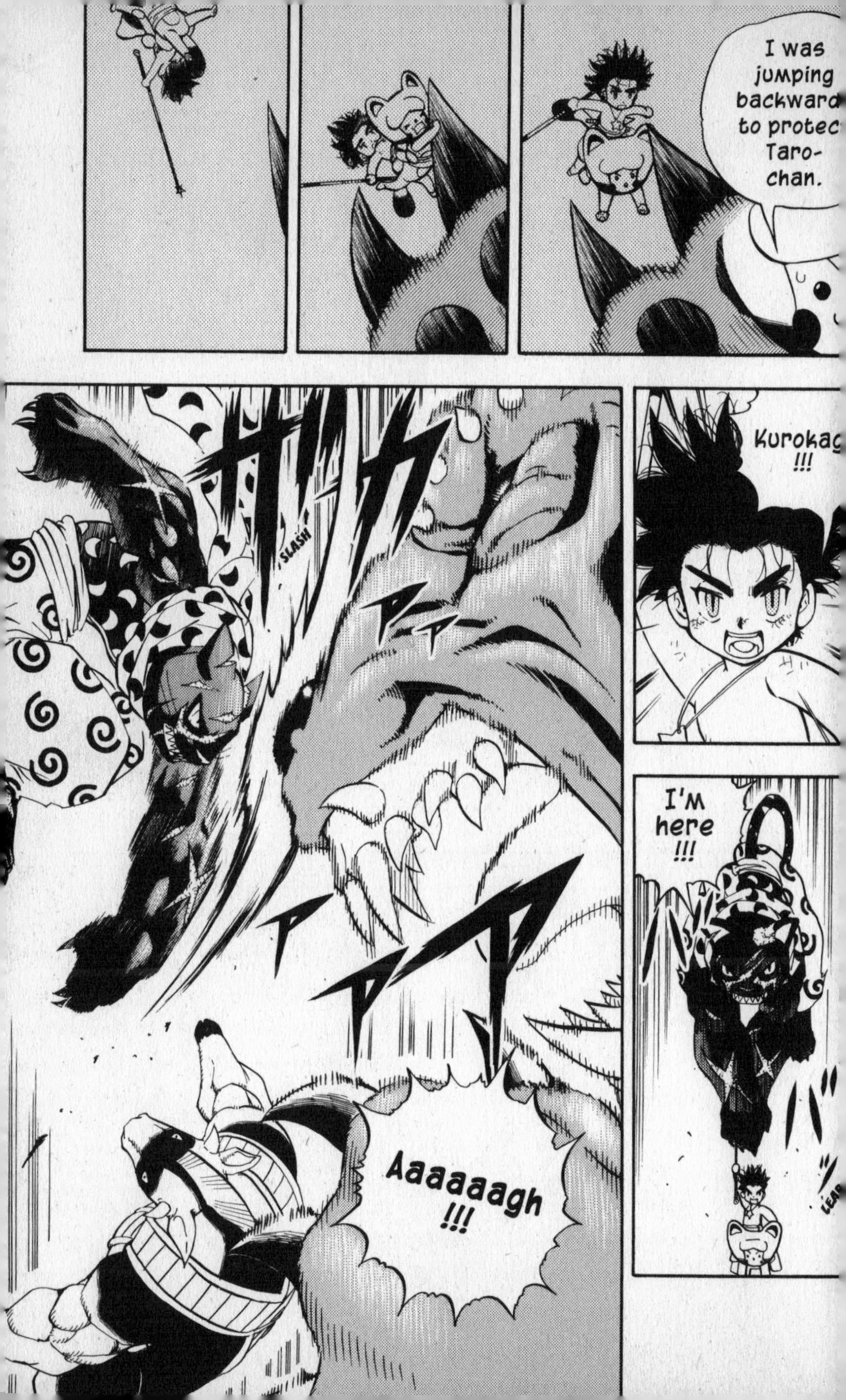
I was jumping backward to protec Taro-chan.
Kurokag !!!
I'M here !!!
SLASH
Aaaaaaagh !!!

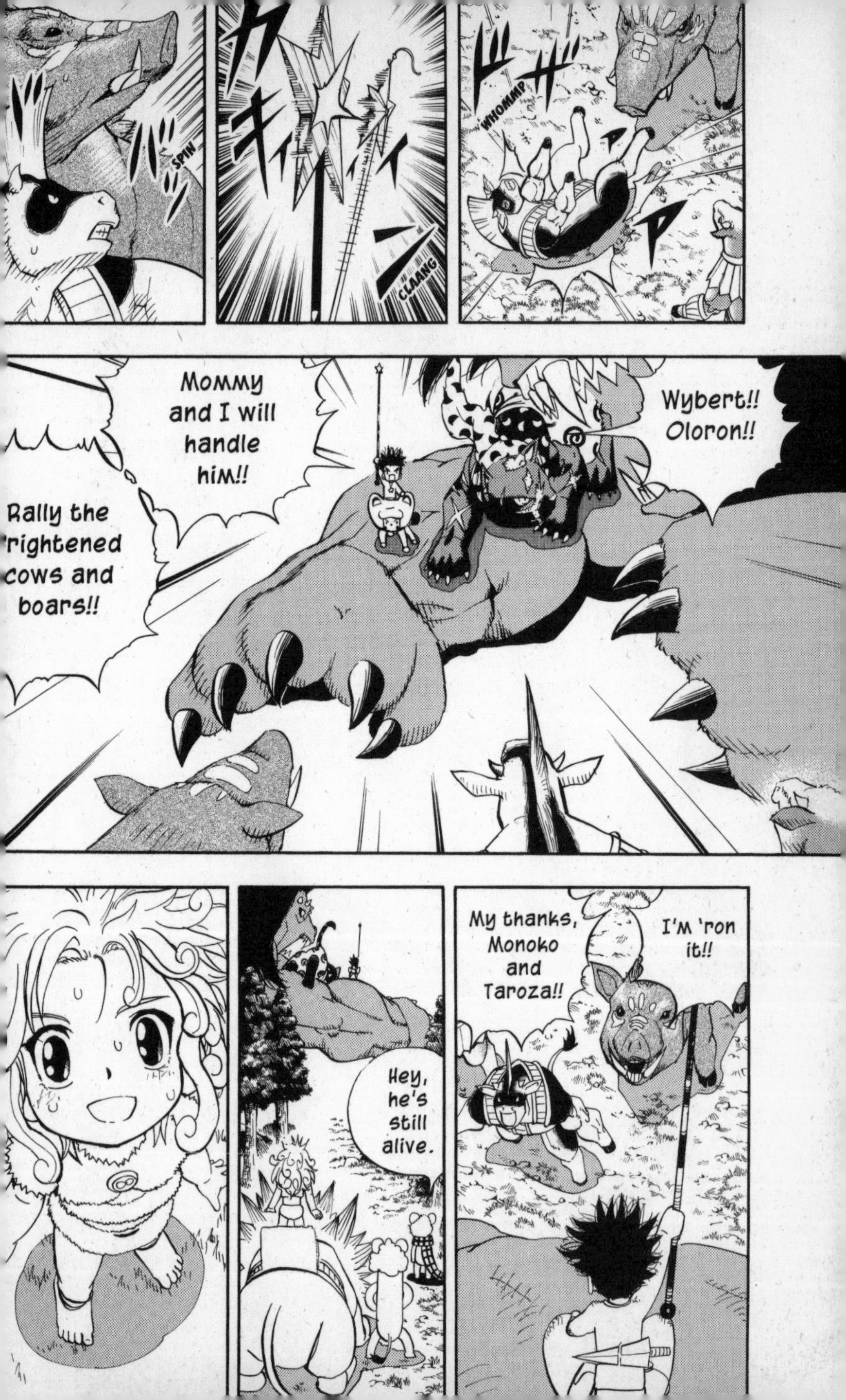
WHOMMP
CLAANG
SPIN
Wybert!! Oloron!!
Mommy and I will handle him!!
Rally the rightened cows and boars!!
I'm 'ron it!!
My thanks, Monoko and Taroza!!
Hey, he's still alive.

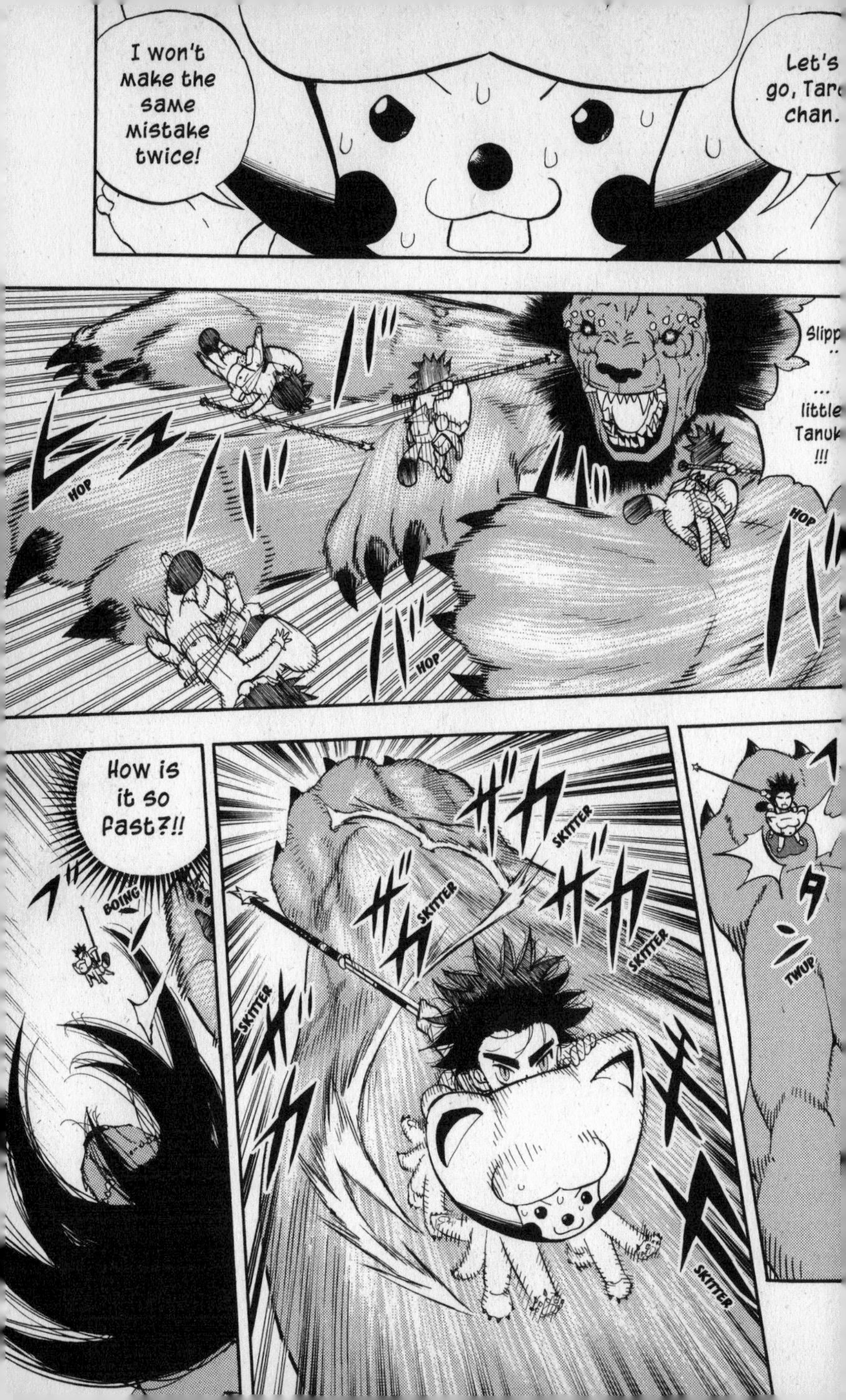

Let's go, Tar chan.
I won't make the same mistake twice!
Slipp.. ... little Tanuk !!!
HOP
HOP
HOP
TWUP
SKITTER
SKITTER
SKITTER
SKITTER
SKITTER
How is it so fast?!!
BOING

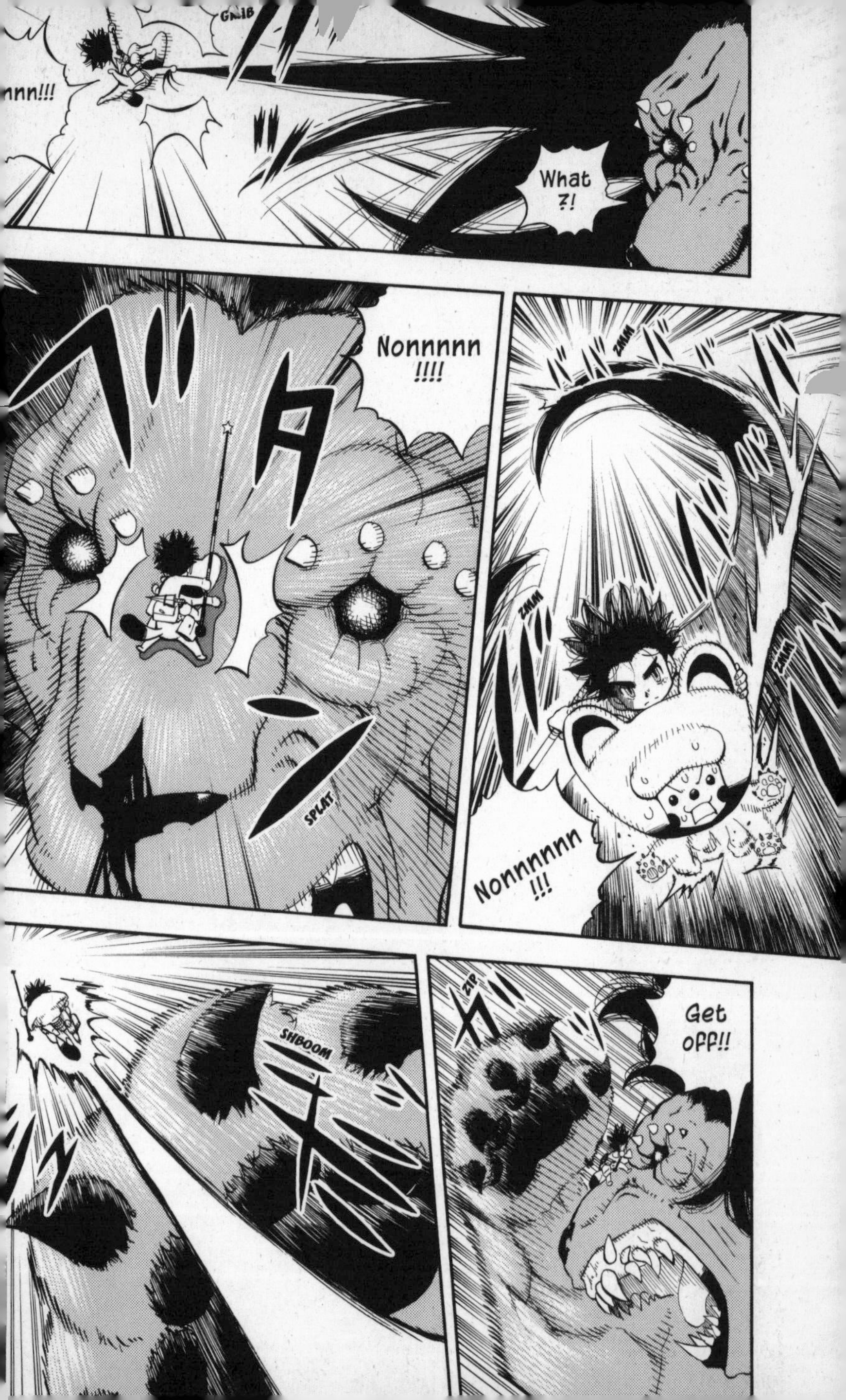
What ?!
nnn!!!
ZMM
ZMM
ZMM
Nonnnnnn !!!
Nonnnnn !!!!
SPLAT
ZIP
Get off!!
SHBOOM

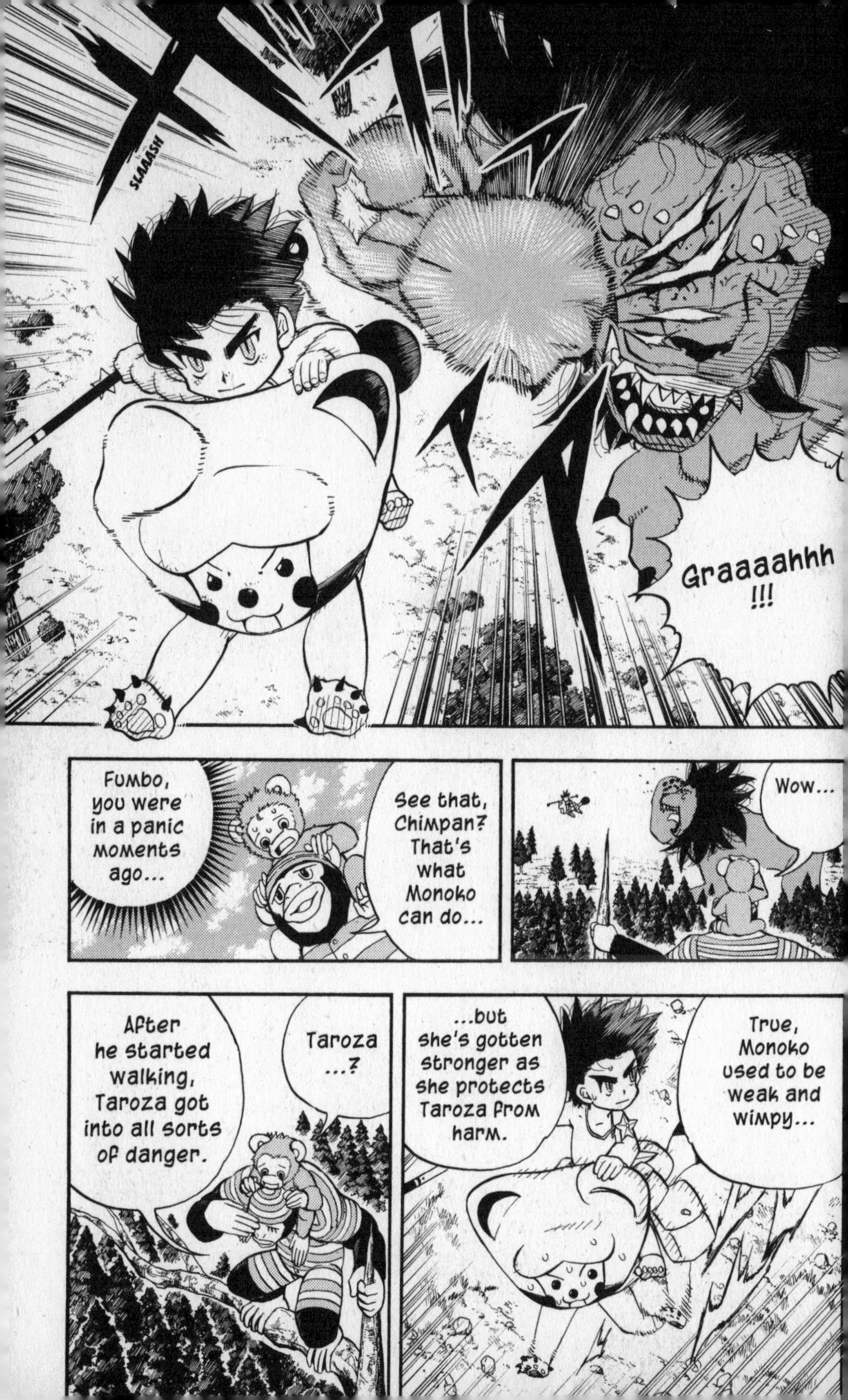
SLAAASH
Graaaahhh !!!
Wow...
See that, Chimpan? That's what Monoko can do...
Fumbo, you were in a panic moments ago...
True, Monoko used to be weak and wimpy...
...but she's gotten stronger as she protects Taroza from harm.
Taroza ...?
After he started walking, Taroza got into all sorts of danger.

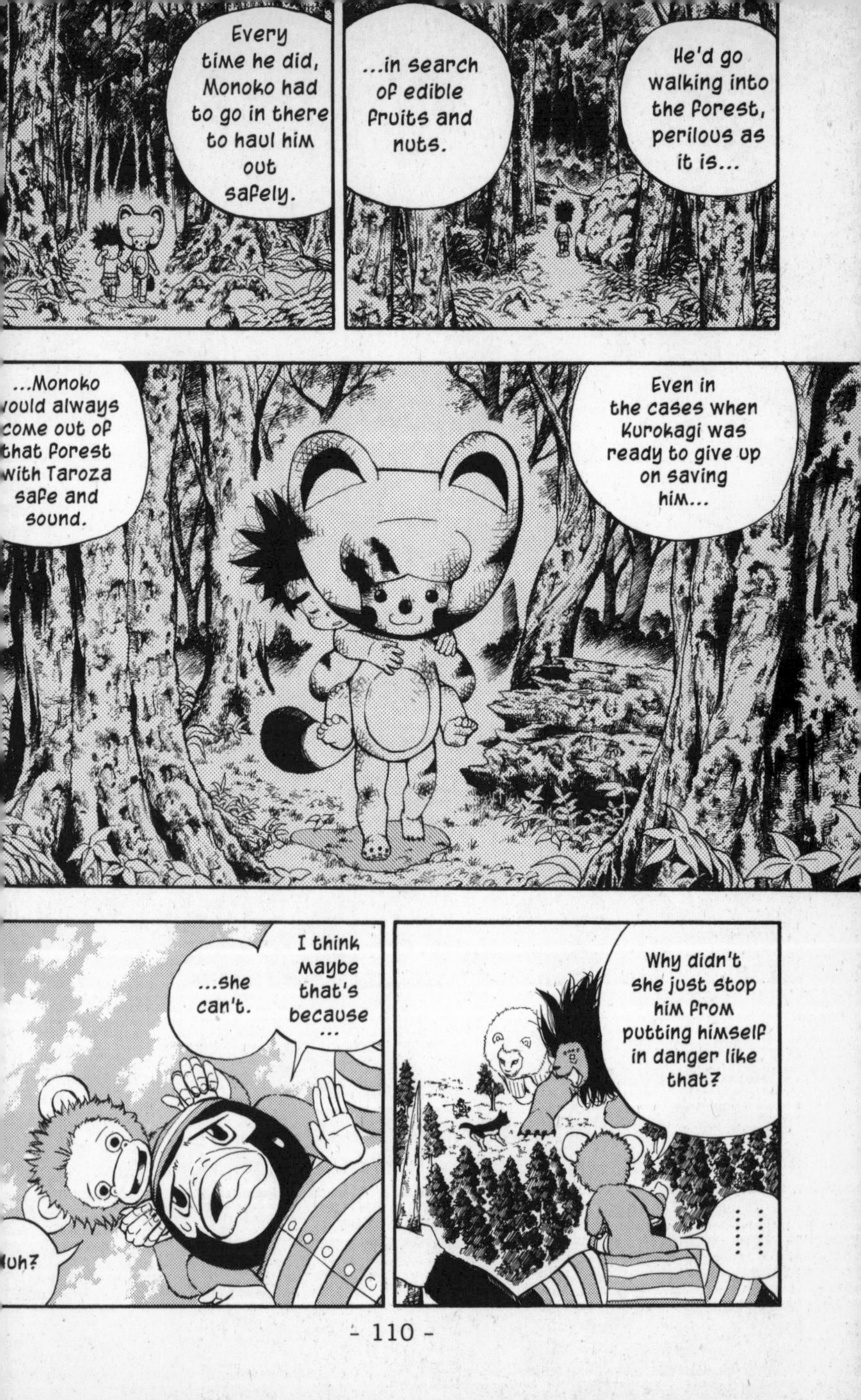

He'd go walking into the forest, perilous as it is...
...in search of edible fruits and nuts.
Every time he did, Monoko had to go in there to haul him out safely.
Even in the cases when Kurokagi was ready to give up on saving him...
...Monoko would always come out of that forest with Taroza safe and sound.
Why didn't she just stop him from putting himself in danger like that?
......
I think maybe that's because...
...she can't.
Huh?

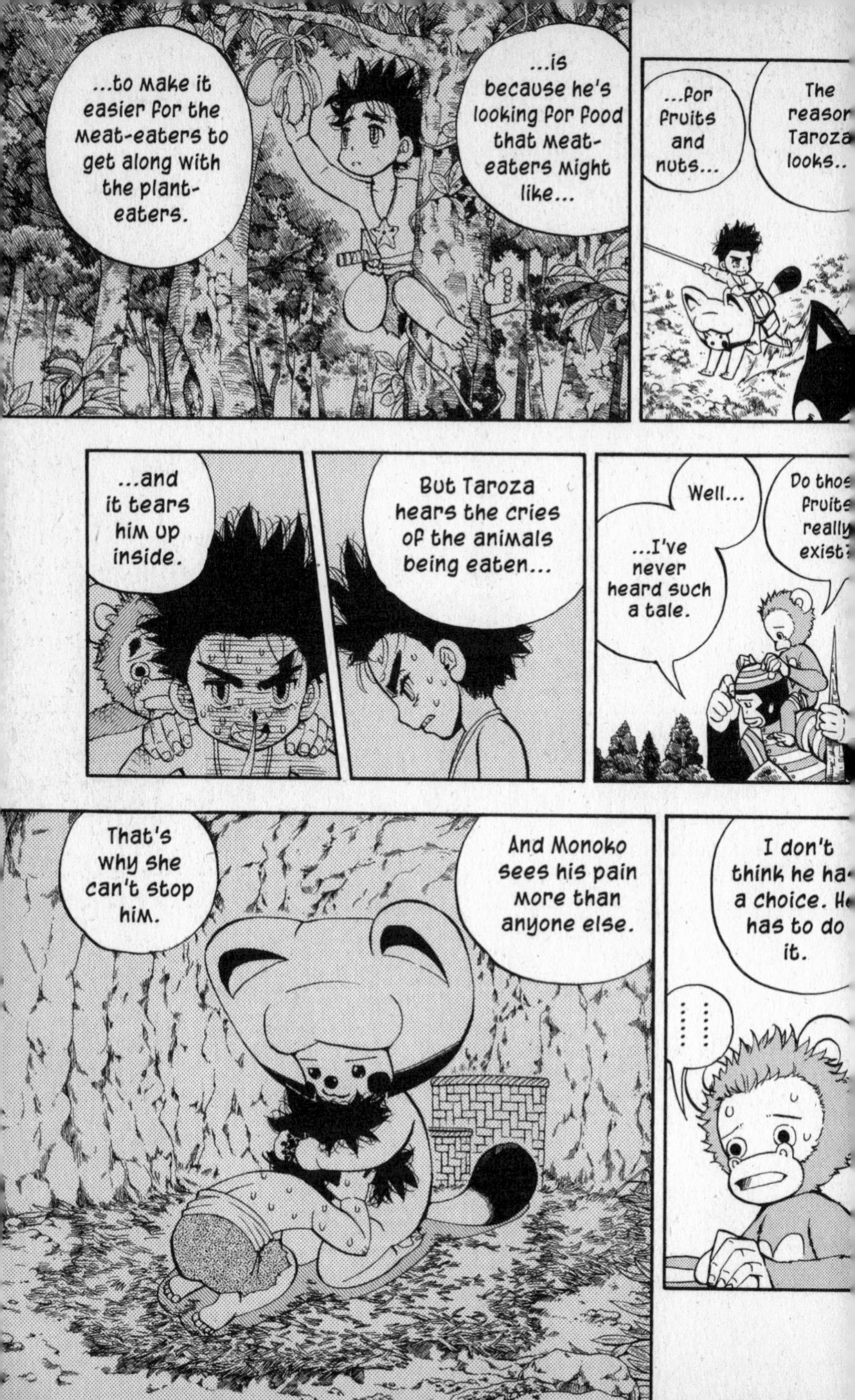
The reaso Taroza looks..
...for fruits and nuts...
...is because he's looking for food that meat-eaters might like...
...to make it easier for the meat-eaters to get along with the plant-eaters.
Do thos fruits really exist?
Well...
...I've never heard such a tale.
But Taroza hears the cries of the animals being eaten...
...and it tears him up inside.
I don't think he ha a choice. H has to do it.
......
And Monoko sees his pain more than anyone else.
That's why she can't stop him.

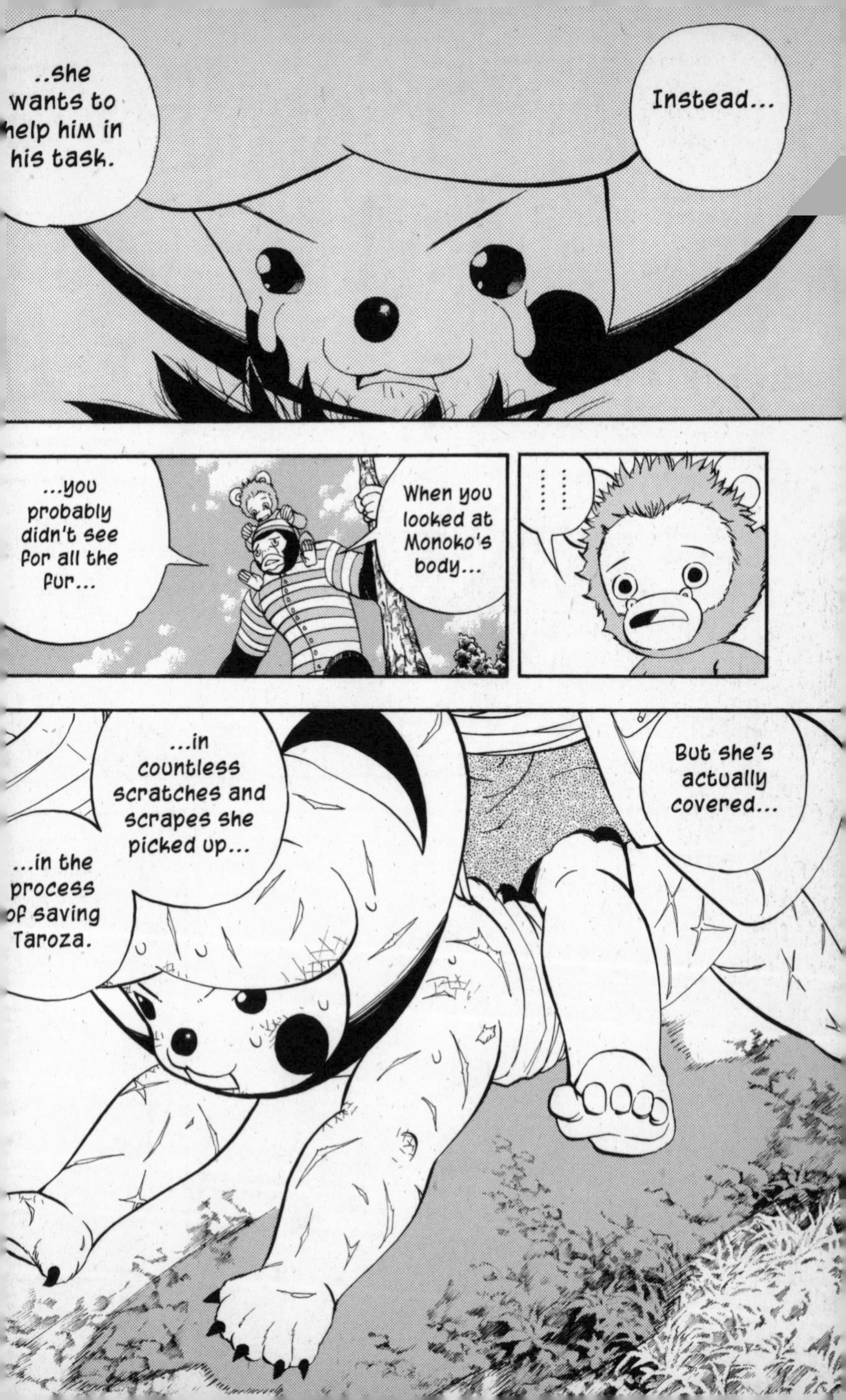
Instead...
..she wants to help him in his task.
......
When you looked at Monoko's body...
...you probably didn't see for all the fur...
But she's actually covered...
...in countless scratches and scrapes she picked up...
...in the process of saving Taroza.

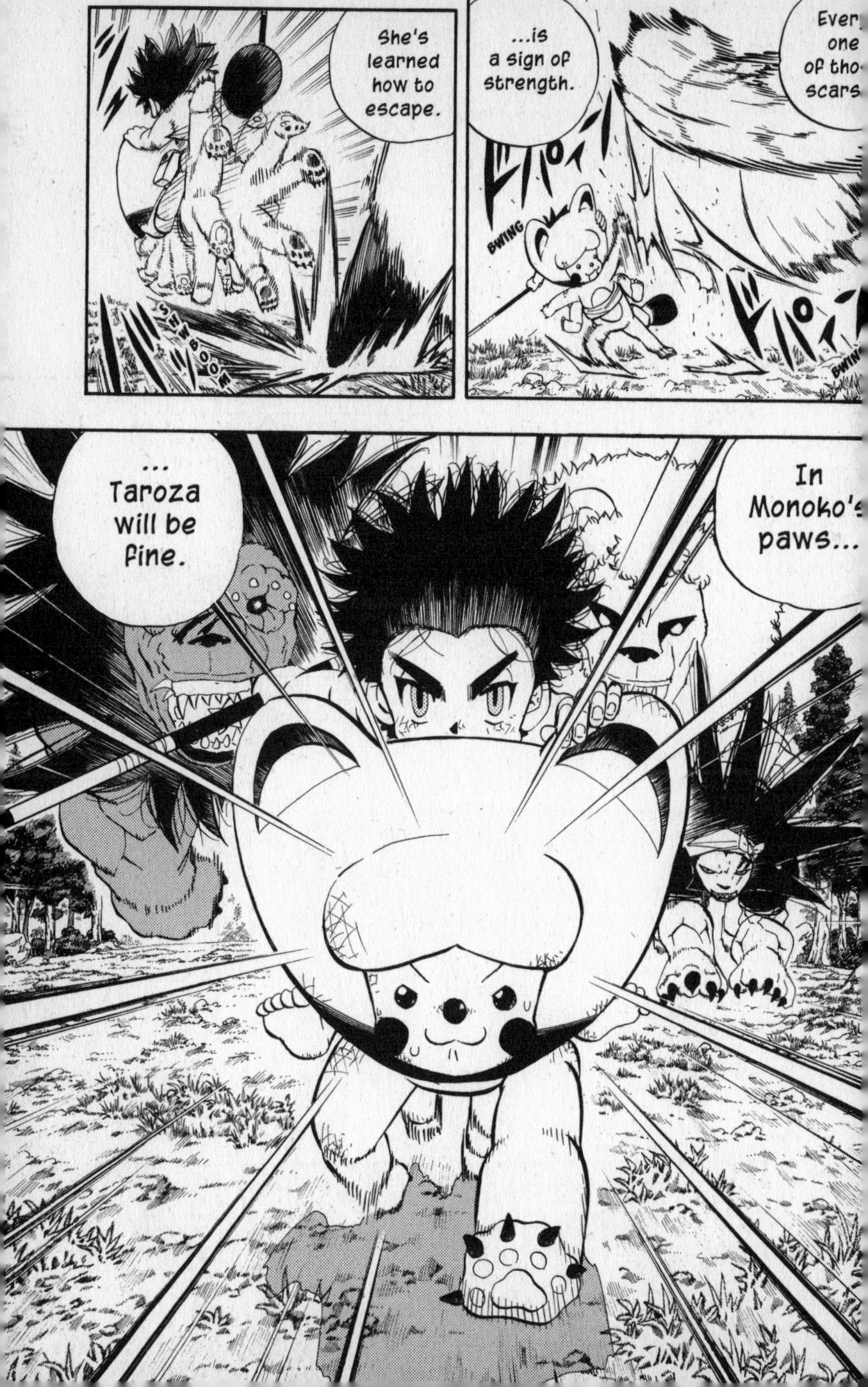
Every one of tho scars
...is a sign of strength.
BWING
BWING
She's learned how to escape.
SHWBOOM
In Monoko's paws...
...Taroza will be fine.

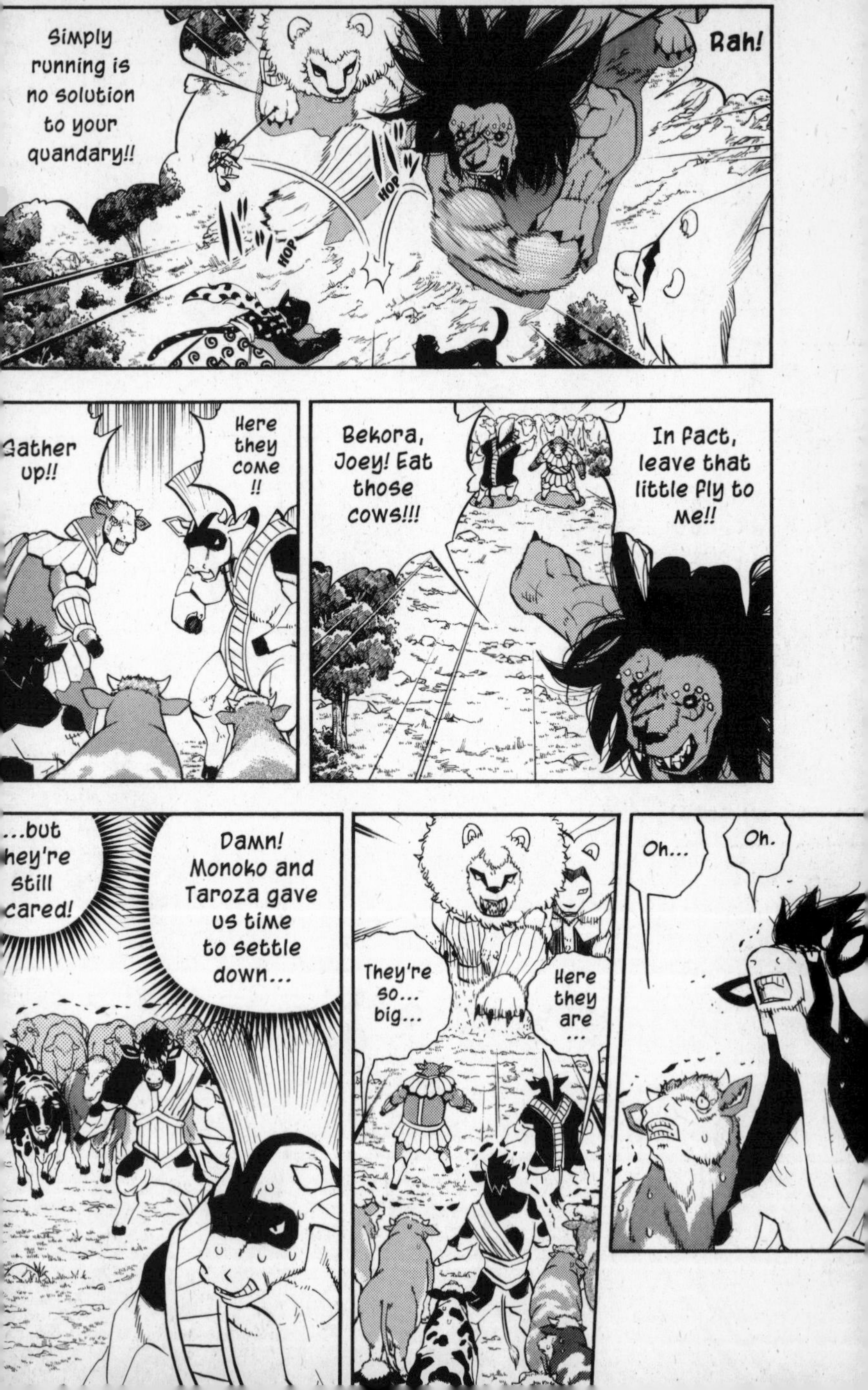

Rah!
Simply running is no solution to your quandary!!
HOP
HOP
In fact, leave that little fly to me!!
Bekora, Joey! Eat those cows!!!
Here they come !!
Gather up!!
Oh.
Oh...
Here they are ...
They're so... big...
Damn! Monoko and Taroza gave us time to settle down...
...but hey're still cared!

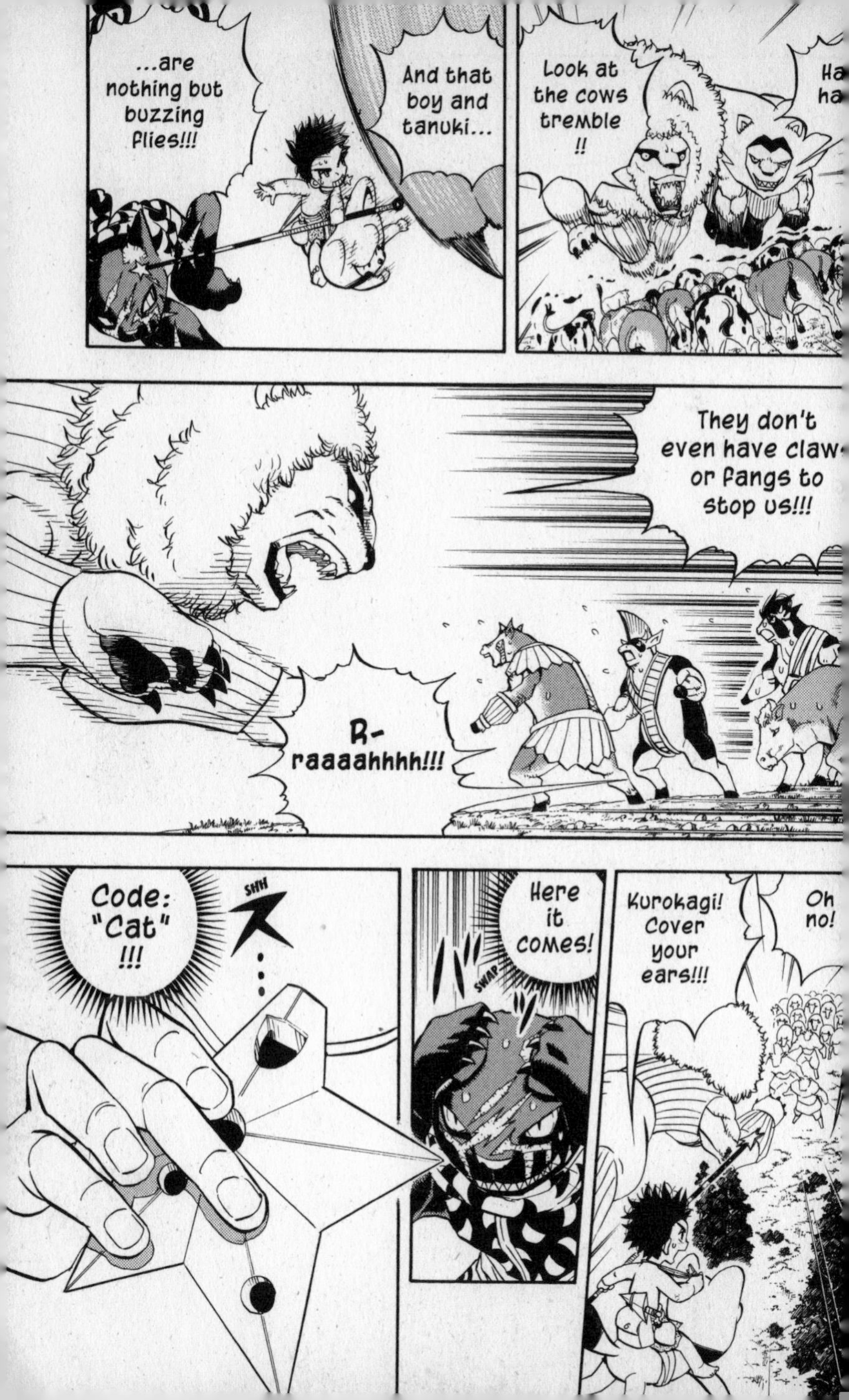

Ha ha
Look at the cows tremble !!
And that boy and tanuki...
...are nothing but buzzing flies!!!
They don't even have claw- or fangs to stop us!!!
R- raaaahhhh!!!
Oh no!
Kurokagi! Cover your ears!!!
Here it comes!
SWAP
Code: "Cat" !!!
SHH

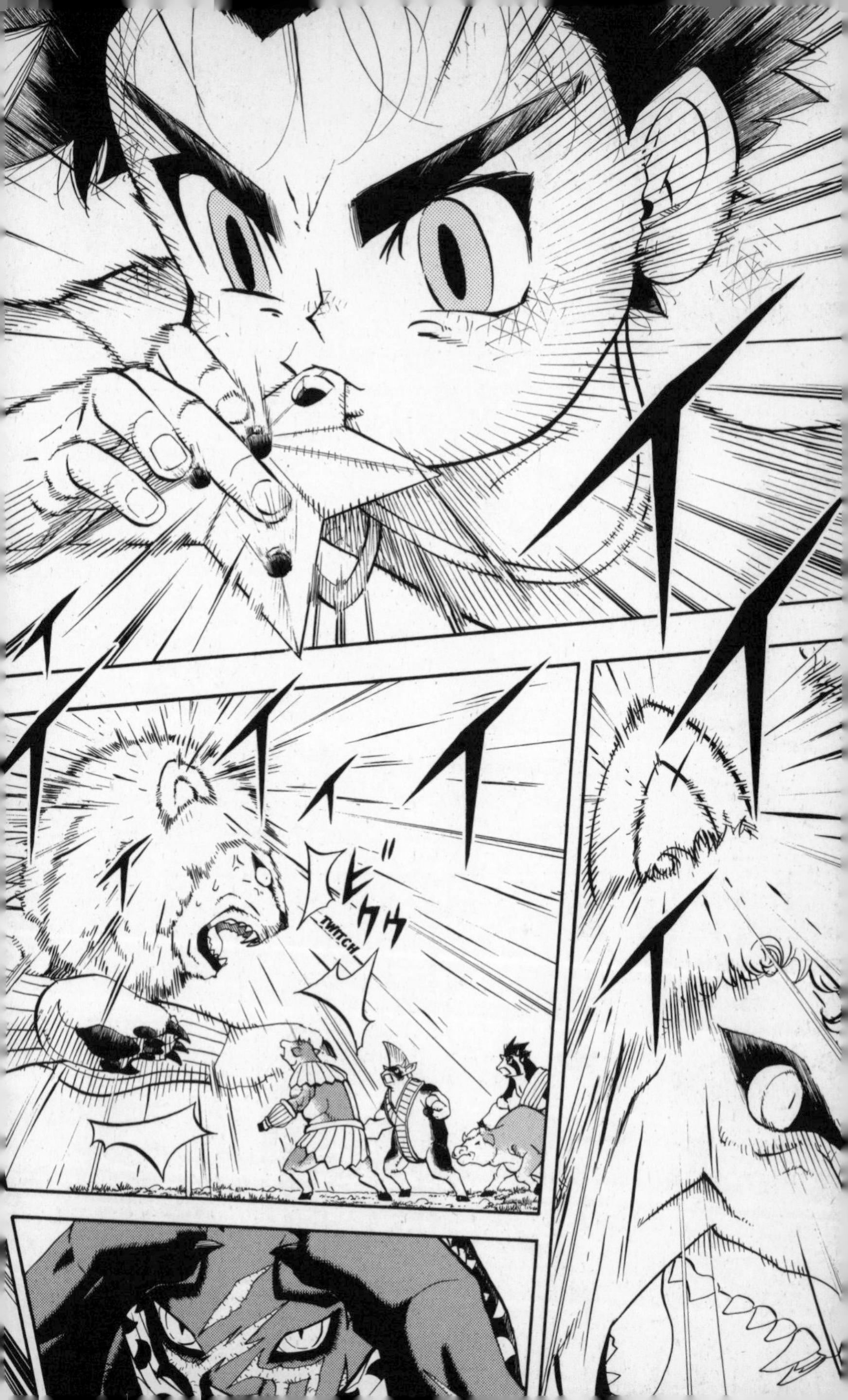
TWITCH

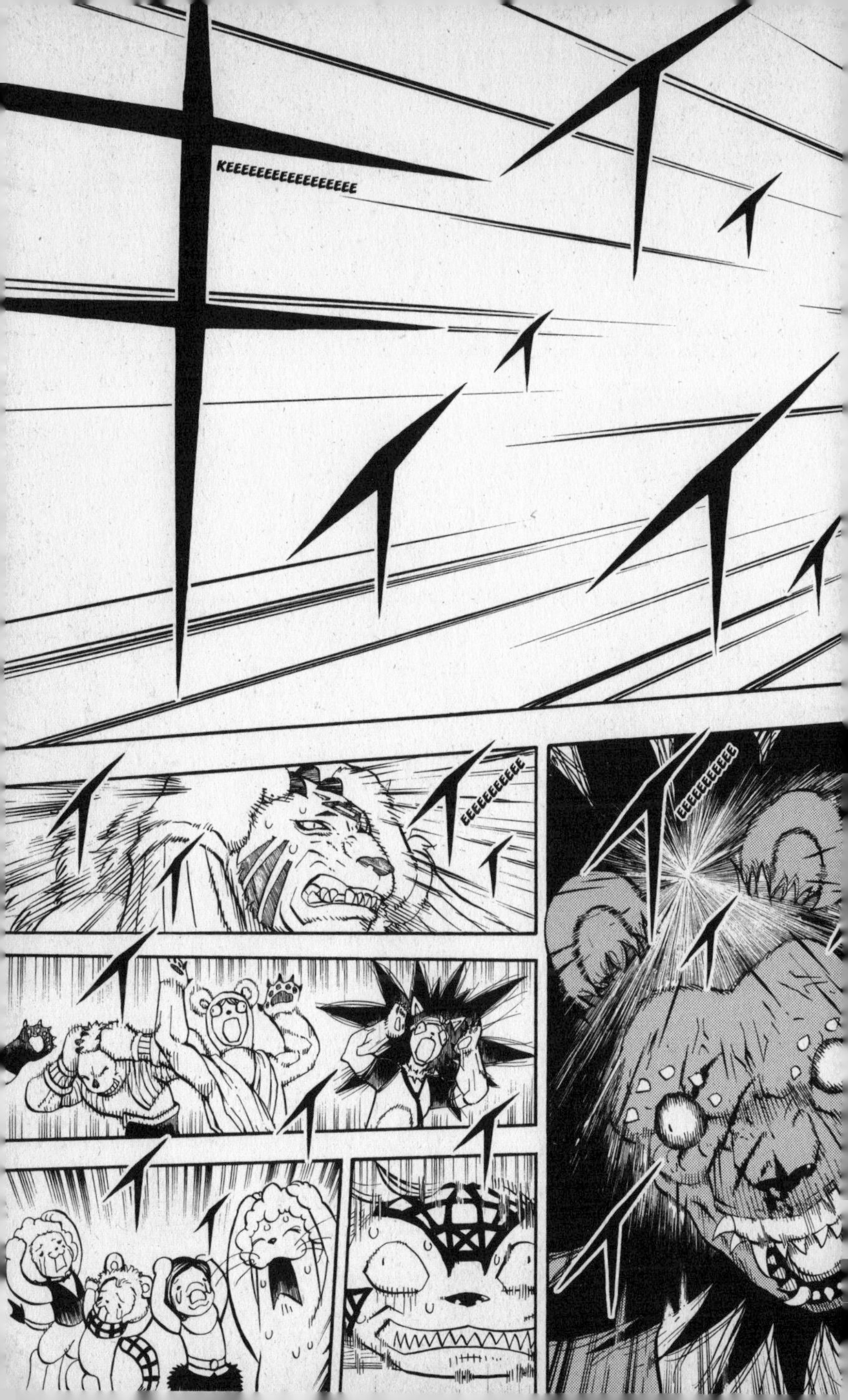
KEEEEEEEEEEEEEEEEE
EEEEEEEEEEE
EEEEEEEEEEE

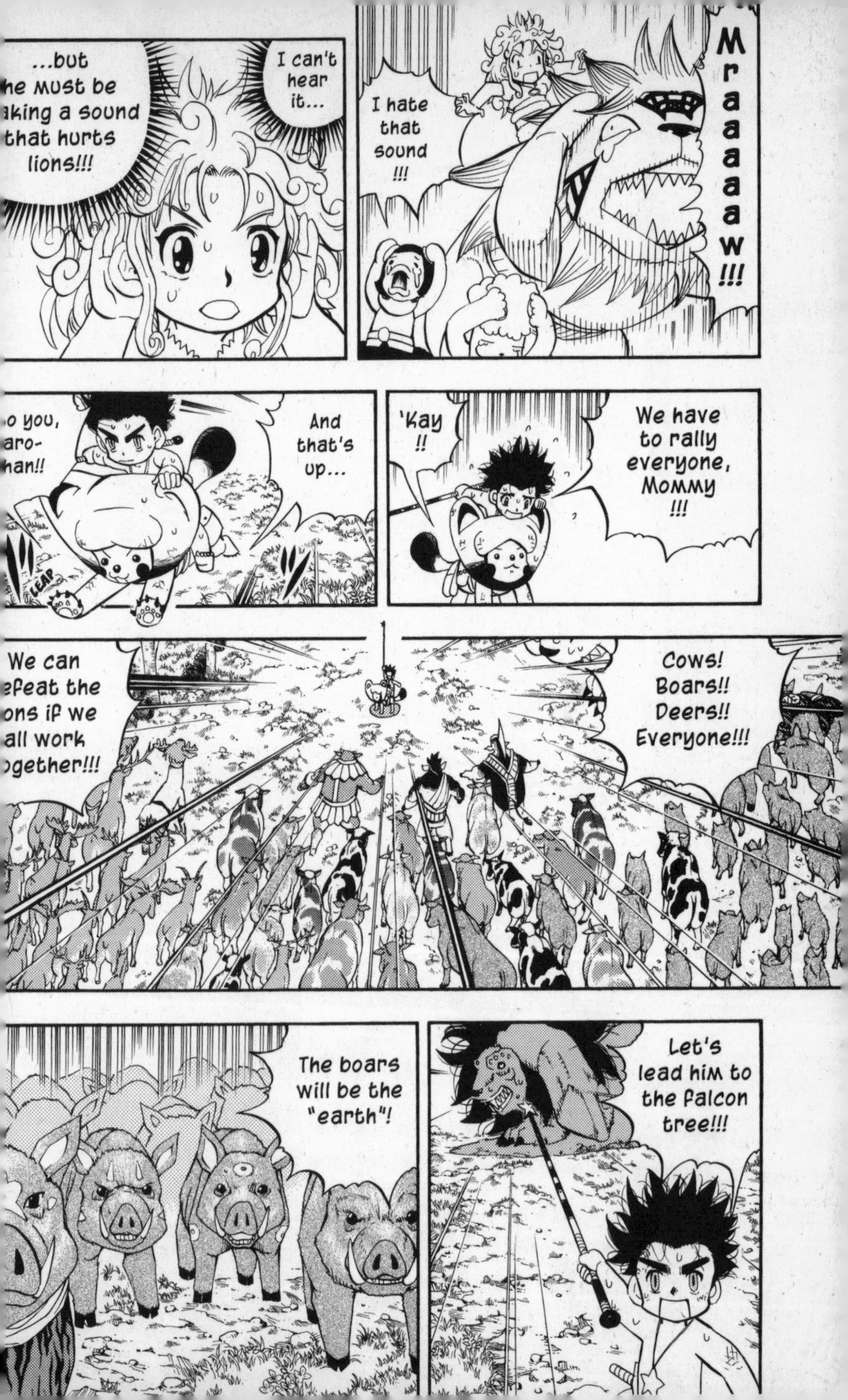

Mraaaaaw!!!
I hate that sound!!!
I can't hear it...
...but he Must be aking a sound that hurts lions!!!
We have to rally everyone, Mommy!!!
'Kay!!
And that's up...
o you, aro-han!!
LEAP
Cows! Boars!! Deers!! Everyone!!!
We can efeat the ons if we all work ogether!!!
Let's lead him to the falcon tree!!!
The boars will be the "earth"!

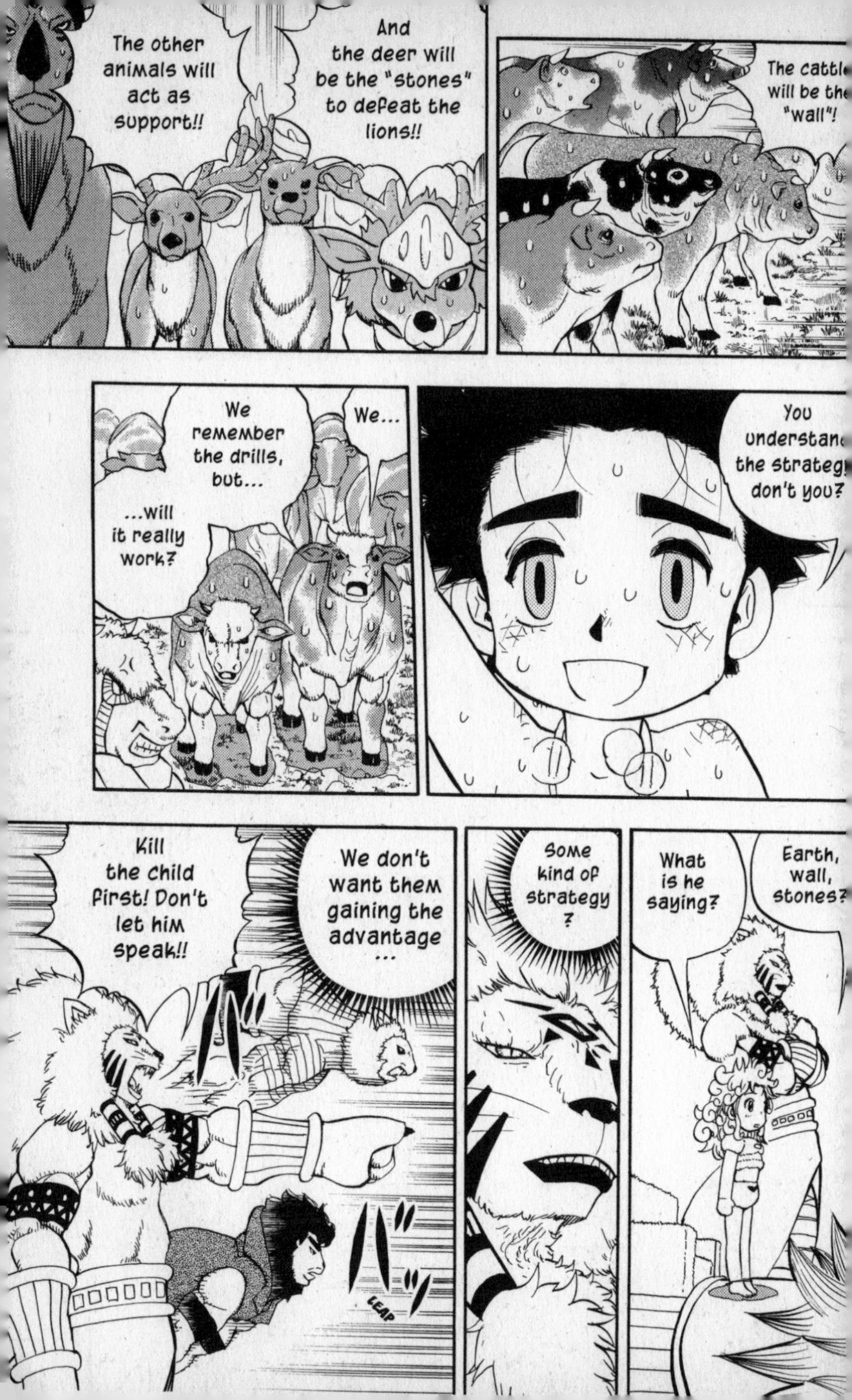
The cattl will be th "wall"!
And the deer will be the "stones" to defeat the lions!!
The other animals will act as support!!
You understan the strateg don't you?
We...
We remember the drills, but...
...will it really work?
Earth, wall, stones?
What is he saying?
Some kind of strategy?
We don't want them gaining the advantage...
Kill the child first! Don't let him speak!!
LEAP

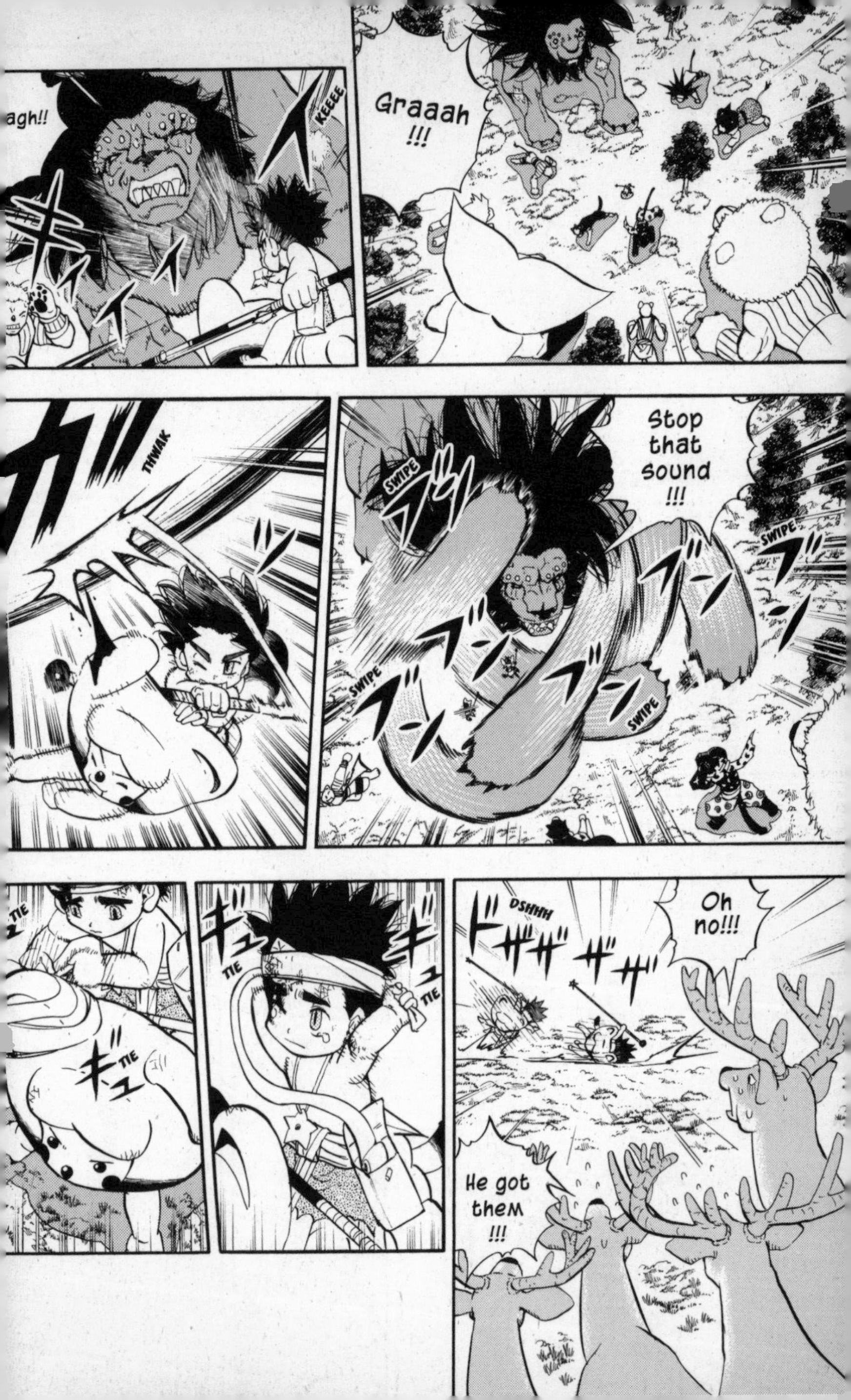
Graaah !!!
KEEEE
agh!!
Stop that sound !!!
SWIPE
SWIPE
SWIPE
SWIPE
THWAK
Oh no!!!
DSHHH
He got them !!!
TIE
TIE
TIE
TIE

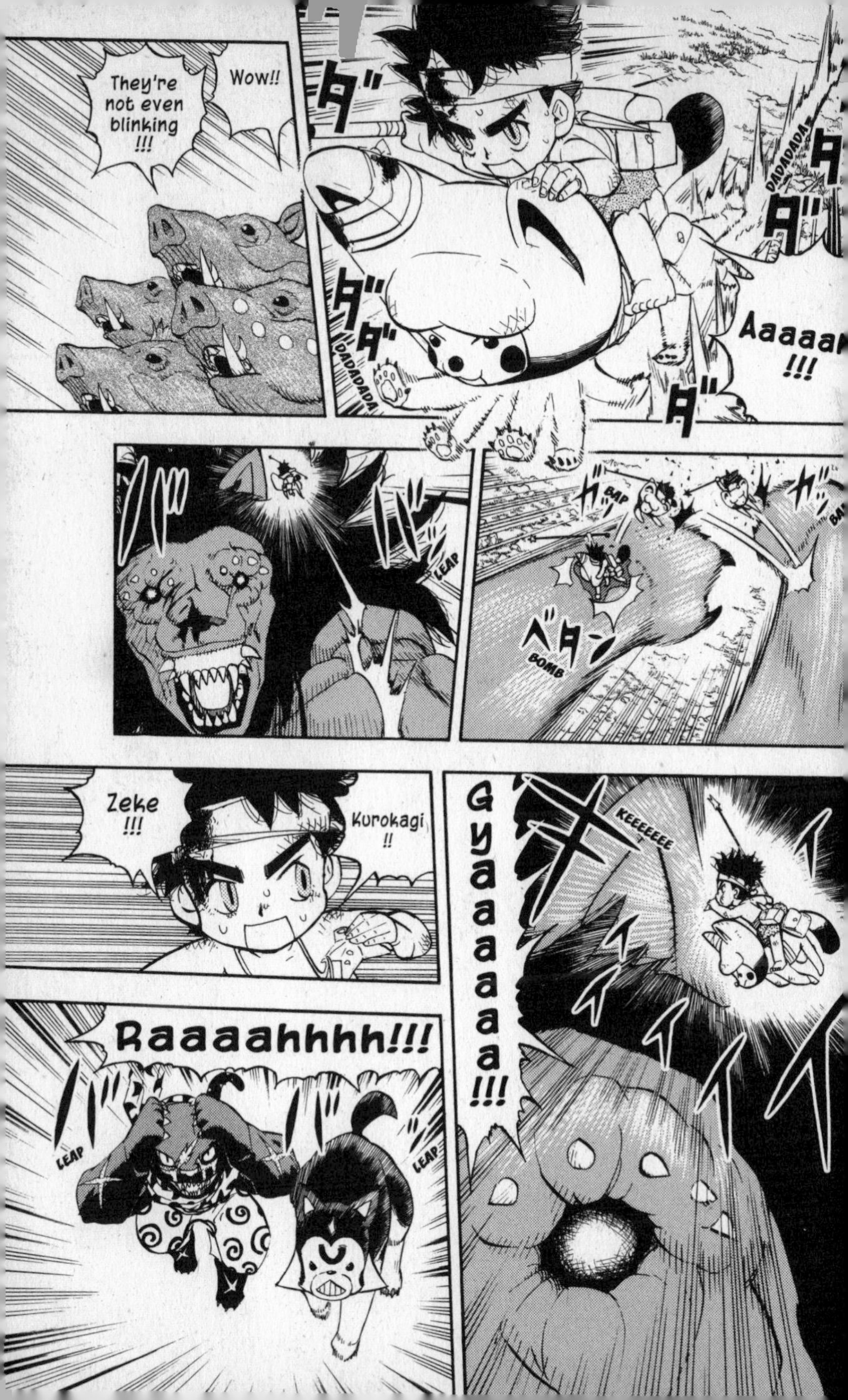
DADADADA
Aaaaa
!!!
DADADADA
Wow!!
They're not even blinking!!!
BAP
BOMB
LEAP
Gyaaaaaaaa!!!
KEEEEEEE
Kurokagi!!
Zeke!!!
Raaaahhhh!!!
LEAP
LEAP

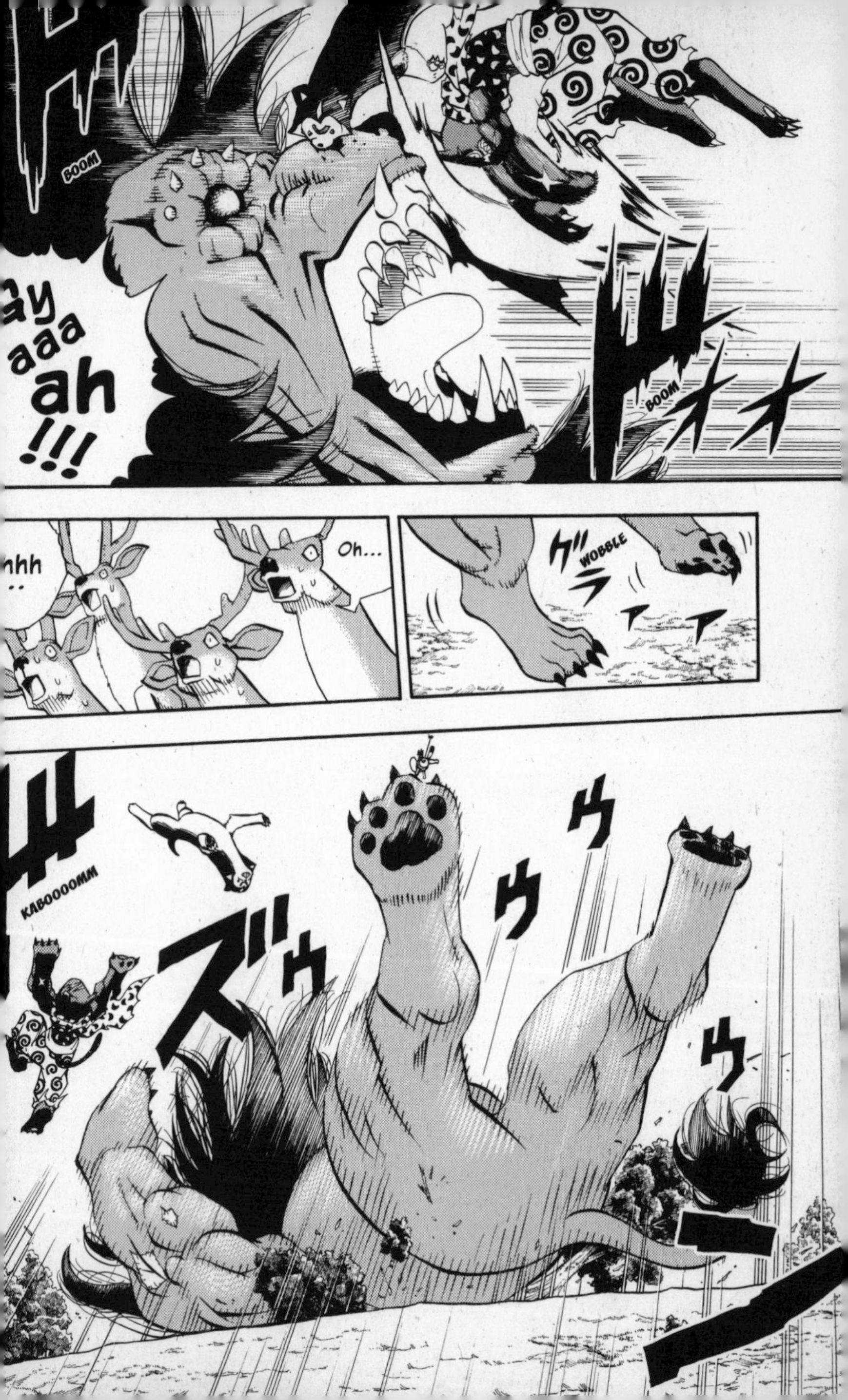

BOOM
ドオオ
BOOM
ay
aaa
ah
!!!
グラァァ
WOBBLE
Oh...
hhh
..
ズウウウウ
KABOOOOMM

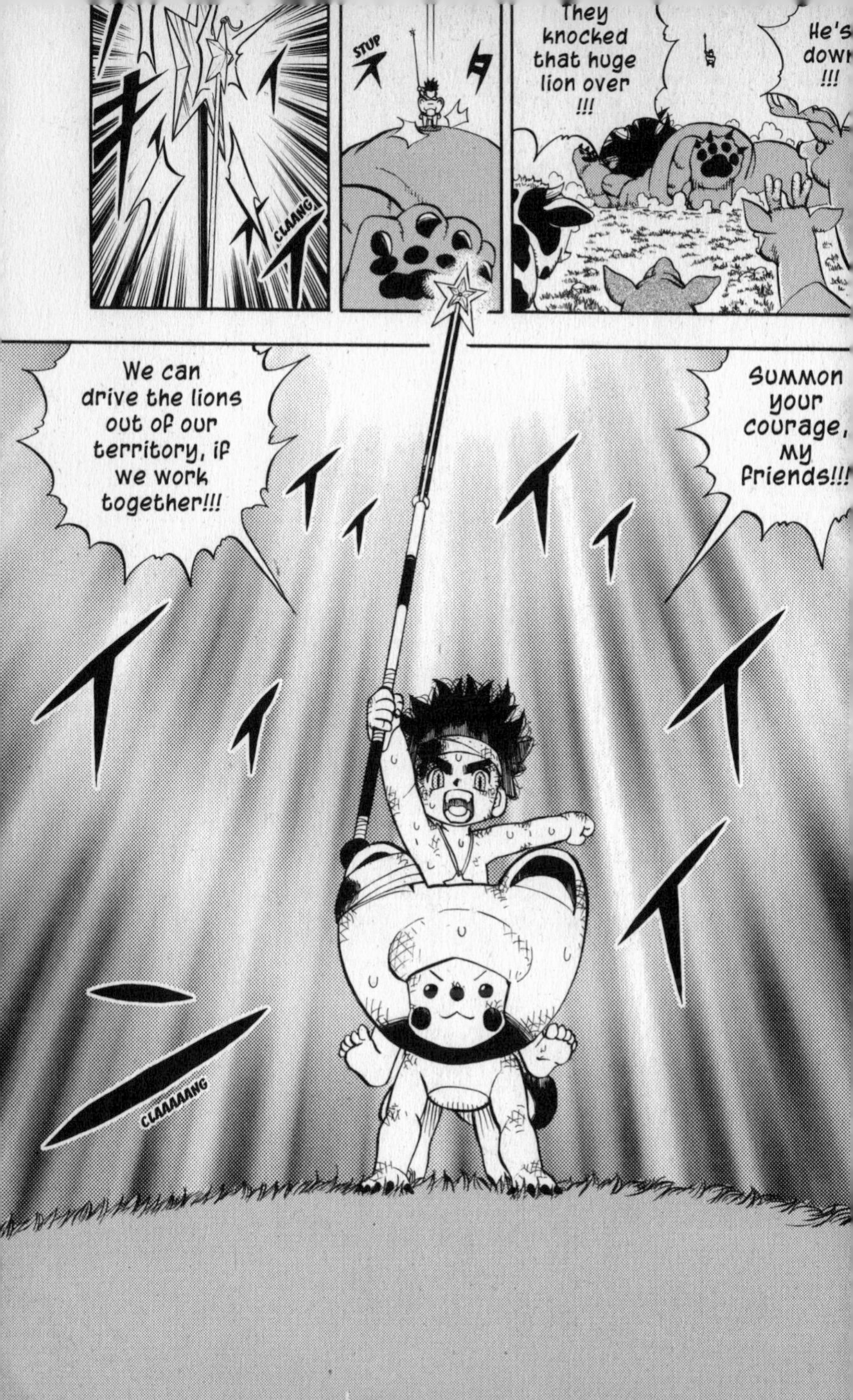
He's down!!!
They knocked that huge lion over!!!
STUP
CLAANG
Summon your courage, my friends!!!
We can drive the lions out of our territory, if we work together!!!
CLAAAAANG

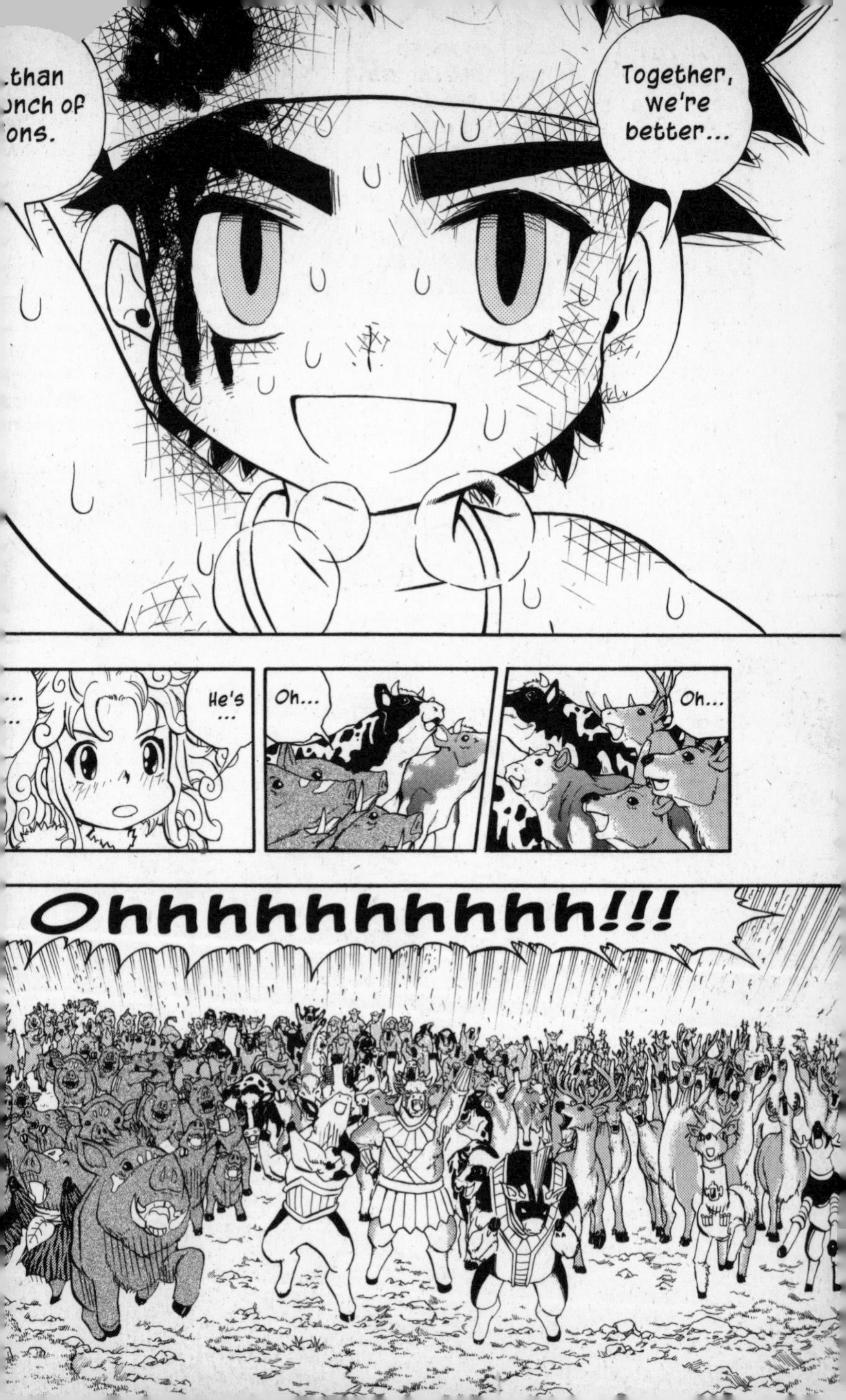

Together, we're better...
.than unch of ons.
Oh...
Oh...
He's ...
Ohhhhhhhhhh!!!

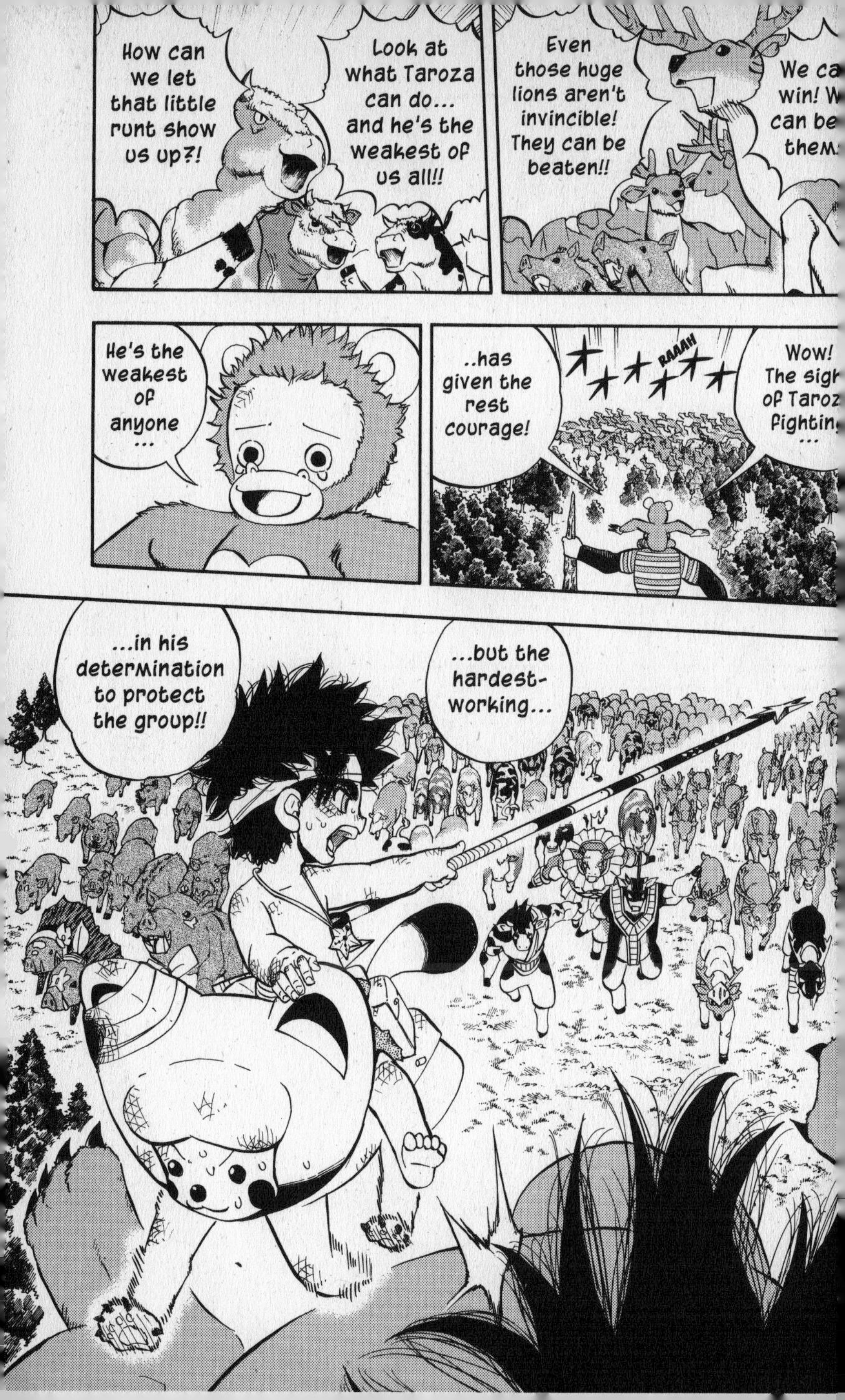
We ca
win! W
can be
them!
Even those huge lions aren't invincible! They can be beaten!!
Look at what Taroza can do... and he's the weakest of us all!!
How can we let that little runt show us up?!
Wow! The sig
of Taroz
fightin
...
RAAAH
..has given the rest courage!
He's the weakest of anyone ...
...but the hardest-working...
...in his determination to protect the group!!

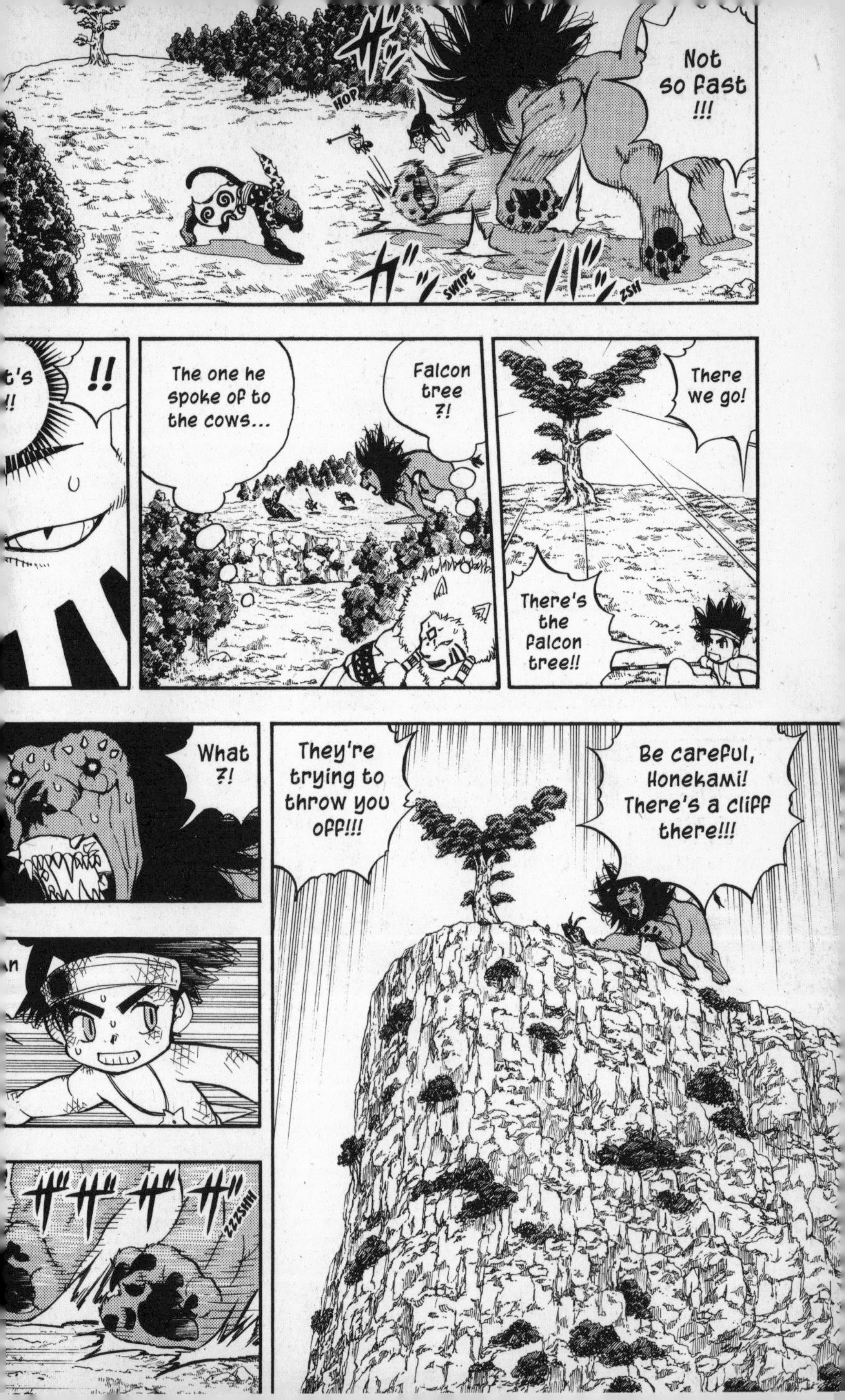
Not so fast!!!
HOP
SWIPE
ZSH
There we go!
There's the falcon tree!!
Falcon tree?!
The one he spoke of to the cows...
!!
Be careful, Honekami! There's a cliff there!!!
They're trying to throw you off!!!
What?!
ZZZSHH

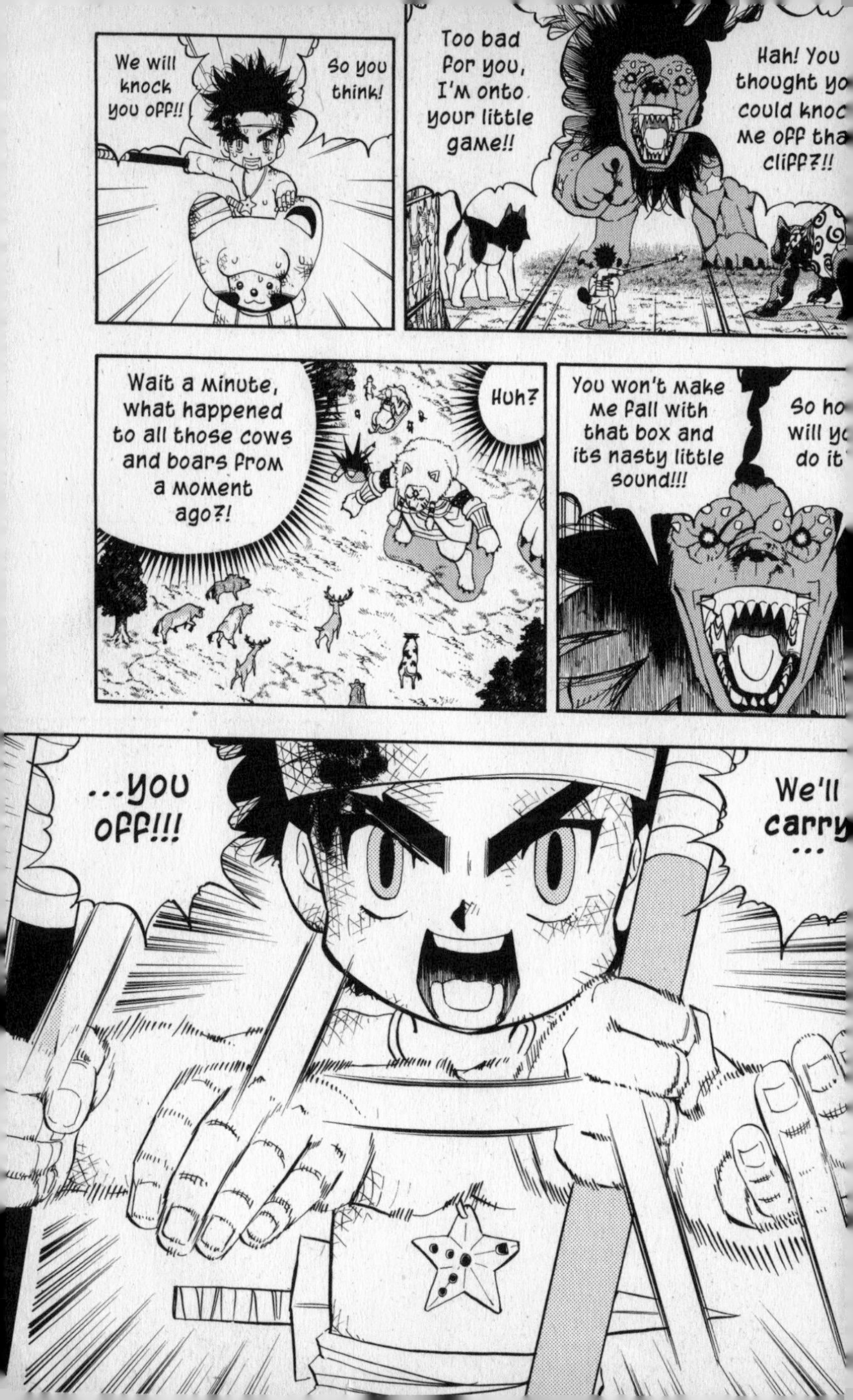

Hah! You thought yo could knoc me off tha cliff?!!
Too bad for you, I'm onto your little game!!
So you think!
We will knock you off!!
So ho will yo do it
You won't make me fall with that box and its nasty little sound!!!
Huh?
Wait a minute, what happened to all those cows and boars from a moment ago?!
We'll carry ...
...you off!!!

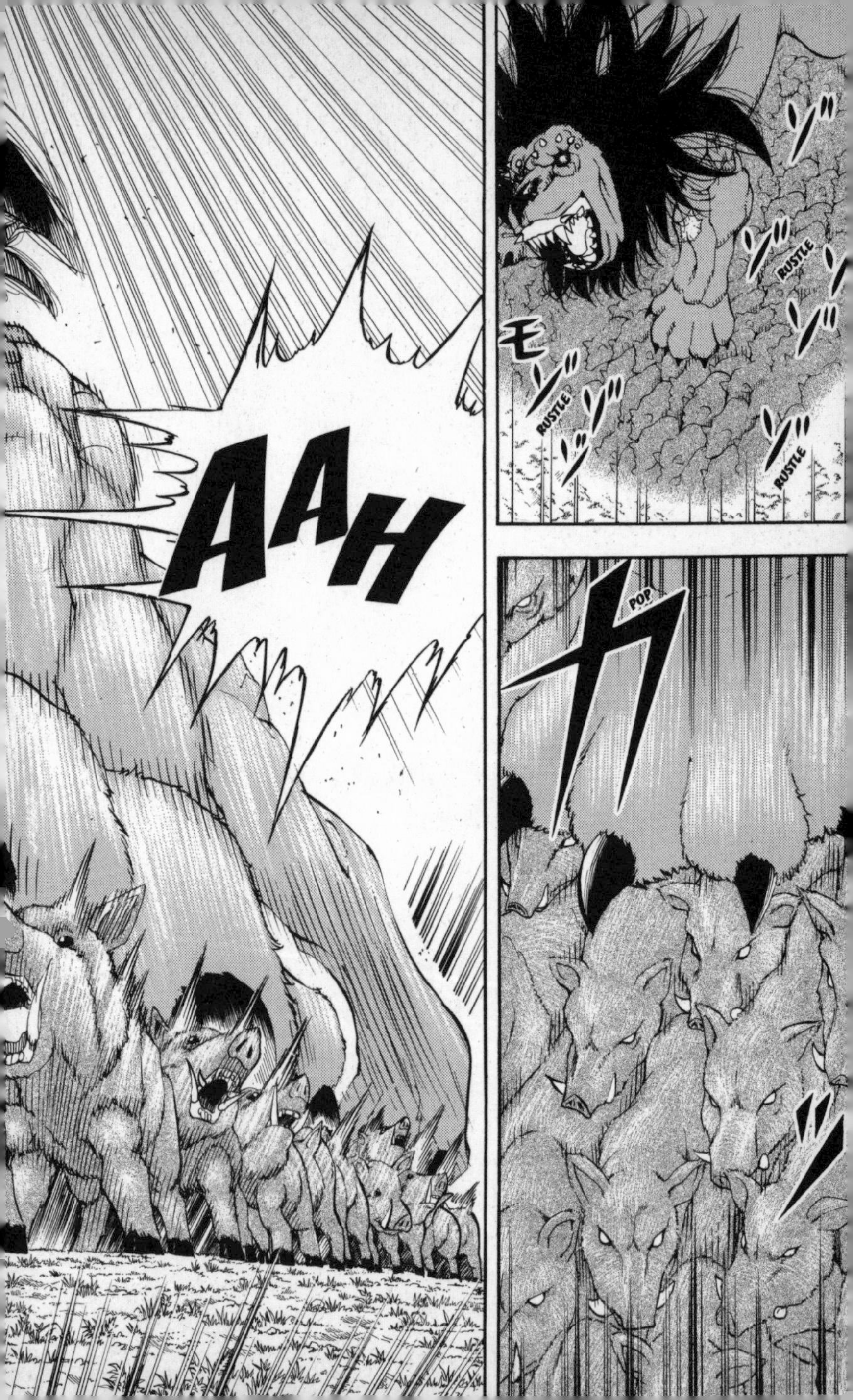
RUSTLE
RUSTLE
RUSTLE
POP
AAH

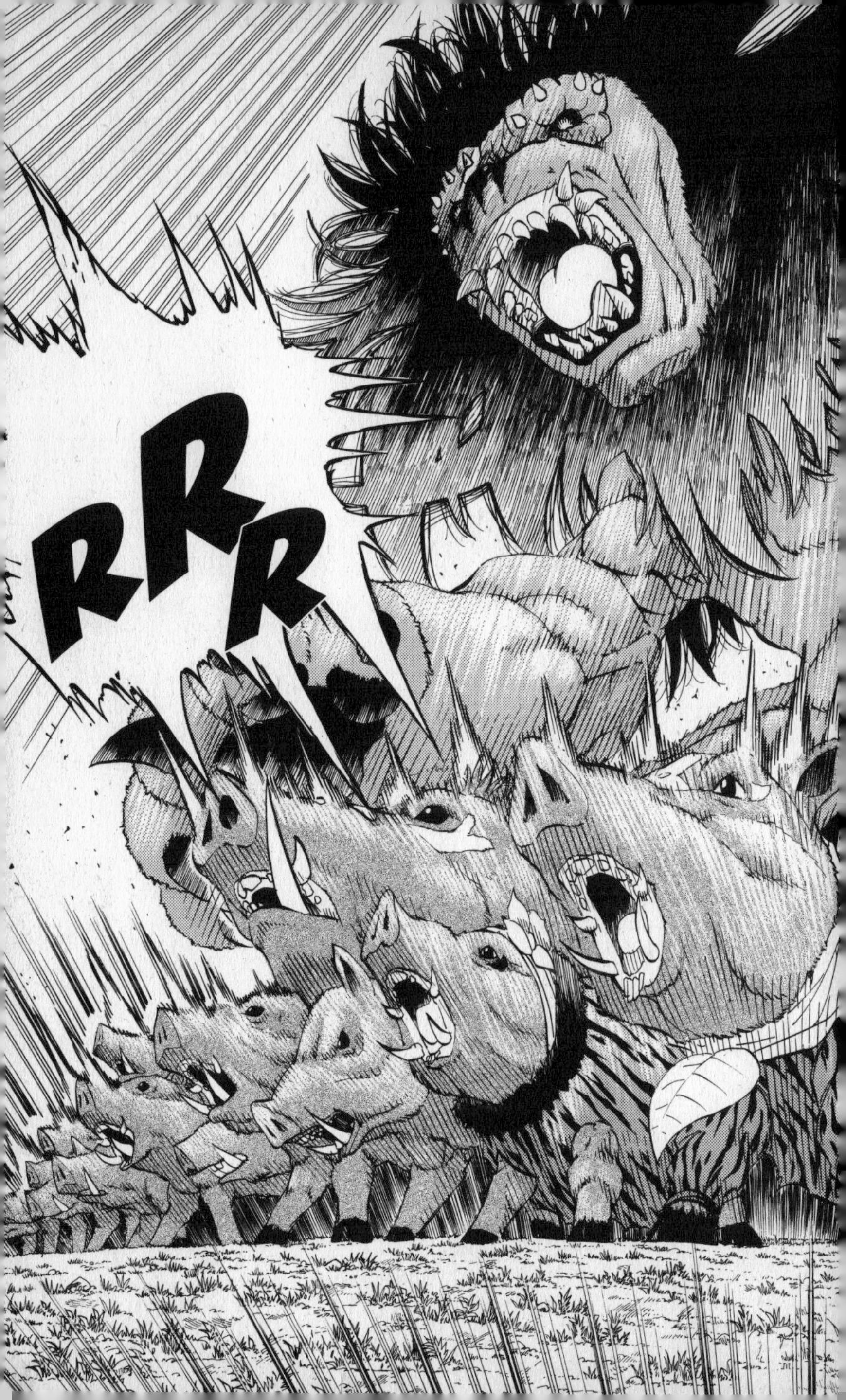
RRR

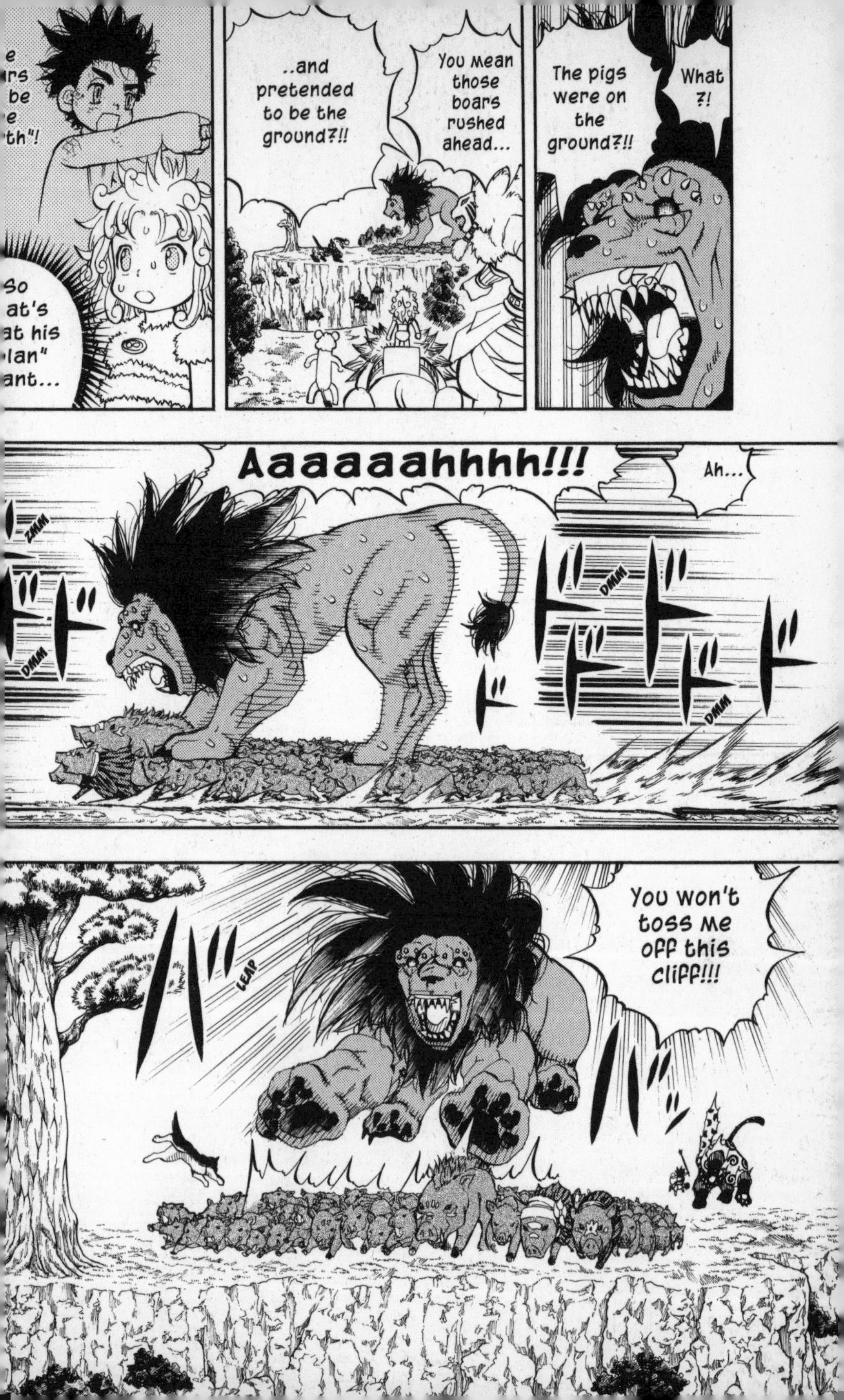
What?!
The pigs were on the ground?!!
You mean those boars rushed ahead...
..and pretended to be the ground?!!
Ah...
Aaaaaaahhhh!!!
DMM
DMM
ZMM
DMM
You won't toss me off this cliff!!!
LEAP

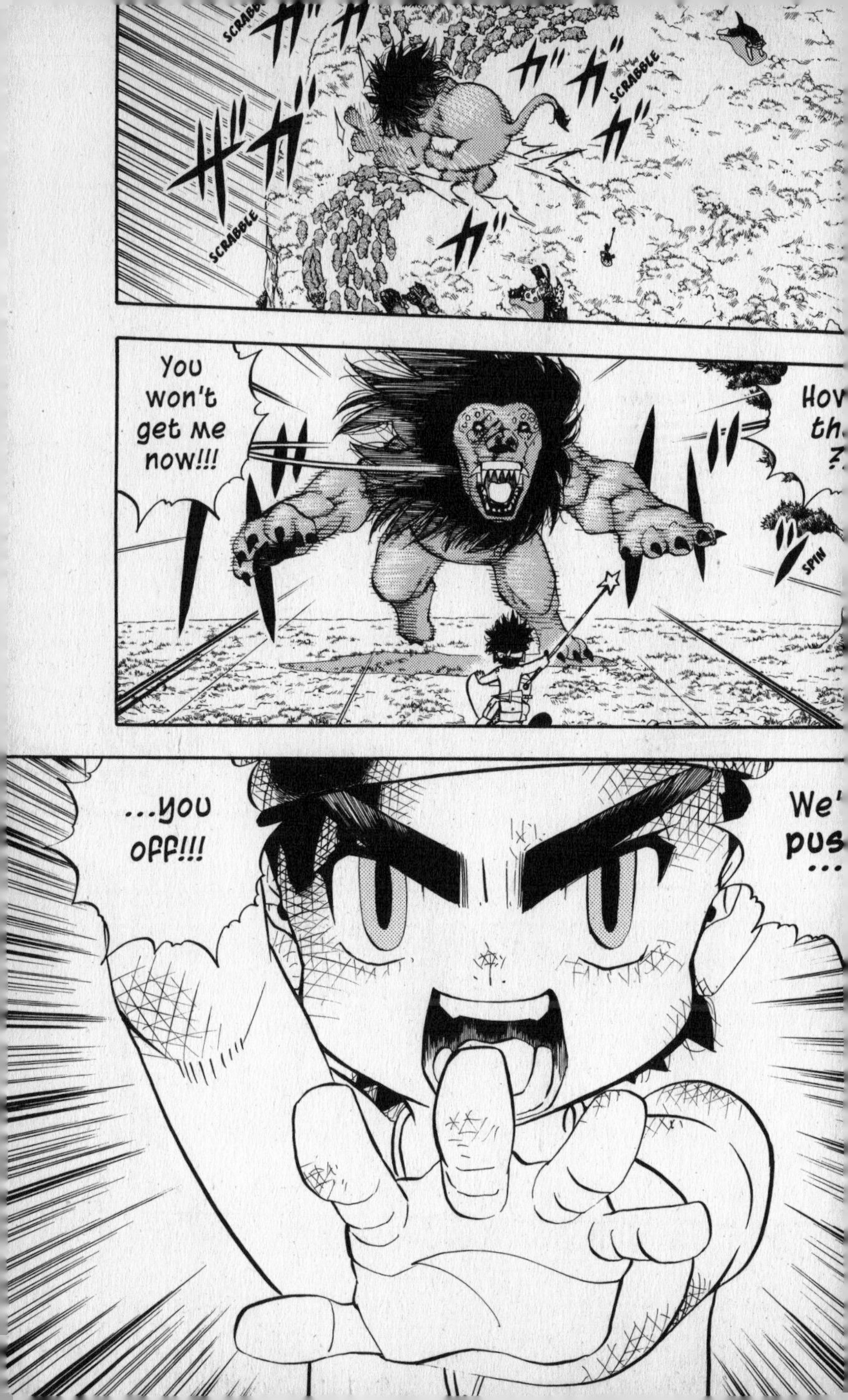
SCRABBLE
SCRABBLE
SCRABBLE
Hov th ?
SPIN
You won't get me now!!!
We' pus ...
...you off!!!

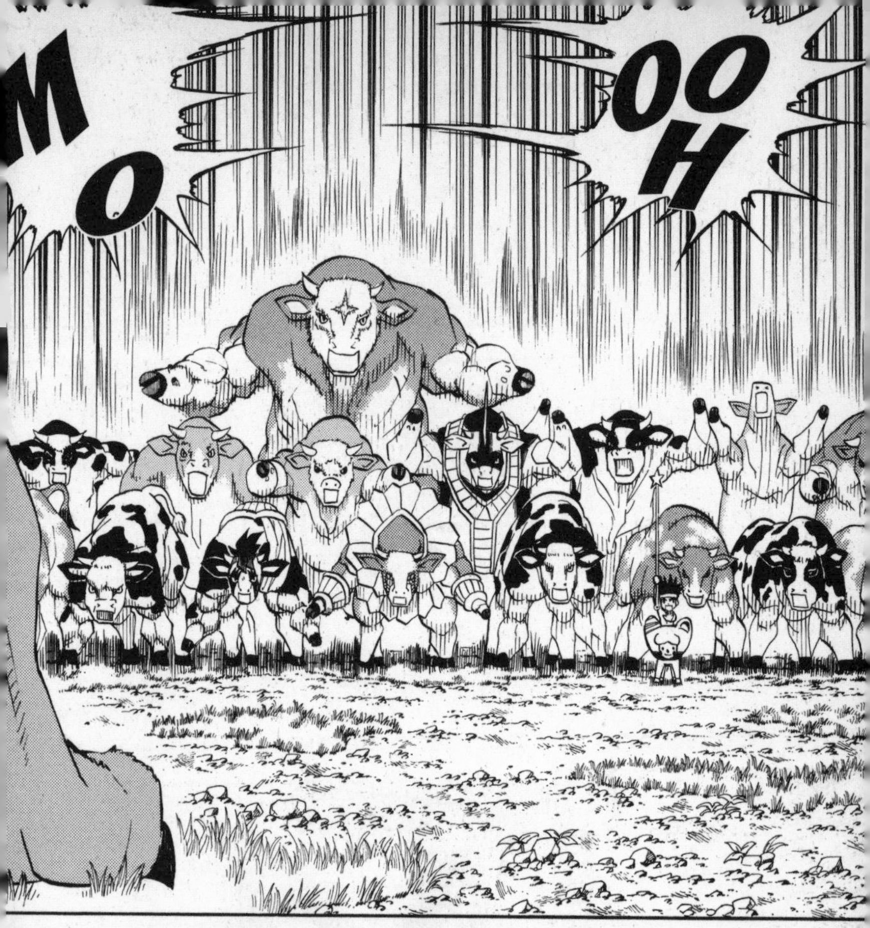
MOOOH
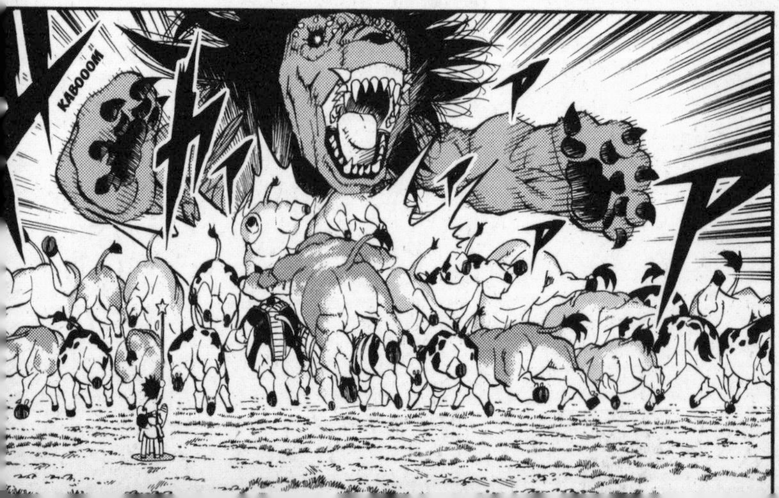
KABOOOM

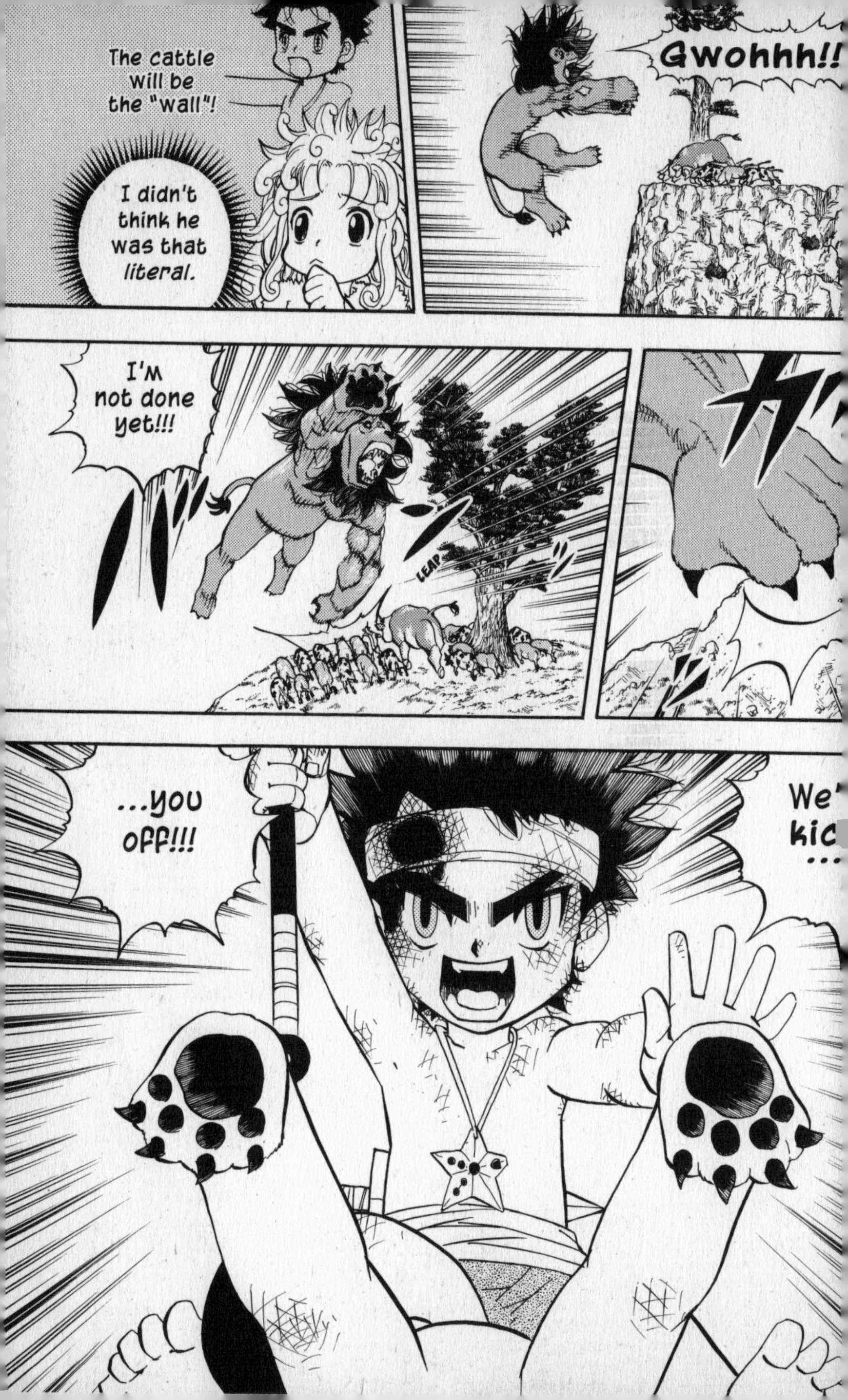
Gwohhh!!
The cattle will be the "wall"!
I didn't think he was that *literal.*
I'M not done yet!!!
LEAP
We' kic ...
...you off!!!

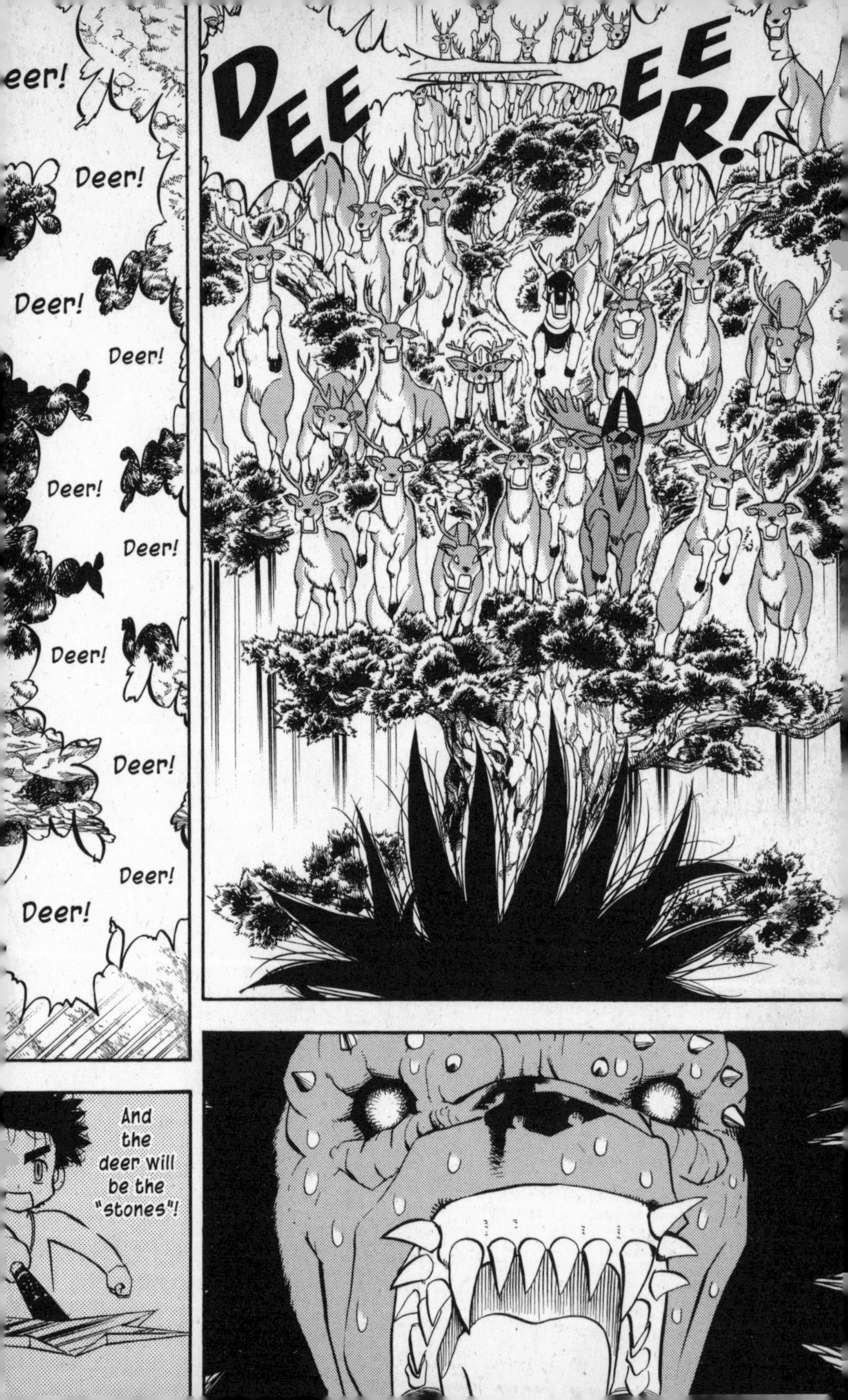
DEEEER!
eer!
Deer!
Deer!
Deer!
Deer!
Deer!
Deer!
Deer!
Deer!
Deer!
And the deer will be the "stones"!

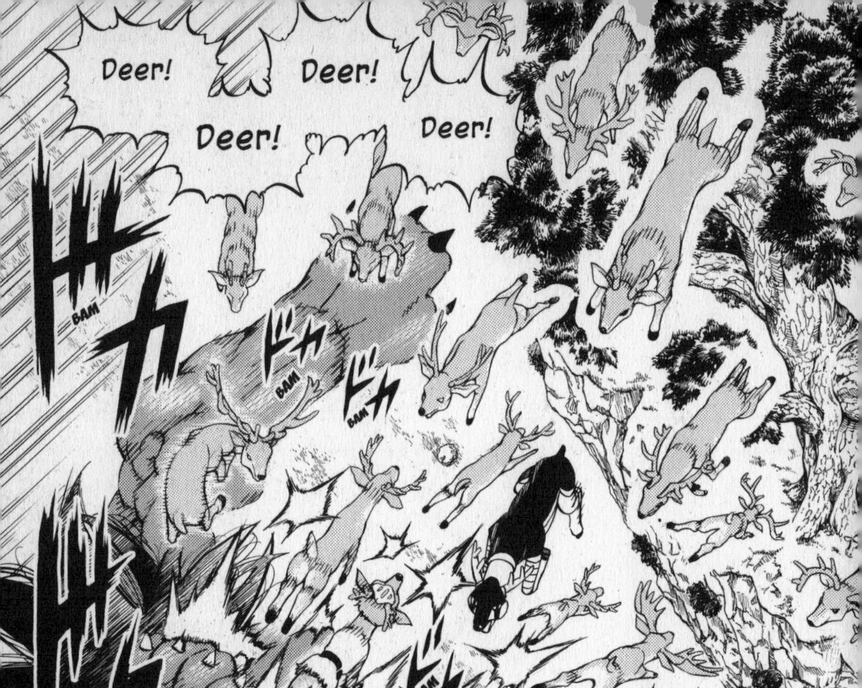
Deer!
Deer!
Deer!
Deer!
BAM
BAM
BAM
BAM
BAM
BAM
BAM
BAM
BAM
BAM
BAM

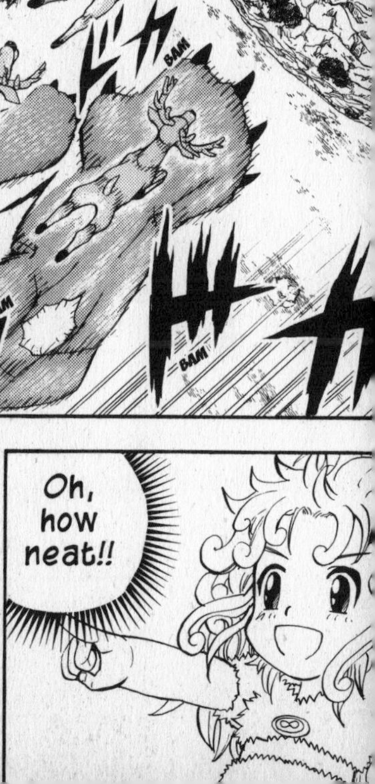
Oh, how neat!!

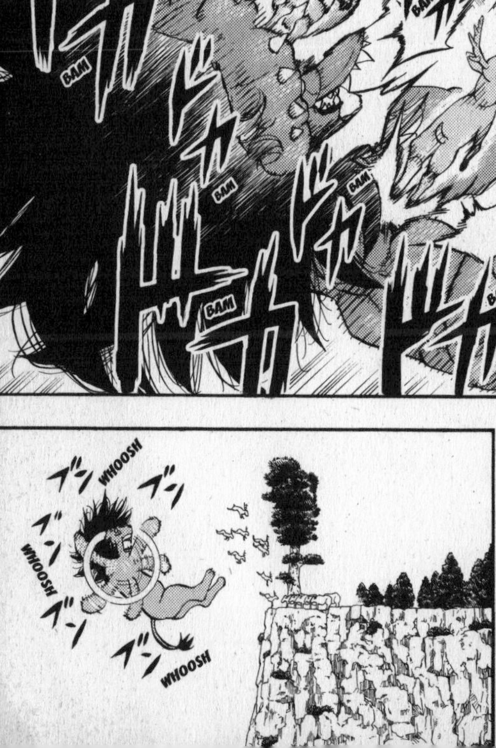
WHOOSH
WHOOSH
WHOOSH

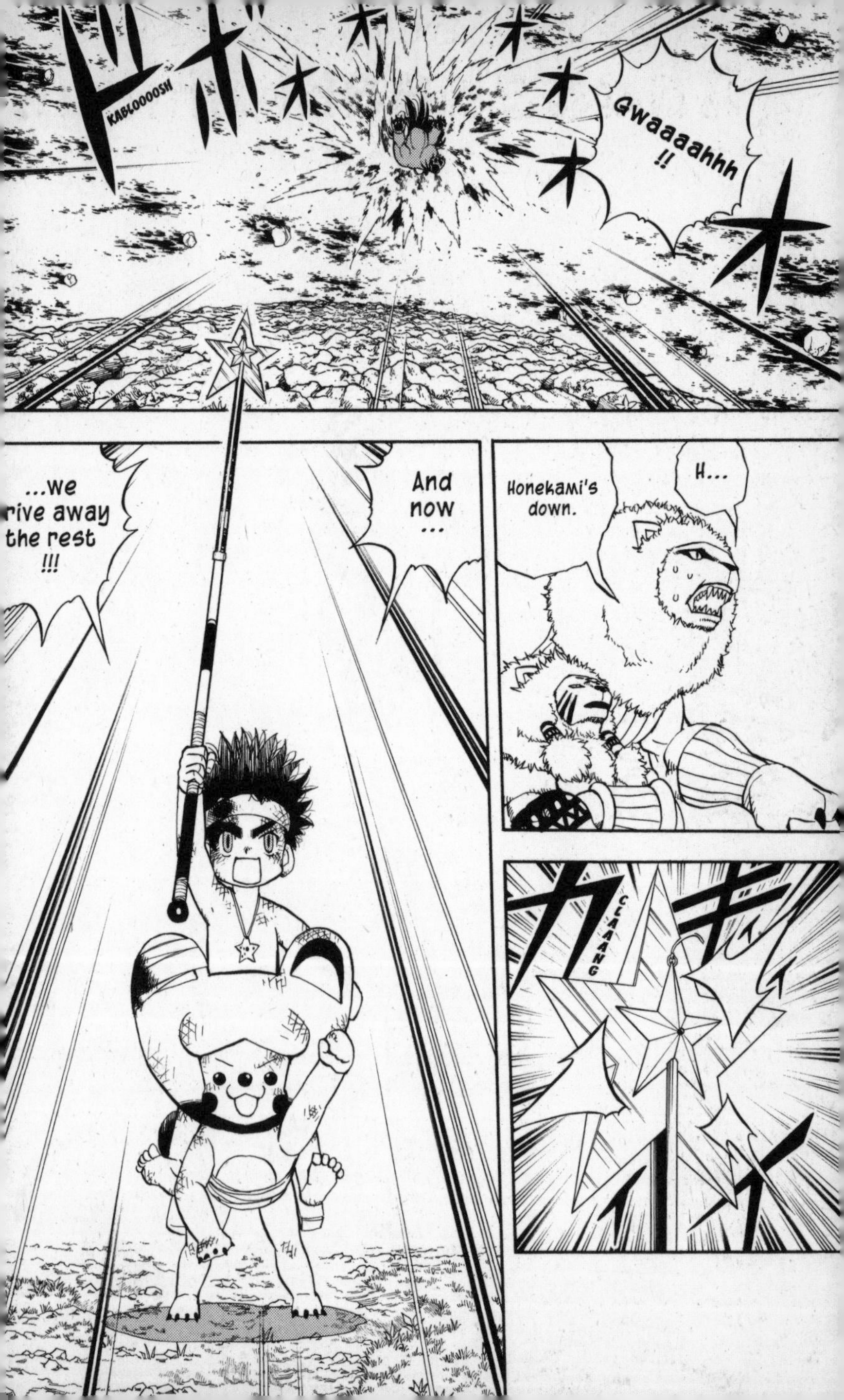
Gwaaaaahhh !!
KABLOOOOSH
H...
Honekami's down.
CLAAANG
And now ...
...we rive away the rest !!!

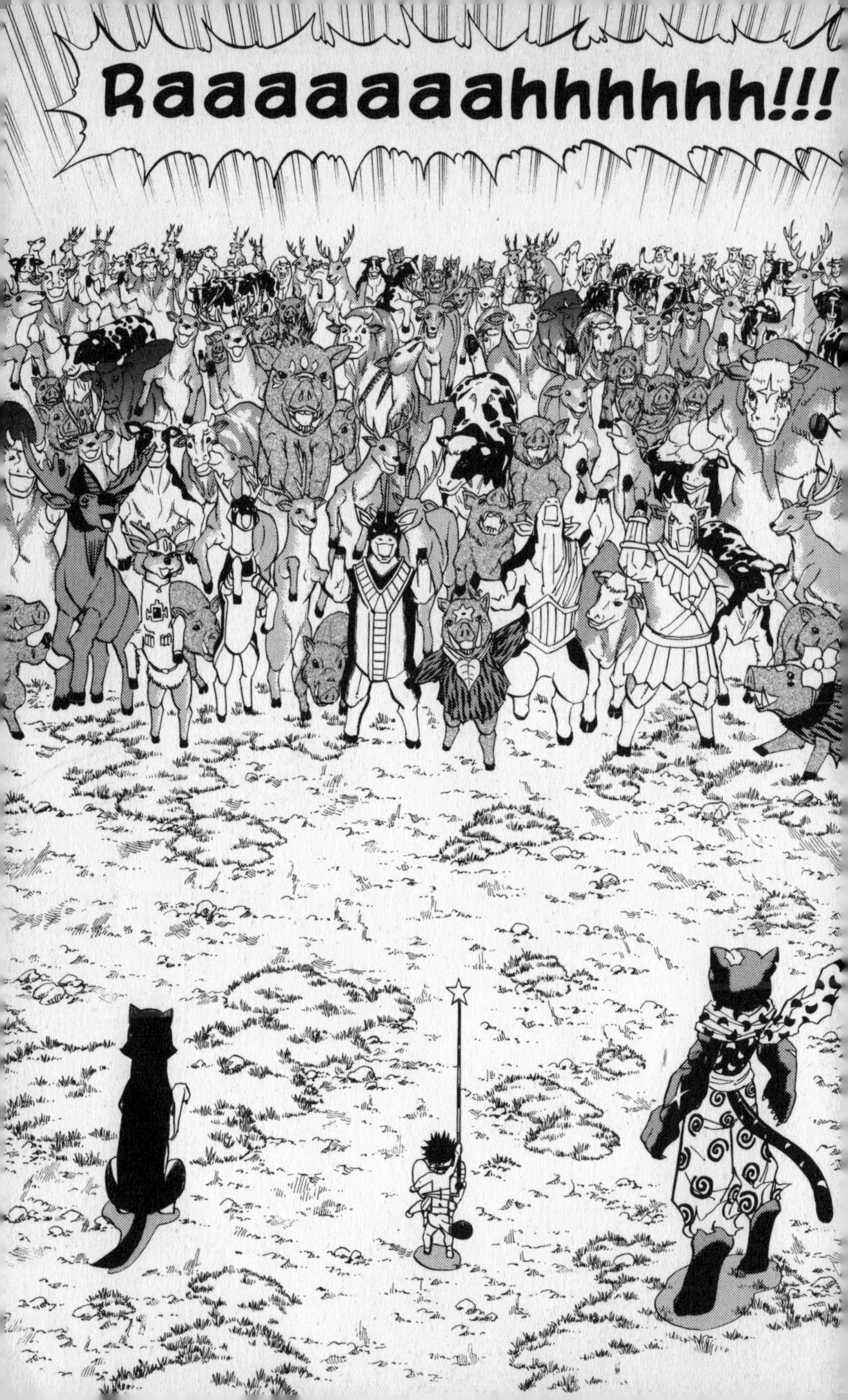
Raaaaaaaahhhhhh!!!

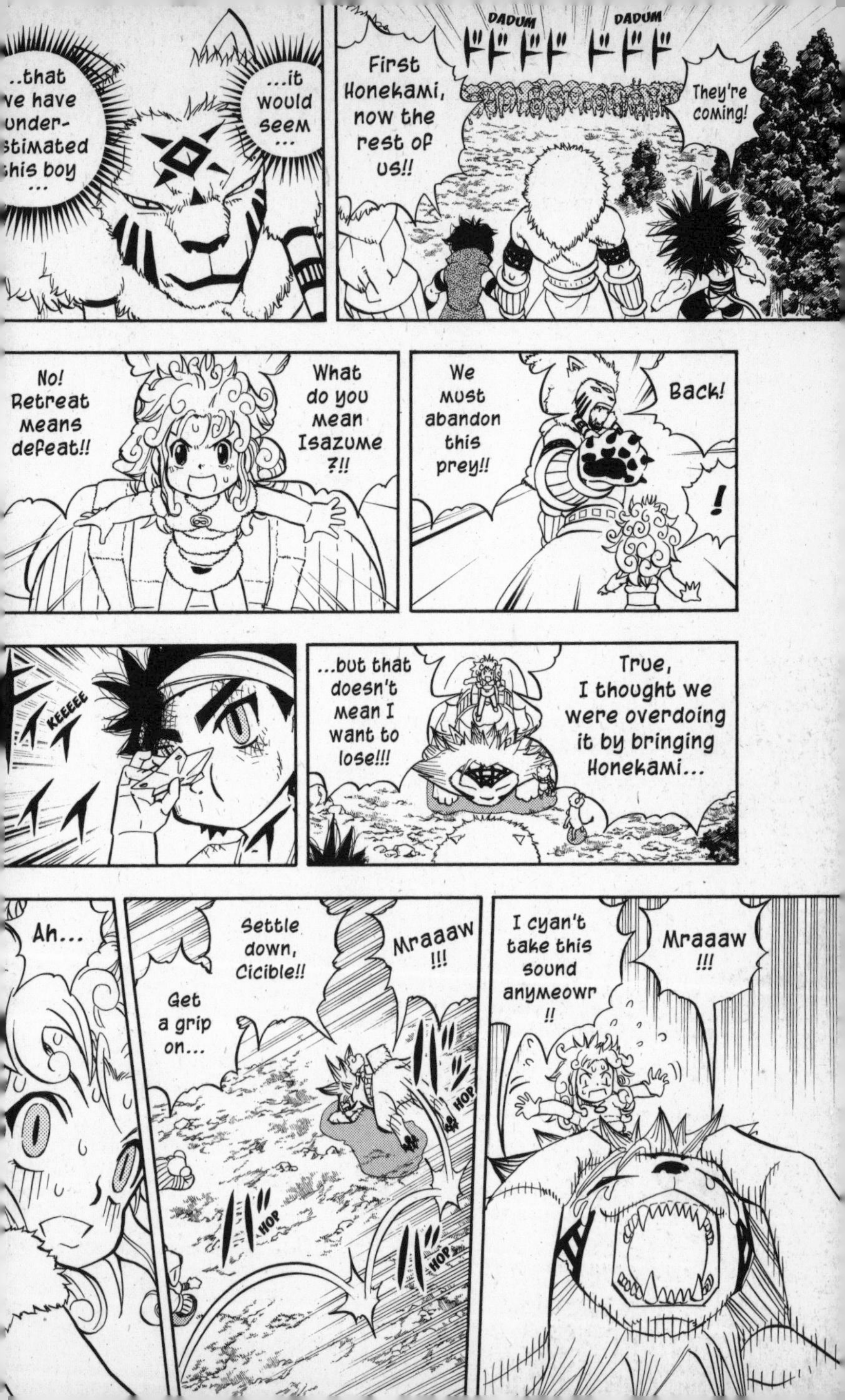

DADUM
DADUM
They're coming!
First Honekami, now the rest of us!!
...it would seem...
..that ve have under-stimated his boy...
Back!
We must abandon this prey!!
!
What do you mean Isazume?!!
No! Retreat means defeat!!
True, I thought we were overdoing it by bringing Honekami...
...but that doesn't mean I want to lose!!!
KEEEEE
Mraaaw!!!
I cyan't take this sound anymeowr!!
Mraaaw!!!
Settle down, Cicible!!
Get a grip on...
HOP
HOP
HOP
Ah...

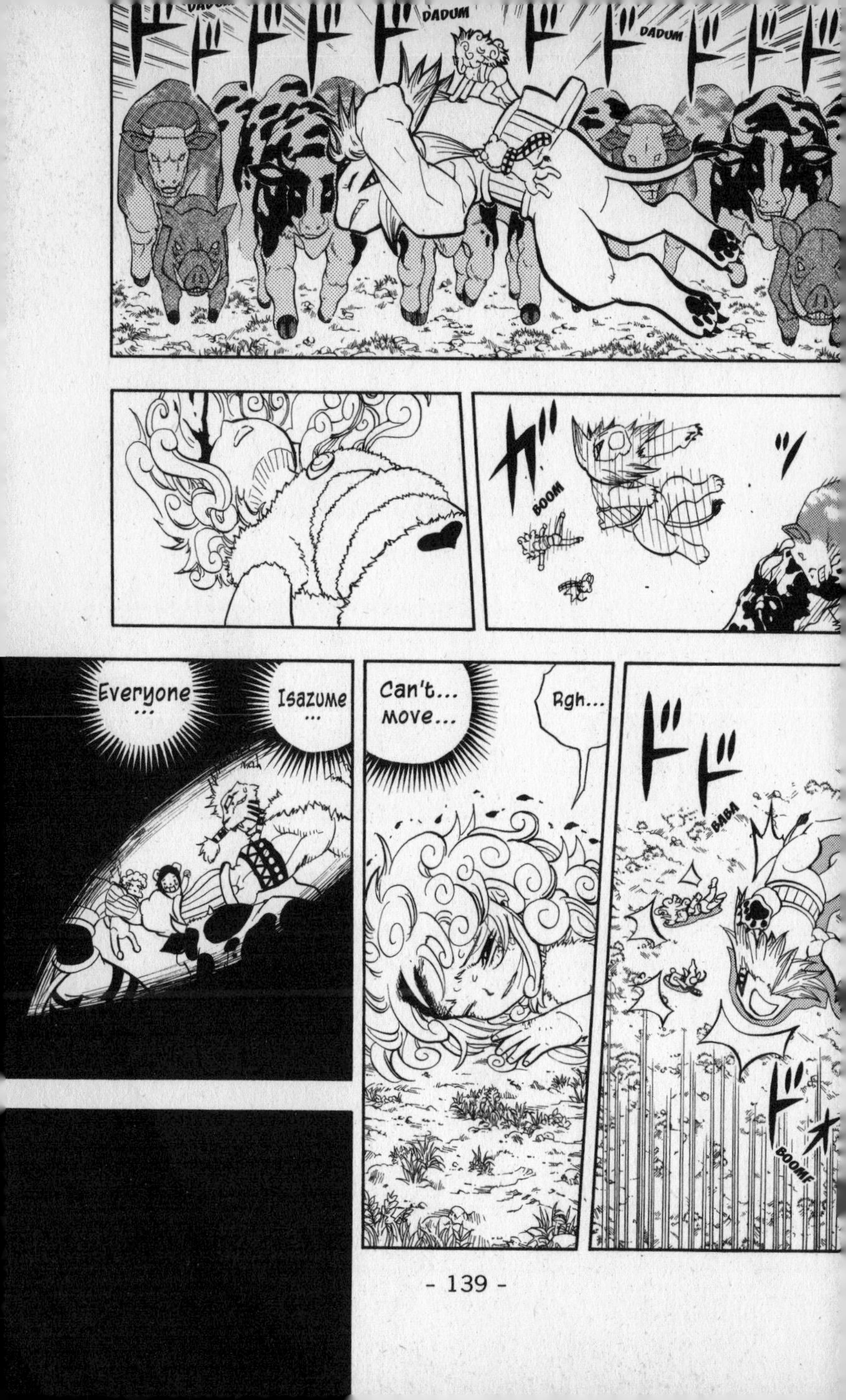
DADUM
DADUM
BOOM
BABA
BOOMF
Rgh...
Can't... move...
Isazume...
Everyone...

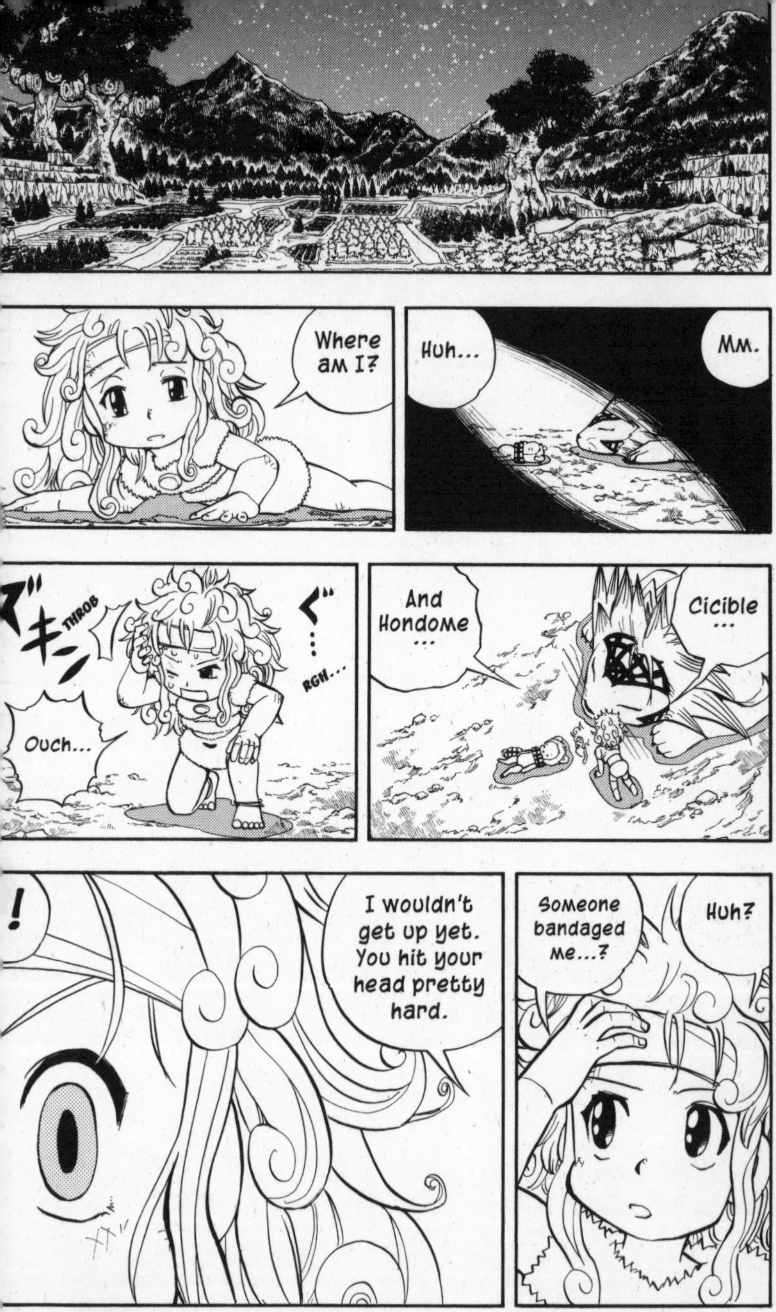
Mm.
Huh...
Where am I?
Cicible...
And Hondome...
RGH...
THROB
Ouch...
Huh?
Someone bandaged me...?
I wouldn't get up yet. You hit your head pretty hard.
!

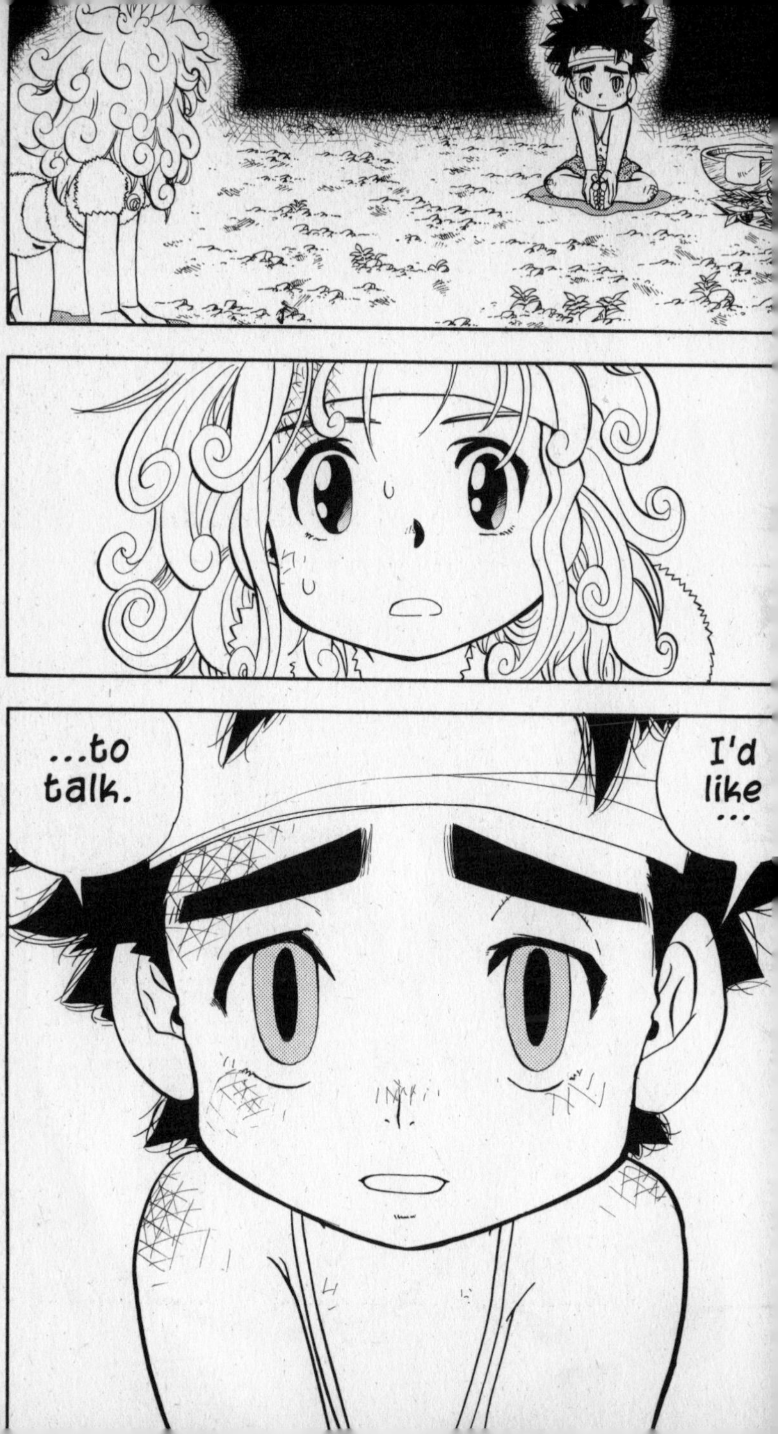
I'd like...
...to talk.

To be continued in Volume 4, Word 11

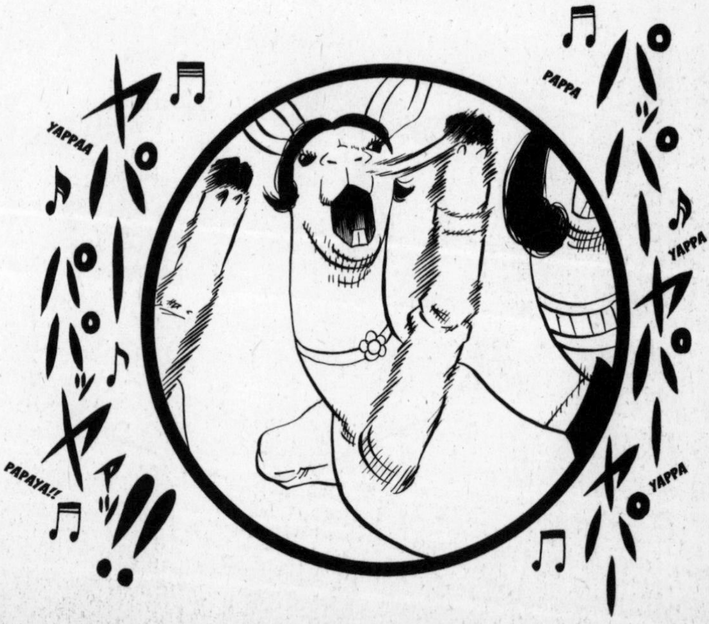
PAPPA
YAPPA
YAPPA
YAPPAA
PAPAYA!!

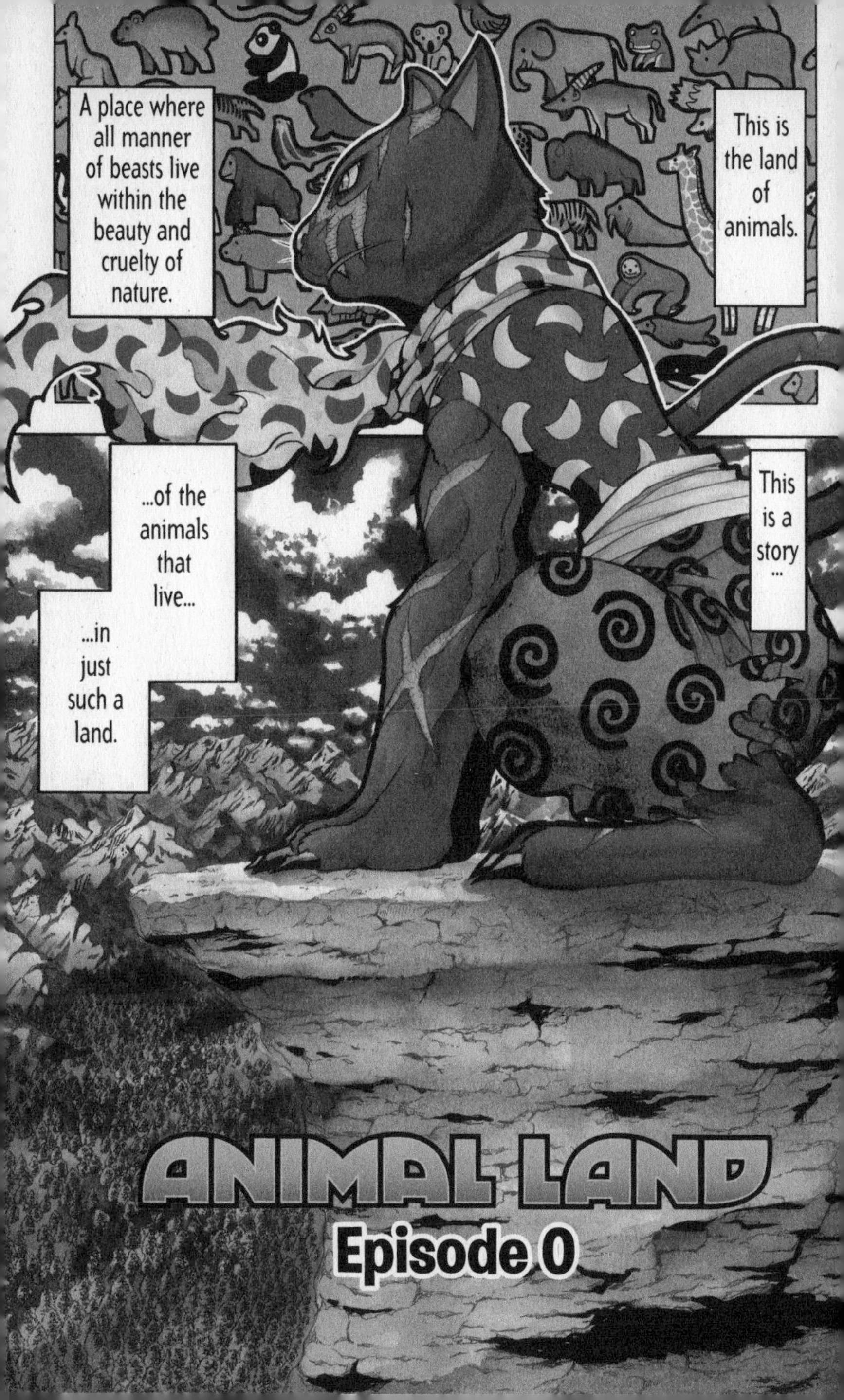
This is the land of animals.
A place where all manner of beasts live within the beauty and cruelty of nature.
This is a story...
...of the animals that live...
...in just such a land.
ANIMAL LAND
Episode 0

Episode 0

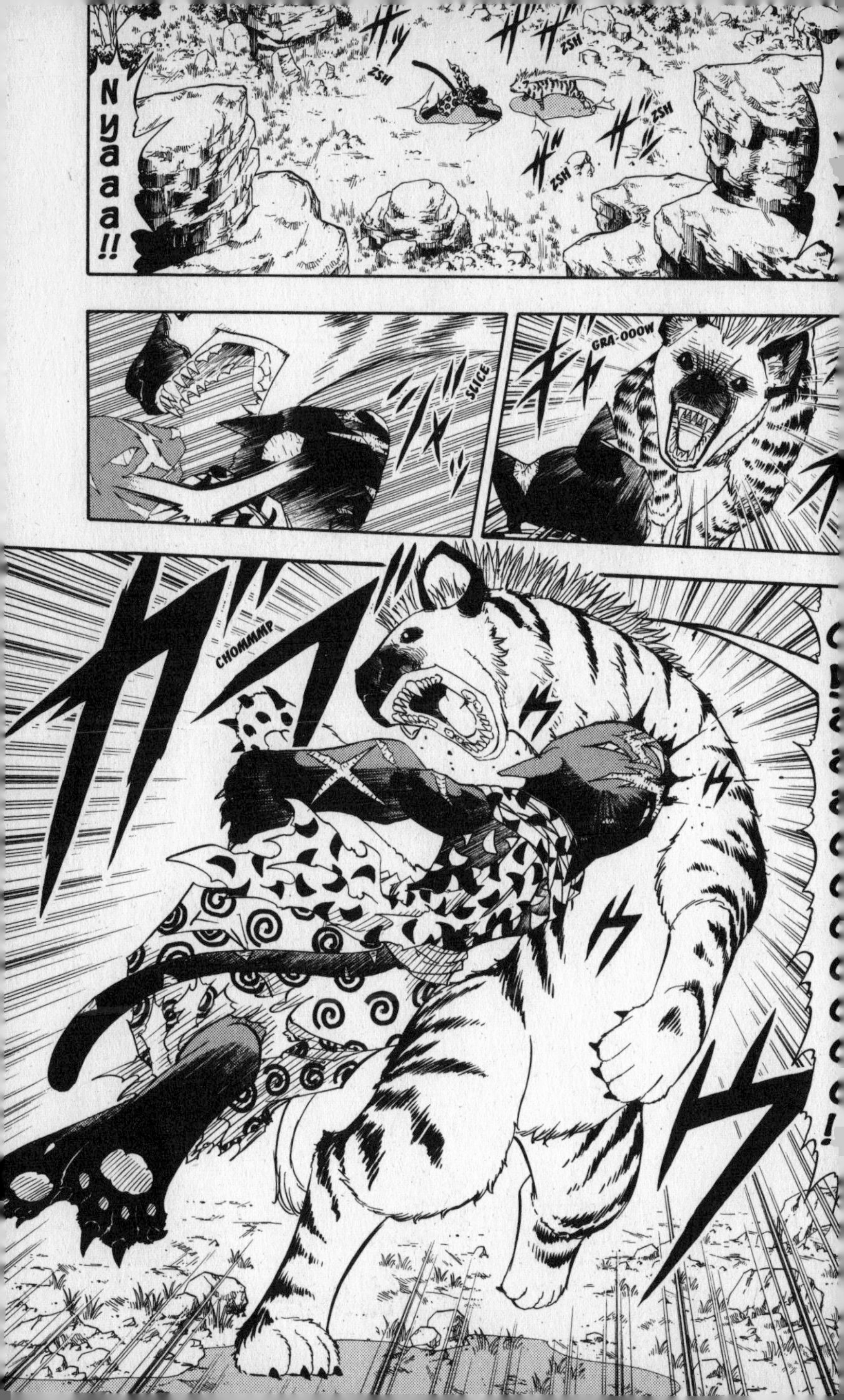
Nyaaaa!!
ZSH
ZSH
ZSH
ZSH
GRA-OOOW
SLICE
CHOMMMP

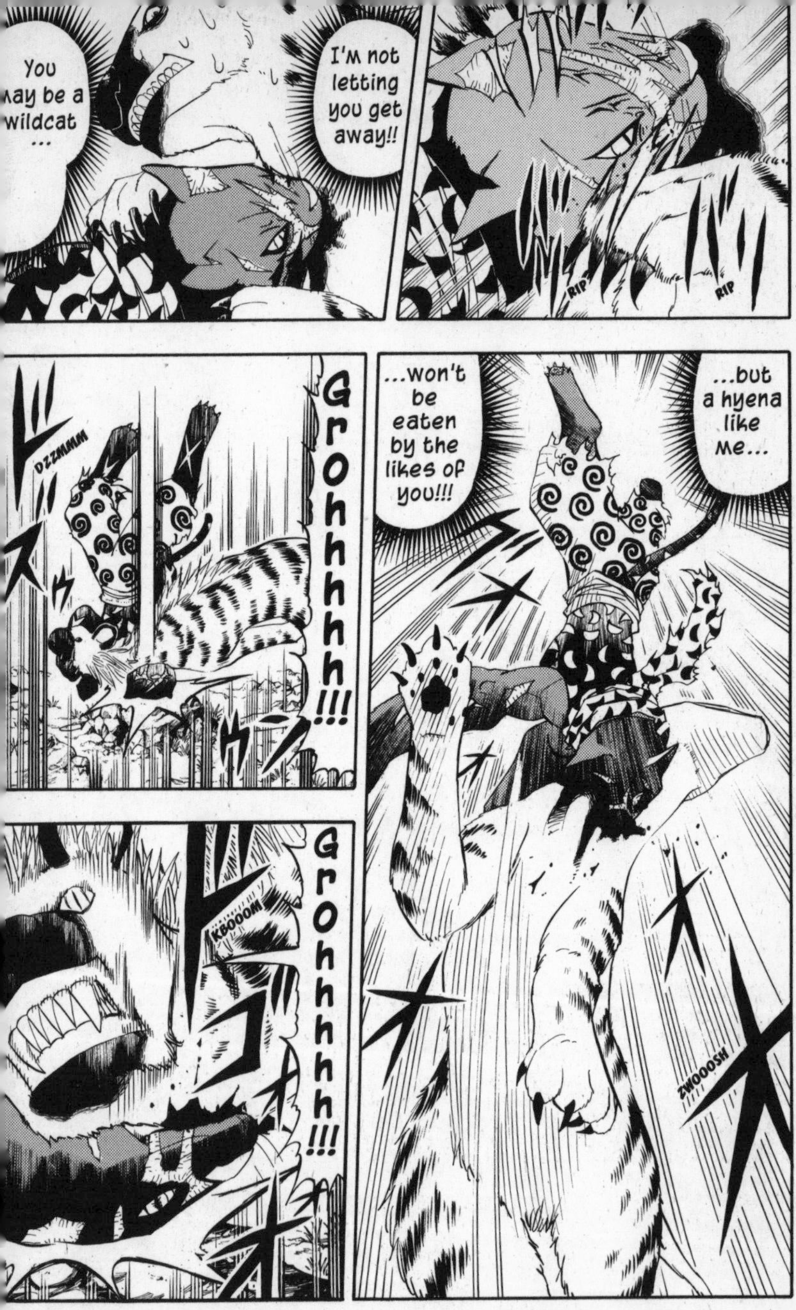
RIP
RIP
I'm not letting you get away!!
You may be a wildcat ...
...but a hyena like me...
...won't be eaten by the likes of you!!!
ZWOOOSH
DZZMMM
Grohhhhh!!!
KBOOOM
Grohhhhh!!!

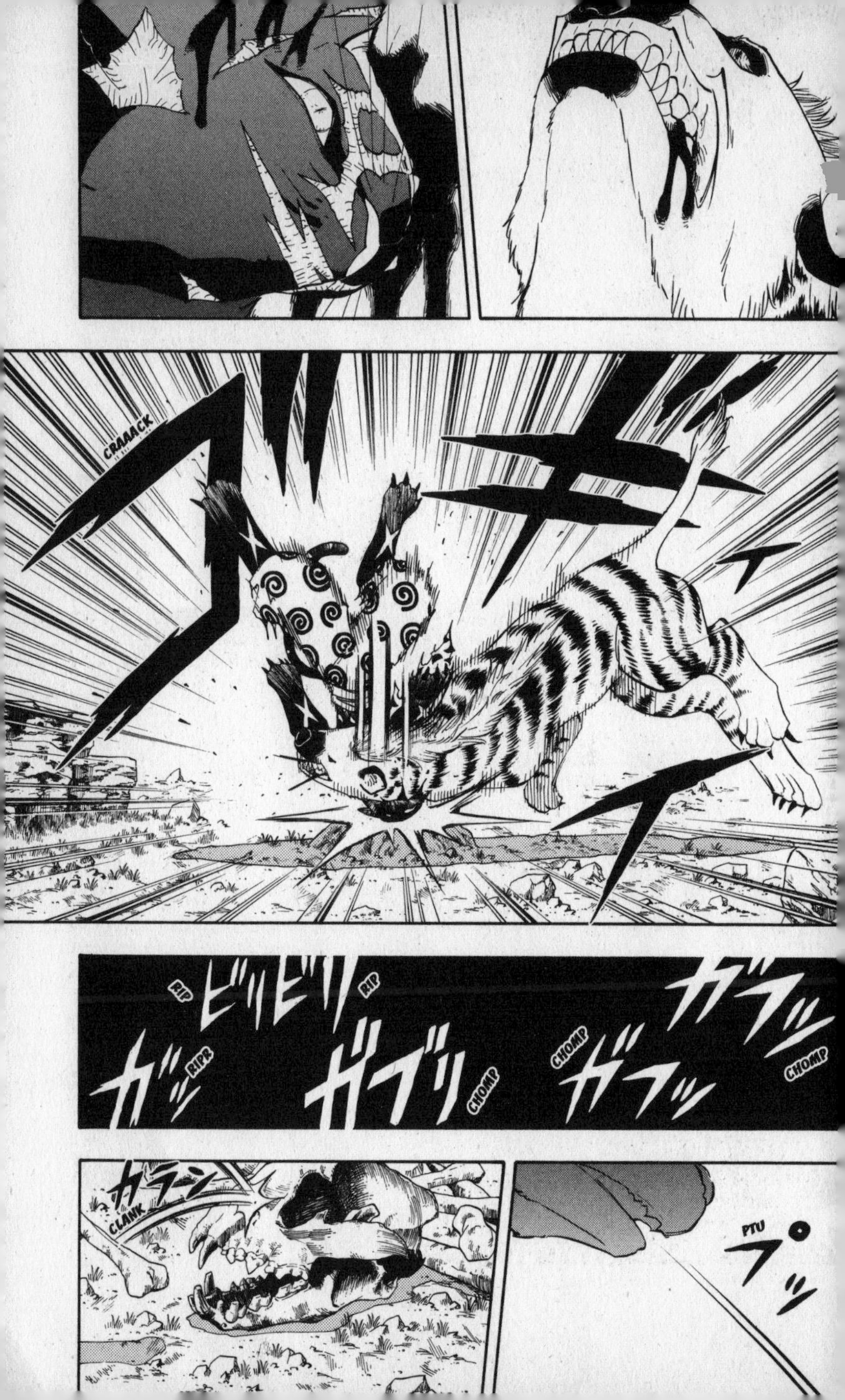
CRAAACK
CHOMP
CHOMP
CHOMP
RIP
RIP
RIPR
PTU
CLANK

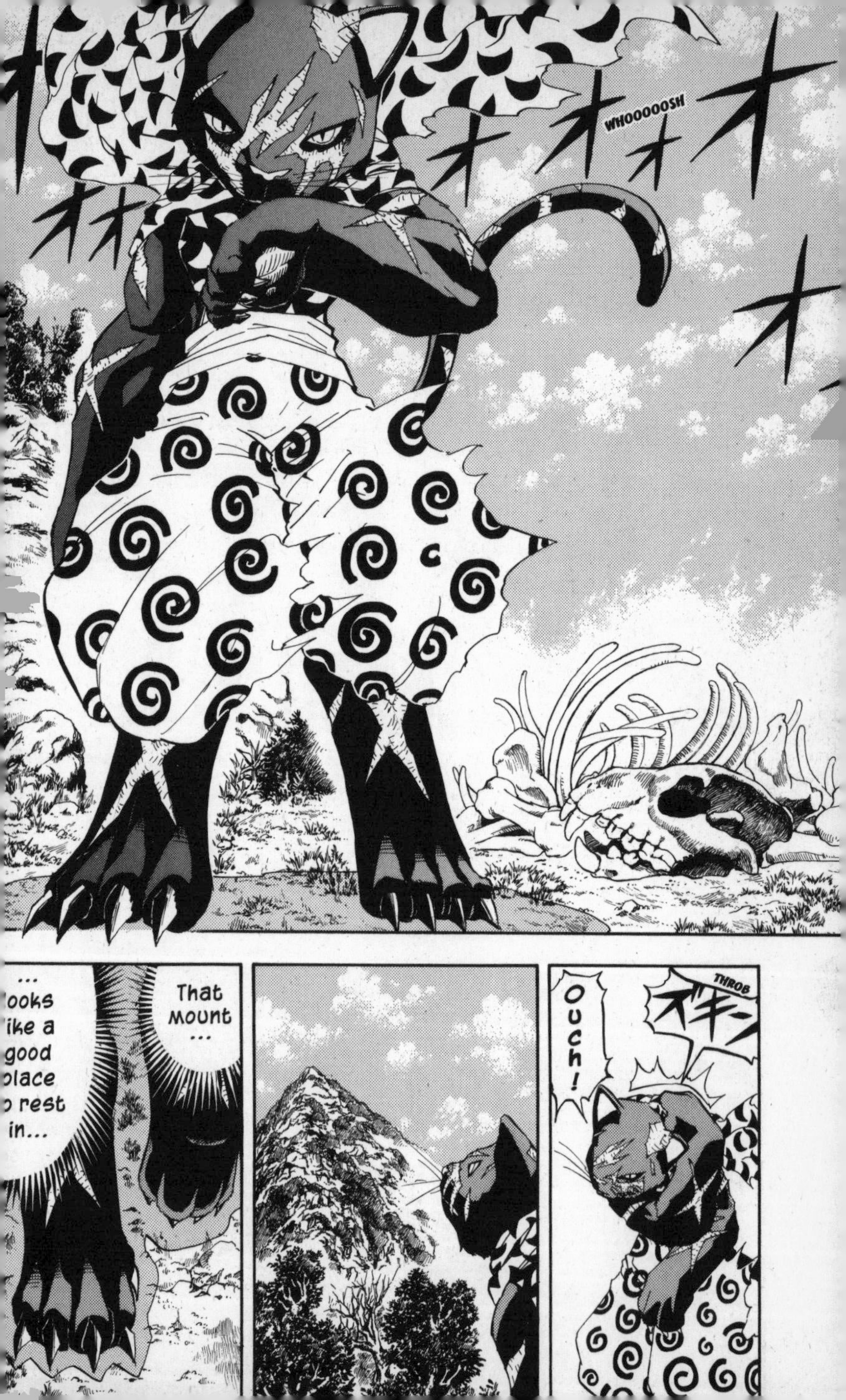
WHOOOOOSH
THROB
Ouch!
That mount ...
... ooks ike a good lace o rest in...

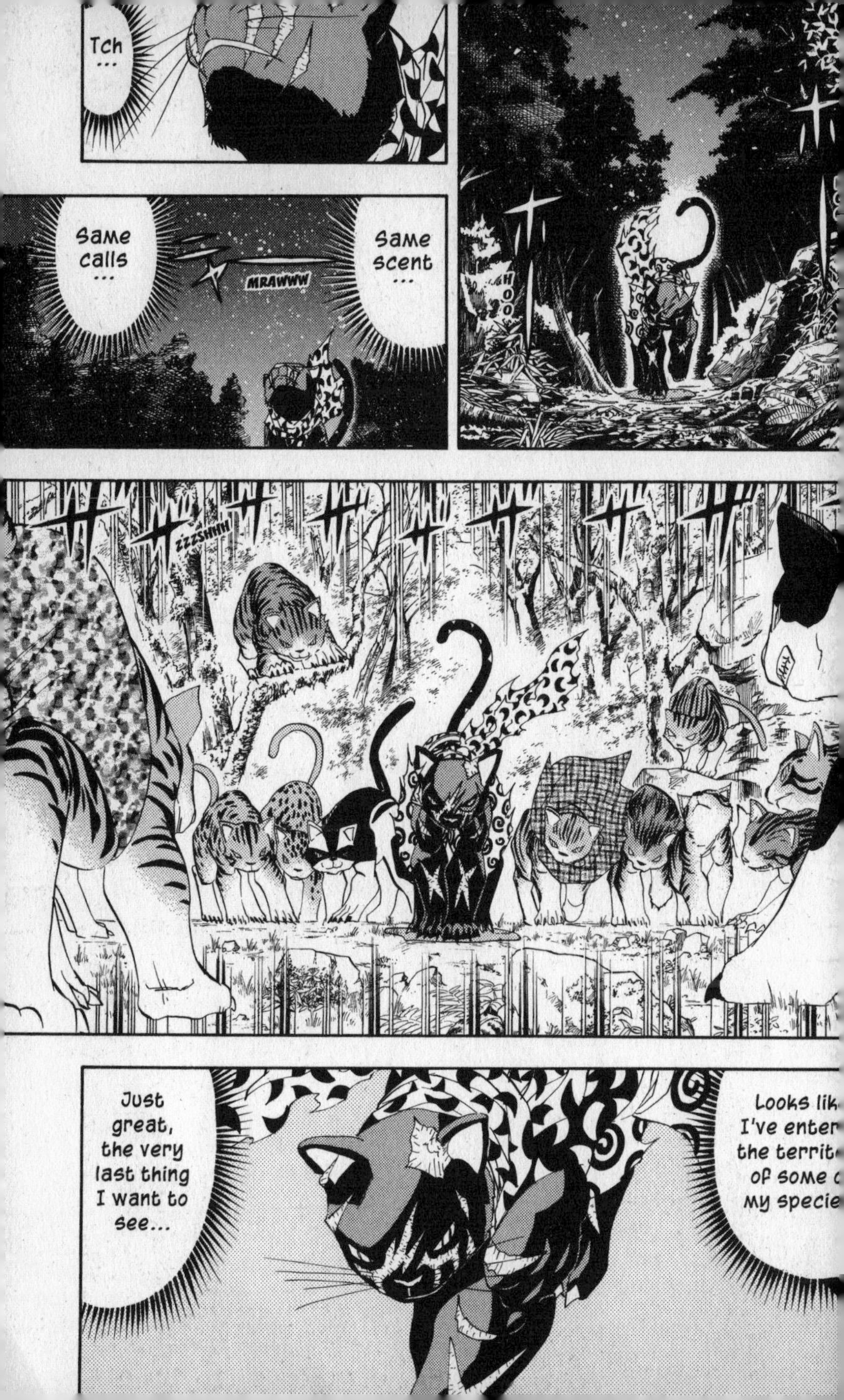
HOO
Tch ...
Same scent ...
MRAWWW
Same calls ...
ZZZSHHH
Looks lik I've enter the territ of some o my specie
Just great, the very last thing I want to see...

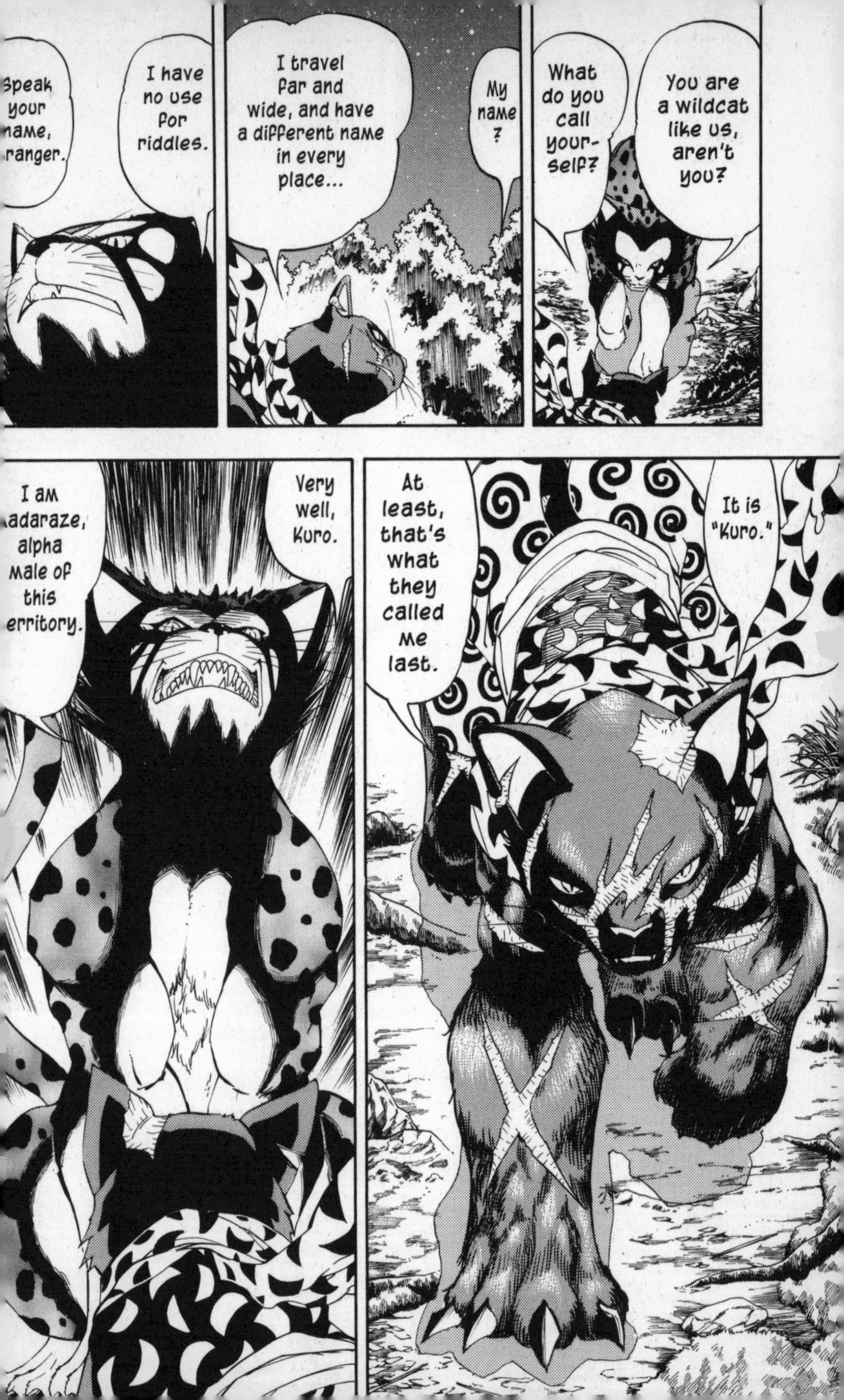
You are a wildcat like us, aren't you?
What do you call your-self?
My name?
I travel far and wide, and have a different name in every place...
I have no use for riddles.
Speak your name, ranger.
It is "Kuro."
At least, that's what they called me last.
Very well, Kuro.
I am adaraze, alpha male of this erritory.

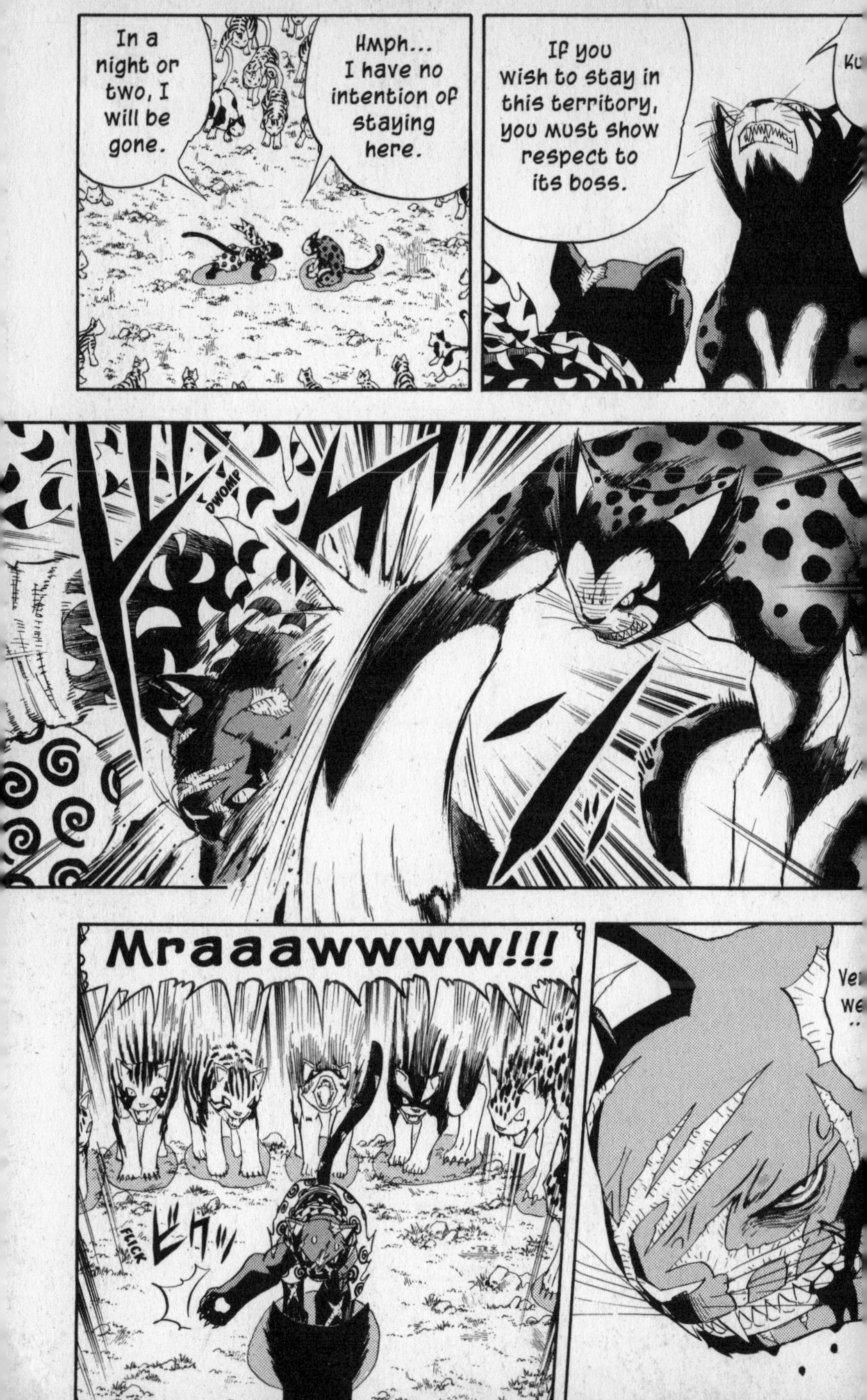
Ku
If you wish to stay in this territory, you must show respect to its boss.
Hmph... I have no intention of staying here.
In a night or two, I will be gone.
DWOMP
Ve
we
Mraaawwww!!!
ビクッ
FLICK

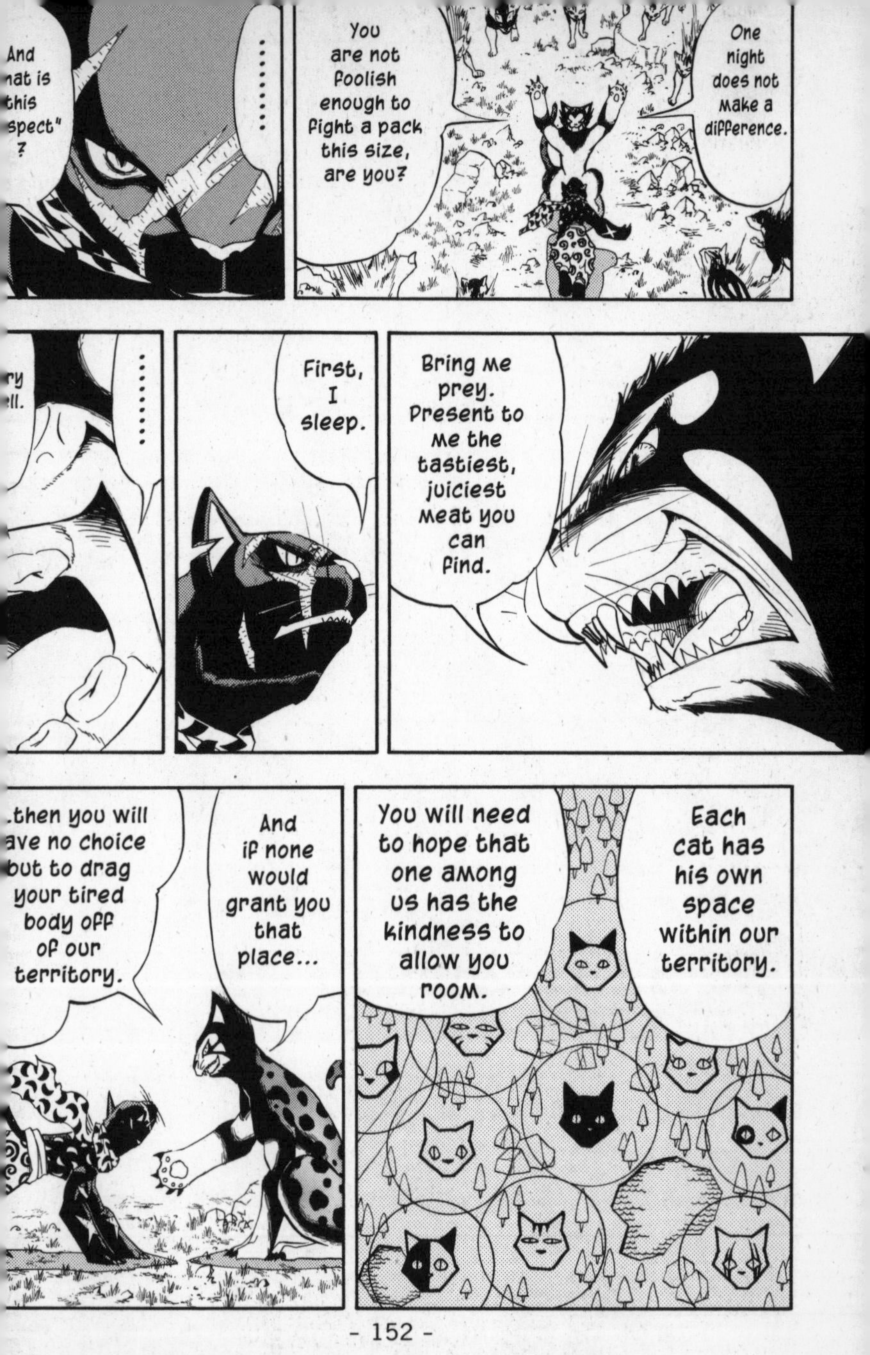
One night does not make a difference.
You are not foolish enough to fight a pack this size, are you?
....
And nat is this spect" ?
Bring me prey. Present to me the tastiest, juiciest meat you can find.
First, I sleep.
....
Each cat has his own space within our territory.
You will need to hope that one among us has the kindness to allow you room.
And if none would grant you that place...
.then you will ave no choice but to drag your tired body off of our territory.

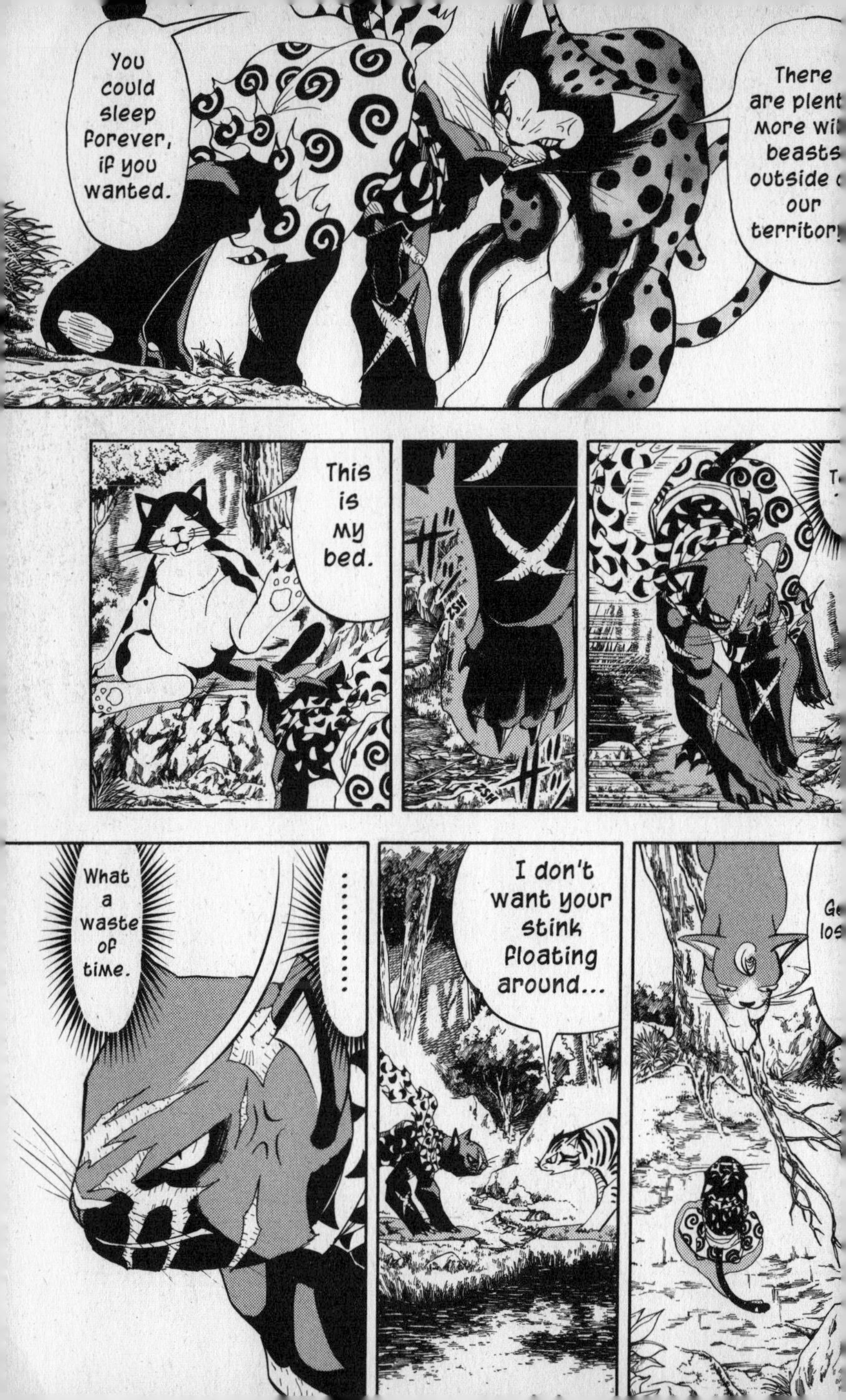
There are plent More wi beasts outside our territor
You could sleep forever, if you wanted.
ZSH
ZSH
This is my bed.
Ge los
I don't want your stink floating around...
....
What a waste of time.

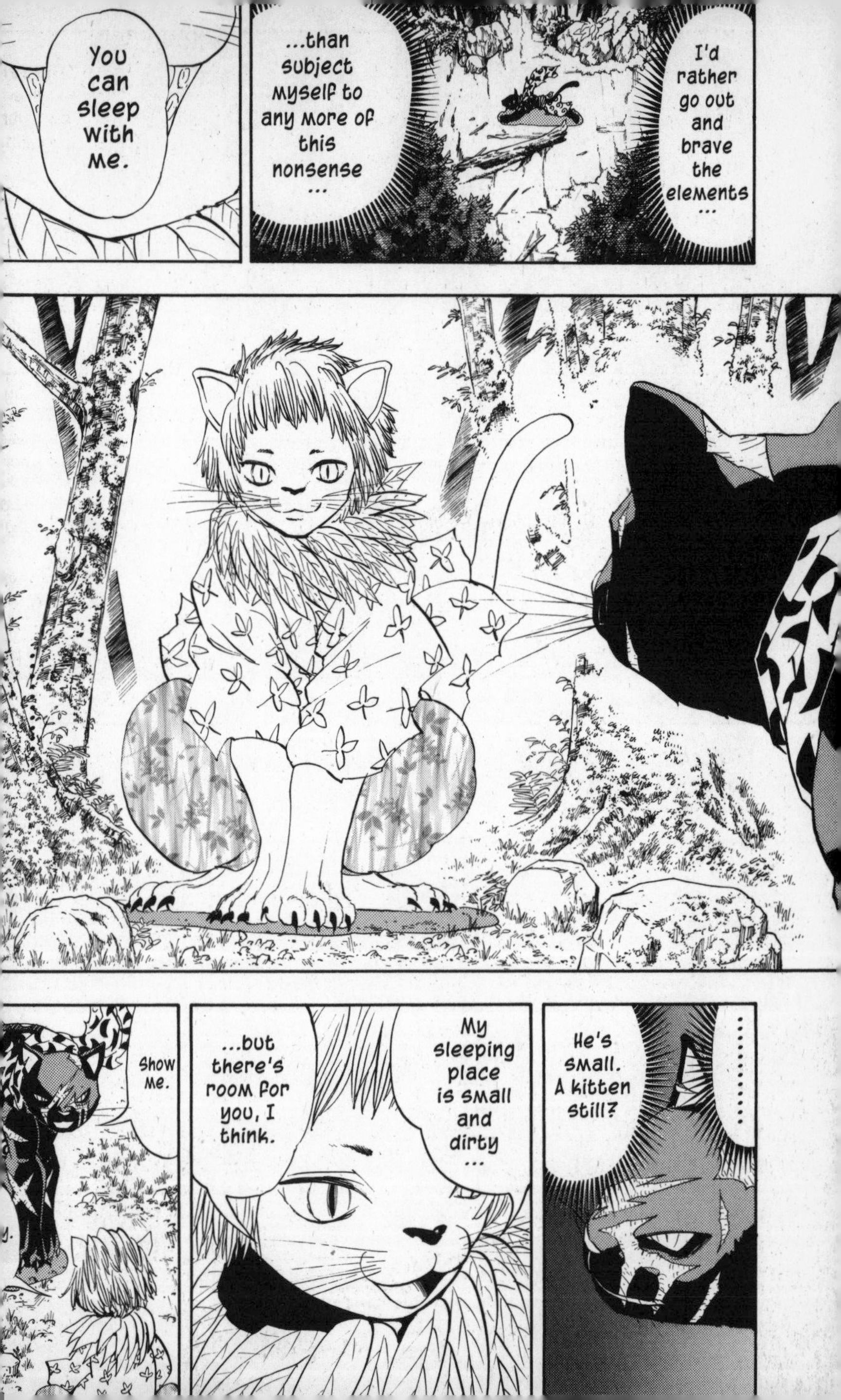
I'd rather go out and brave the elements ...
...than subject myself to any more of this nonsense ...
You can sleep with me.
......
He's small. A kitten still?
My sleeping place is small and dirty ...
...but there's room for you, I think.
Show me.

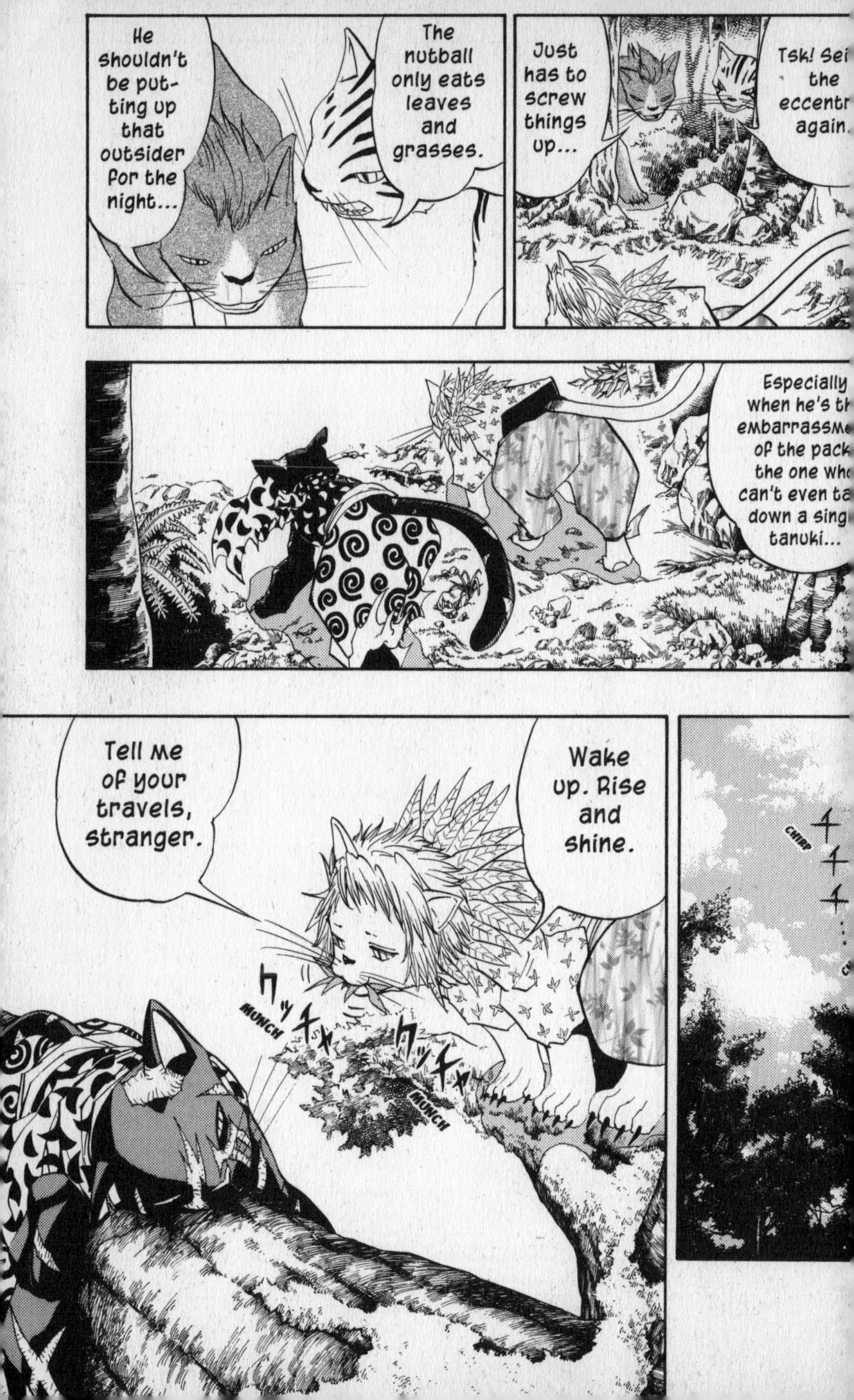

Tsk! Sei the eccentr again.
Just has to screw things up...
The nutball only eats leaves and grasses.
He shouldn't be putting up that outsider for the night...
Especially when he's th embarrassm of the pack the one wh can't even ta down a sing tanuki...
CHIRP
Wake up. Rise and shine.
Tell me of your travels, stranger.
MUNCH
MUNCH

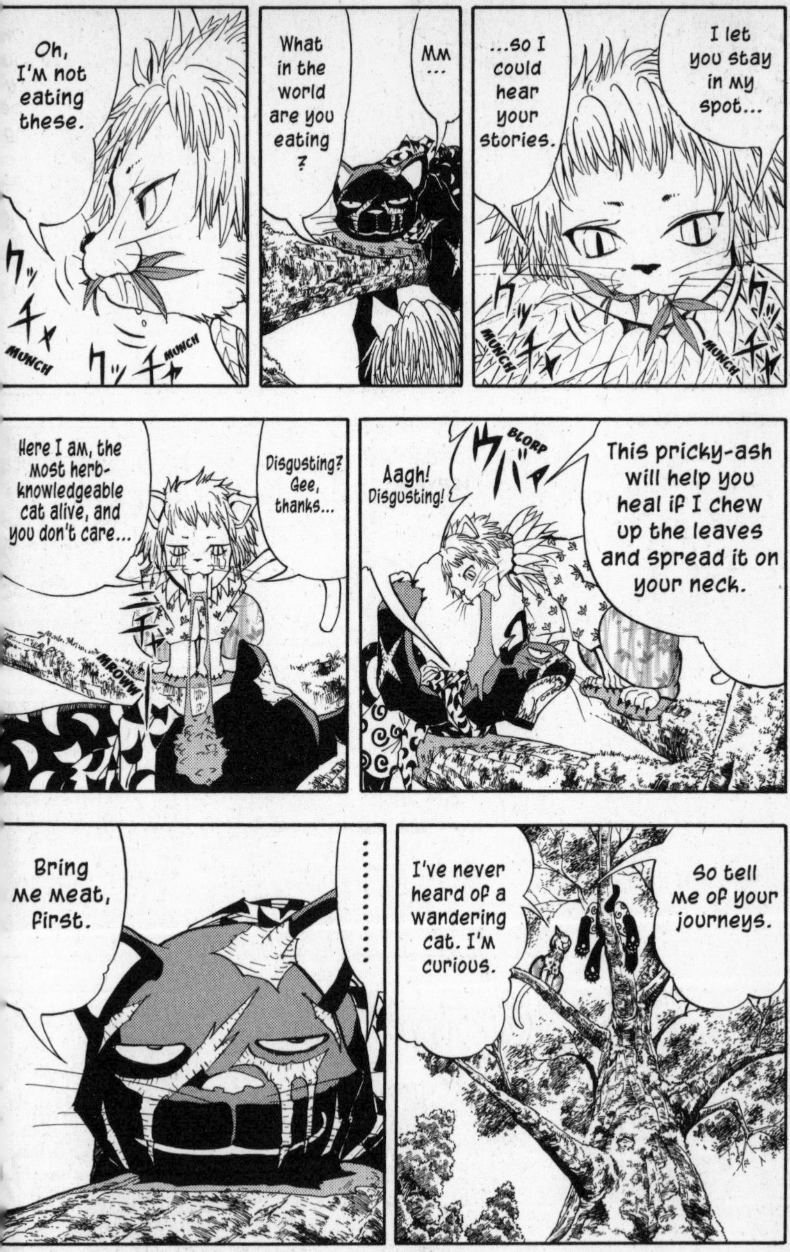
I let you stay in my spot...
...so I could hear your stories.
MUNCH
MUNCH
Mm...
What in the world are you eating?
Oh, I'm not eating these.
MUNCH
MUNCH
This pricky-ash will help you heal if I chew up the leaves and spread it on your neck.
BLORP
Aagh! Disgusting!
Disgusting? Gee, thanks...
Here I am, the most herb-knowledgeable cat alive, and you don't care...
MROWW
So tell me of your journeys.
I've never heard of a wandering cat. I'm curious.
......
Bring me meat, first.

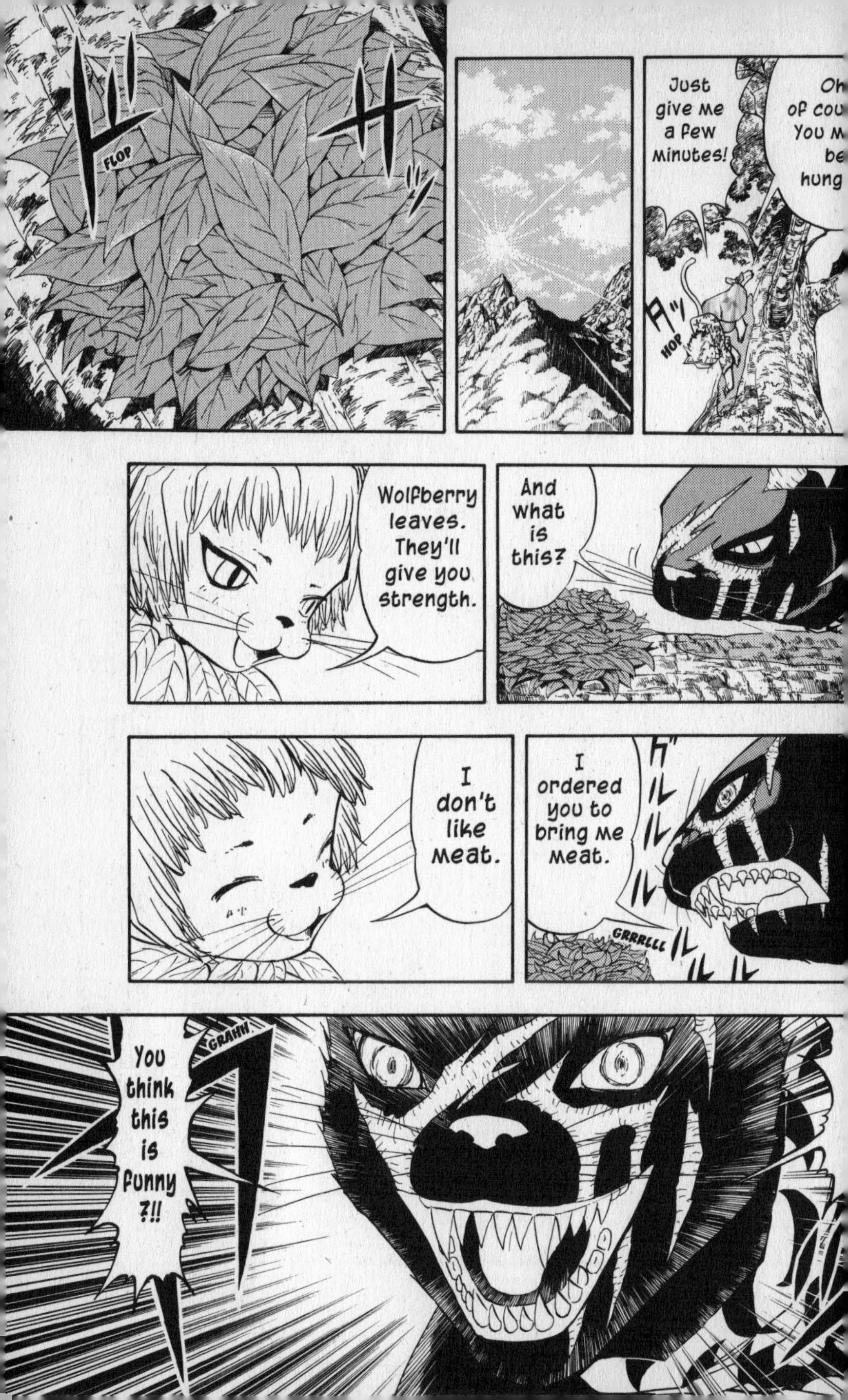
Oh of cou You m be hung
Just give me a few minutes!
HOP
FLOP
And what is this?
Wolfberry leaves. They'll give you strength.
I ordered you to bring me meat.
GRRRLLL
I don't like meat.
GRAHH
You think this is funny ?!!

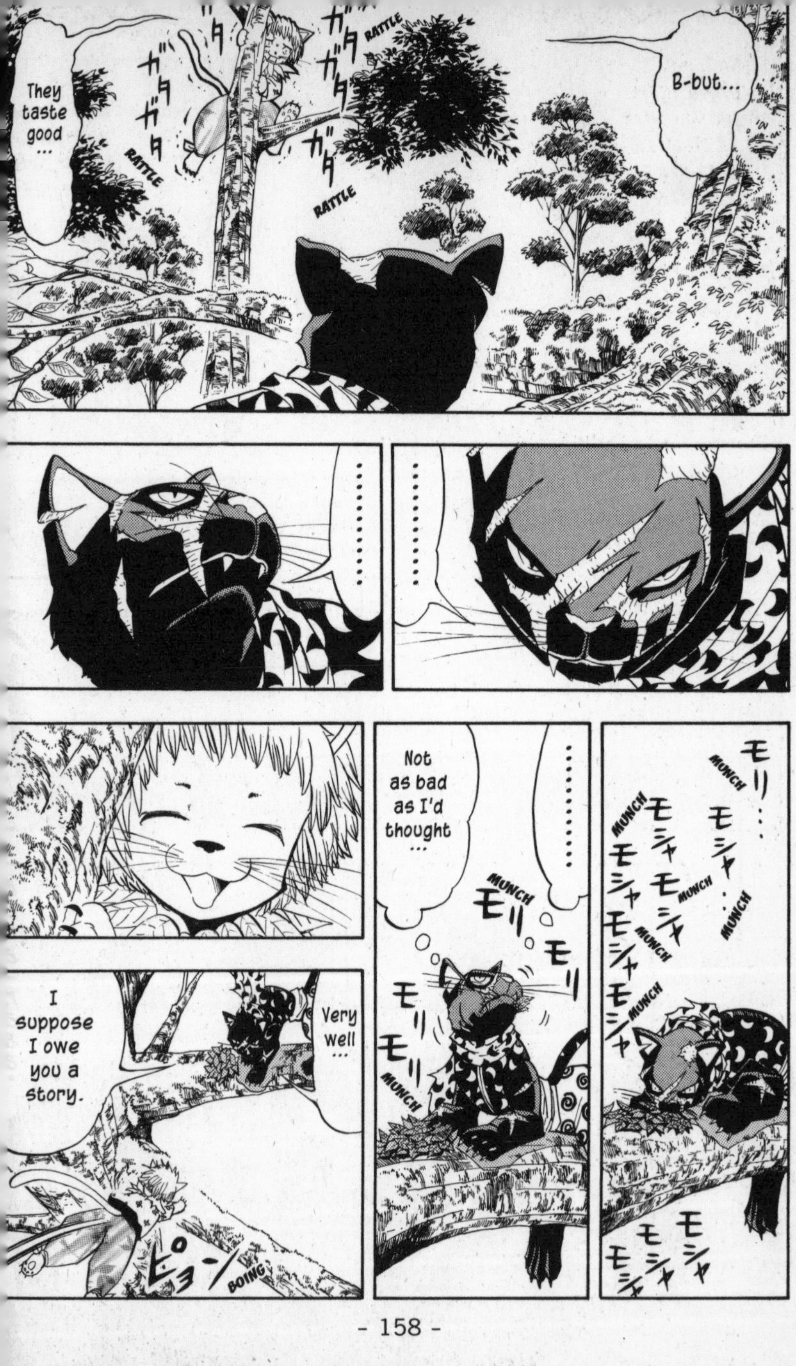
B-but...
ガタ ガタ ガタ RATTLE
ガタ ガタ RATTLE
ガタ RATTLE
They taste good ...
......
......
モリ... MUNCH
モシャ... MUNCH
モシャ モシャ MUNCH
モシャ モシャ MUNCH
モシャ モシャ MUNCH
モシャ モシャ
モシャ
......
Not as bad as I'd thought ...
モリ MUNCH
モリ
モリ モリ MUNCH
Very well ...
I suppose I owe you a story.
ピョーン BOING

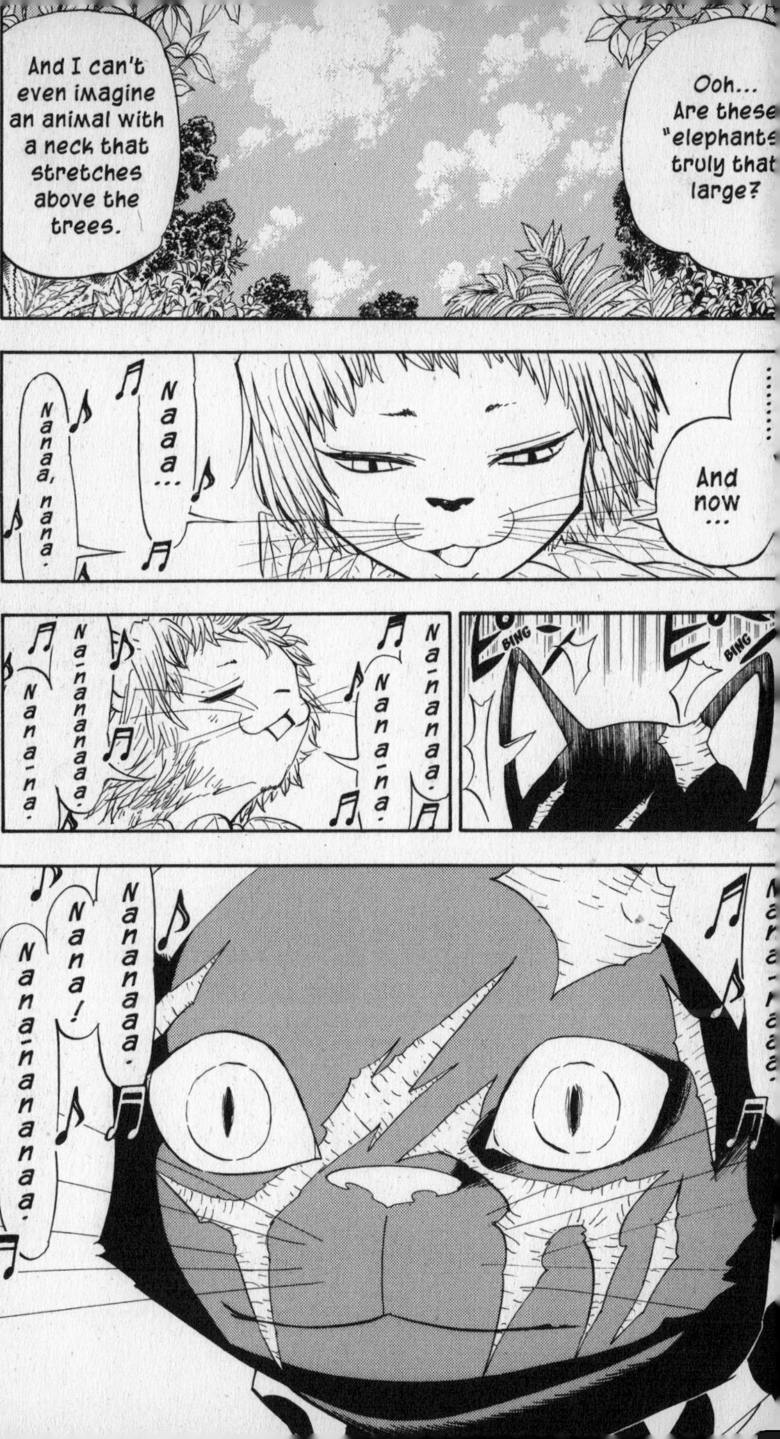
Ooh... Are these "elephants truly that large?
And I can't even imagine an animal with a neck that stretches above the trees.
......
And now...
Naaa...
Nanaa, nana.
BING
BING
Na-nanaa.
Nana-na.
Na-nanananaa.
Nana-na.
Nananaaa.
Nana!
Nana-nanananaa.

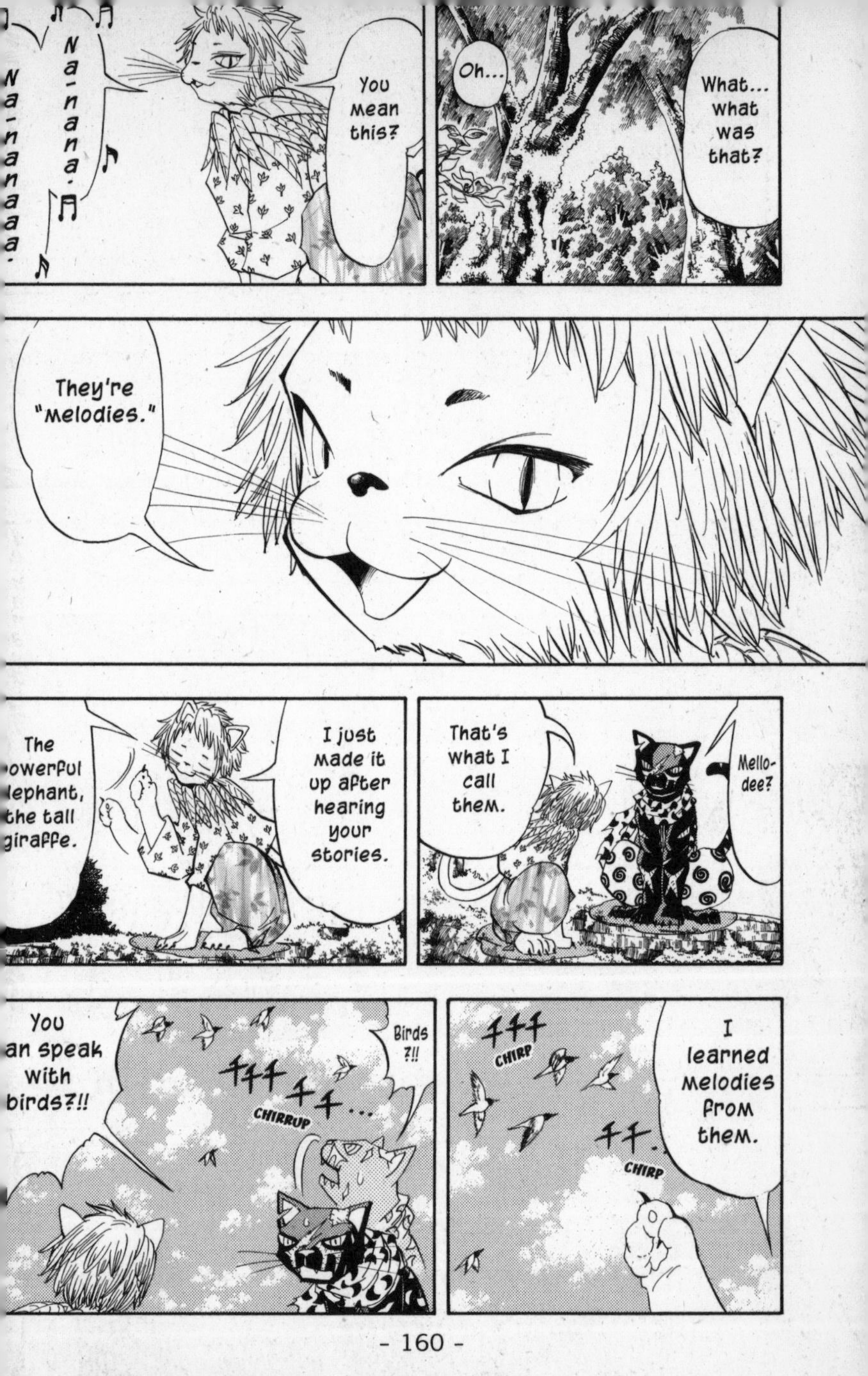
What... what was that?
Oh...
You mean this?
Na-nana-na.
Na-nanaaaa.
They're "melodies."
Mello-dee?
That's what I call them.
I just made it up after hearing your stories.
The owerful lephant, the tall giraffe.
I learned melodies from them.
チチチ
CHIRP
チチ.
CHIRP
Birds?!!
チチチ チチ...
CHIRRUP
You an speak with birds?!!

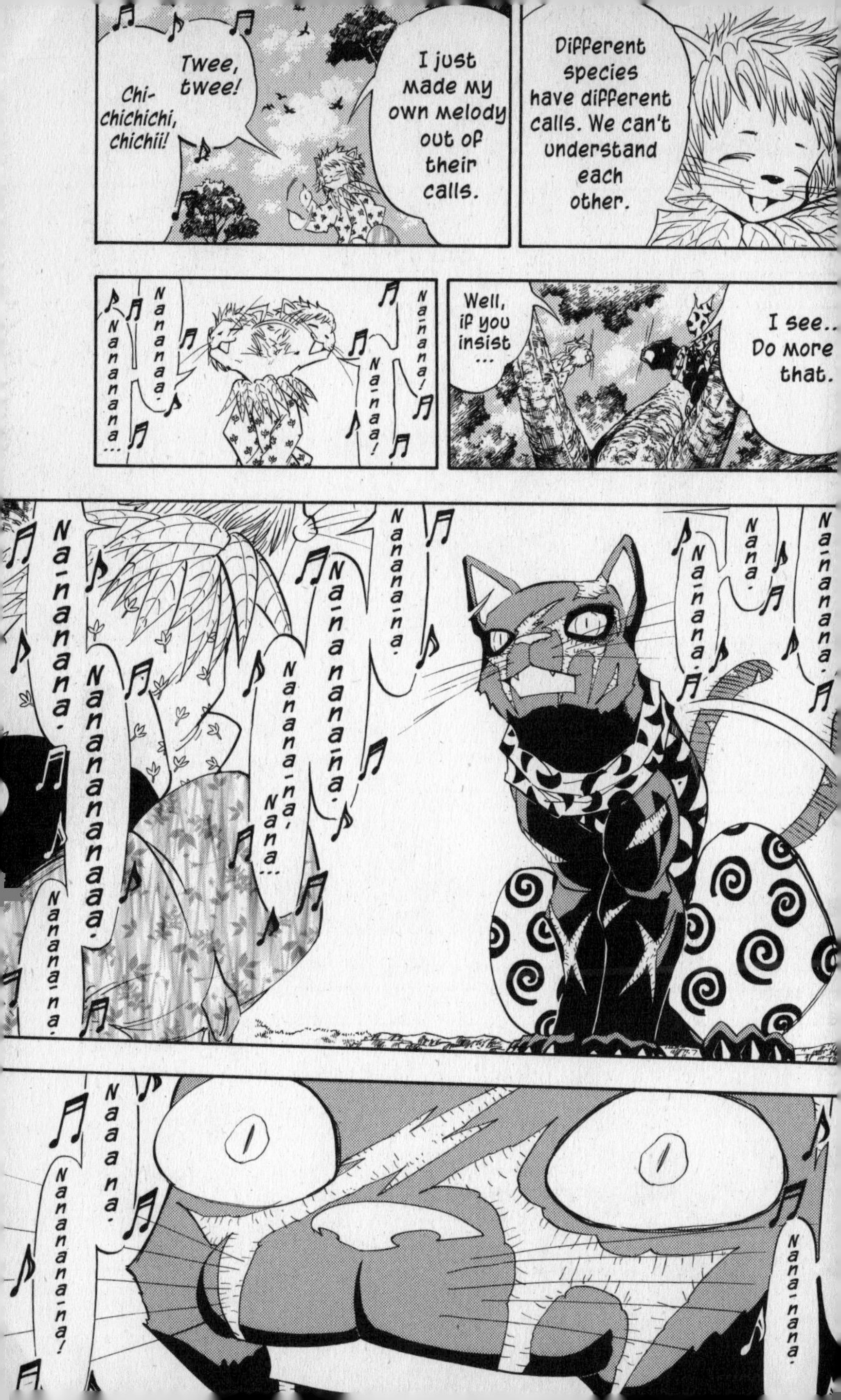

Different species have different calls. We can't understand each other.
I just made my own melody out of their calls.
Twee, twee!
Chi-chichichi, chichii!
I see.. Do more that.
Well, if you insist...
Na-nana!
Na-naa!
Nananaa.
Nananana...
Na-nanana.
Nana.
Na-nana-na.
Na-nana-na.
Na-nanana-na.
Nanana-na, Nana...
Nanananaaa.
Na-nanana.
Nanana-na-na.
Nana-nana.
Naaana.
Nanana-na-na!

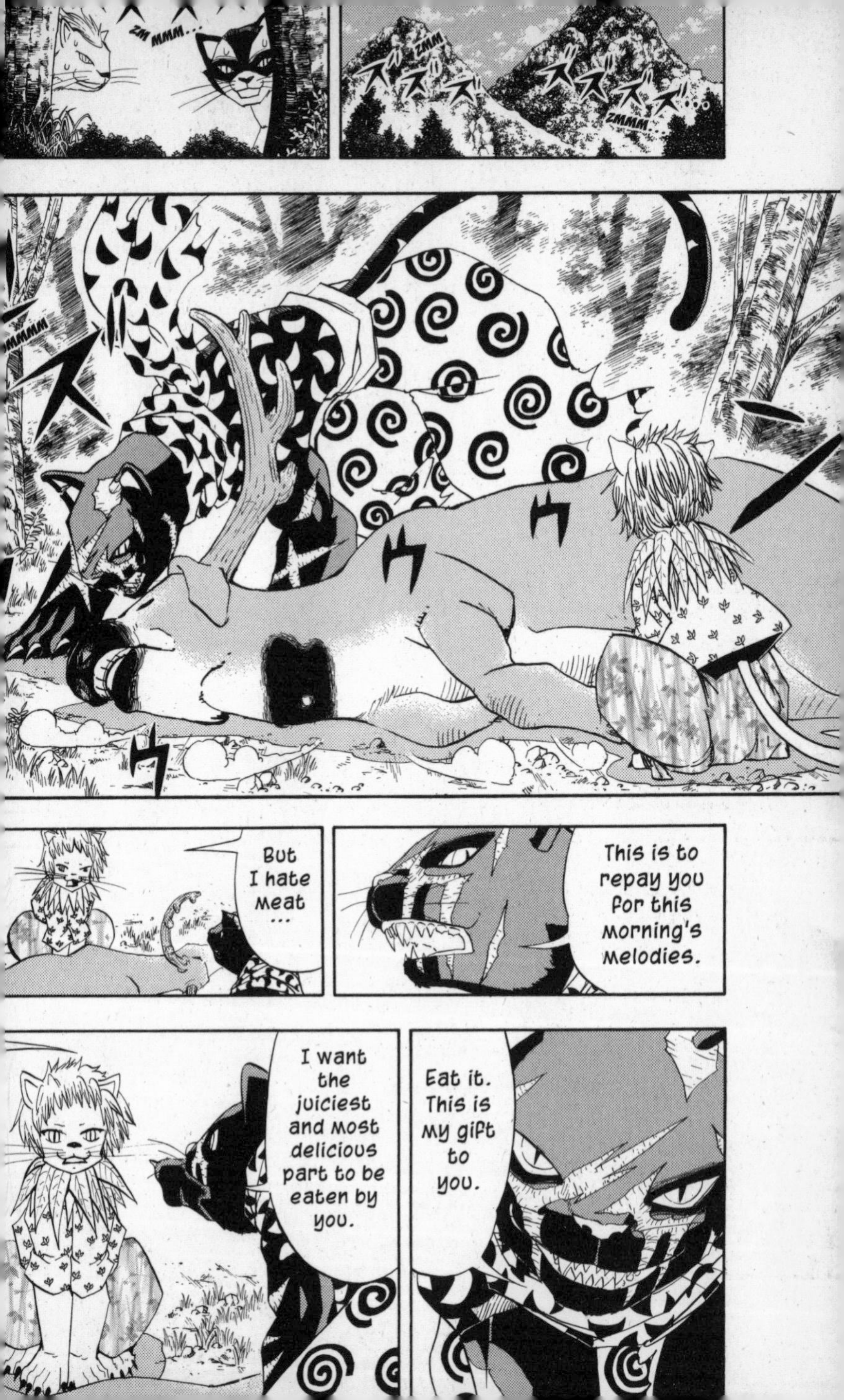
ZMM
ZMMM...
ZM MMM...
This is to repay you for this morning's melodies.
But I hate meat ...
Eat it. This is my gift to you.
I want the juiciest and most delicious part to be eaten by you.

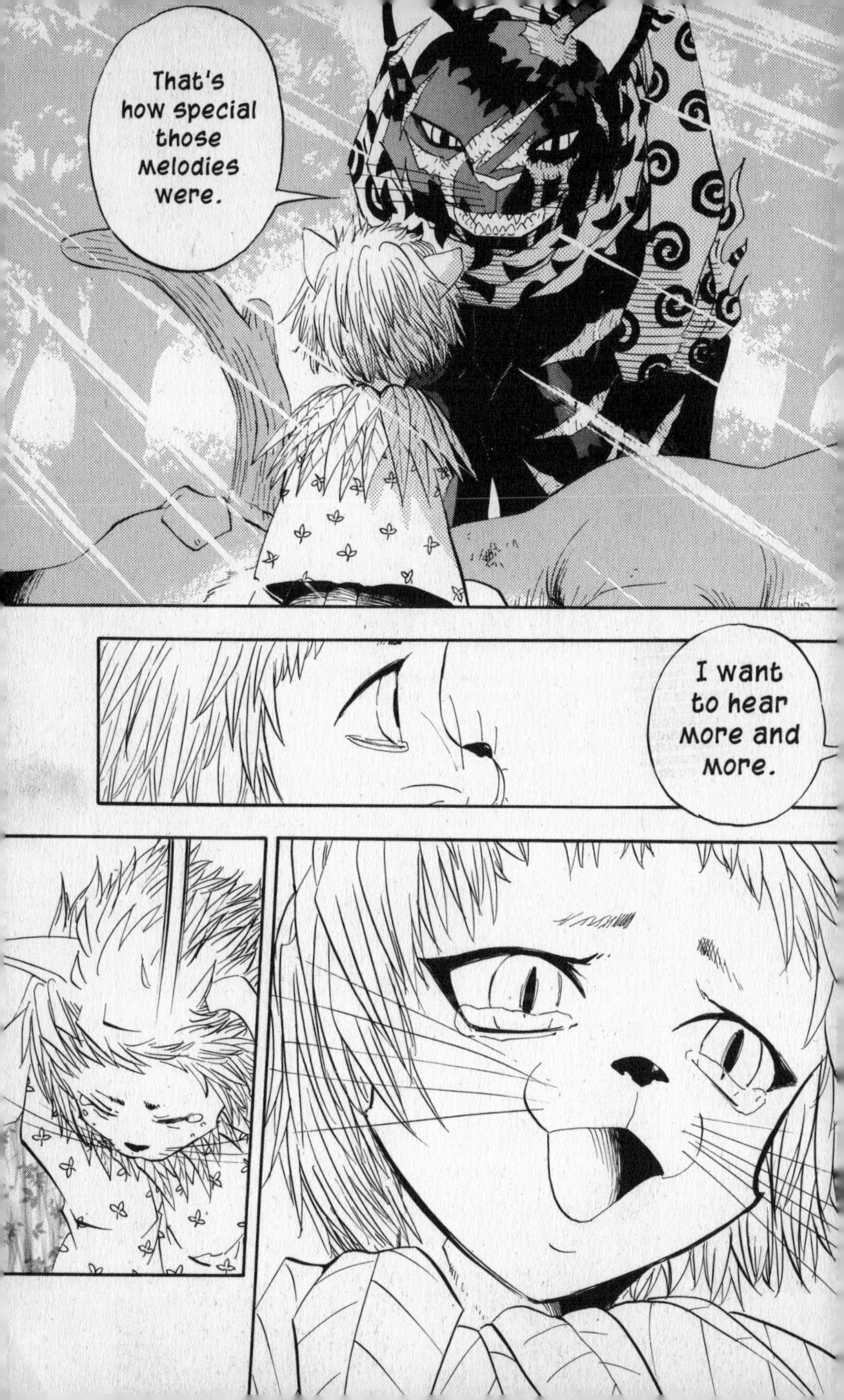
That's how special those melodies were.
I want to hear more and more.

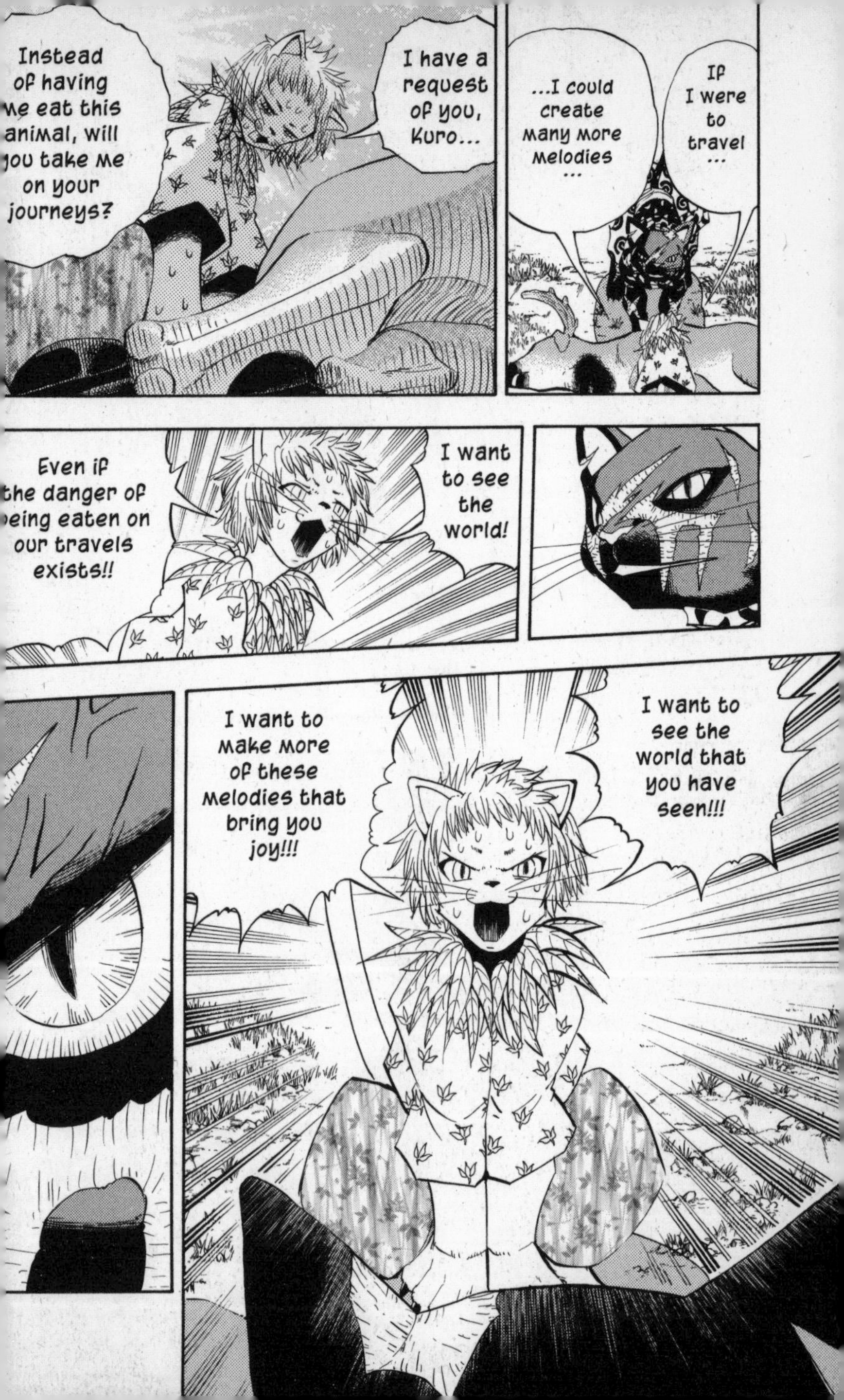
If I were to travel ...
...I could create many more melodies ...
I have a request of you, Kuro...
Instead of having me eat this animal, will you take me on your journeys?
I want to see the world!
Even if the danger of eing eaten on our travels exists!!
I want to see the world that you have seen!!!
I want to make more of these melodies that bring you joy!!!

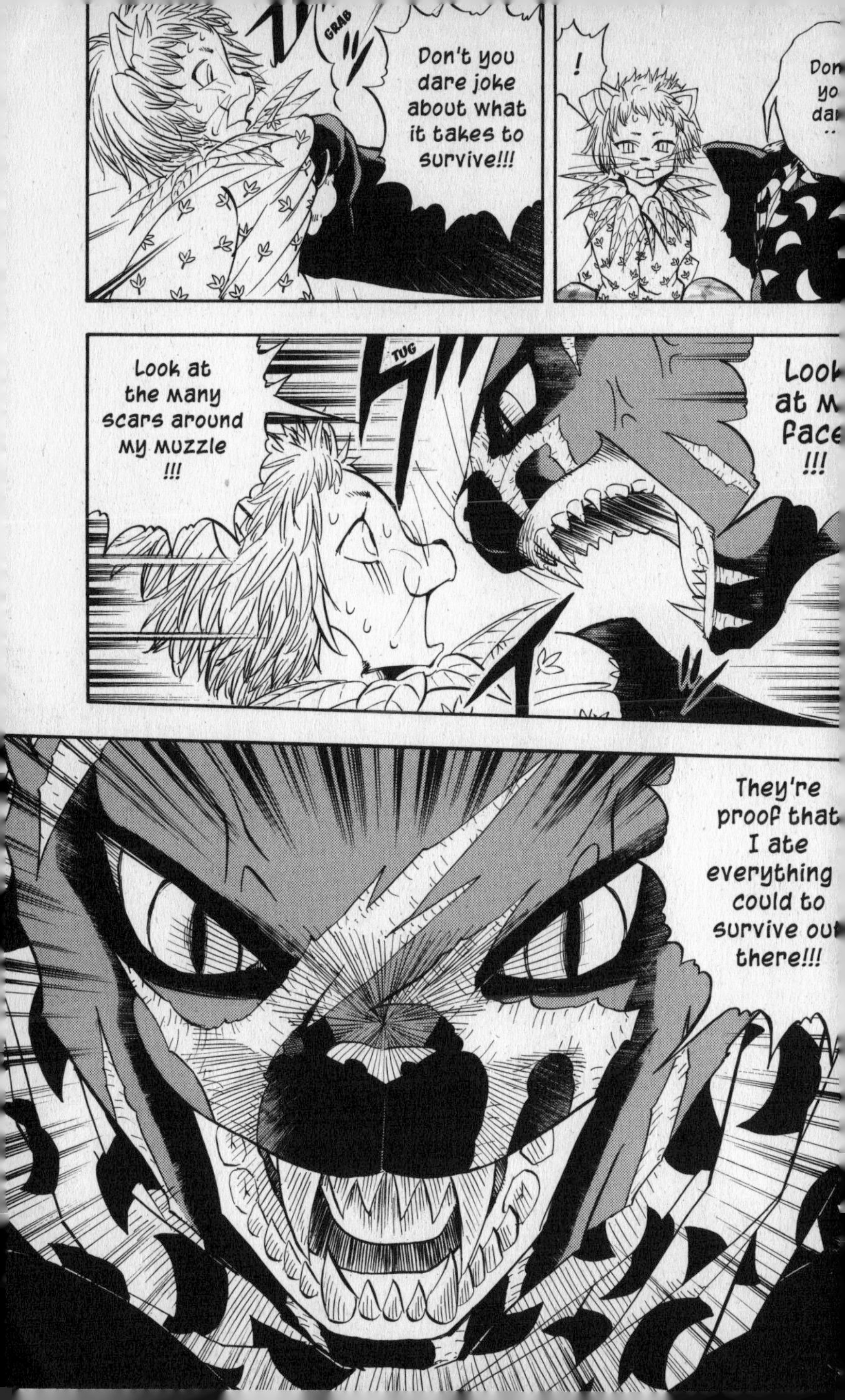

Don yo dar ..
!
GRAB
Don't you dare joke about what it takes to survive!!!
Look at M face !!!
TUG
Look at the many scars around my muzzle !!!
They're proof that I ate everything could to survive ou there!!!

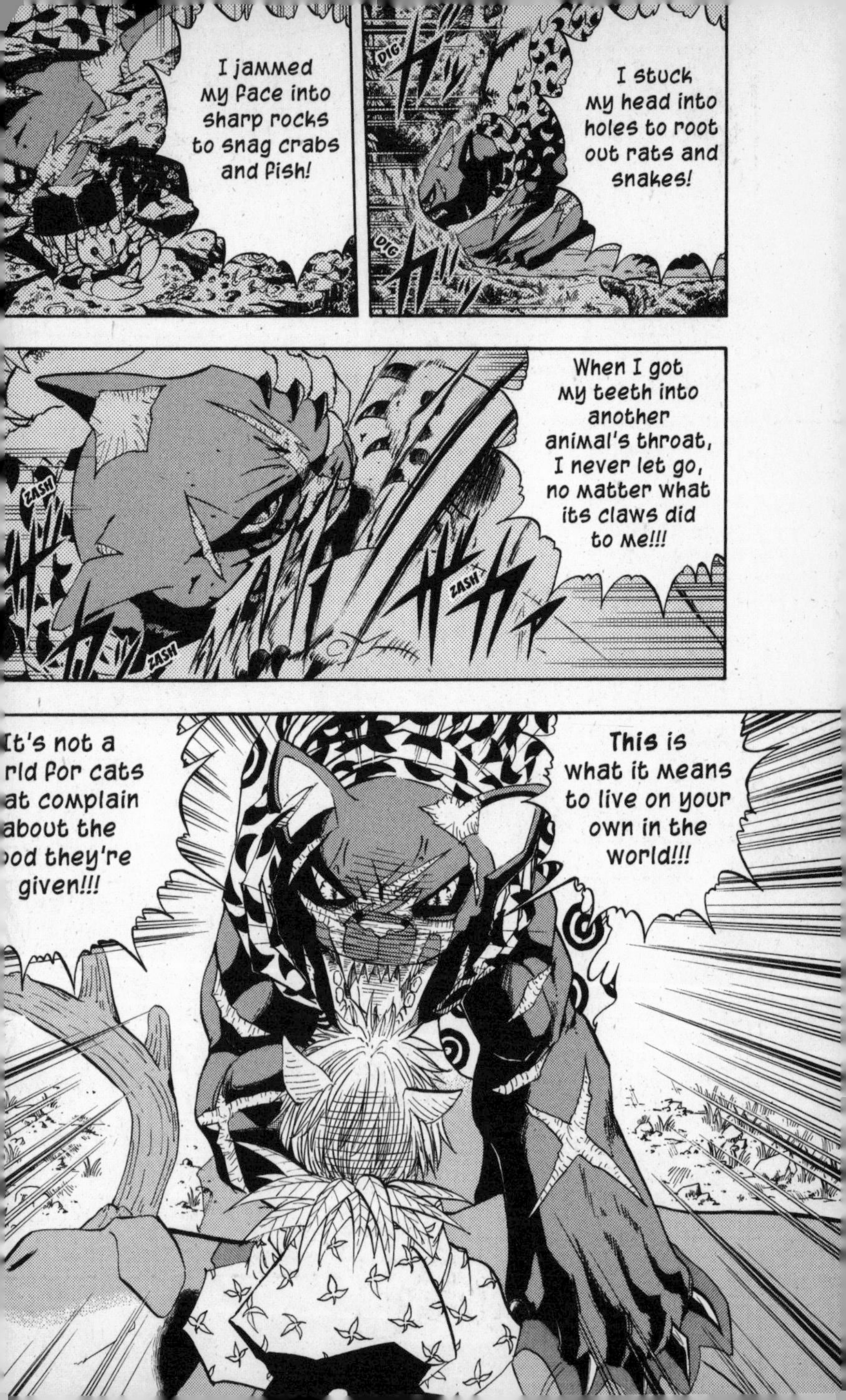
I stuck my head into holes to root out rats and snakes!
DIG
DIG
I jammed my face into sharp rocks to snag crabs and fish!
When I got my teeth into another animal's throat, I never let go, no matter what its claws did to me!!!
ZASH
ZASH
ZASH
This is what it means to live on your own in the world!!!
It's not a rld for cats at complain about the od they're given!!!

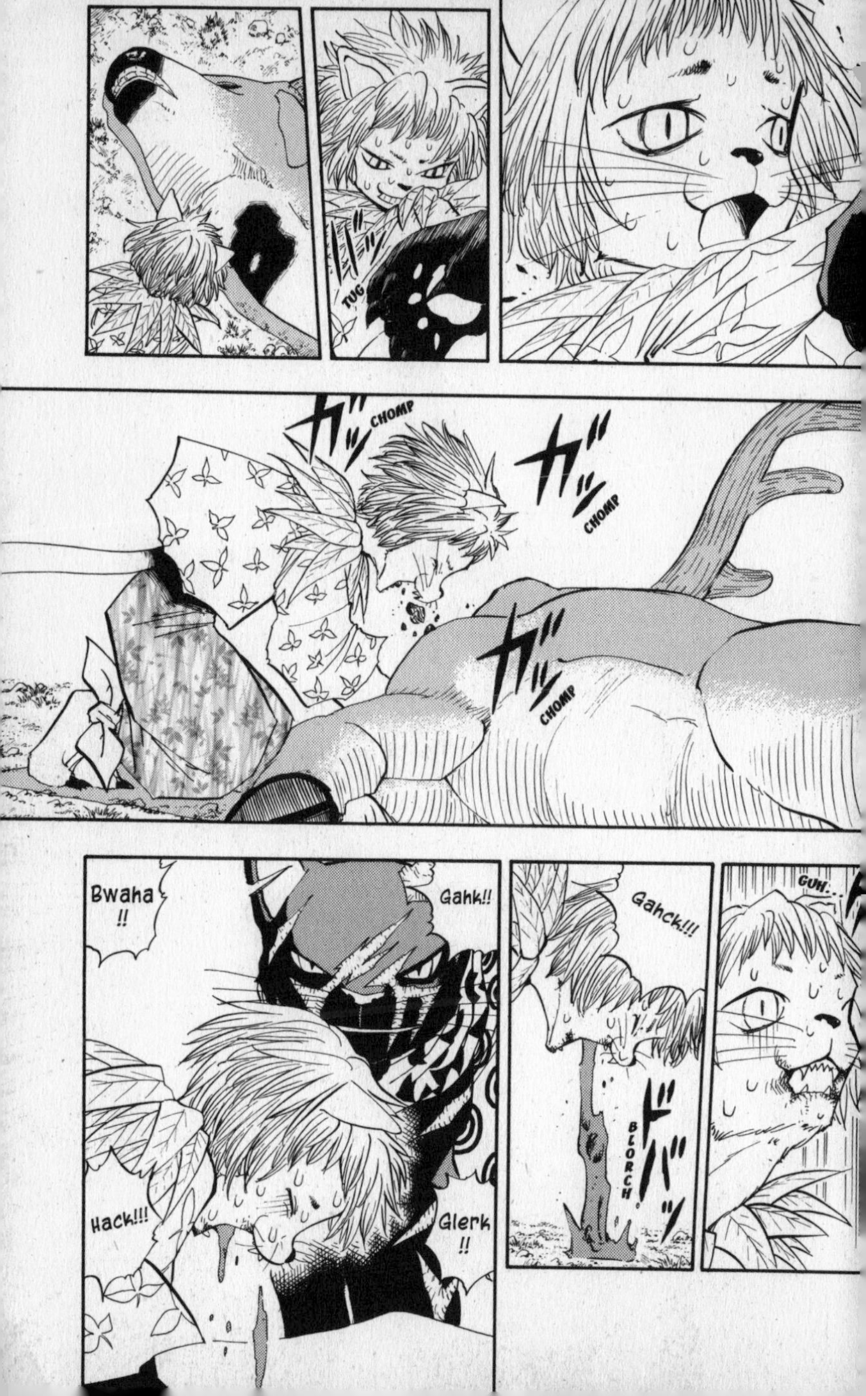
TUG
ガッ
CHOMP
ガッ
CHOMP
ガッ
CHOMP
GUH...
Gahck!!!
ドバッ
BLORCH
Gahk!!
Bwaha!!
Glerk!!
Hack!!!

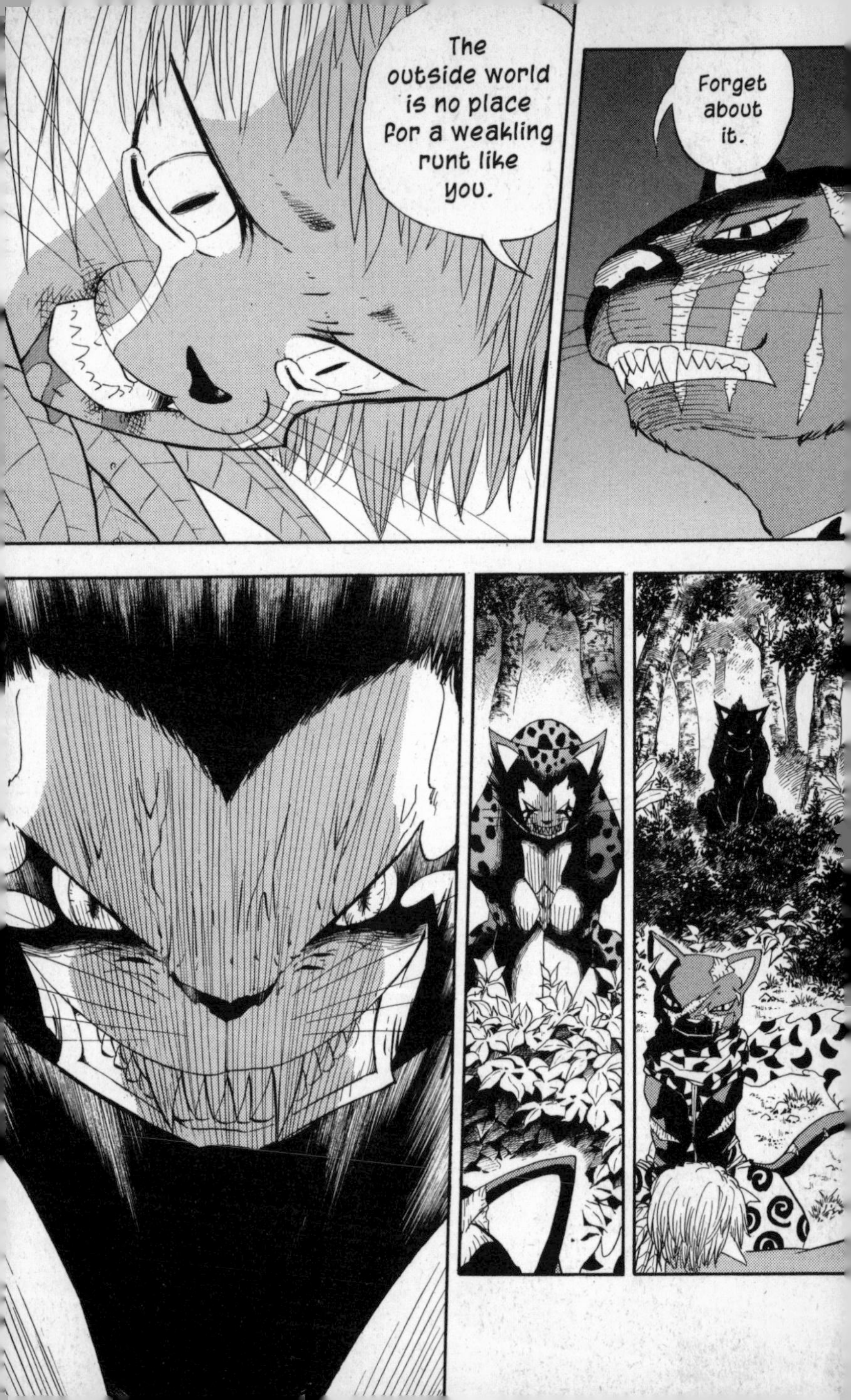
Forget about it.
The outside world is no place for a weakling runt like you.

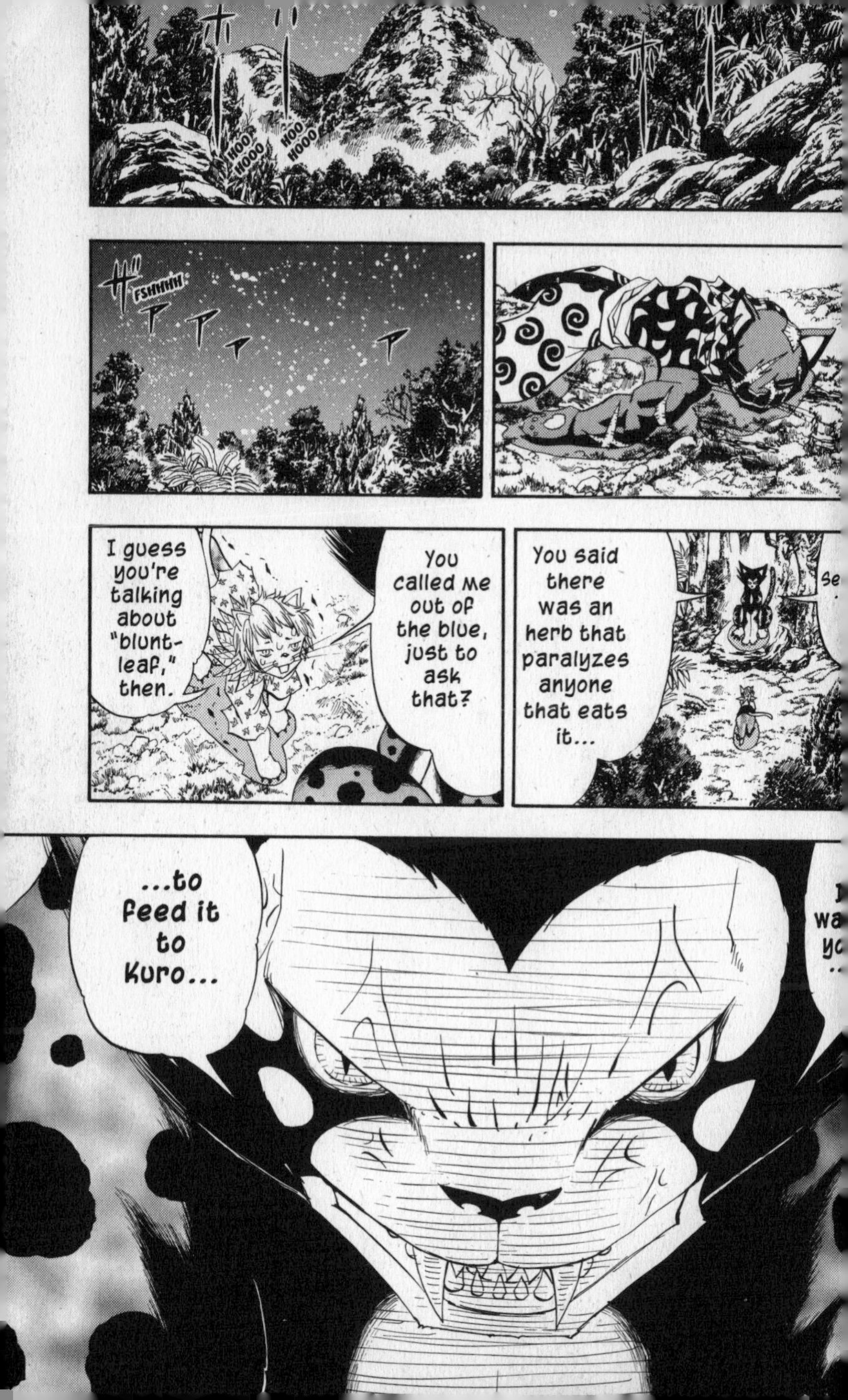
HOO HOOO
HOO HOOO
FSHHHH
You said there was an herb that paralyzes anyone that eats it...
You called me out of the blue, just to ask that?
I guess you're talking about "blunt-leaf," then.
...to feed it to Kuro...

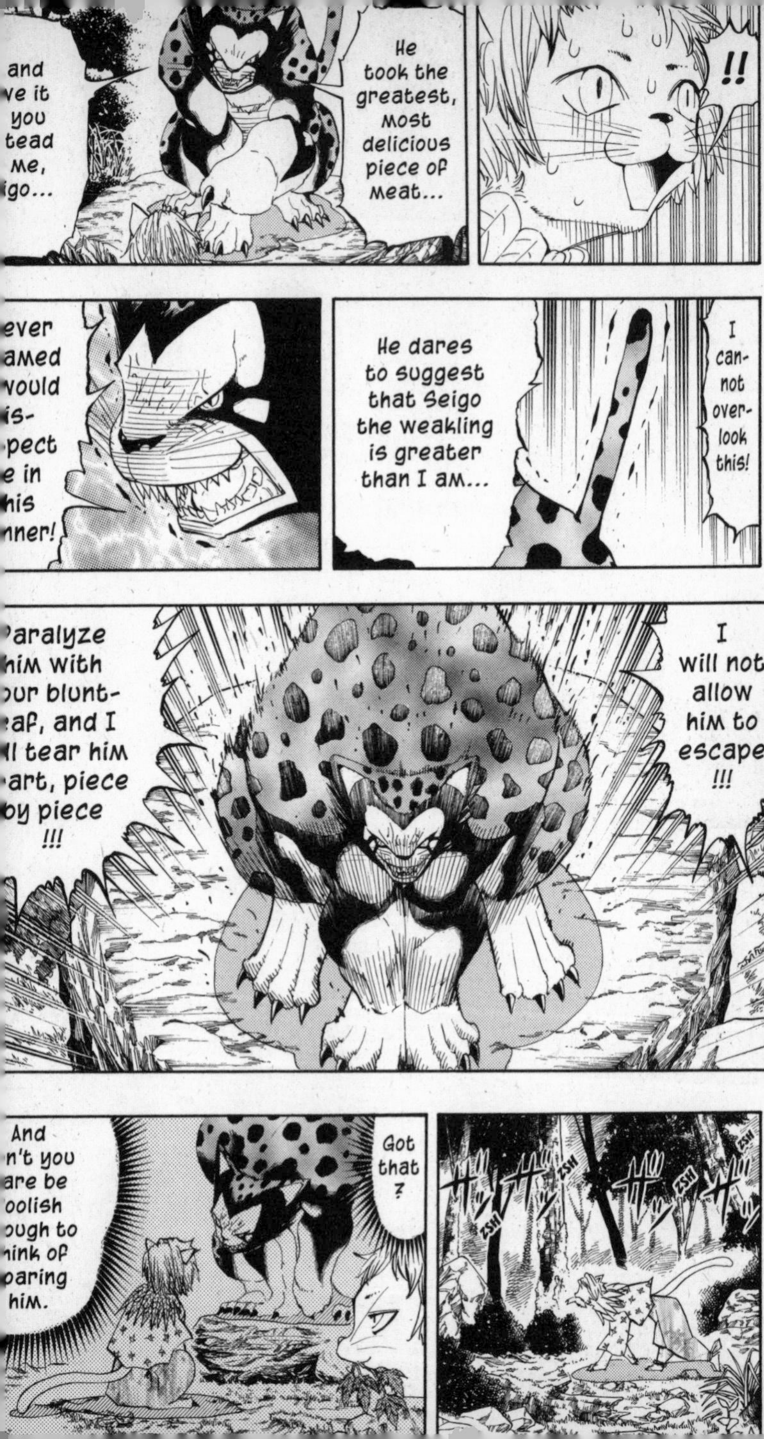
!!
He took the greatest, most delicious piece of meat...
and ve it you tead me, igo...
I can-not over-look this!
He dares to suggest that Seigo the weakling is greater than I am...
ever amed vould is- pect e in his nner!
I will not allow him to escape !!!
Paralyze him with our blunt- af, and I ll tear him art, piece by piece !!!
ZSH
ZSH
ZSH
ZSH
And n't you are be oolish ough to hink of paring him.
Got that ?

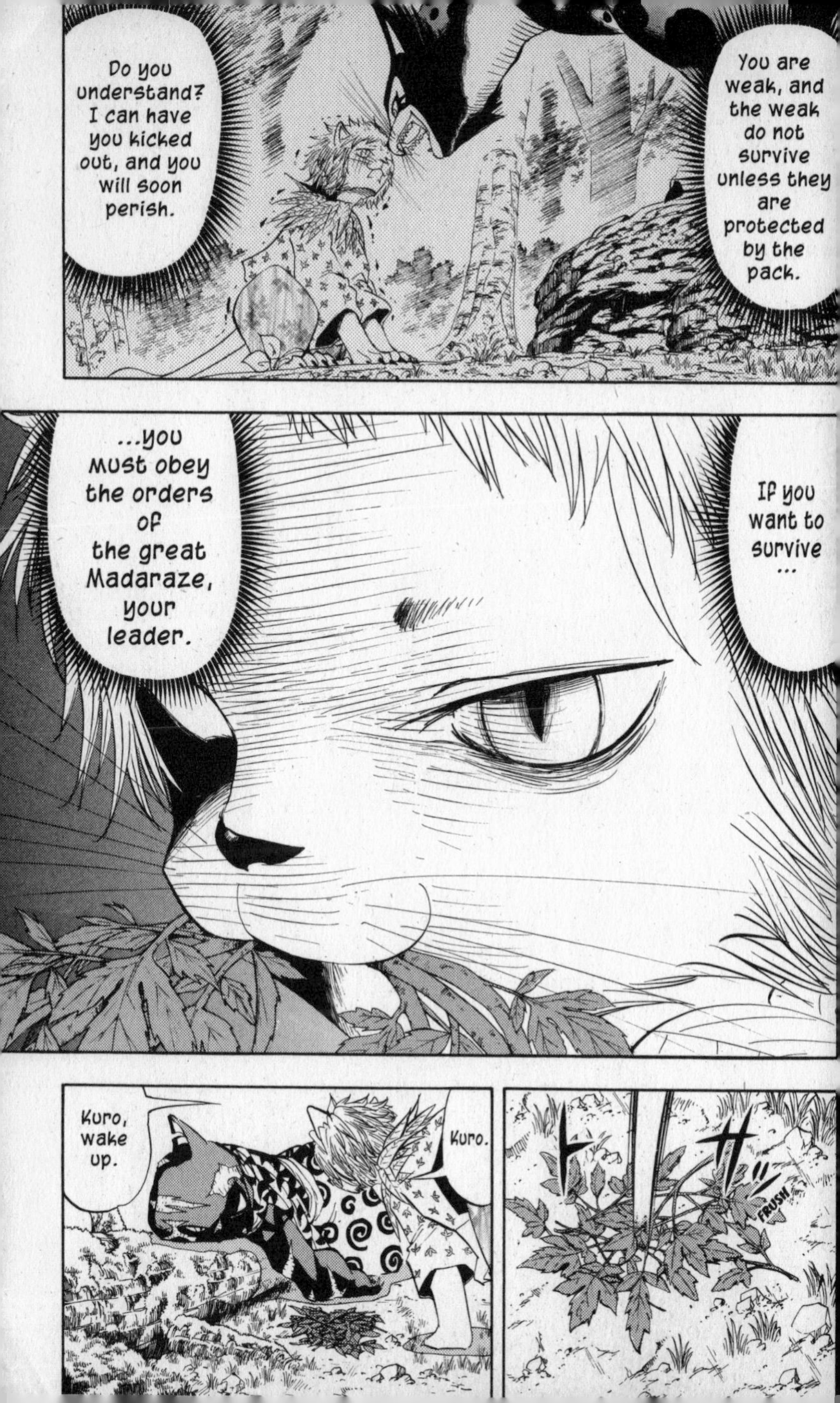
You are weak, and the weak do not survive unless they are protected by the pack.
Do you understand? I can have you kicked out, and you will soon perish.
If you want to survive ...
...you must obey the orders of the great Madaraze, your leader.
FRUSH
Kuro.
Kuro, wake up.

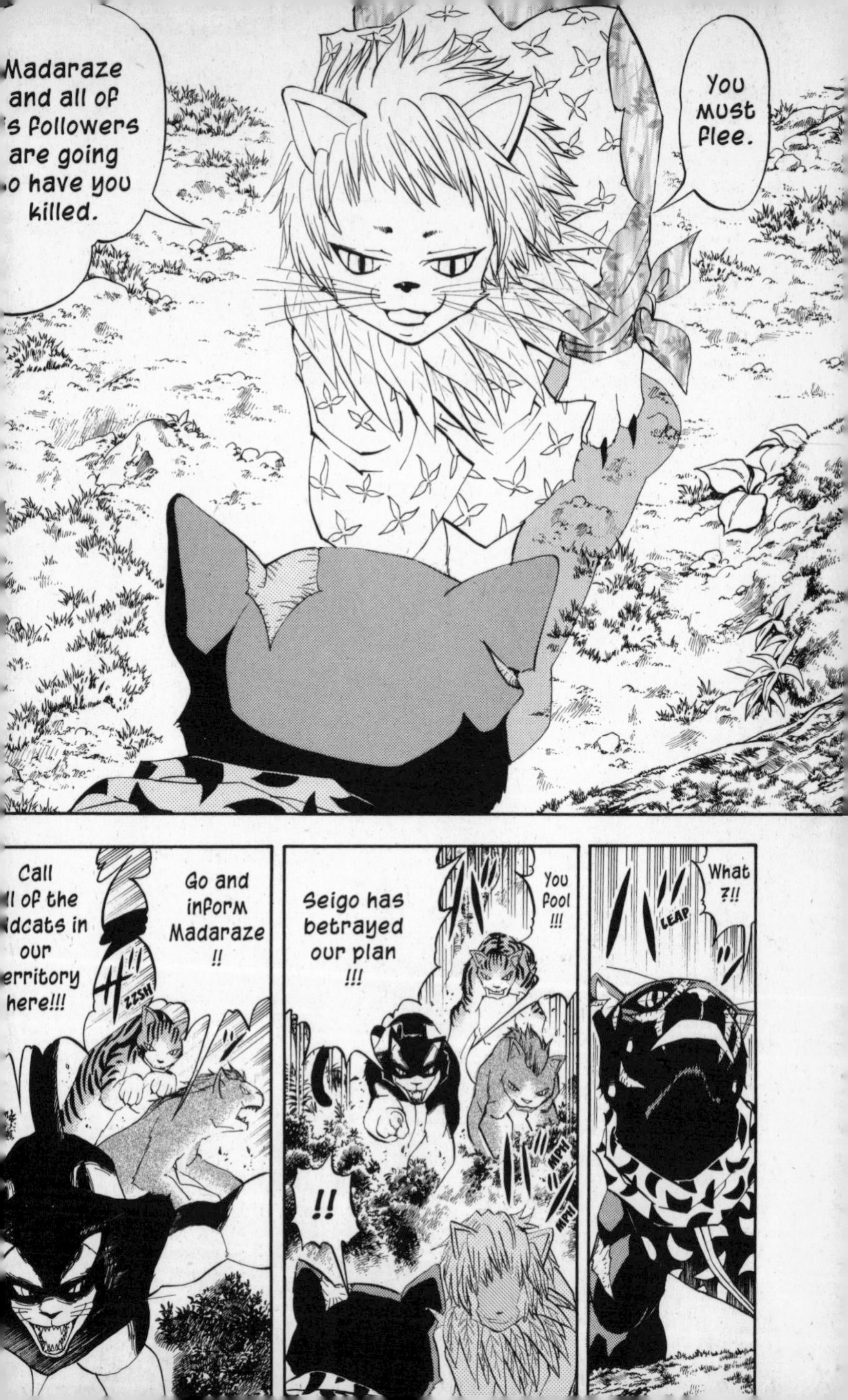
You must flee.
Madaraze and all of 's followers are going o have you killed.
What ?!!
LEAP
You fool !!!
Seigo has betrayed our plan !!!
!!
MPH MPH
Go and inform Madaraze !!
Call ll of the dcats in our erritory here!!!
ZZSH
!!

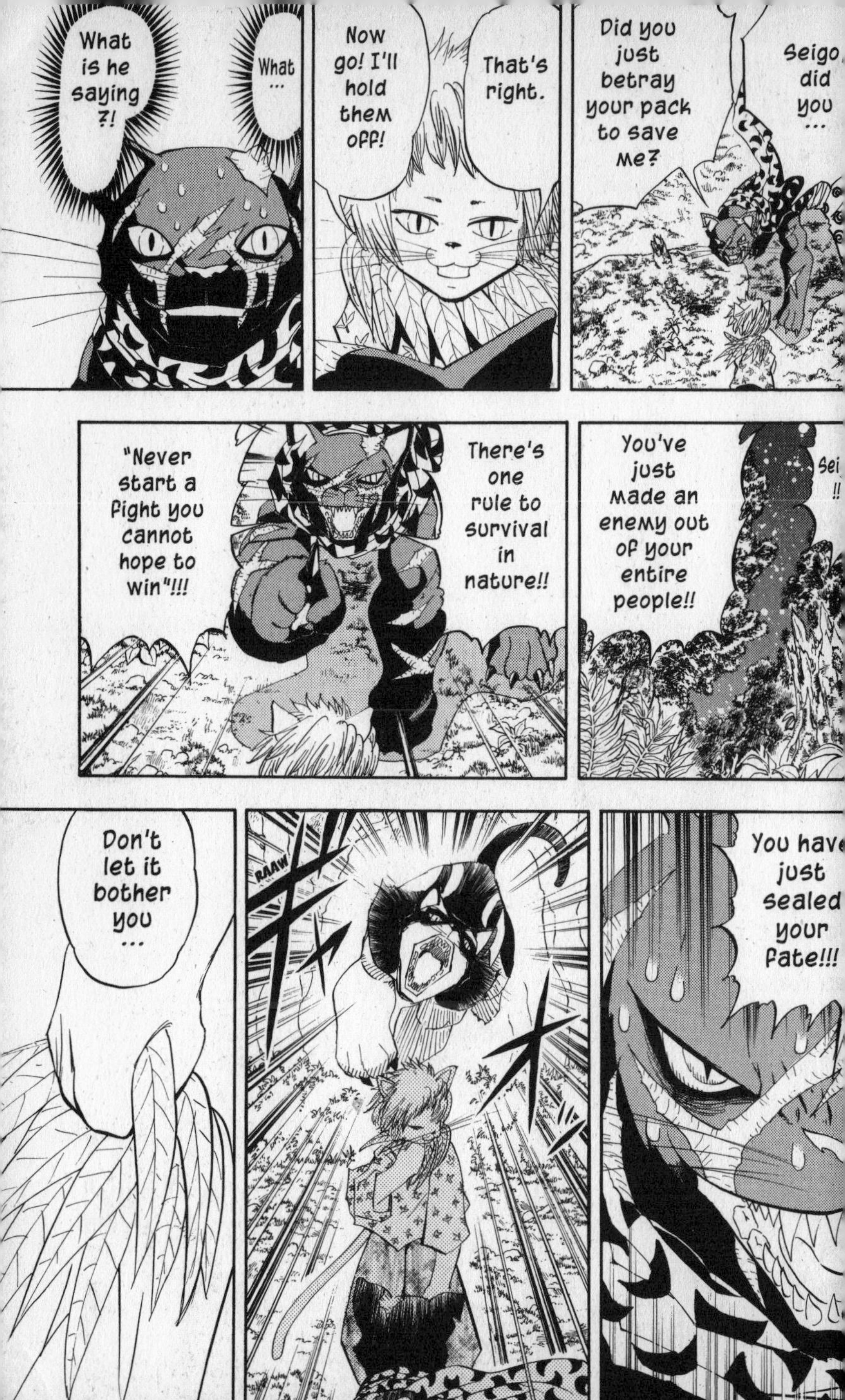
Seigo did you ...
Did you just betray your pack to save me?
That's right.
Now go! I'll hold them off!
What ...
What is he saying?!
Sei !!
You've just made an enemy out of your entire people!!
There's one rule to survival in nature!!
"Never start a fight you cannot hope to win"!!!
You have just sealed your fate!!!
RAAW
Don't let it bother you ...

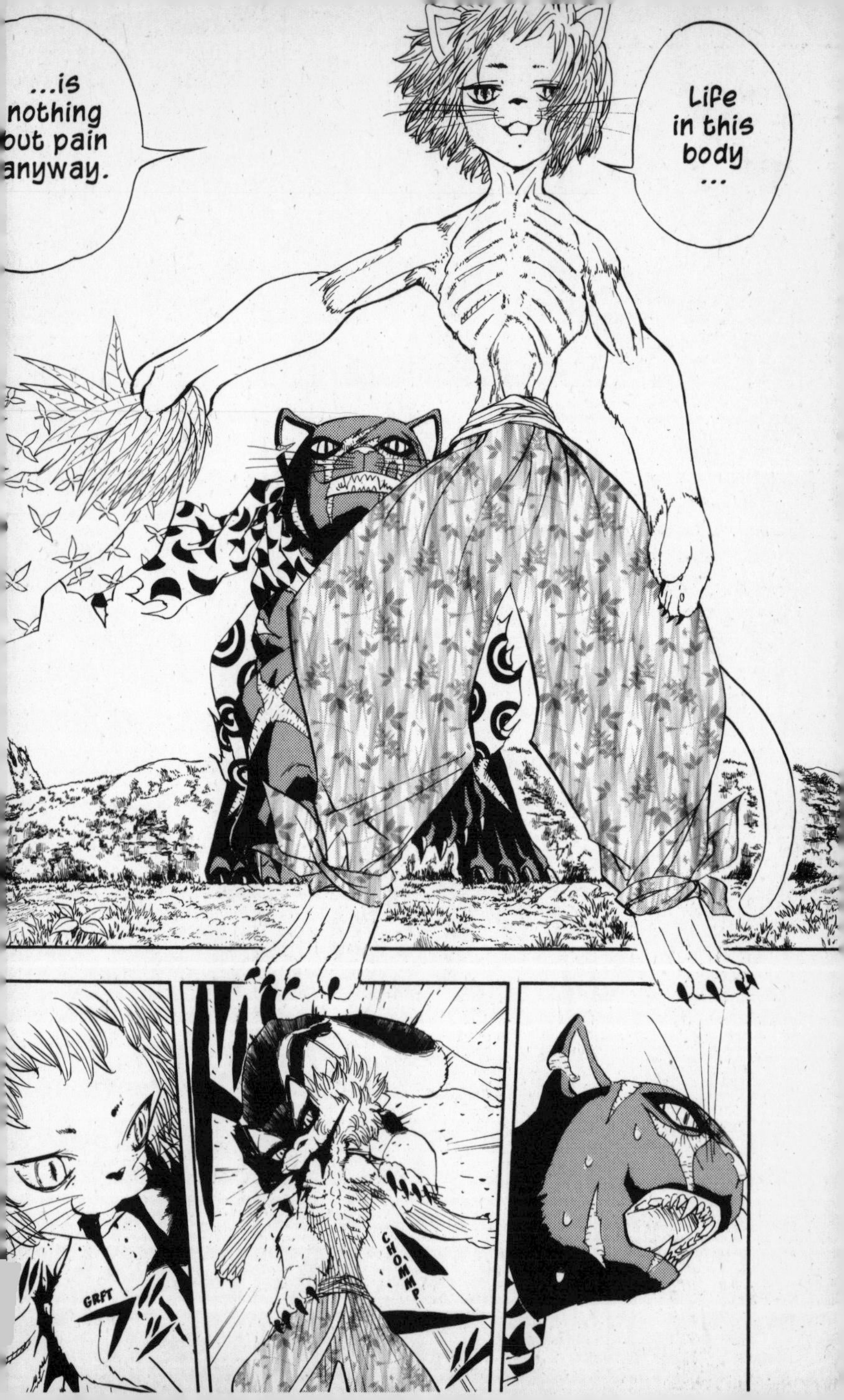
Life in this body ...
...is nothing but pain anyway.
CHOMMP
GRFT

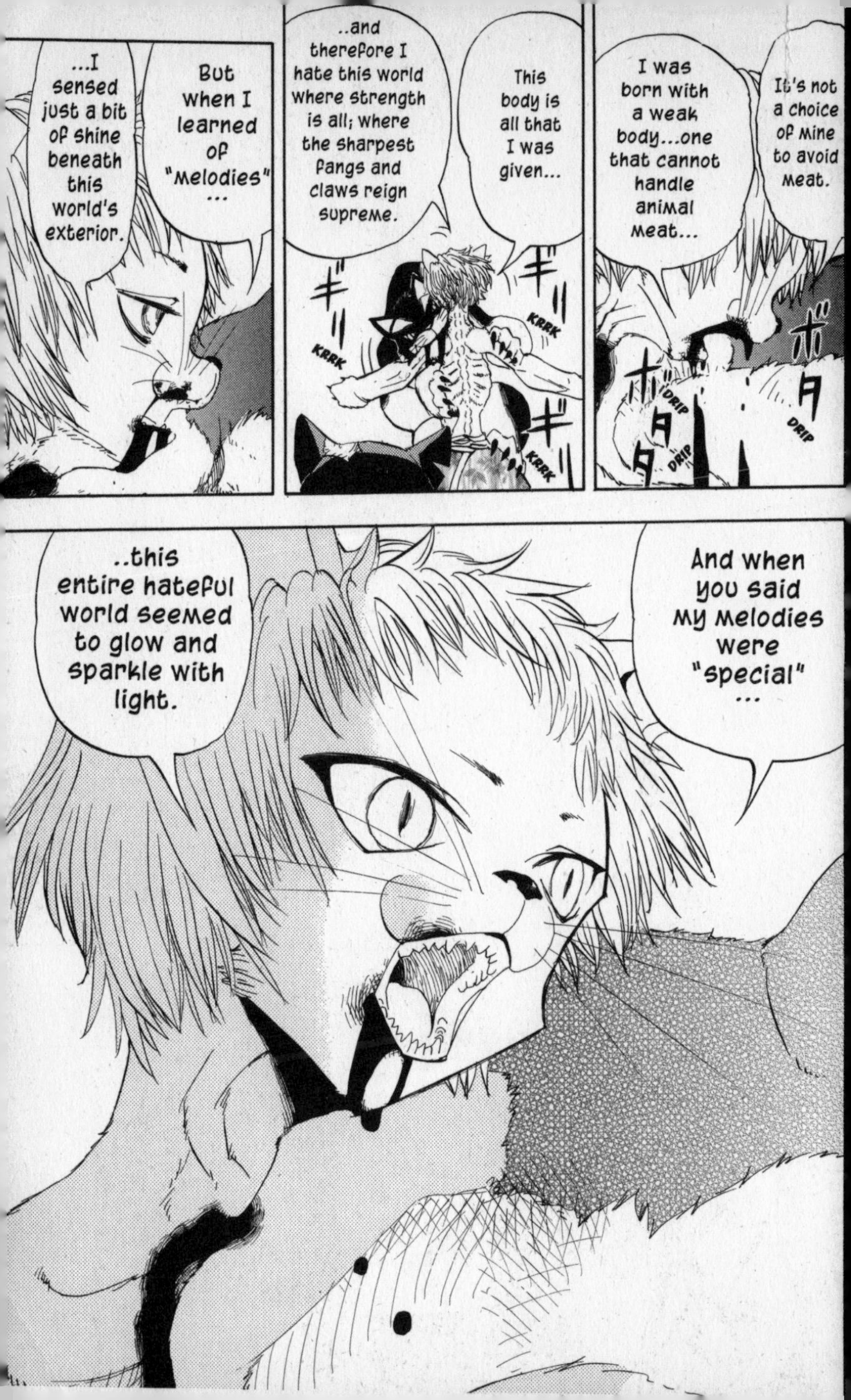
It's not a choice of mine to avoid meat.
I was born with a weak body...one that cannot handle animal meat...
ボタ
DRIP
ボタ
DRIP
DRIP
This body is all that I was given...
..and therefore I hate this world where strength is all; where the sharpest fangs and claws reign supreme.
ギリ
KRRK
ギリ
KRRK
ギリ
KRRK
But when I learned of "melodies"...
...I sensed just a bit of shine beneath this world's exterior.
And when you said my melodies were "special"...
..this entire hateful world seemed to glow and sparkle with light.

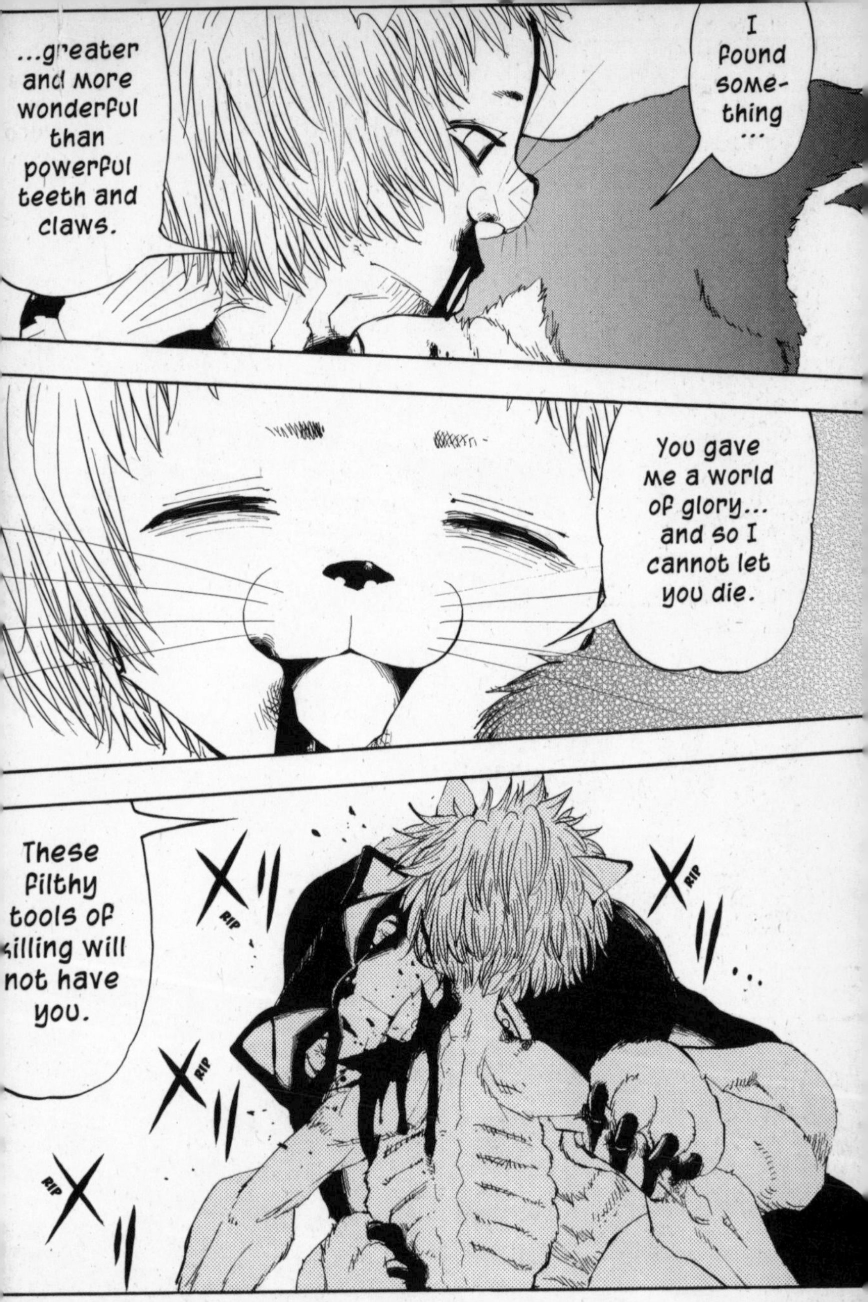
I found some-thing ...
...greater and more wonderful than powerful teeth and claws.
You gave me a world of glory... and so I cannot let you die.
RIP
...
RIP
These filthy tools of killing will not have you.
RIP
RIP

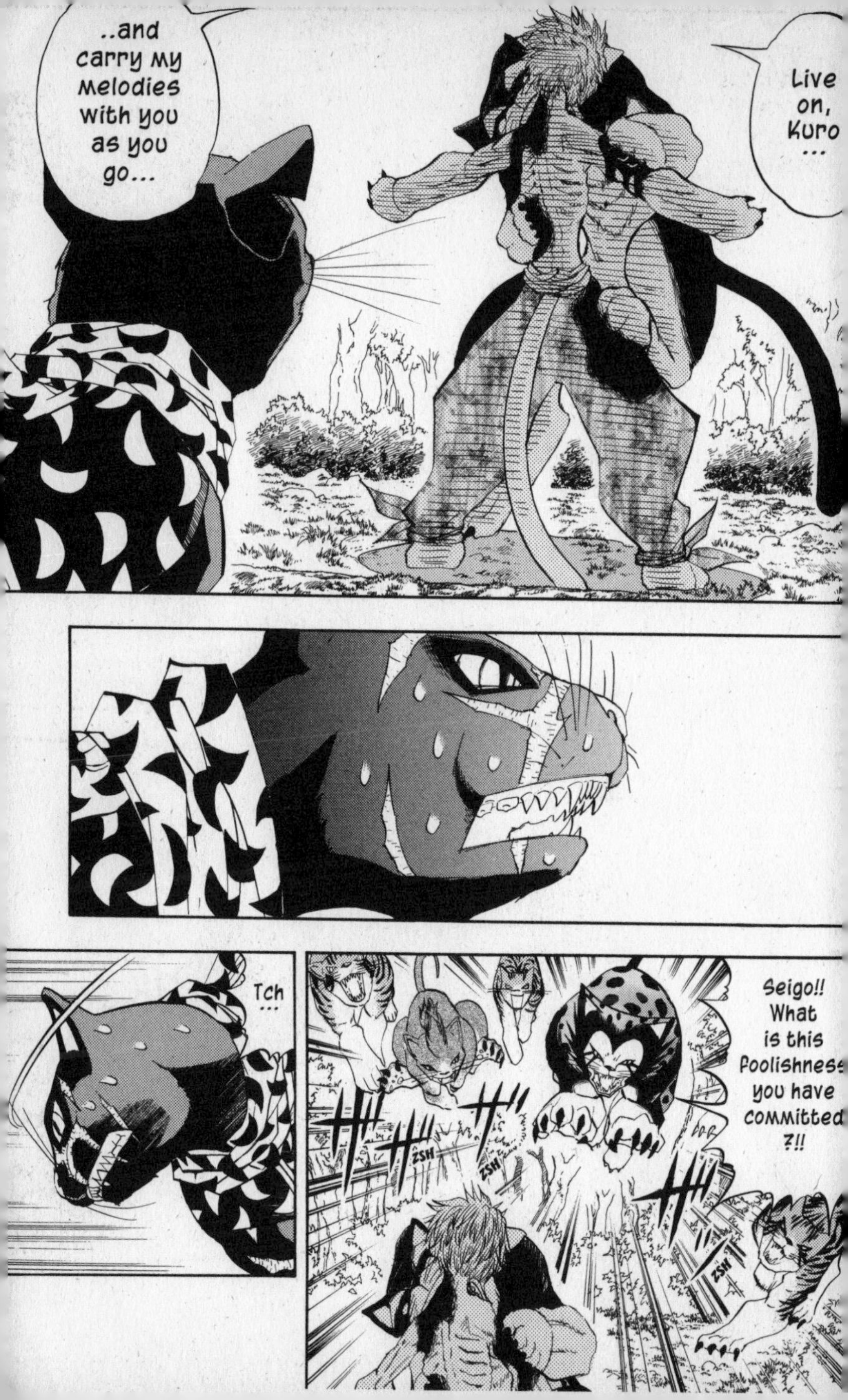
Live on, Kuro...
..and carry my melodies with you as you go...
Seigo!! What is this foolishness you have committed?!!
ZSH
ZSH
ZSH
Tch...

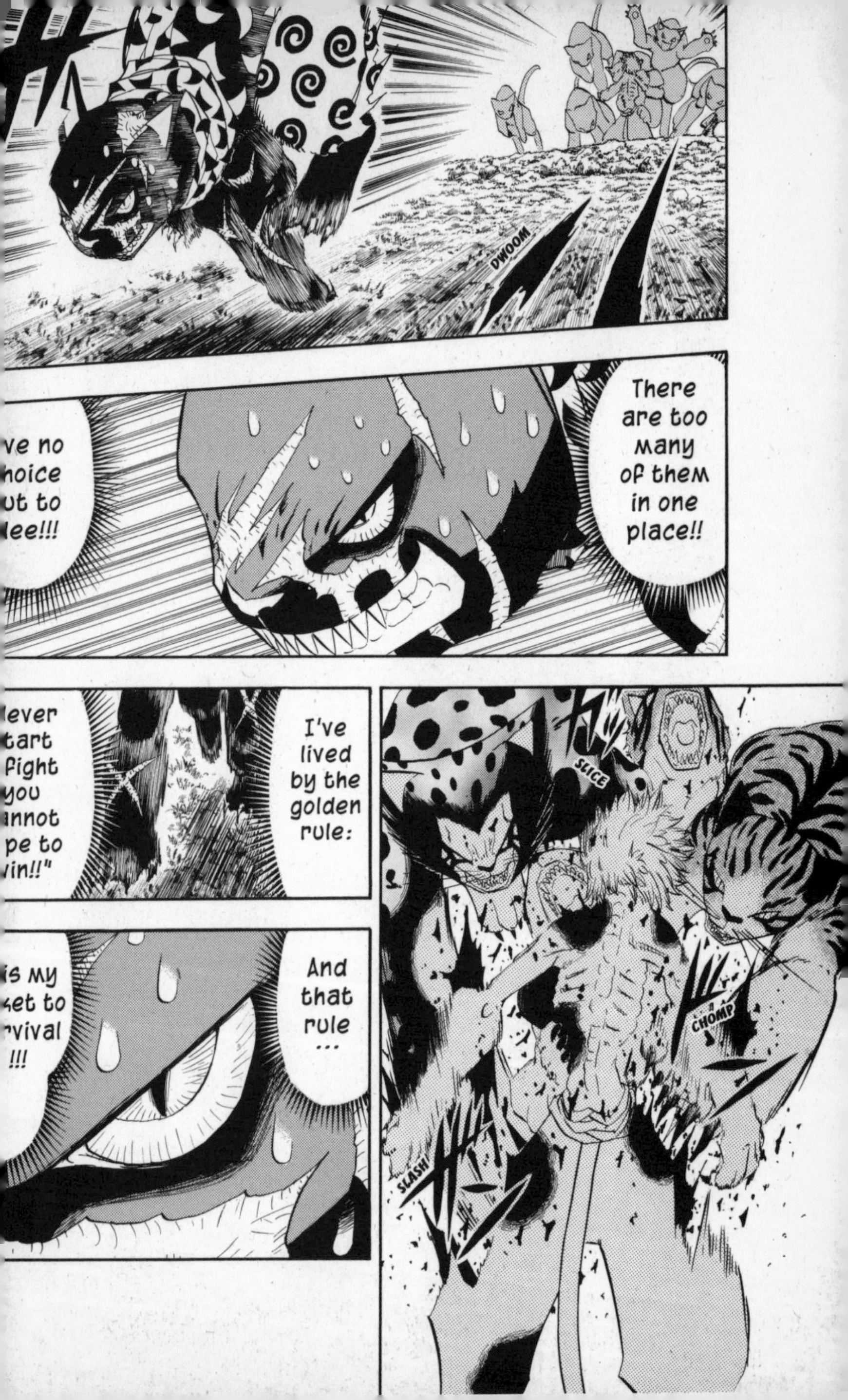

DWOOM
There are too many of them in one place!!
ve no hoice ut to lee!!!
SLICE
CHOMP
SLASH
I've lived by the golden rule:
lever tart fight you annot pe to vin!!"
And that rule ...
is my ket to rvival !!!

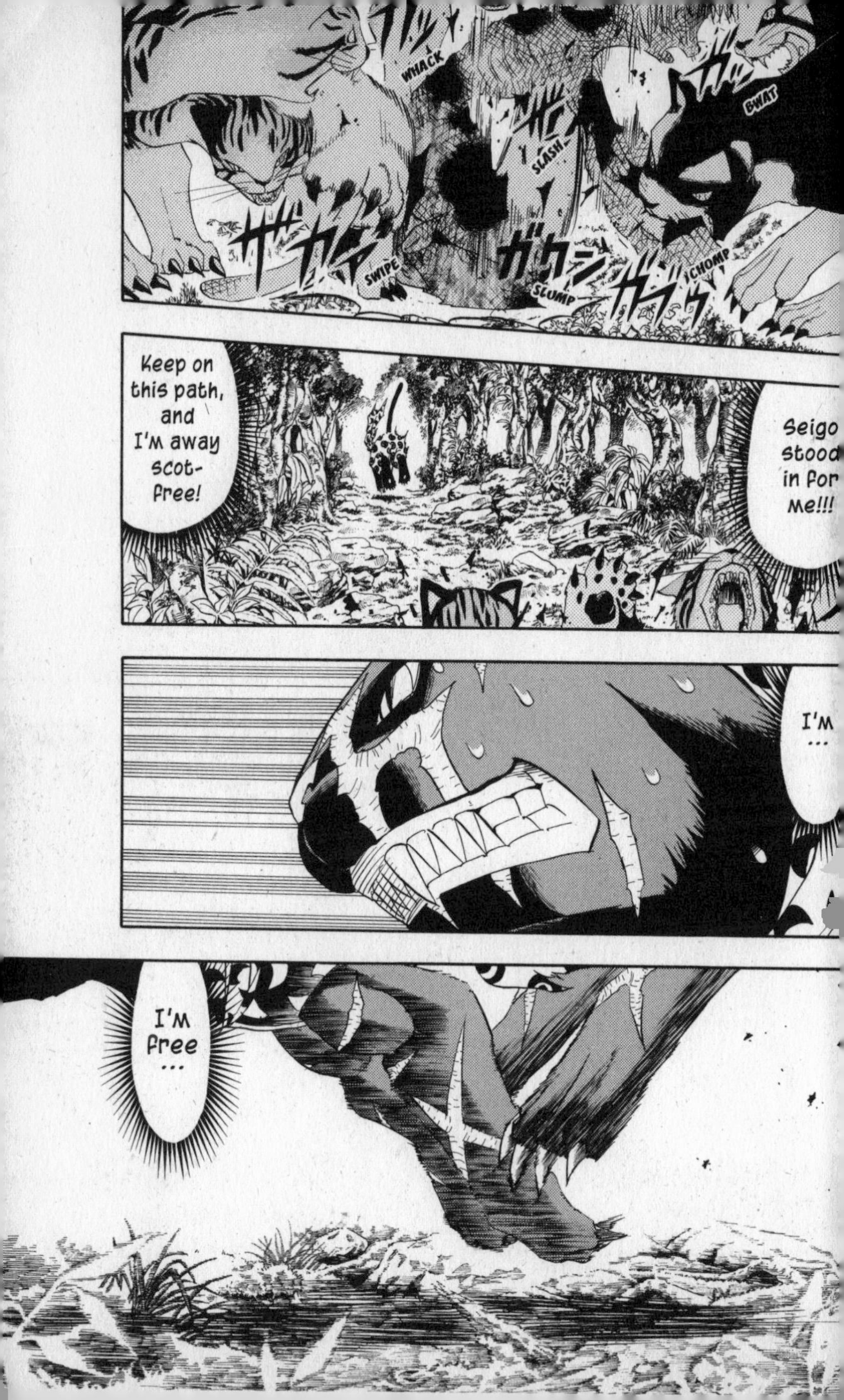
BWAT
CHOMP
SLASH
SLUMP
WHACK
SWIPE
Seigo stood in for me!!!
Keep on this path, and I'm away scot-free!
I'm ...
I'm free ...

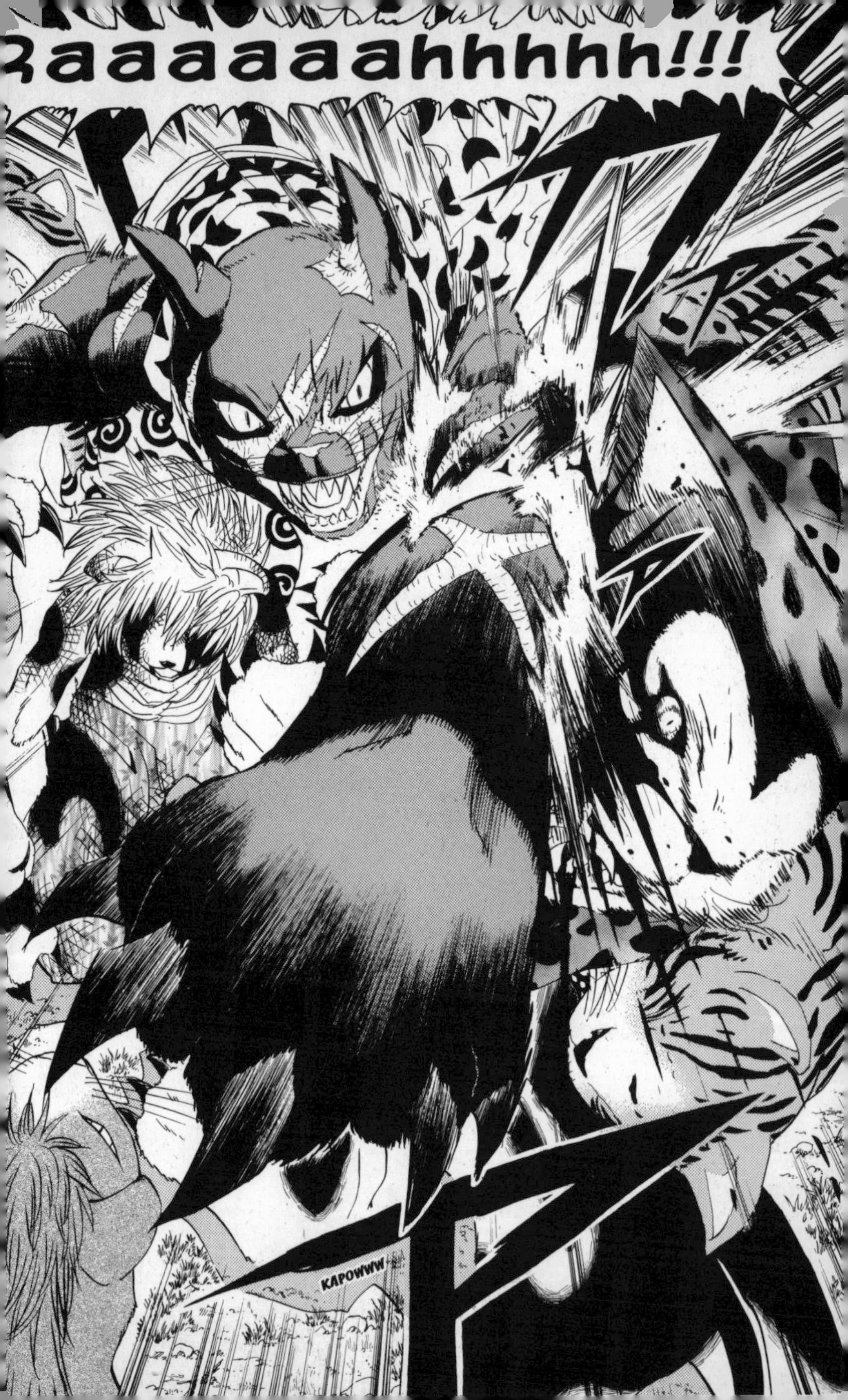
Raaaaaaahhhhh!!!
KAPOWWW

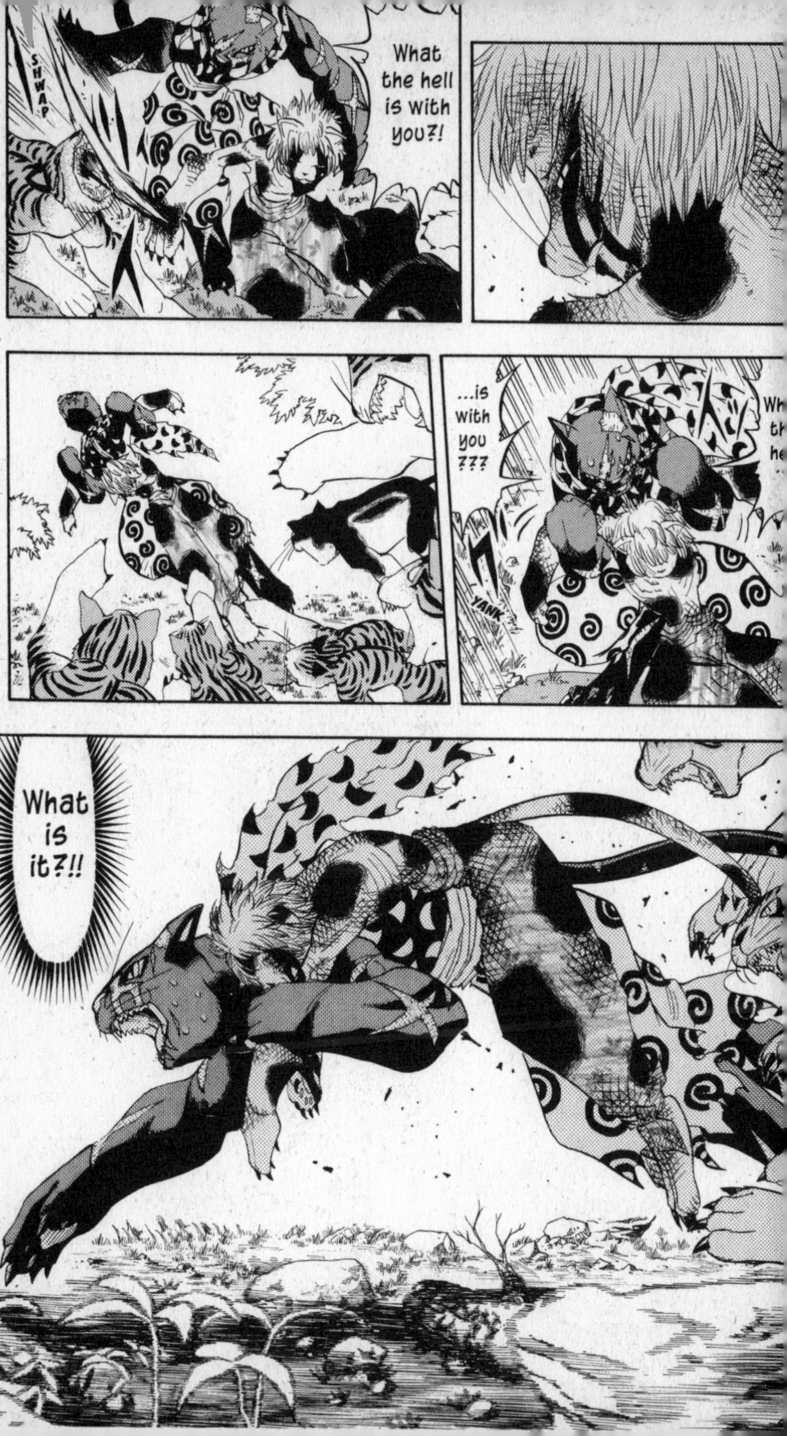
What the hell is with you?!
SHWAP
...is with you???
YANK
What is it?!!

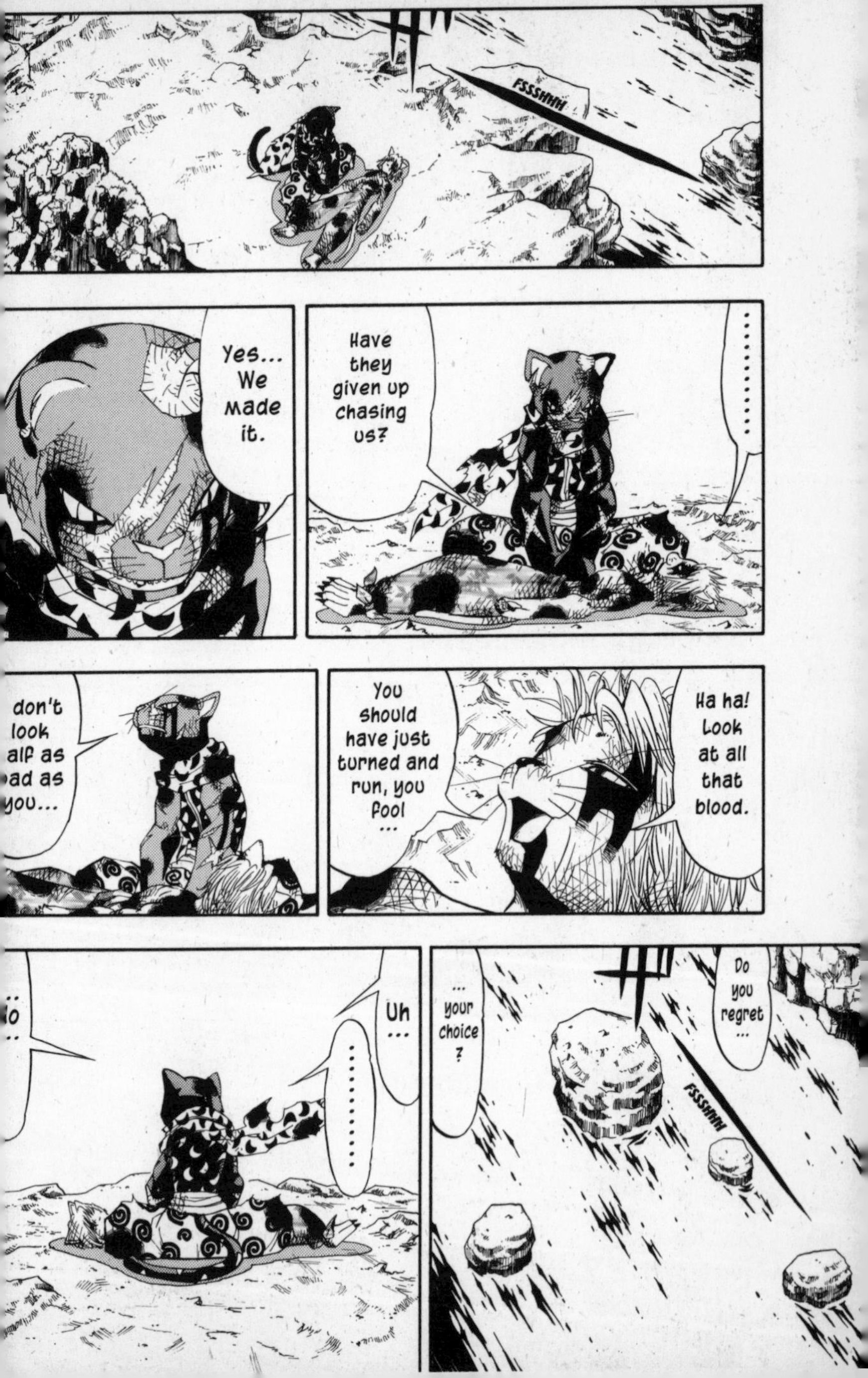
FSSSHHH
......
Have they given up chasing us?
Yes... We made it.
Ha ha! Look at all that blood.
You should have just turned and run, you fool ...
don't look alf as ad as you...
Do you regret ...
FSSSHHH
... your choice ?
Uh ...
......

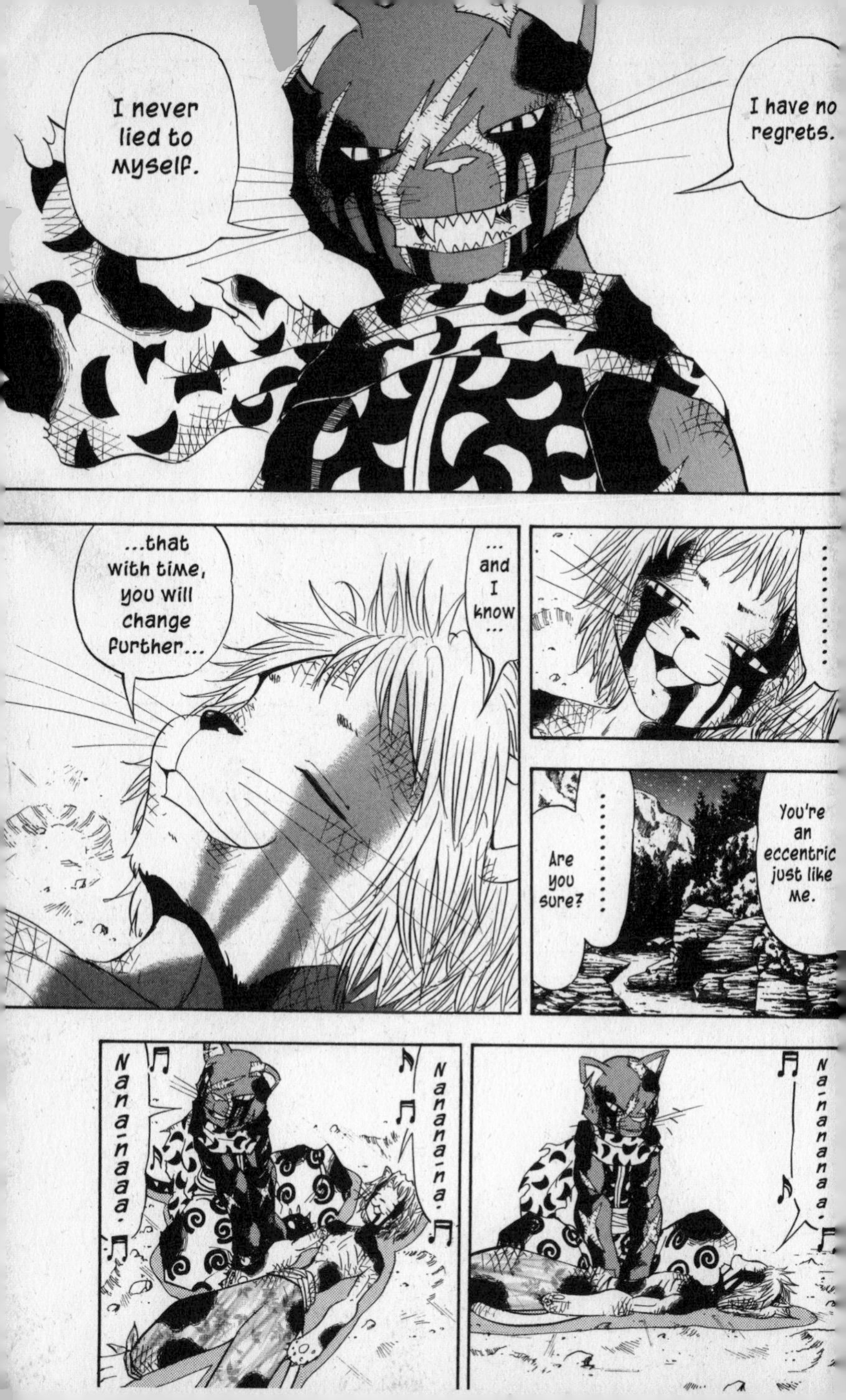
I have no regrets.
I never lied to myself.
......
You're an eccentric just like me.
......
Are you sure?
...and I know...
...that with time, you will change further...
Na-nananaa.
Nananana.
Na-naaa.

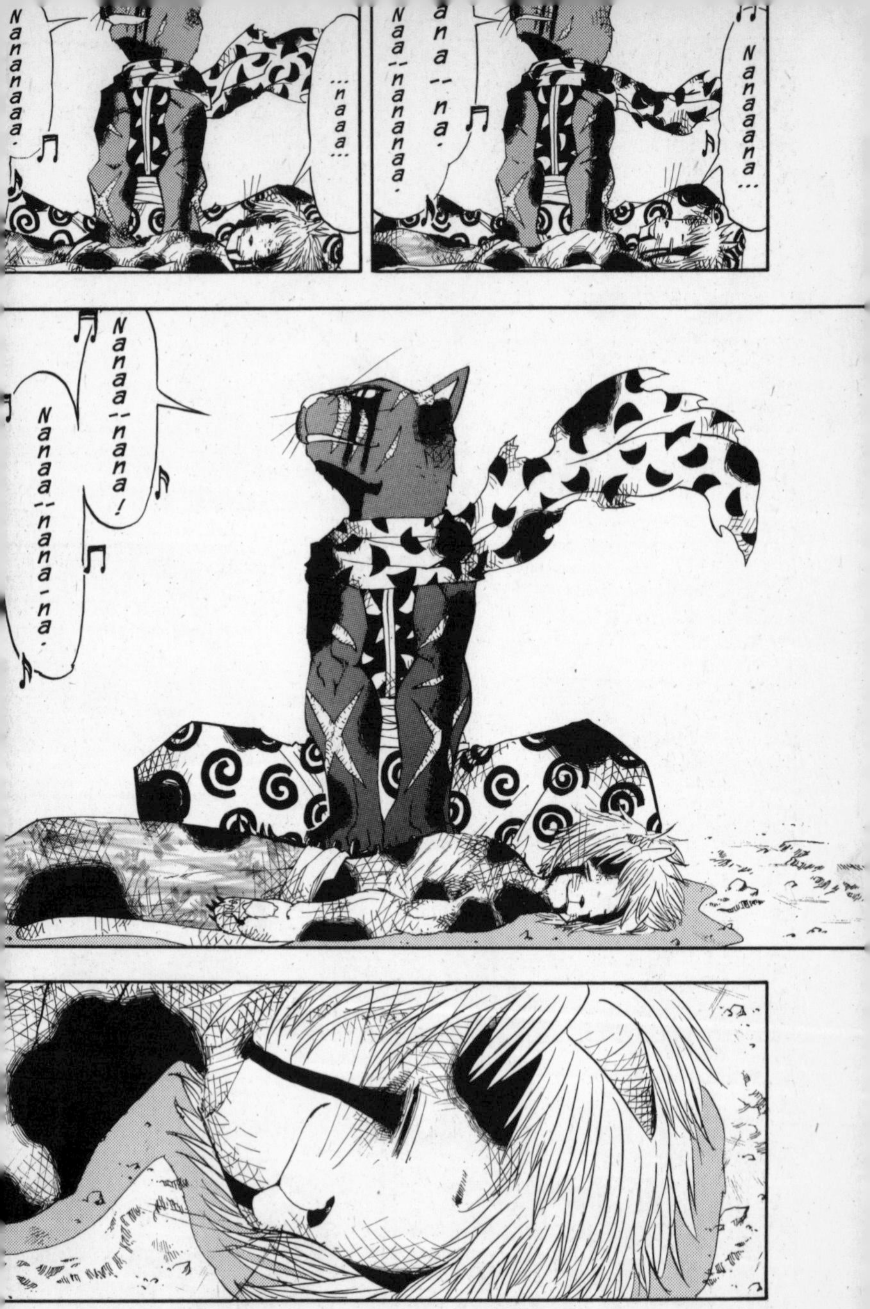
Nanaaaana...
ana~na.
Naa~nananaa.
...naaa...
Nananaaa.
Nanaa~nana!
Nanaa~nana-na.

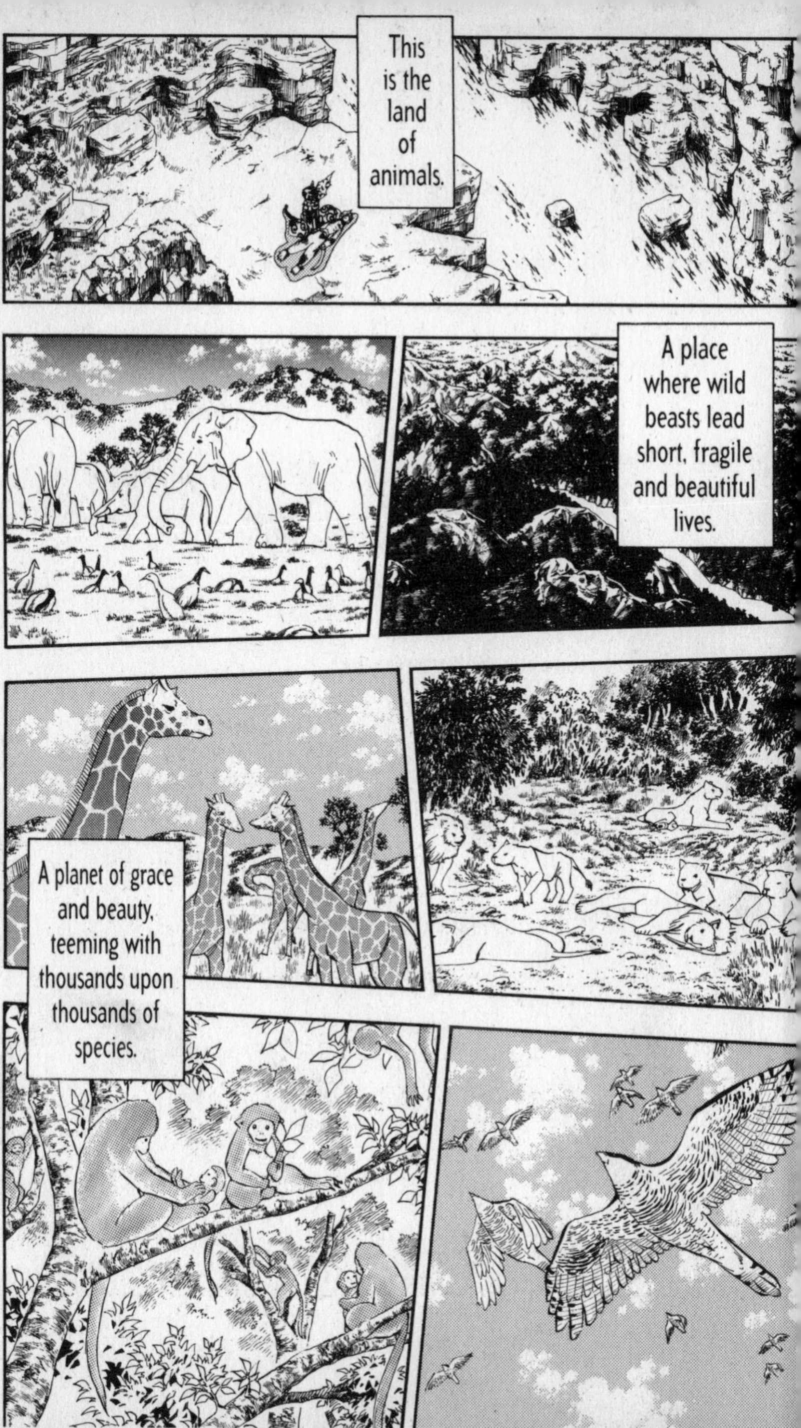
This is the land of animals.
A place where wild beasts lead short, fragile and beautiful lives.
A planet of grace and beauty, teeming with thousands upon thousands of species.

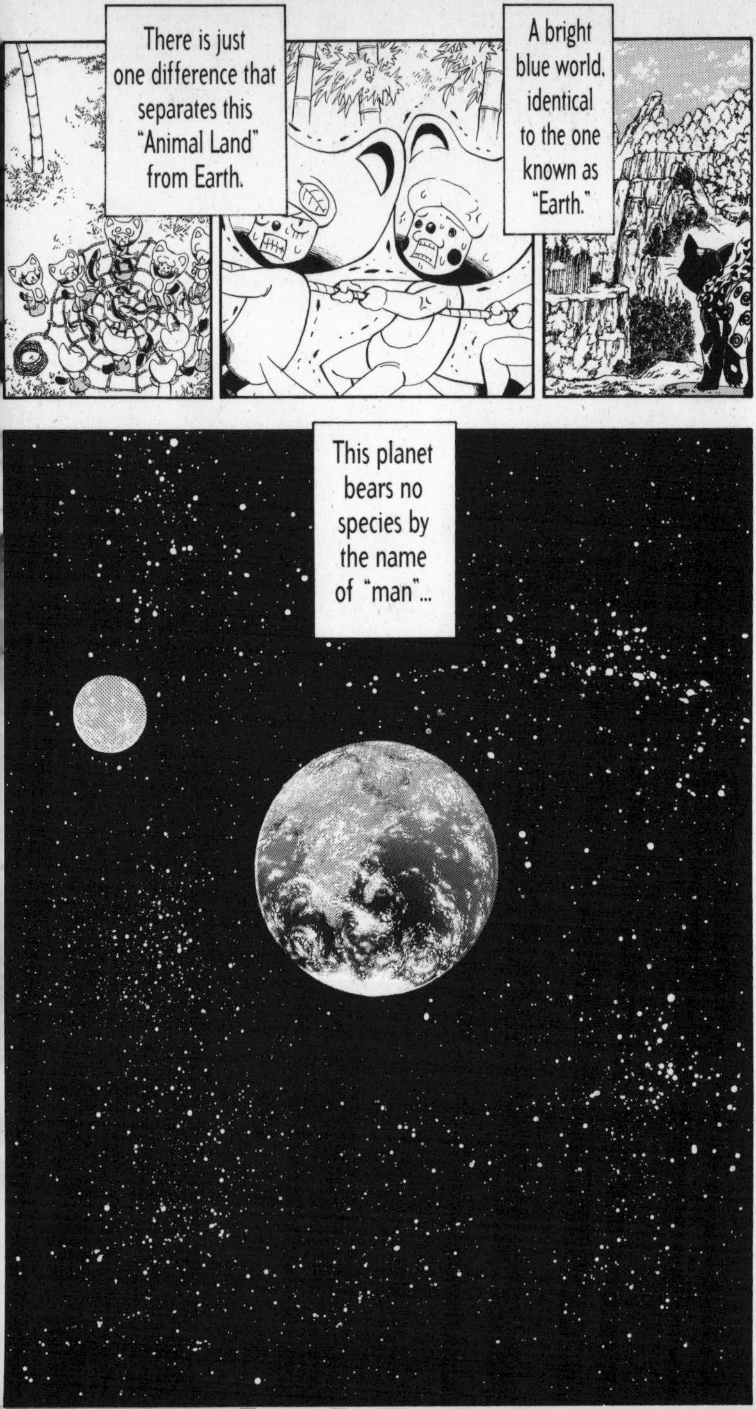
A bright blue world, identical to the one known as "Earth."
There is just one difference that separates this "Animal Land" from Earth.
This planet bears no species by the name of "man"...

Animal Land Episode 0 End

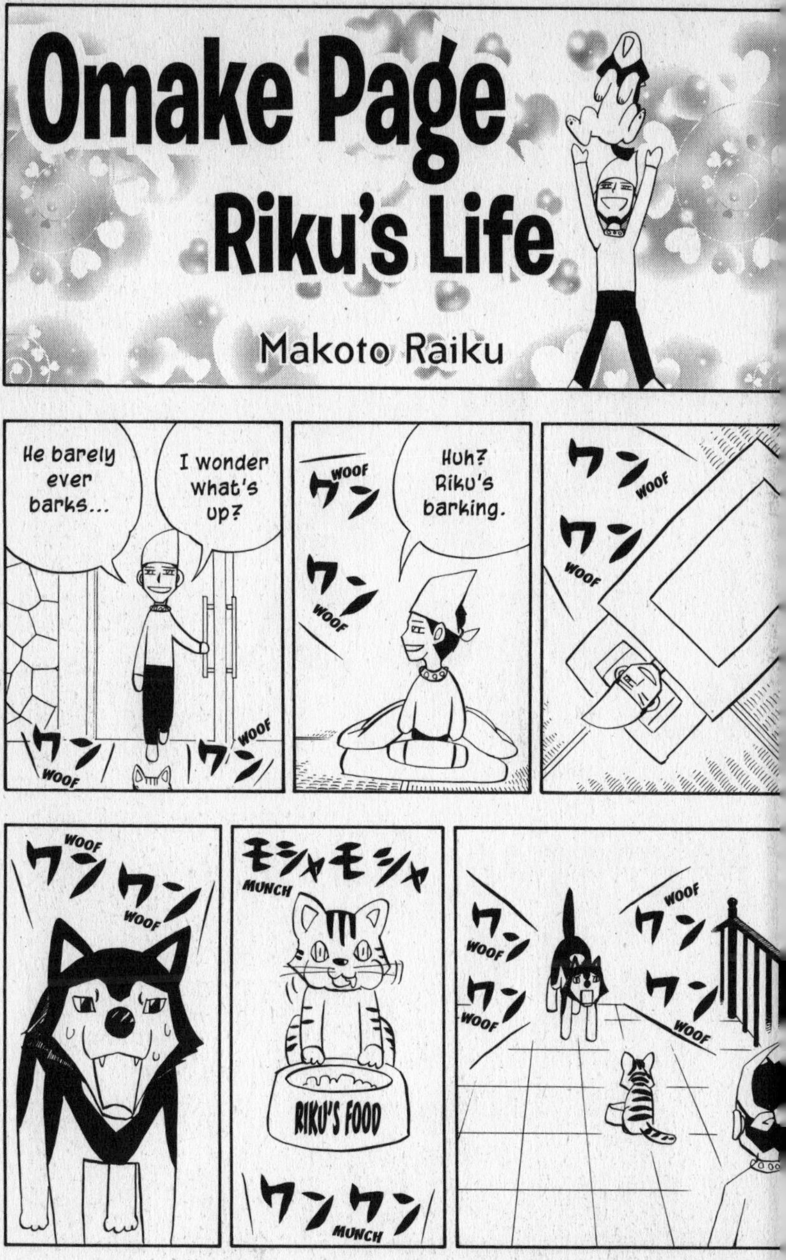
Omake Page
Riku's Life
Makoto Raiku
ワン WOOF
ワン WOOF
ワン WOOF
ワン WOOF
Huh? Riku's barking.
I wonder what's up?
He barely ever barks...
ワン WOOF
ワン WOOF
ワン WOOF
ワン WOOF
ワン WOOF
ワン WOOF
モシャモシャ MUNCH
RIKU'S FOOD
ワンワン MUNCH
ワン WOOF
ワン WOOF

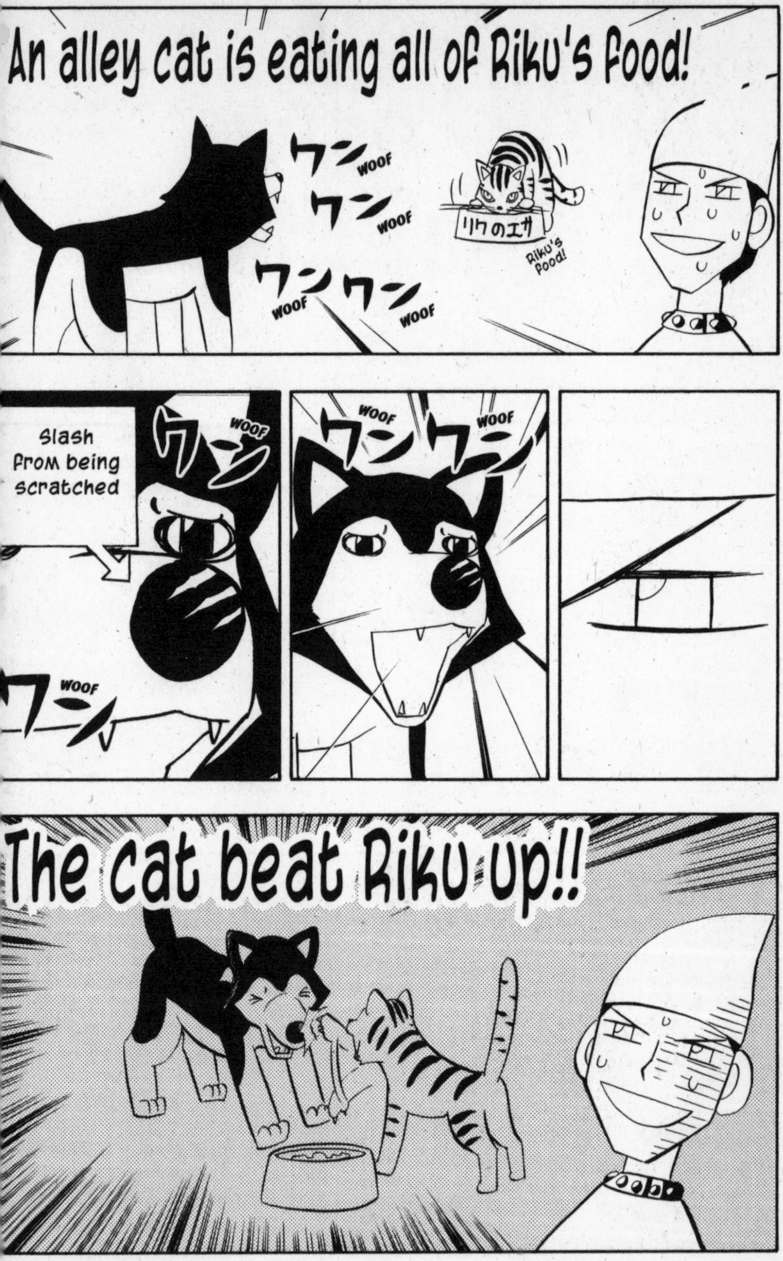
An alley cat is eating all of Riku's food!
リクのエサ
Riku's food!
ワン
WOOF
ワン
WOOF
ワン
WOOF
ワン
WOOF
ワン
WOOF
ワン
WOOF
ワン
WOOF
Slash from being scratched
ワン
WOOF
The cat beat Riku up!!

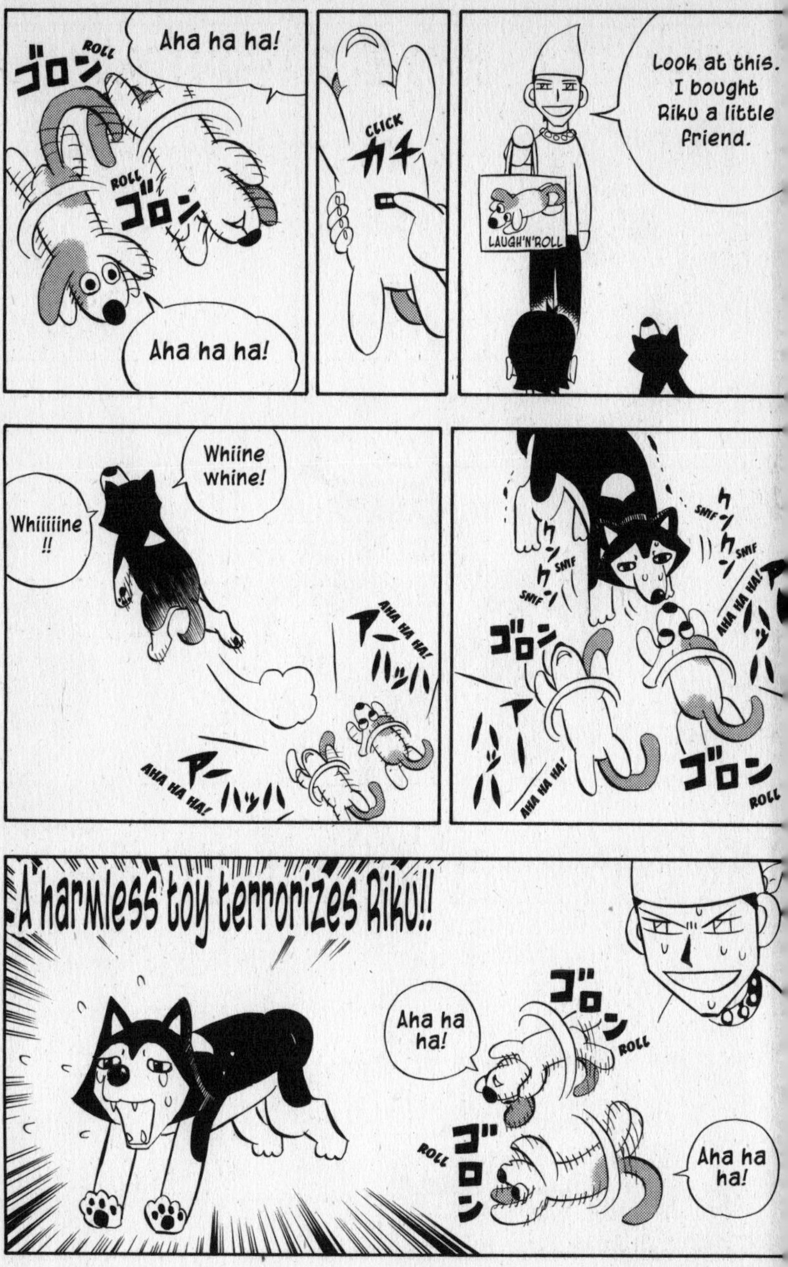
Look at this. I bought Riku a little friend.
LAUGH'N'ROLL
CLICK
カチ
Aha ha ha!
ゴロン
ROLL
ゴロン
ROLL
Aha ha ha!
クンクン
SNIF
クンクン
SNIF
アーハッハ
AHA HA HA!
ゴロン
ROLL
ゴロン
アーハッハ
AHA HA HA!
Whiine whine!
Whiiiiine !!
アーハッハ
AHA HA HA!
アーハッハ
AHA HA HA!
A harmless toy terrorizes Riku!!
ゴロン
ROLL
Aha ha ha!
ゴロン
ROLL
Aha ha ha!

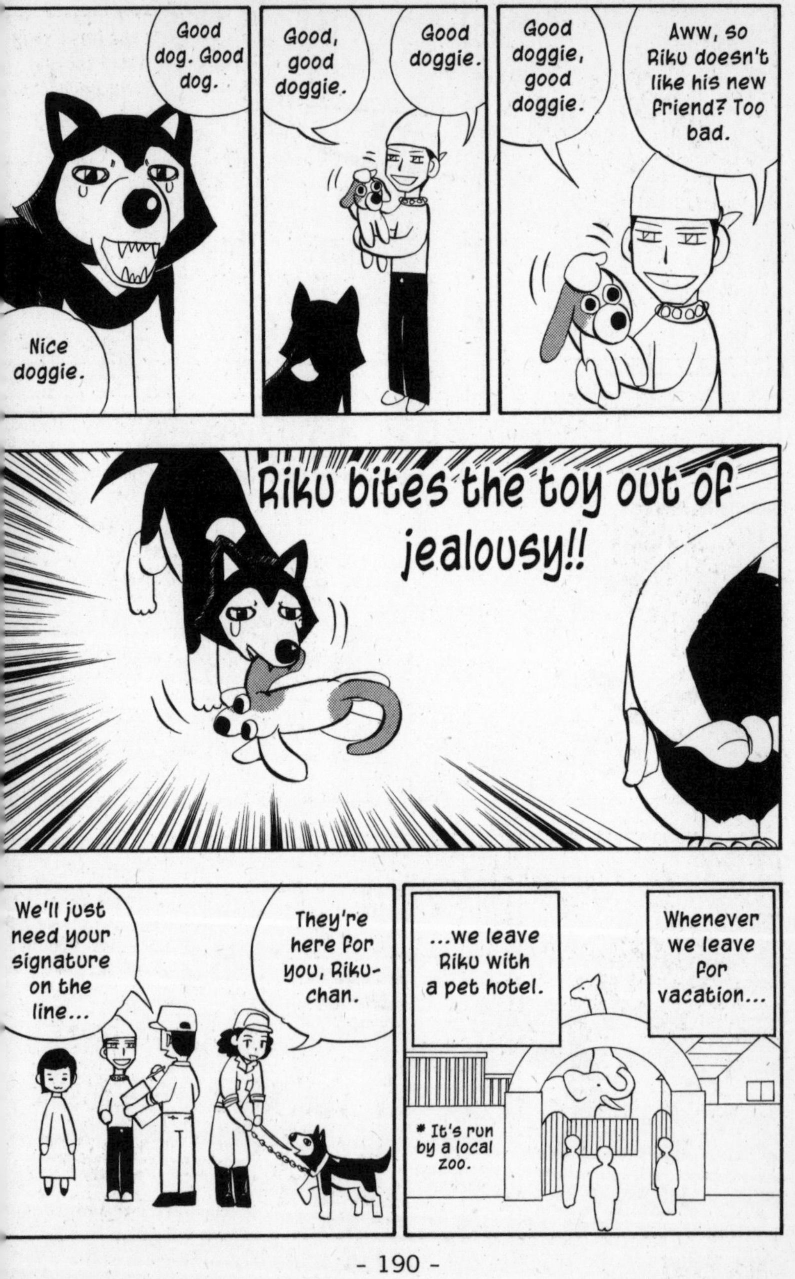
Aww, so Riku doesn't like his new friend? Too bad.
Good doggie, good doggie.
Good doggie.
Good, good doggie.
Good dog. Good dog.
Nice doggie.
Riku bites the toy out of jealousy!!
Whenever we leave for vacation...
...we leave Riku with a pet hotel.
* It's run by a local zoo.
They're here for you, Riku-chan.
We'll just need your signature on the line...

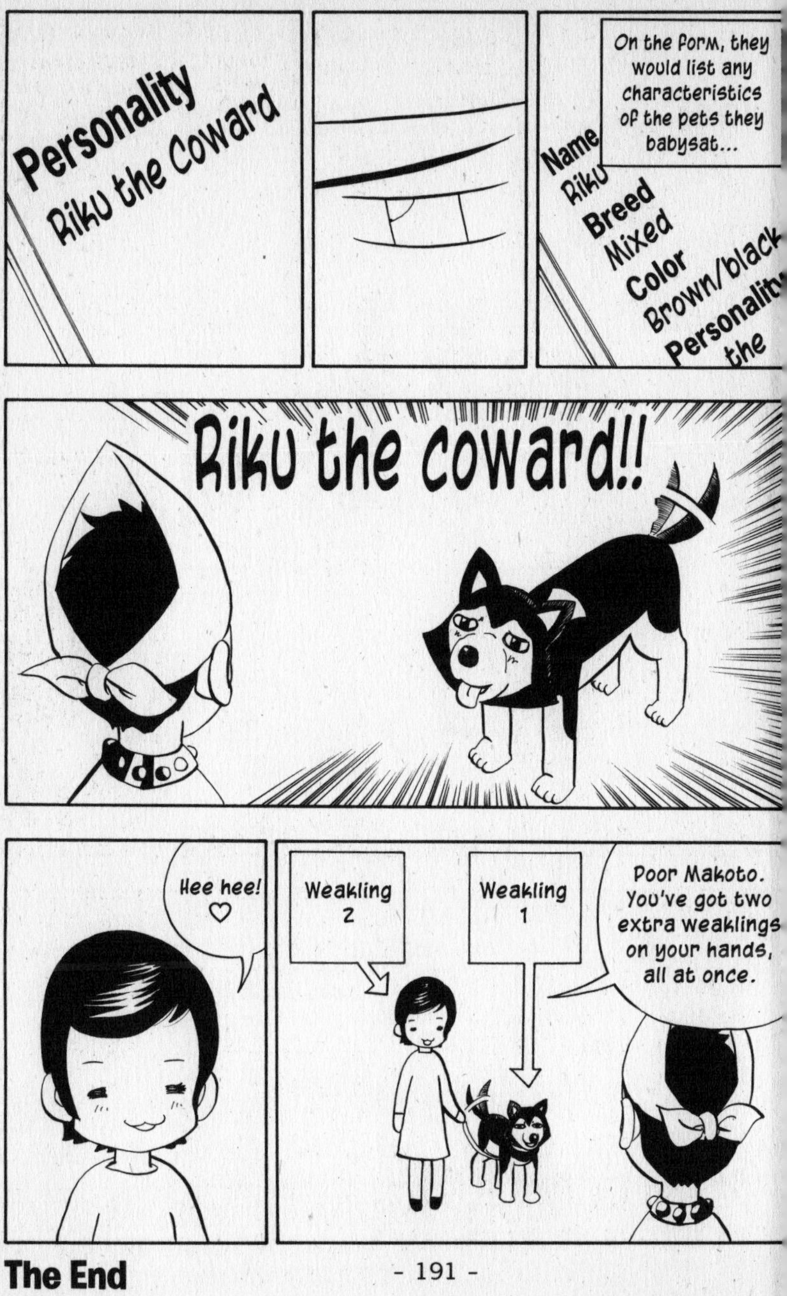
On the form, they would list any characteristics of the pets they babysat...
Name
Riku
Breed
Mixed
Color
Brown/black
Personality
the
Personality
Riku the Coward
Riku the coward!!
Poor Makoto. You've got two extra weaklings on your hands, all at once.
Weakling 1
Weakling 2
Hee hee! ♡

The End

Pepper's Life

by Makoto Raiku

Aaah-ahaaaah!!!
PLOOP
RIP
AAAAAH!

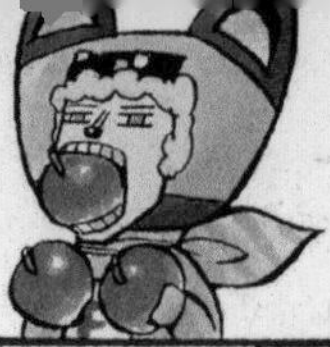

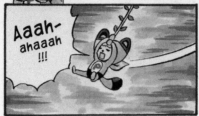

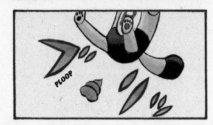

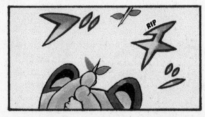

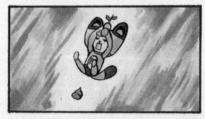

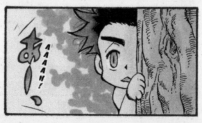

Translation Notes

Japanese is a tricky language for most Westerners, and translation is often more art than science. For your edification and reading pleasure, here are notes on some of the places where we could have gone in a different direction with our translation of the work, or where a Japanese cultural reference is used.

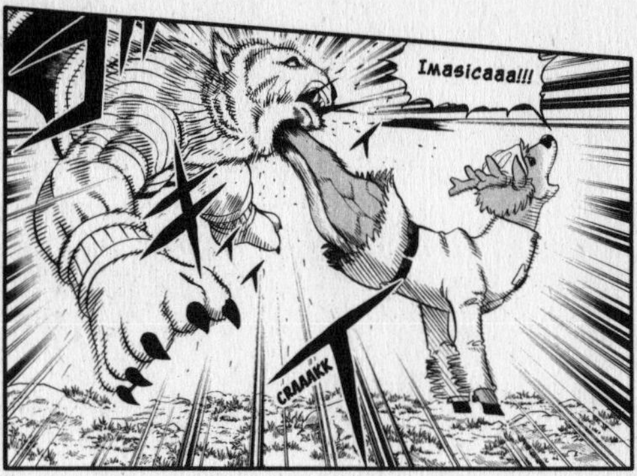

Imasicaaa!!!
CRAAAKK

Imasicaä, page 64
This deer (and her costume) is a parody of the character Nausicaä from Hayao Miyazaki's manga/anime classic, Nausicaä of the Valley of the Wind. In Japanese, the end of the name Nausicaä (shika) is a homonym for "deer."

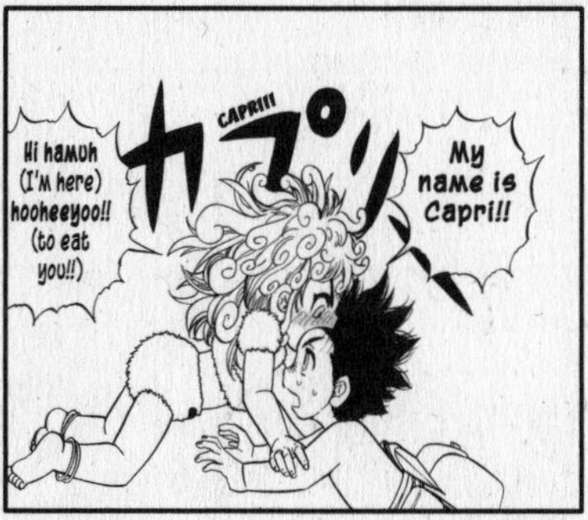

My name is Capri!!
CAPRI!!
Hi hamoh (I'm here) hooheeyoo!! (to eat you!!)

Capri, page 76
Princess Capri's name is a play on kapuri, the Japanese onomatopoeia for a "chomping" noise. As you can see from her introduction to Taroza, that's no coincidence.

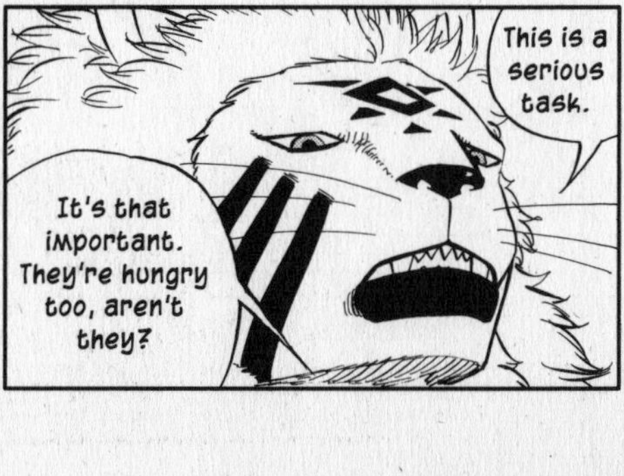

This is a serious task.
It's that important. They're hungry too, aren't they?

Isazume, page 86
The name "Isazume" sounds like "fierce claws" in Japanese.

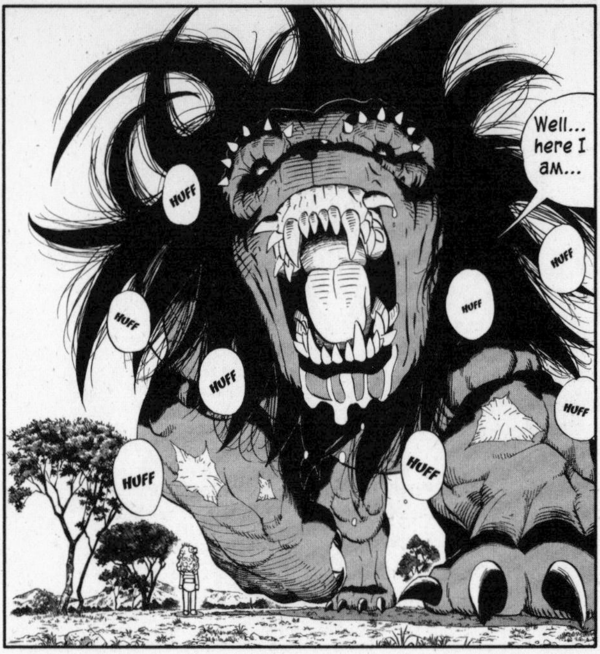
Well... here I am...
HUFF
HUFF
HUFF
HUFF
HUFF
HUFF
HUFF
HUFF

Honekami, page 87

The name "Honekami" sounds like "bone biter" or "bone cruncher" in Japanese.

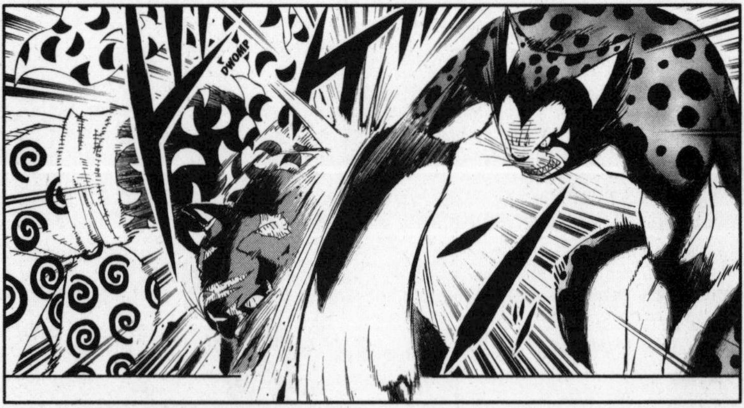
DWOMP

Madaraze, page 150

The name "Madaraze" sounds like "spotted back" in Japanese.

Preview of
Animal Land, volume 4

We're pleased to present you a preview from
Animal Land, volume 4. Please check our website
(www.kodanshacomics.com) to see when this volume
will be available in English. For now you'll have to
make do with Japanese!

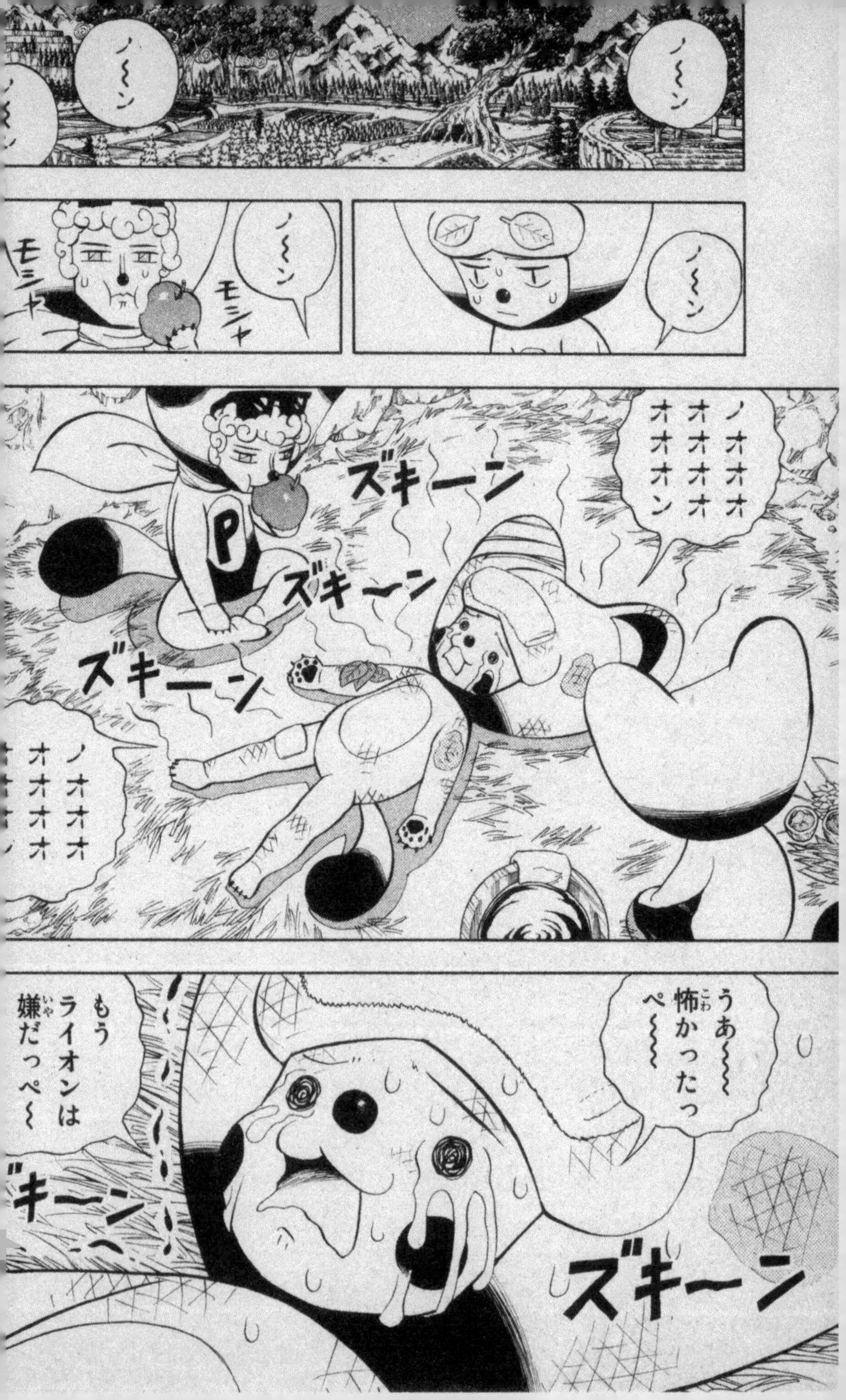
ノ〜ン
ノ〜ン
ノ〜ン
ノ〜ン
ノ〜ン
モシャ
モシャ
ノオオオオオオオオオオン
ズキーン
ズキ〜ン
ズキーン
ノオオオオオオオ
うあ〜〜〜 怖かったっぺ〜〜〜
もう ライオンは 嫌だっぺ〜
ズキ〜ン
キ〜ン

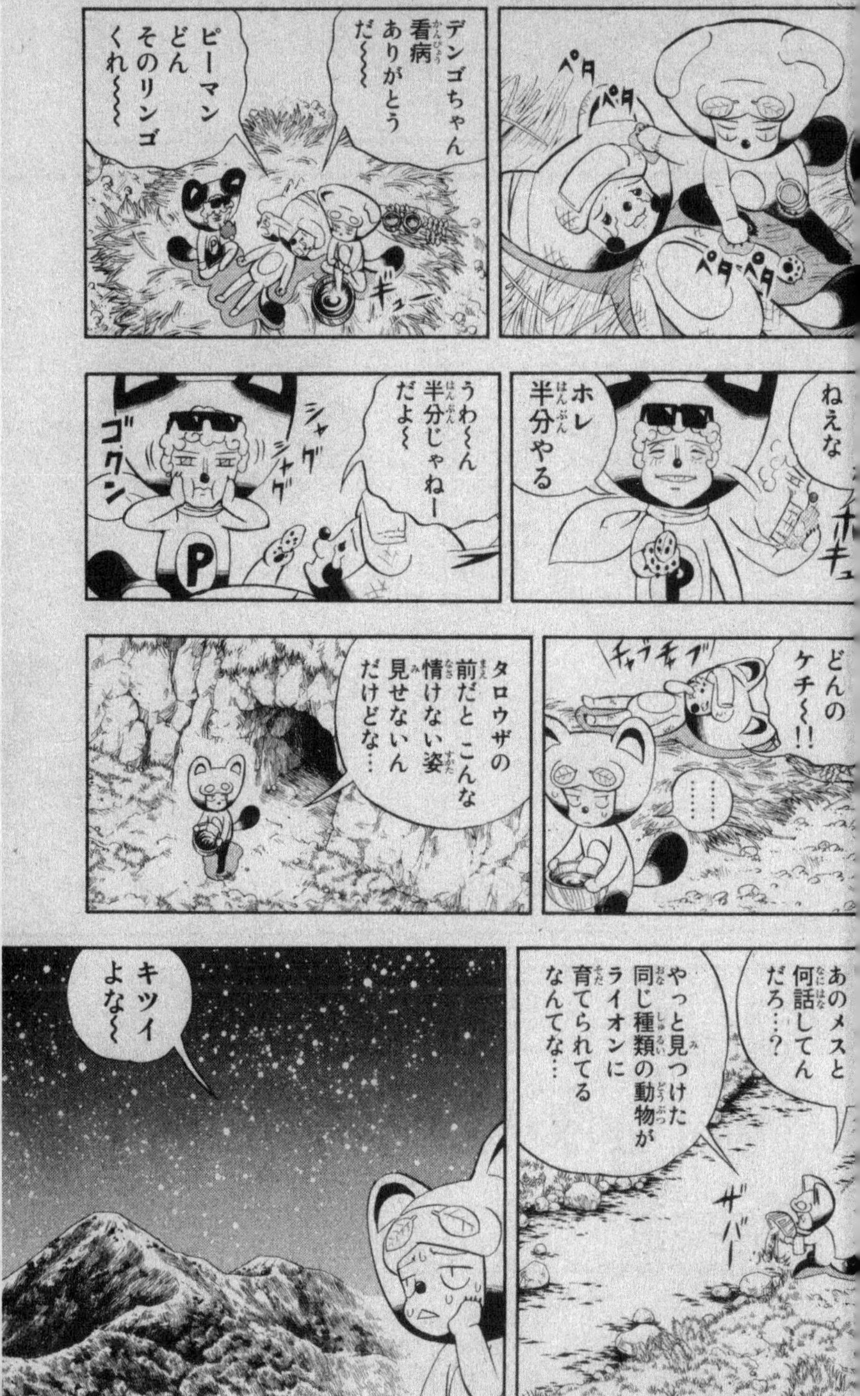
ペタ
ペタ
ペタペタ
デンゴちゃん看病ありがとうだ〜〜〜
ピーマンどんそのリンゴくれ〜〜〜
ギュー
ねえな
ホレ半分やる
ボキュ
うわ〜ん半分じゃねーだよ〜
シャグシャグ
ゴクン
どんのケチ〜!!
チャブチャブ
……
タロウザの前だとこんな情けない姿見せないんだけどな…
あのメスと何話してんだろ…?
やっと見つけた同じ種類の動物がライオンに育てられてるなんてな…
ザバー
キツイよな〜

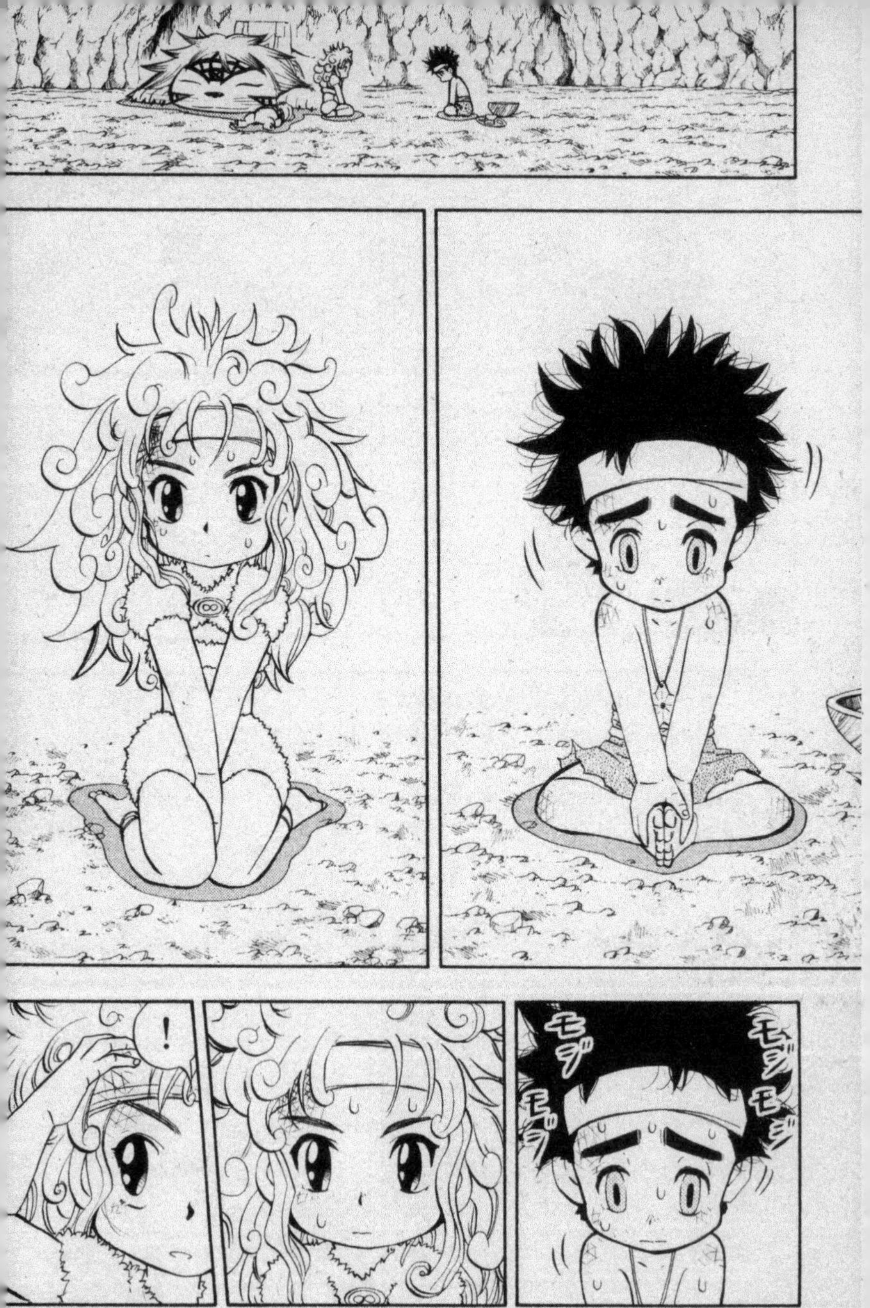
モジモジ
モジモジ
!

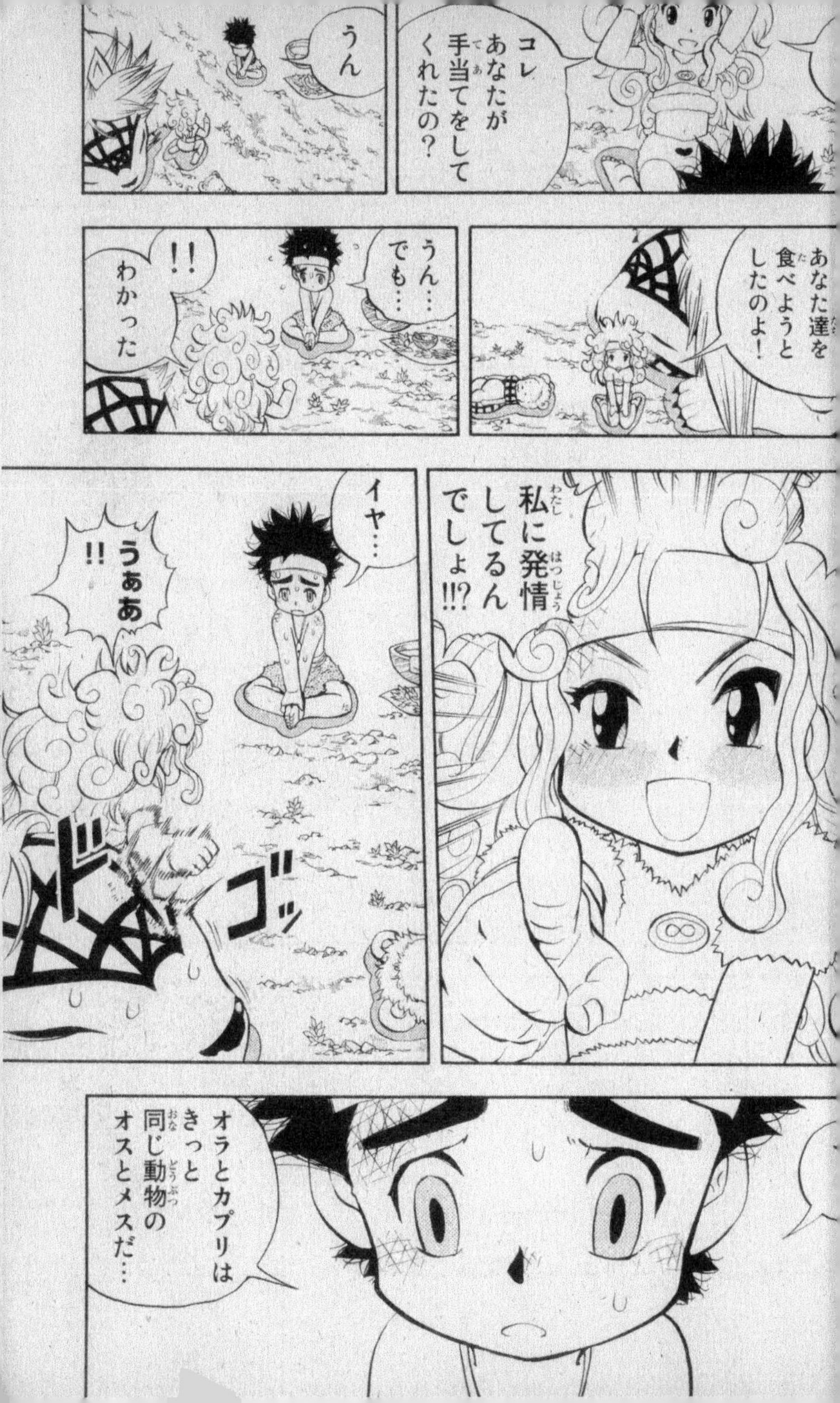
コレあなたが手当てをしてくれたの?
うん
あなた達を食べようとしたのよ!
うん…でも…
!!わかった
私に発情してるんでしょ!!?
イヤ…
うぁあ!!
ドゴッ
オラとカプリはきっと同じ動物のオスとメスだ…

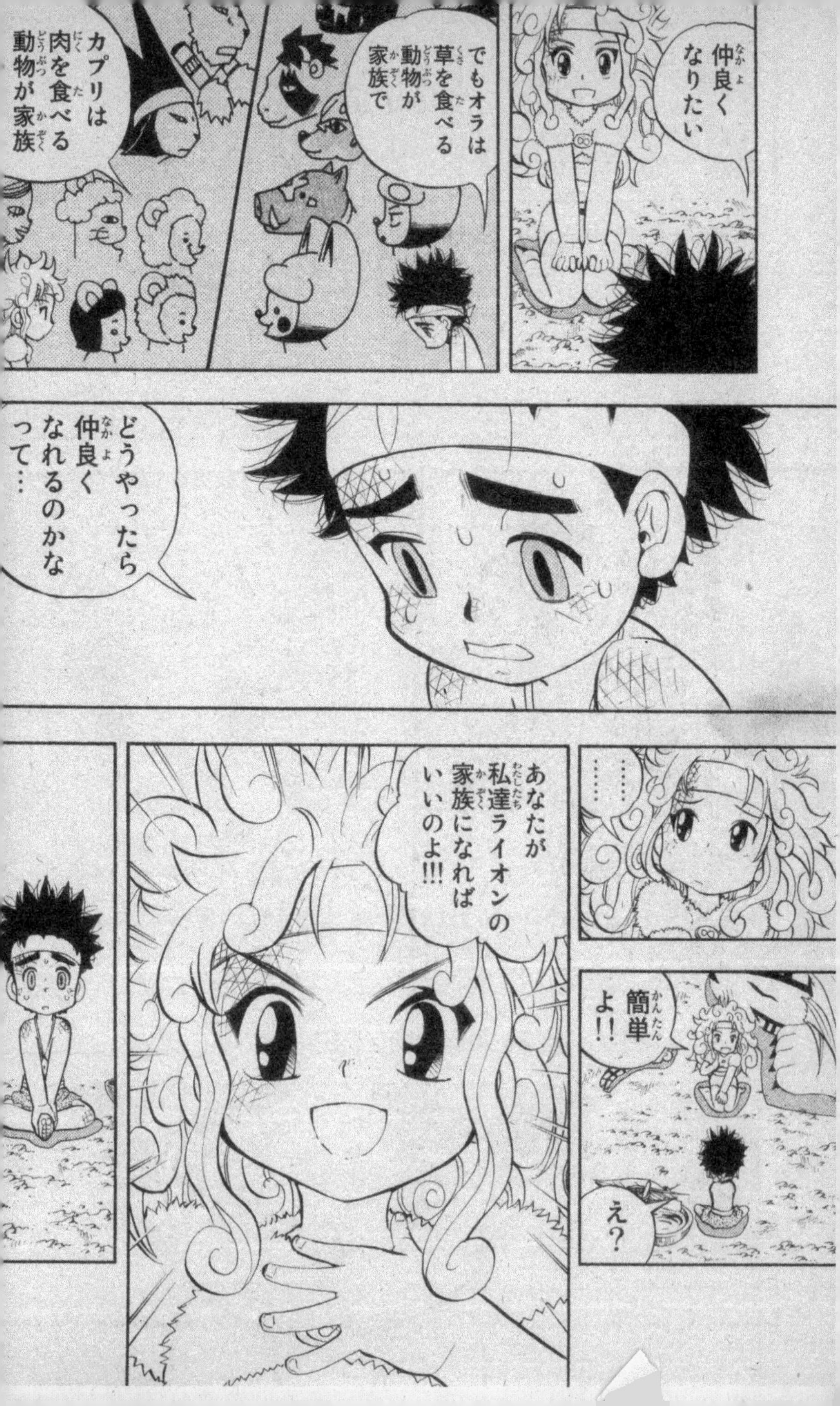
仲良くなりたい
でもオラは草を食べる動物が家族で
カプリは肉を食べる動物が家族
どうやったら仲良くなれるのかなって…
……
簡単よ!!
え?
あなたが私達ライオンの家族になればいいのよ!!!

You are going the wrong way!

Manga is a completely different
type of reading experience.

To start at the beginning, go to the end!

That's right! Authentic manga is read the traditional
Japanese way—from right to left, exactly the opposite of
how American books are read. It's easy to follow: Just go to
the other end of the book, and read each page—and each
panel—from right side to left side, starting at the top right.
Now you're experiencing manga as it was meant to be.